1st Edition

Also by Albert Murray:

The Omni-Americans
South to a Very Old Place
The Hero and the Blues
Trainwhistle Guitar
Stomping the Blues

GOOD MORNING BLUES

The Autobiography of

GOOD MORNING BLUES

Count Basie

AS TOLD TO

ALBERT MURRAY

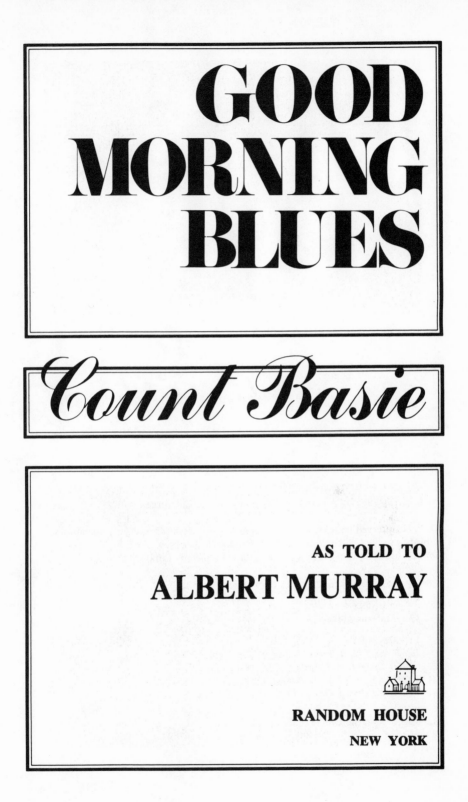

RANDOM HOUSE

NEW YORK

Library of Congress Cataloging in Publication Data

Basie, Count, 1904–
    Good morning blues.

    Includes index.
    1. Basie, Count, 1904–1984. 2. Jazz musicians—
Biography. I. Murray, Albert. II. Title.
ML422.B25A3   1985   785.42′092′4 [B]   85–2439
ISBN 0–394–54864–7

Manufactured in the United States of America
98765432   24689753   23456789
First Edition

TO MY MOTHER,
LILLY ANN CHILDS BASIE

The familiar concept of temperament—the torn hair, the blazing eye, the groaning, the throwing of manuscript into the fire—is totally inapplicable to him. This quietness of spirit has led some critics to interpret his gentleness as weakness and to characterize his music as superficial. Much of the world's education in music came from the romantics, in whose eyes rebellion burned bright and who hurled their private life into their scores . . . [but] Neither in his life nor in his music was he intent upon proving anything. Pleasure is the first, the most obvious reaction to his work. He intended it so, for he believed that music should delight.

—Marcia Davenport, *Mozart*

They know I'm there in the cause of happiness.

—Louis Armstrong

When I woke up again from another one of those little catnaps that I had been slipping in and out of all that afternoon on the trip from London, the train was just coming to the outskirts of Liverpool. I was still sleepy. I'm almost always ready to grab myself a few more winks when I'm en route with the band from one town to another like that. But for some reason I didn't nod back off right away that time. I moved over closer to the window of the compartment and looked out, and that was when I found myself remembering things from my childhood days again.

Because what I saw as we rumbled on toward the city limits were the back ends of the kinds of tenement row houses that you always see in that part of every town, no matter which country you're traveling in, and what all of that brought back to my mind was the backyard of our old house on Mechanic Street in Red Bank, New Jersey, a few years before the First World War.

What got me started were the clotheslines. I don't remember what I had been dreaming about or anything like that, but as soon as the scenery changed from the countryside to the suburbs and I saw all of those pieces of laundry strung out and flapping in the breeze on all of those sagging lines across all of those back porches, my mind flipped from England all the way to New Jersey and how the clothesline in our backyard used to look every Monday morning when I was growing up, and then what I was also thinking about was my mother.

It was September, but the weather in Great Britain must have started turning chilly already, because, as I recollect it now, the first thing I remembered about our old backyard was how it used to look and feel in the wintertime, when I used to have to go out there early in the morning and shovel a path through the snow and then take a wet towel and knock the ice off the lines so my mother could hang out the first batch of white pieces when they were ready to come out of the rinse tubs.

My mother, God rest her lovely soul, used to take in washing, as folks used to say, which meant that she did all of the washing and ironing of all the clothes and household linen for several well-to-do families around town. So what those clotheslines outside the window of my cozy compartment on the way to Liverpool really made me think about was how I always felt about her having to do that rubbing and scrubbing over those hot suds and all of the squeezing and starching and shaking out and hanging out and taking in and ironing and pressing to help my father make ends meet, and how I used to promise her that when I grew up she would never have to do that kind of work anymore because I was going to take care of her and buy her a lot of beautiful things and also be somebody that she would be proud of.

I don't know how long I just sat there going back over that part of my childhood in Red Bank before somebody came and stuck his head into the compartment to check on me. But I do remember who it was. It was Douglas Torbutt, who was the road manager for Harold Davidson Productions' promotion of the British leg of our European tour that fall, and I can also remember what I told him when he asked me what I was doing.

"Oh, nothing much, Dougie," I said without really turning to look in his direction. "Just going back a bit. Just sort of reminiscing a bit about some things that happened a long time ago."

That's all I remember saying, and I probably just sort of mumbled that, and he might have thought that I was thinking about a piece of music. I don't know. Anyway, he and I had known each other for about six years, and during that time he had become one of my close pals in Britain. So he could tell right away that I was wrapped up in something, whatever it was, and he just mentioned something about how many minutes before the train was due to be pulling into the Liverpool terminal and cut on back out, probably to check with the band manager.

So then there was just me by myself again, and I went on remembering Red Bank and some of the things I used to tell my mother over and over. Sometimes just the thought of all of those baskets of laundry was almost more than I could bear, and I would just go over to her and hug her and say, "One of these days. You just wait and see. I promise. You just wait till I grow up."

I still remember myself telling her something like that, and I also remember myself hearing what she always used to say back to me. I never will forget that.

"I'm already proud of you, Billy," she used to say, sometimes stroking me on the cheek and patting me on the head, and sometimes holding me by both shoulders. "You're a very big help to me already. You're a good boy, Billy. You're such a good boy, and you will go far in the world, and my prayers will go with you and be with you."

Memories like that kept coming back to me, and by the time we pulled into the part of town where the freight yards began, I had started to consider something that I had been putting off for about twenty-five years at least. I finally began to think about making some kind of written account about some of the things I have done to keep the promises I made to my mother.

For years people have been trying to get me to do a book about myself or to let somebody else do one about me, and up to that afternoon I had always put them off. But by the time I stepped off the train, I had definitely made up my mind, and not long afterwards I actually started putting a few memories on tape and also jutting down little notes about a few things.

But the problem was that I couldn't ever seem to find enough free time to break away from my everyday routine and really get the thing going. So after about a dozen years of making those litle tapes and notes and then forgetting what the hell I did with some of them, I finally decided to bring in a co-writer and see if I could work things out with him, the same way that I've spent all of these years working up materials for the band with my staff arrangers, ever since I first got the idea and started co-writing arrangements with Eddie Durham for Bennie Moten in Kansas City.

As my main man in the research department, my co-writer also likes to think of himself as Count Basie's literary Count Basie; in other words, he comps for me pretty much as I have always done for my soloists and also my sections and also for my band as a whole. And of course, we have also done quite a bit of four-handed piano playing, just like Bennie Moten himself and I used to do, sometimes with two separate pianos and sometimes on the same keyboard.

What the two of us have tried to put together is a book about some of the people and places and happenings that I think have been important to me, in my career as a musician and a bandleader. One thing the two of us agreed on at the very outset was that we were not going to be sidetracked into a lot of unhip gossip-magazine chitchat about people's private lives. I did not write any of the words for "Sent for You Yesterday" and "Going to Chicago" and "Don't Tell On Me," or any of those other tunes either. I never have been a songwriter, so I don't have any lyrics to explain by revealing something that I've been keeping secret all these years. And even if I had written any of those lyrics, I still wouldn't say anything about them that's going to scandalize somebody.

Anyway, I said I didn't want to get into things like that, because I really don't think those things are very important. But that didn't mean we were going to leave out anything just because it is personal. I just don't intend to bring up anything that might add up to a lot of gossip and speculation that don't really have anything to do with playing music the way I play it.

As I think back on that afternoon en route to Liverpool now, I realize that one good reason for finally deciding about a book was that it was a great year for the band. Along with our full Stateside schedule, we had spent part of May and June on our first tour of Japan, with stopover gigs in Honolulu going and coming. We had spent all of August in Sweden and Belgium. We had spent the first week of September in Germany, and we were back for our sixth tour in England, where we had already played a command performance and had been presented to the queen on our second trip there.

Another thing I realized was how far I had actually been able to go beyond anything that I remember having in mind when I used to make all of those promises to my mother. But on the other hand, there is also that little four-bar riff that my co-writer likes to run down. He says that as a child you are forever putting yourself in the place of the heroes in whatever storybooks you know about. So he says, "When you set out from home to seek your fortune in the world at large, you really are trying to accomplish something that will turn the bright-eyed little honeybunch or sly-eyed little rascal into a prince or king or duke, or even a Count." Those are his words, not mine. But if this book turns out to be a little like a fairy tale, that's all right with me too.

CONTENTS

PART ONE

1904 = 1951

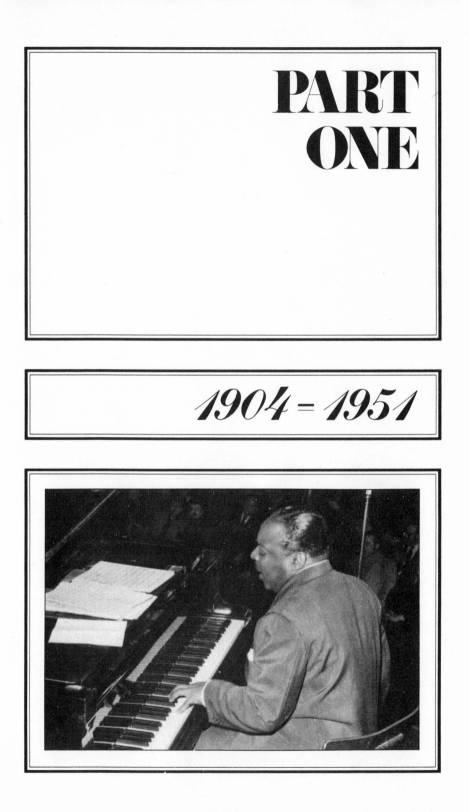

THE BLUE DEVILS

1927 - 1929

The first time I ever heard the fabulous territory band from Oklahoma City known as the Blue Devils was one midsummer morning out in Tulsa. I was lying in bed upstairs in the Red Wing Hotel, which was really a two-story boardinghouse right across Greenwood Avenue from the Dreamland Theatre, where I was working as the piano player on the TOBA circuit in a vaudeville show billed as Gonzelle White and the Big Jazz Jamboree.

Back in those days the TOBA was the main entertainment-business network serving colored people. It was really a string of independent show-places, like the old Lincoln Theatre in Harlem, the Howard in Washington, Bailey's 81 in Atlanta, the Lyric in New Orleans, the Palace in Memphis, the Booker T. Washington in St. Louis, and some others. The initials stood for Theatre Owners Booking Association. But there were some performers who used to say those letters meant "Tough On Black Artists," and to some others that meant tough on you-know-what—part of the anatomy. As for myself, I was having the time of my life just being a road-show musician, and all of the ups and downs were part of the game.

After all these years I still have not forgotten how the Blue Devils sounded that morning in Tulsa, and I also remember that at first I thought I was hearing a phonograph record. I am pretty sure that it was around eleven o'clock. I don't think it was any later than that, because I hadn't

3

come in until after daybreak, and it seemed as if I'd just closed my eyes. I know for sure that the weather was very hot and sticky that day, and I was not just tired and sleepy but also, I'll just say, a little groggy from a little too much sampling of a local beverage called Chock that I had just recently been introduced to in a back-alley joint where I had been hanging out every night after closing time at the Dreamland. So it took me a minute or so to realize that I was awake.

But I had already recognized the melody as soon as I heard about a half-chorus. It was an old tune called "In the Barrel," and it was being played by a big band, and right away the trumpet player made me think of Louis Armstrong. I'm pretty sure that's the main reason I thought it was on a record, one of Louis's new ones, or at least one with a group I hadn't heard before. Of course, another reason could have been all that Chock I was hearing it through. Anyway, there was something about it that really got to me, and I started wondering just where the hell the phonograph was.

From where I was, it sounded like somebody was playing it in one of the rooms not more than a few doors away. Because there was one of those long, narrow hallways up there, and during that time of the year everybody used to leave the doors and windows open so that whatever little breeze there was could circulate. Anyway, I couldn't stay where I was with all that music going on. So I sat up in my BVD's, rubbing my eyes and trying to clear my head. Then I pulled on my pants and went groping past two or three rooms and didn't see anything and didn't seem to be getting any closer, and that's when I started calling out, asking who was playing that new record, and somebody said it wasn't a record.

"That's the Blue Devils downstairs out there advertising that dance in that place next door tonight."

So I looked out and saw where they were and rushed back to my room and pulled on something to wear outside and went down and joined the crowd around the back of the truck they were using as their portable bandstand. I just stood there listening and looking, because I had never heard anything like that band in my life. It turned out that the trumpet player who had made me think I was hearing a new Louis Armstrong record was named Oran Page and was also known by the audience as Hot Lips.

I forgot all about my hangover and about catching up on my sleep. I just wanted to hear those guys play some more. Then when the main singer came out and did his number, that's how I heard the one and only Jimmy Rushing the first time. I had never heard anything about him before either, but there was already something special about him even then. He already had his own way of handling an audience. You could see that as soon as he came forward.

The leader was the heavyset, pleasant-looking fellow playing the bass horn and doubling on the baritone. His name was Walter Page, and at that time the band was known as Walter Page and his Blue Devils. But you could also hear the musicians addressing him by his nickname, which was Big 'Un. You could also tell right away that they didn't just respect him because he was the boss; they really liked him and felt close to him because he was also one of them.

Everybody seemed to be having so much fun just being up there playing together, and they looked good and sounded good to boot. There was such a team spirit among those guys, and it came out in the music, and as you stood there looking and listening you just couldn't help wishing that you were a part of it. Everything about them really got to me, and as things worked out, hearing them that day was probably the most important turning point in my musical career so far as my notions about what kind of music I really wanted to try to play was concerned. Not to get ahead of the story, I'll just say when I look back at just about every step I've taken since I ran into those guys that morning, I can see quite a lot to bear out the old saying "Once a Blue Devil, always a Blue Devil."

I'd say that there were about ten pieces in that band at that time, maybe eleven with Jimmy Rushing, but I'm not really sure, and every time I try to remember the lineup, I'm always afraid that I'm getting somebody who was in there later on. I'm absolutely sure that Buster Smith was in there on alto and clarinet though, because you could never forget the first time you heard him play. I'm also pretty sure that Ernie Williams was in the band at that time, but I'm not so sure about what he was doing that day. He might have been playing drums, because sometimes he did that, and he was also the entertainer, and he was also one of the singers. So was "Lips" Page. But I don't think I knew that Ernie was a singer and entertainer until later on.

I think Joe Keys might have been in there with Lips on trumpet, and the other reeds could have been Reuben Roddy on tenor and Ted Manning on first alto. Buster Smith was playing third. I think Dan Minor was the trombone player at that time, and Reuben Lynch was the banjo player. I know all of these fellows were in the Blue Devils around that time, but I can't honestly say that I actually saw every one of them up there on the platform that day. But the one that really stumps me is the piano player. I don't know why I can't remember him. I've been told that a guy named Turk Thomas was probably playing piano at that time, so it might have been him or it may have been Charles Washington. But I don't remember what he looked like or sounded like or anything. All I can say is that I didn't pay any special attention to him. That's all I can say, because I just can't explain it.

When the truck moved on to the next stop, I followed along with some of the crowd, just like I used to follow the circus parade around town back home in New Jersey when I was a kid, and the more I heard them, the more I liked them. And you could also tell that the people in Tulsa also liked them. I don't remember whether I knew anything about the so-called territory bands at that time, but you got the impression that the Blue Devils already had a big reputation in that part of the country and that Tulsa was a part of their stomping ground, and I do mean stomp, which, as I found out later, was a very popular word in that part of the country in those days. A lot of tunes were called stomps, and a lot of bands were called stomp bands.

Then, back at the Dreamland Theatre later on in the afternoon, some of them came by and heard me playing the ballyhoo for the Gonzelle White show out on the sidewalk at the entrance. There was a drummer and there was a trumpet, and I was playing the upright piano that was rolled out there from somewhere inside the lobby, and we would play a couple of numbers, and the barker would spiel the come-on for the show. Playing for that was what we used to call ballying or playing the ballyhoo. We used to bally before the show, and then sometimes we used to roll the piano back out there again and bally between shows.

It was while we were playing out there that afternoon that I looked out and saw some of the Blue Devils in the crowd. I was very happy about that and couldn't wait to meet them, and when we finished, somebody introduced me to Jimmy Rushing. So we talked, and he told me they were playing a dance right upstairs next door to the Red Wing that night, and Jimmy was the one who introduced me to Walter Page, who was also somewhere nearby, and I also liked him right away. So the three of us talked, and then Jimmy mentioned something about the dance again.

"He'd like to hear the band."

"Well, why don't you come on up when your show is over," Page said. "Me and Rush will be checking the door. You're welcome to come on in."

Naturally I said I'd be there, and that's how I happened to go up there after our show at the theater and hear the Blue Devils really doing their thing, and I just couldn't get over it. I just thought it was the greatest thing I had ever heard in my life. They were together, and they had their own thing. Hot Lips Page was really the standout personality of that band at that time. Once he began singing and playing that horn, everything was there. I also liked the way Jimmy Rushing sang. He wasn't really a blues singer in those days. He was really a ballad singer. But there was a blues flavor about the way he was singing, even back then. And there was also Buster Smith on clarinet and alto sax, and he had his own original style. He had a different style from everybody.

——

In a way, that was the first big band I ever heard. Because all I had heard back in New York before I hit the TOBA circuit were the groups they used in small cabarets, and I think maybe the most they had in those places was something like five pieces—maybe piano, drums, and maybe a trombone and a cornet, and somebody on reeds. Something like that was the biggest thing I was around or had played with. I hadn't been around any of the clubs where any of the big bands were working, except for one time, when Fess Williams played at the Savoy when it opened, a few months before I left New York.

Fess Williams and another band led by Vernon Andrade were playing there the night I went up there with somebody on a pass or something. But to tell the truth, I really didn't pay much attention to the music that night. I was mainly interested in seeing the Savoy. As far as digging the band was concerned, it really didn't mean much to me. I just wanted to see the glamour of the place and the beautiful hostesses, and it was just a great thing for me just to be there.

I knew about Fletcher Henderson and his band, because I remember that while I was working at Leroy's up on Fifth Avenue at the corner of 135th Street before I left to go on the road with the show the third time, I knew that Louis Armstrong had come to New York and joined Fletcher. But I had never had a chance to hear that band back then. I don't think I heard the Fletcher Henderson band in person until some years later on. I heard the records, and I heard him on the radio, but I don't think I heard him in person until I had been in Kansas City for a while. I never heard the band that Charlie Johnson had in Smalls' Paradise. I didn't even know about Jimmy Harrison playing in that band for a while. I knew Jimmy when he was working with June Clark in the place Smalls used to have over on Fifth Avenue before he opened the Smalls' Paradise on Seventh.

—

Anyway, the Blue Devils was the first big band I ever had a chance to get close to and really listen to, and it was the greatest thing I had ever heard. I had never heard the blues played like that. What we were playing in the show was music for the acts. The musicians didn't have any feature spots or anything like that on the program. We didn't actually have a real band. We had a piano and drums, bass horn, trumpet and sax; and many times the horns would lay out, and it was just piano and drums. We just followed what the dancers did. Then when the comedians were on we'd pick out the tempo they wanted to dance by. As strange as it may seem to many people today, we didn't have any blues singers in the Gonzelle White show.

I had heard the blues Bessie, Mamie and Trixie Smith, Viola McCoy, Victoria Spivey, and Ida Cox, and singers like that were putting out on records back in those days, but I hadn't ever really paid any attention to them, and I hadn't ever played the blues. I hadn't got my first real taste of the blues until the burlesque show I first left New York with played in Kansas City that second time, and Elmer Williams and I went out walking along Troost Avenue one night and came to all those joints that started at Eighteenth Street.

Not that the Blue Devils were just playing the blues. They were not really playing all that much blues that night. But they were still bluesy. But the main thing about that band was that they had their own special way of playing everything. They would get some kind of signal for the next number, and they would stomp off and they were gone! I didn't try to analyze it or anything like that. I just dug it, and right away I knew that that was for me, without even thinking about it. Sometimes you hear new things and it scares you. But this time I just wanted to play with them. I don't know why I thought I could, which is why it's so strange that I don't remember who the piano player was. I didn't think I could take him because I had his number or anything like that. It didn't have anything to do with cutting anybody, I just wanted a chance to play. Just hearing it made me want to play.

Between the sets I went on talking with Jimmy Rushing and meeting other members of the band, and somewhere along the line I mentioned that the show I was with was due to go into Oklahoma City when we left Tulsa; and that's when Jimmy told me about his father running a little restaurant right next door to the Aldridge Theatre, which was where all the traveling shows played. Jimmy and the Blue Devils were on their way out on a series of dance dates around in the Oklahoma and Kansas territory and wouldn't be back in for several weeks, I guess it was. But he told me to look up his father at the restaurant, and I said I would.

That was how I first got to know about the Blue Devils, and as much as I enjoyed it, I did not have any idea what a big change it was going to make in my life one day.

I remember thinking about how great it would be if I could ever have a chance to play in a band like that. But that's about as far as that went at that time. I'm pretty sure that I didn't have any notions about actually joining them or anything like that, because I also liked being a road-show musician out on the circuit with Gonzelle. I don't remember having any serious thoughts about giving that up yet. But as a musician I knew that those musicians were something else.

I guess they must have pulled out that next morning. But the Gonzelle White show stayed on in Tulsa for about at least another few more days after our last night at the Dreamland Theatre, and I spent my time playing in an alley joint.

I was always looking for some action like that in every town the show came into in those days; and this time I had met a local man-about-town called Pencil, and he put me next to things. He had heard about the little guy playing piano down at the theater, and he came to the show and sat in the front row and stayed around all that evening and introduced himself and asked me what I was going to do after the show, and I said something like "Well, nothing much." Or something like that. And he said why not come on run with him.

So he took me back into one of those alleys, and there was a house back in there, and there's where he introduced me to that local Oklahoma brew called Chock, which is short for Choctaw beer. They also had a piano in there, and the old guy playing it was named Goodman. It was a good piano too, and I had started playing it and drinking that Chock and having some fun, and after a few nights I got to be sort of like the king around there for a while.

So when we stayed on in town for a few days after the show was over, I didn't have anything to worry about. I was all right with Pencil and the gang he hung out with. And I didn't have to worry about a meal ticket either, because Gonzelle had given everybody a meal ticket, and you could eat downstairs at the hotel, which I didn't have to do, because I was running with Pencil and the gang and the eating was good and there was plenty to drink.

But then, all of a sudden, things got a little rough there for me. Because another show was opening at the Dreamland Theatre, and they had a left-handed piano player named Seminole. He was from back east, but I don't remember having heard about him before. I had met most of the baddest piano players around New York and New Jersey, including Willie "the Lion" Smith, James P. Johnson, Fats Waller, the Beetle, Don Lambert, Freddy Tunstall, but not Seminole. So I had never been warned about him. *He had a left hand like everybody else had a right hand.* I mean, he was doing everything with his left hand that I was doing with my right hand. He was terrible. He was with the show, and everybody went to the opening, and afterwards they invited him around to this alley joint. And he *de-throned* me. *Took my crown!* That shows how quickly they can forget you. The cat took over and said no hard feelings, man. But that was all for Basie in Tulsa.

That's how I met Seminole, and he could *play.* I hadn't met him back in New York, and I didn't know about the kind of reputation he had with guys around Harlem like James P. Johnson and Willie "the Lion" Smith, but I met him out there and I never will forget him. By the way, I've also been told that he was also one hell of a guitar player, a left-handed guitar player. I can believe it.

We left for Oklahoma City in another day or so, and it was a good thing for me. It saved my face. Because I didn't have to walk around being second guy.

I got my chance to sit in with the Blue Devils a few weeks later when they came back home to Oklahoma City. The Gonzelle White show was still there because after we finished that week at the Aldridge Theatre we did not have anything else to go to, and they were trying to line up something somewhere.

I had gotten in touch with Jimmy Rushing's father in his little restaurant by the theater. So that was one local person I knew, and soon after we got there, I also met a nice little lady named Mrs. Breux, who owned the Aldridge and was also a school official of some kind. They had a piano with a funny little organ attachment, and I played it, and she said anytime I wanted to play just come on in and play. So I used to do that quite often and pick up a little change.

I also met a guy in Oklahoma City by the name of Honey Murphy. He had a little upstairs place there that used to be like an after-hours spot, and I used to go up there and play anytime I wanted to, and I became something like the house piano player. The Big Jazz Jamboree was sort of semi-broken up for a while, but Oklahoma City was not a bad town. I had my spots where I could go. There was a section of several blocks along Second Street, called Deep Second, and that's where most of the action was.

I also had myself another little alley gig going for me. There was a lady that had a house back up in there. She sold a delightful vintage from the corn products, which had no label but was very tasty. I was a youngster, and I was drinking everything in those days. So I used to be the house piano player in there too. There were a lot of good pianos in those alleys. In those days, everywhere you went you could just about count on finding a pretty good piano in those joints. And this very nice lady used to cook too. Before long I had my spots where I could eat and drink all picked out. I used to go down there in the afternoons and play a while because I knew what time they ate around there. And I had my thing up there with Honey Murphy at night. So I was covered as far as food and my juice and pocket change was concerned.

It was also while I was in Oklahoma City that time that a show came through called *Rock Dinah*, and they had a little young cat in the band playing the greatest trumpet I'd ever heard in my life. His name was Roy Eldridge. That's where I first met him. And they also had another cat in there that was playing saxophone. His name was McTeer, and he had a brother that played banjo, and later on I found them and had them with that first group I started with in Kansas City. But I never will forget hearing Roy Eldridge that first time. He was *something*. I went back and told all the guys in the show to go down there and hear that little cat.

I remember that layover in Oklahoma City as a wonderful experience.

You didn't have to worry about rent because Gonzelle would be taking care of everybody's hotel-room expenses, and you could eat on the meal tickets. I had found myself some alley joints and had my thing going, and I was picking up a little change, and I got to know some wonderful people, especially in Honey Murphy's place. That's where everybody got together after hours.

I can also remember Slaughter's Drug Store. I used to hang out there, and there was a dance hall upstairs on the top floor of that building. I can also remember Halley Richardson's shoeshine parlor.

Another person I got to know when I was in Oklahoma City that time was a guy called Crip. He was a cook in the restaurant across the street from the Aldridge Theatre, and he loved music. So he used to come and listen to me playing the organ. He was a good cook, and he used to make some wonderful hot biscuits and rolls, and I would go by and hang out and talk with him and he would let me have my breakfast free every morning before the customers started coming in.

Jimmy Rushing's father's place was a little snack bar where you could get a sandwich and soda and candy and fruit and stuff like that. I think he lived upstairs. I think he might have owned that little building. The place across the street where Crip worked was a regular restaurant. There were three or four tables in there, maybe more, and there was also a counter. I don't know whether Crip owned the place or not. I don't think so. But I really don't know.

Then I was in there with Crip one morning and we got to talking and he said, "Doe [meaning Jimmy Rushing] and them Old Blues Devils'll be getting back in town this morning. You going to be waiting for them?" And I said, "You know I'm going to wait up for them, because I want to go to that breakfast dance."

I had seen the placards around town, and I knew they were going to play a breakfast dance at Slaughter's Hall. That was where all the big dances were held. Breakfast dances were very popular back in those days. So I waited, and they pulled in, and when Jimmy Rushing came to the restaurant to have his breakfast, he remembered me and we got to talking, and I told him I'd like to go up there with him and hear the band again. And so it happened that the piano player was having a health problem of some sort and was not up to making it to work that night.

So Jimmy asked me would I like to play this one with them. And I jumped at that, and he called Walter Page and reminded him of me in Tulsa and said why don't we get him to go in there with us, and Page told him it was okay. So I went to the place where I was staying and put on a coat and tie, and I was the happiest guy in the world. I was on my way to play my first gig with all those wonderful cats. I can still remember how excited I was about the whole thing.

But when I got there, the guys at the door stopped me. I've forgotten what was actually said, but it had to be something about either having an advance ticket or paying cash at the box office, and when I told whoever it was that I was playing with the band, they just looked at me and shook their heads, as if to say, "What's this cat trying to pull?"

"Playing what?"

"Piano."

"Aw, come on, man. This is a hometown band. We all know who the piano player is."

So somebody finally had to go in the back somewhere and find Walter Page, and he told them to let me come on in.

That breakfast dance was a real great highlight for me. I mean it was the kind of thrilling experience that you knew you would always get a special kick out of just remembering. As for their book or repertory, I don't remember seeing any sheet music up there. *The band just played.* Somebody just called out something. They played a lot of heads, and by the time they worked a tune over once, that was it. If I had seen any sheet music, I don't think I would have known what to do with it. But I could get with those heads, and I could comp, and I also tried to lay a few stride choruses from back east in there on them, and I guess it must have come out pretty good, because they didn't run me out of there.

I've forgotten how much they paid me for that gig, and I am sure that it didn't really mean anything at that time. The main thing was having a chance to sit in with those Blue Devils.

I also got a chance to play another dance with them there, and when the Gonzelle White show got ready to pull out, Walter Page gave me an address to use in case something happened and I wanted to come with them one day.

=

After Oklahoma City the show moved on back to Kansas City and went back into the Lincoln Theatre on Eighteenth Street. But when we finished that run at the Lincoln Theatre, the Gonzelle White show was stranded again, and this time it broke up for good. But just about everybody stayed around Kansas City, which was a great town for musicians and entertainers. I don't remember what my plans were at that time, but in the meantime I got sick and had to go to the hospital.

I forget how long I actually stayed in the hospital but it must have been for three weeks or maybe a month or more. I was not in the Phyllis Wheatley Hospital, which was right off Eighteenth Street, not far from the Yellow Front Saloon. I was in the General Hospital downtown in the area near Union Station and outside the room where I was, there was a hill that sloped right down to the window by my bed.

That's something I will never forget, because somehow my good old road buddy, whose name was Temple and who was the drummer in the Gonzelle White show, found out that he could come that way and visit me without having to check with the nurses, and he started coming by with some barbecue and pop and other little snack goodies for me and some home brew for himself, and he would sit on the slope right outside the window, and we'd talk and have a ball. I don't know how he ever found out how to come that way. I don't even know how he found out that I was in the General Hospital, unless he was the one who took me there.

But every night he'd be out there with that good old Kansas City barbecue or something else for me, and he'd sit on that slope drinking his brew and tell me all about what was going on around town. One thing I remember is that Temple always had me falling out laughing about what was the latest news about what Harry Smith was doing. Harry Smith was the trumpet player in the show, a hell of a trumpet player, and he also did a great dance routine. He was always doing something comical, especially after he had had a little taste of something, which he had quite often.

Naturally I didn't want my folks back home in the east worrying about me, so I didn't let them know that I was sick. As a matter of fact I really didn't keep in close touch with home during those early days. I guess I really must have taken for granted that everything was still just like it was when I left and would be the same whenever I went back, which I didn't have any notion of doing soon.

Every time I was lucky enough to get a little extra change I always sent a little money order back to my mother. But to tell the truth I didn't ever give her many details about the kind of life I was leading knocking about in the world of show business. I really didn't say any more in those letters than you put on a post card, and that's just about the same kind of information I was getting back from her when my mail would finally catch up with me. That was about what my contact with home amounted to, and as long as I didn't get any Special Delivery letters or Western Union messages or long distance calls I told myself that everything was OK; because that was the way you learned the bad news in those days. When you saw the Western Union messenger boy's bicycle, the first thing that popped into your mind was *come at once*.

While I was in the hospital, my beard grew out, and they finally got a barber to come out there and shave me. Then one day they told me I would have to get dressed and go outside, and I did, and everybody was looking at me because they said I had spinal meningitis and they hadn't expected me to pull out of that. I was sitting there and they kept looking at me, and I said, "All that's wrong with me is y'all starving me to death. That's what wrong with me."

So then they were going to test me because they didn't believe me.
So they took me in another room where there was a piano. This was
the room where the doctors and nurses went for relaxation and recreation.
They said they were going to test me to see what effect the illness had
had on me. So they told me to play something on the piano.

"Play the piano?" I said. "What for?"

"We want to see if you can play."

"Of course I can play," I said. "What you want to hear?"

And then I had to play for them every day up there. And then it got
so they would let me come out of the hospital and go and see a show
anytime I wanted to go and see a new show. As long as I got back to
the hospital that evening to go to bed. I had that privilege.

But then, after a while, I said to myself, "Let me get out of here. What
am I doing in here?" And I told somebody else I was about to leave,
and I remember whoever it was saying, "Yeah, I know. They putting
you out. You been in there trying to duck some rent, and they caught up
with you."

—

After I came out of the hospital, I fooled around in the area of the
Eastside Hotel awhile. It was nice since I hadn't been very far from that
part of Eighteenth Street. I hadn't ever been as far as up to Paseo, because, to tell the truth, that looked like the beginning of another little
town, where you had to be a little different from the way folks back over
here were. Over where I was staying was not quite as high class as things
seemed to be between Vine Street and Paseo.

But I said to myself, "I'm going to pass there anyhow." So I went on
up there one Sunday and went on across the boulevard, and I looked
around and there was Street's hotel on the corner, a big, fine, beautiful
hotel. At Eighteenth and Vine there was a pool hall, a barbershop, the
Subway Club downstairs in the same block as the barbershop. I said to
myself, "Well, looka here, this is it." There was also a big barbecue stand
in the next block. So I kept on walking, and further up Eighteenth Street
there was a little dime-movie place. So I went in there, and they had a
piano that had all kinds of sound effects on it to go with the silent pictures.
It even had the sound for horses' hooves for the cowboy pictures. Naturally
I was very interested in that.

I didn't get any farther up Eighteenth Street than that dime-movie place
that first time. But when I took another walk up there the next week, I
made a turn on Vine Street, and that's when I came to the Eblon. It was
a little movie theater, and there was a special little sign announcing that
they had just recently installed a Wicks organ, a manual Wicks, which
hadn't been in there more than two or three weeks, I guess.

So I happened to have twenty-five or thirty cents in my pocket, and I used one of my treasured dimes for admission and went in and sat down front as I always did when there was an organ in the theater. There was a woman in there playing the organ while the picture was on. Then at the end of the main feature there was a seven-piece band that came on and played for the cartoons and short subjects. The leader was a violin player called Gooby Taylor, and the drummer was Baby Lovett, one of the local musicians I had met in some joint before going in the hospital. When they finished, they went out into the alley, and I went out and joined them, and Baby and I got to talking, and I said I saw you up on Twelfth Street, and we talked on and talked on. And I said I'd like to play that organ in there.

"What you mean?" he said giving me a funny glance.

"I'd like to play it," I told him. "I can play that thing."

He knew that I was a piano player because he had heard me sitting in at one of the joints. But he didn't know I could play organ too. He said something about the woman coming back and telling Gooby, but I kept on after him.

"Do you know how to turn it on?"

"Yeah," he said, "I know how to turn it on."

"Well, turn it on."

But he just looked at me. "You're sure you know what you're doing?"

"Shit yeah, man," I said. "I can turn it on myself. All you got to do is put that switch on back there."

"Look, you going make me lose my job," he said, and then he said, "Go ahead, but if anything happens, I don't know you. Hell, I don't even know how you got down there."

The woman still wasn't back from wherever she went for lunch or whatever she went out to do, and the feature picture was back on again. So I finally got him to go back there and turn the switch on, and I went in and started. There was a sad scene up on the screen. The audience really should have been just about ready to cry. But I opened up with the "Bugle Blues" on the organ, and the kids in there for the matinee started clapping right after I hit the break. Two or three of them breaks and the house was rocking.

That's when Jap Eblon, the owner of the theater, came running down there. Baby Lovett was sitting there, and Baby saw him coming and said, "Oh, shit, I'm gone." But I just went on playing, and Jap Eblon came running on down to the organ and said, "What the hell are you doing sitting down there?" And I said something. I don't know what I said. And he said, "Come on up here." He was a rough-talking old son of a gun.

"Come on up here."

So he took me back up to his office and set me down there.

"Don't you know you ain't supposed to come in here and play that organ? Did you ask somebody?"

"No, I didn't see nobody."

"Who told you?"

"Nobody," I said. "I just wanted it play it."

Then he just sat there and looked at me. Then he shuffled some papers on his desk. Then he looked at me again.

"You want a job?"

That's exactly how it happened. That was just about the last thing I had expected, but I wasn't too surprised to take him up on it.

=

Then when I came back downstairs and went back where the musicians were, Lovett was waiting. "Should I pack my drums?"

"No, man," I said. "Everything's all right. I'm working here now."

I don't know what Jap Eblon said to the woman when she came back, but I went to work there that next week. I have been told that her name was Virginia Harding and that she was from Sedalia, and that later on she used to work in the Crown Drug Store on Eighteenth Street. If I ever went in there and saw her, I never made any connection between her and what happened at the Eblon. I only remember that she was playing that organ the way it was supposed to be played according to what was written on the cue sheets, and I just played and made up my little things as I went along.

I had played the organ for silent movie pictures before, but I hadn't had any experience working with cue sheets. They used to send them in with musical themes to go with the moods of the different scenes. But I wasn't really very sharp about reading music in those days. I could spell it out if I really had to, but it was really easier for me just to pick things up as I went along. Once I heard it, I had it and could put something with it. So I invented my own themes. I had learned that from my friend Fats Waller at the Lincoln Theatre back in Harlem.

=

I worked in the Eblon for a while, maybe a few months, and all during the same time I was beginning to get around to more and more of those joints where all of that fabulous Kansas City action was. More and more people were beginning to know that I was there, because they heard me and saw me in the Eblon, and there were also those places in the area of the Yellow Front Saloon that I already knew about from the time that the Big Jamboree first came into town. As a matter of fact, I had already met the one and only Piney Brown, the number-one man-about-town, probably the day Gonzelle's show arrived in Kansas City.

Anyway, I was making the scene and trying to dig what was going down, and sometimes also picking up a little extra change from the kitty, a bowl that some clubs had on the piano for the customers to leave a little contribution for the musicians. In some places there was a piano, and you could just go in and play, and other places might also have a set of drums, and then there were other places where a lot of musicians hung out and they were noted for jam sessions that sometimes went on all night.

I really was just stumbling around finding out about those places in those early days, but it was during this time that I decided to name myself the Count. I knew about King Oliver, and I also knew that Paul Whiteman was called the King of Jazz. Duke Ellington was also getting to be one of the biggest new names in Harlem and also on records and the radio, and Earl Hines and Baron Lee were also important names. So I decided that I would be one of the biggest new names; and I actually had some little fancy business cards printed up to announce it. COUNT BASIE. Beware the Count is Here. Somebody showed me one of those cards years later, and I imagine whoever that was still has it. I sure would give a lot to see it again.

Now as for what was happening with me and the ladies during those early days in Kansas City, I figure that ain't nobody's business. But truthfully, what was going on is not really worth going into. I was just out there hitting on whatever I could get next to, with no strings attached. Of course, if any of them had strings attached to somebody else, I'm damn sure not going to mention that.

Meantime I still couldn't get those Blue Devils out of my mind. So I wrote Walter Page and told him what I was doing and everything, and after a little while I got a telegram back from him asking me if I would like to join the Blue Devils. So right away I got in touch with him on the phone, and we talked, and then I showed the telegram around and said, "Well, I got this telegram from Paris. They want me to come to Paris," because the address on the telegram was Paris. But it was Paris, Texas. I didn't let them see that part.

I went to Jap Eblon and told him I wanted to go down there and see what they were doing, and that is how I left Kansas City to go and join that wonderful band of Blue Devils.

—

The telegram had come from Paris, Texas, but I actually joined the band back in Oklahoma City, and they were planning to go back to Texas, which was just great for me because I don't think I had been down that far when I was with the show. But we hung around town for a while, and I got back in touch with Miss Breux at the Aldridge Theatre and Honey Murphy and the Deep Second scene again, and then we started out playing through Oklahoma on our way down into Texas.

That was another part of their territory, and they were really kings all down through there, and I got to play all those towns like Dallas and Fort Worth. We hung around Dallas a little bit and went down to San Antonio and Houston; and everywhere that band went they were well loved, and you didn't have to worry about food or where you were going to stay. Because you could always stay at somebody's house. We had a whole lot of friends down there, and it was just great, and I enjoyed everything about it. I was with that band. I was with the Blue Devils. I was a Blue Devil, and that meant everything to me. Those guys were so wonderful.

A special thing that was so wonderful about that mob was the way they felt about each other. I didn't know what kind of salary I was supposed to get. It wasn't important. It was not a salaried band anyway, and you never heard anybody squawking about finances. We played mostly on a very little guarantee, and then we got the rest from whatever the door receipts were. So what usually happened was that Big 'Un would get the money, and after we'd bought the gas and figured out the expenses to get to the next town, we'd divide the rest among ourselves, and when the married musicians had special family bills back home, what we made on the next dance we'd play would go to help them. That was what I found out about how the Blue Devils worked. And I understand that a lot of territory bands operated like that in those days. They were called commonwealth bands. It was just like a beautiful family.

In Dallas we stayed in one big rooming house, which had a piano, and that's where I remember us rehearsing quite a bit. We had just bought some big arrangements on something, and we worked on those. They were big stock arrangements, something I had never seen before, let alone worked with. And we had made up some wonderful head arrangements there, and to me they were better than any music you could get in stocks because they really swung. They were leaping.

While we were in Dallas, Jimmy Rushing got in touch with a girlfriend of his who worked in a restaurant, and during a certain time of day he could go around there and get himself a free meal. I had been there and had seen him do it a few times. So one day while he was fooling around in the pool room or somewhere I got hungry and I slipped around there and told his girl friend that Jimmy said he won't be around today and said for me to eat his meal. And I ate my head off and cut out, and later on he went around there and sat at the table and she kept walking by without bringing him anything, and at first he thought she was just busy and then he started wondering. Then she finally came and stood looking at him.

"Hey, what you doing here?"

"Aw now, baby. Don't I come here every day?"

"Yes," she said, "but you sent Basie around here."

"What?" I don't even have to imagine the look on his face. I know that bulb began to light up right there.

"Basie was here and said you were not coming so I gave him your meal."

Old Jimmy came back and just sat and cut his eyes at me for hours, as if to say, "You dirty dog. You lowdown dirty dog." Then all he did was shake his head and walk away. But finally he had to laugh about it, and he was still telling about that until he died some forty-odd years later.

Dallas was some town. They loved the Blue Devils all through Texas. San Antonio was also great. The first time I played in Galveston with them we had an early dance date at the Galvez Hotel, but just before we got there something happened to our transportation. I guess it must have been about fifteen or twenty miles from the outskirts of town. I don't remember exactly what happened, but I remember that we made it into a filling station somehow and the man telling us it won't be ready this afternoon. You can get it tonight. He said that was the best he could do.

So what Big 'Un had to do was get one of those old open-tailgate trucks. He put the drums and the bass and all of us inside with a couple of guys sitting in the back with their feet hanging out. And that's how we made it on into town and drove up to the Galvez Hotel. We got down and unloaded our things and the man took us into a funny little room back there and we put on our uniforms and played that gig and came out and got back on that truck and went back and picked up our car, and then we had to drive back into Galveston again to spend the night.

But it was worth it to get back into town. Because Galveston was leaping. Everything was there. Now I'm not saying I participated. But a good time was had by all, and of course, I was there. You have to get around town and see things. And I did, and there was a lot to see. As far as I was concerned, that was the greatest town in Texas. But I still am not saying that I participated, or anything like that.

The Blue Devils wore good-looking uniforms. I can remember wearing Oxford gray and also some Gamble stripes. In those days you had to have a uniform. Bands that didn't have their own special costumes didn't look professional. It was like a baseball team with uniforms. You looked like a sandlot outfit. They didn't want bands that didn't have them. There were no strange-looking musicians with all that ring-around-the-collar stuff and all that in those days. You had to be pressed and clean with everything shined up. All you have to do is look at some pictures of the orchestras in those days and you'll see how well they were dressed. All of the orchestras were like that.

Which reminds me of how careful Lips Page used to be when it came to his clothes. He had a couple or three fine special suits, and at that time he and I were the same size. So one night we were supposed to go out somewhere, and I said I couldn't go because I didn't have anything to match up, and he said, "That's all right. Why don't you borrow one of my suits?" And I said okay. I figured that would be great. Because he had three real sharp, truly great outfits. But I didn't know what I was getting myself into. I couldn't get rid of him. Everywhere I went he was right there with me, saying, "Don't lean on that."

Or he'd say, "Hey man, that chair is kinda dirty."

"Hey, Baisie, watch it sitting down."

He couldn't think of anything else all night but that suit of his I was wearing. That was one of the most uncomfortable evenings I've ever had in my life. I never was so glad to get back home and take off a suit.

But the main man for clothes in the Blue Devils' band in those days was Ernie Williams. Ernie used to work in a tailor shop when the Devils were in Oklahoma City. So he was a very sharp dresser, and he used to help keep the band looking good. He was not a tailor. He didn't make suits or anything like that, but he could press and he could mend things and make alterations.

I was with the Blue Devils for some months. I don't remember exactly how many, and I'm not very certain about any of the actual dates, whether it was August or October, but I do remember that at first it was warm, and that when it got cold I was still with them for a while. It could have been three months or maybe about four or even as many as six. But I am pretty certain that I didn't stay with them throughout the winter.

It seems like the time I spent with them was much longer than it actually was. Because so much happened. You can cover a lot of territory in a few months on the road, working the way we were working. Because we were not playing on any jobs by the week. Sometimes we might be around town for a while, like when we were working out of Dallas. But mostly we would be playing one-night stands. We'd come in and play a dance and move on to the next town on our schedule. We were not playing with any shows or any theatres, and there was no such thing as a concert for that kind of band in those days. So we were always on the go, and we hit a lot of places.

By the way, as Dan Minor told my co-writer in an interview a couple of years ago, I was calling myself Count Basie when I joined the Blue Devils. Dan was the trombone player when I first saw that band out in Tulsa, and he was still with them all during the time I was one of them. According to Dan, nobody really paid any attention to the name I had given myself until one day when Ted Manning, then tenor player and I got into an argument about something. And it went on and on until Ted finally said something like "Basie you call yourself the Count, well, man, you're just about the most raggediest-assed count I've ever seen." Naturally from that day on, anytime anybody mentioned anything about Count, everybody knew who that was.

When we would come back into Oklahoma City and lay off before heading out for somewhere else, everybody else was like at home. That's where some of them who were married had their families, and most of the others already had regular places to stay. I think I was the only Indian in the bunch. But since I had been there before, I had already made a few friends around town too, and I had my little alley joints, and I could also go by Jimmy Rushing's father's restaurant and catch Jimmy in there and eat free.

During this time, one of the other places I used to hang out in from time to time was Halley Richardson's shoeshine parlor. He also had a little something going on in the back room there, and maybe a few other little things on the side. He was also known as Big Halley. I know one reason for it. This was during the days of Prohibition. He used to come into a dance wearing an overcoat, and he was big, fat Halley. But he really wasn't as fat as he appeared to be. When he came in, there was some extra fat under his coat, and he would get thinner and thinner as the dance went on.

Jimmy Rushing and I got to be very good friends on the road with the Blue Devils, and we used to hit those alleys and find the joints together. Me and old Rush. We were some pair. We just wanted to have a good time. Me playing the piano and him singing. We used to do that in every town. We'd go out, and when we came to a joint with a piano in it, that was our chance to get with it. The places that didn't have a piano were not so hot as far as I was concerned, because I couldn't do my thing. But that didn't always stop Jimmy. One night we were in some town somewhere and I came walking down one of those alleys and heard all this singing up ahead, and when I got there, I still didn't hear any piano in the background. And when I went in, I found that son of a bitch in there singing by himself with no piano anywhere in sight or out of sight either.

"Hey," I said, "what you doing, Rush?"

He just looked at me and shook his head smiling sheepishly.

And he looked at me and said, "Well, I be durned."

"Yeah," I said. "I caught you, didn't I?"

He had rushed on in there and was singing his can off with no music, nothing. I kidded him for days about that. I don't think he was that hungry or hard up or anything like that. I think he just liked the looks of the place or something, or saw somebody in there that he wanted to get next to.

In those days old Rush was not anything like as heavy as he was later on. He was plump, but not what you'd call fat, and he was also a very good dancer. I found that out when I went to a couple of dances with him. And sometimes when we were playing somewhere, he'd get a partner and get out there on the floor and dance his old butt off. He was light on his feet, and he could really move. He was also a very fast runner back in

those days. Later on in the Bennie Moten band I remember how sometimes when the bus stopped for a break on the road somewhere, he and
Bennie, who was about the same size at that time, used to race each other
along the highway. They were both fast. Sometimes they used to race
each other running backwards, something old Bojangles Robinson was
very notorious for doing.

There were no heaters in those old canvas-top touring cars that the
Blue Devils were traveling in while I was on the road with them, and
sometimes when the weather turned cold and the wind started coming
through the bulges and cracks in those old snap-on isinglass enclosure
panels, we used to wrap newspapers around our legs. But once we got
ourselves a little jug or two and packed ourselves in there as close as
we did, you could keep pretty warm. But it was a little rough out there
during that time of the year.

I can also remember how cold it was while we were in Kansas City.
On the morning they came by Temple's house to pick me up to go to
Topeka, I was still in bed, and I thought about that weather outside and
I said, "Man, I can't make it." But I was the one who had talked them
into stopping off in Kansas City. Because I knew the Kansas City people
should hear that band. So we came and about half of the band stayed
with Big 'Un's relatives, and we got the others settled somewhere. I
already had a place to stay—Temple's alley down the street from the
Eblon Theatre. But we couldn't find any place to play, until I finally went
to Bob, the guy I had met who had a little chicken shack, and I talked
him into taking the band there for a couple of nights. There was no money
up front. We would get a little cut of whatever they took in, and we had
the commission of bootleg whiskey, and they gave us a meal. That was
about the best we could do in Kansas City that time.

So when they came and knocked on my door that cold morning, I said,
"Man, I just can't make it." But I knew I had to go back out with them
again. Old Rush and the rest of them talked me out of quitting for the
time being. And we went on to Topeka and on to Wichita. But every time
it got cold from then on, I told myself I had to start thinking about getting
out of here now.

From Topeka we went on down to Wichita and played a dance and
stayed there for a week or so trying to line up our next job. I never will
forget what happened there. Because when Big 'Un finally got us a gig
to go down and play a big dance in Oklahoma City and we decided to get
down there two or three days ahead of time, we found out that we didn't
have enough money for everybody to check out of the hotel. So they had
to leave me and Lips Page and a few instruments there until Big 'Un got
to Oklahoma City and picked up the advance and wired back the ransom
money.

After the big dance we went out again and did a few jobs down in Texas, where it was somewhat warmer than Kansas. Then when we came back into Oklahoma that time, we had a little layoff. That was when I went by the tailor shop where Ernie Williams worked and saw a hat I liked. I think it cost something like three or four dollars, but that was a lot back in those days and I couldn't afford it. But I liked it so much that the owner let me have it on time with no down payment. He said I could take it, and when I got something, I could bring it over and pay him.

But not long after that, Kansas City began calling me again. I liked Oklahoma City fine, but not much was happening with the Blue Devils. We were still laying off, and I started thinking about getting back to the Eblon Theatre and that organ and all of those joints around Kansas City. There was so much happening all the time in Kansas City. There was a lot of action that I hadn't had time to get into yet.

So I saved enough money for train fare from what I was making playing up at Honey Murphy's, and then early one morning I got up and took that hat, which I hadn't paid anything on, and a little note by Jimmy Rushing's father's restaurant and left it there. Then I went on down to the station and took the first train to Kansas City.

I hadn't talked to anybody about what I was going to do. I just sort of eased on out of town. I figured that was the best way, because I really hated to leave those guys, and I know they would have tried every tack I could think of to talk me out of it again.

Anyway they didn't realize what had happened until Jimmy came by the restaurant later on that morning. When I saw him again in Kansas City sometime afterwards, he told me he came into the restaurant and Mister Rushing started right in on him.

"What's the matter? Where's that piano player, that Basie boy?"

And Jimmy told me he himself just let it go by.

"Nothing's the matter. He must not be up yet."

But Mister Rushing kept on.

"I don't think so. I think he's gone."

And Jimmy said, "Oh no."

And Mister Rushing said, "Oh yeah, I think he's gone because he left this hat and this note for you."

What I had written on the note was something about once a Blue Devil always a Blue Devil, but I must go back. I said something about how I hate to leave, but I hope you understand. Please take this hat across the street to the tailor shop and thank Ernie Williams for me. I could have also said I'll be seeing all of you guys again before long, and will also be seeing some of you for a long time to come. Because during that short time I had spent on the road with them I really had become a Blue Devil forever.

RED BANK AND THERE-ABOUTS

1904 = Circa 1923

I had come out west to Kansas City and Oklahoma from New Jersey by way of New York City, passing through quite a few other places on the way. I was born in Red Bank, New Jersey. My father's name was Harvey Lee Basie, and my mother's name was Lilly Ann. According to information recorded in the family Bible that was passed on to me, my father was born in 1870, and the year of my mother's birth was 1875.

So far as I know, both of my parents were born and raised in Chase City, Virginia. But when I was born, on August 21, 1904, they were living in Red Bank, New Jersey. I don't remember anything about how and why they left Virginia, and I don't know how long they had been living in Red Bank before I was born. But I think I'm probably right when I say I believe they already knew each other down in Chase City and got married there and then came north together.

My grandparents on my father's side also lived in Red Bank. I don't remember anything about when they came or how they came, but my guess is that they came after my father and mother had gotten settled, because they lived in our house for a while; and then they went to stay with one of their daughters in Newark. That must have been where they stayed from then on. They didn't come back to live with us anymore that I remember, and I'm pretty sure they didn't go back down to Virginia.

The main thing I remember about my grandmother is how nice and warm her big old bed used to be, especially in the wintertime. I must have been still hardly big enough to toddle about at that time, but I remember how much I used to love to be all snuggled up with her rocking me to sleep.

My recollection of my grandfather is also very vague. But I do remember one thing he did that upset my father very much. He went out into the backyard and cut down one of my father's apple trees just so he could have a clear place to sit out there and smoke his pipe. I remember that my father was very disturbed about that, and I also remember that he was still upset about it even after grandfather left for Newark. My father had two sisters and one brother. One was Aunt Myrtle Basie Morton, who lived in Red Bank, and there was Aunt Mary, who lived in Newark. There was also Uncle James Basie, who also lived in Red Bank, and I remember us visiting his house often, especially on Sundays. I don't know what relatives were still living in Chase City. In fact, I don't remember hearing anybody ever talking about anything that went on down there. And if I ever knew anything about anybody going back down there on a visit, I have forgotten all about it.

My mother's maiden name was Lilly Ann Childs. I never saw any of my grandparents on her side of the family. But I did know her two brothers, Uncle Alex and Uncle Henry. Both of them were ministers. Uncle Alex was Reverend Alexander Childs, the pastor of a big church in Philadelphia, and Uncle Henry was Reverend Henry Childs, who was a pastor in Pittsburgh. If I had any aunts in my mother's family, I don't remember them. I didn't get to know very much about Uncle Henry because we never went to Pittsburgh when I was a child. But we did go to visit Uncle Alex in Philadelphia, and down the street from his house there was one of those fire stations that had a horse-drawn, hook-and-ladder fire engine. When they pulled that thing out on the way to answer an alarm call with all the bells clanging, it was something to witness.

I had one older brother. His name was Leroy, and I think he was probably about eight years older than I was. I can't say that I really remember very much about him because he died while I was still very young. The only special thing I recollect is that he used to go into the kitchen while my mother was away and try to cook up something and then try to hide the evidence. I remember tattling on him one time and getting him punished. I don't remember what he actually did and what I told Mama or why I told on him, but I never will forget the look he gave me afterward. He looked at me and shook his finger in my face.

Red Bank was an important resort town in those days, and my father was the coachman and caretaker for Judge White, who owned one of the big estates along the Shrewsbury River. I never will forget that big house and those grounds, and the pier that ran from the backyard and the beach out to where rowboats were tied up. Sometimes my father used to take me along with him, and when I was big enough, he taught me how to curry the horses, which I liked; and I also liked being around the harnesses and the carriages, and I used to have to put the hay in the rack and help Pop, as I called my father, clean out the stalls.

My father's job as coachman didn't last a very long time, because the automobile was beginning to come into fashion around that time, and before long Judge White bought one. So horses and carriages were moved out, and the stables became the car shed. But Pop didn't become a chauffeur. He still worked for Judge White, but he also began to take care of the grounds of other estates around Rumsen and also some places in Red Bank, and in a while he had a little business of his own.

When the estate people he contracted with went away, he closed their houses for the season and took care of the premises while they were gone; and they would notify him when they were coming back, and he'd have everything all ready for them. Sometimes he also used to take me along to help him on those jobs, and I worked in the gardens and cut grass and scrubbed floors and cleaned rugs and windows and all that kind of stuff, and I hated it.

The Whites drove their own automobile, which, I'm pretty sure, was also the first one I ever rode in. I used to find out when Lady Margarette, as I used to call their daughter, was getting ready to drive downtown, and I'd make it my business to walk up two or three blocks and slow up until I heard her coming, because I knew she was always going to say, "William, are you going into town?"

And I'd say, "Yes ma'am, yes ma'am," and hop in.

She was always very nice to me. I guess she must have been in her early twenties; and sometimes she used to treat me almost as if she were my teacher, and when I started taking piano lessons, she used to have me come into the house and go over the keyboard exercises for her. I can still remember that room and the piano with the neat stack of sheet music that she herself, like a lot of well-to-do ladies during that time, used to know how to play. Not because they were going to be professional or anything like that, but just as a part of what hip, young women in her social circles were supposed to do. I used to sit on that stool and go through my exercises, and she would listen and say, "That's nice, William. Keep practicing, William."

I didn't start out to be a piano player. The first thing I really wanted to be was a drummer.

When Pop was working full-time for Judge White, his pay was forty dollars a month, which must not have been too bad back in those days, because he bought the house we were living in. But of course, my mother worked, too. She was a laundress, or, as folks used to say, she took in washing and ironing. She didn't seem to mind it, but I didn't like to see her doing that at all. I used to look at all those big baskets of clothes, and as far as I was concerned, that was too much work for the little change she was getting paid.

Sometimes it used to start snowing in Red Bank right after Thanksgiving, and there would be snow on the ground until damn near spring. So another task I used to have was delivering those big baskets of clothes on my sled. I'd say my mother used to get paid about fifty cents for each one of those baskets of clothes in those days, not any more than that, and I didn't get anything for making all those deliveries. Except every now and then when she would bake a cake especially for me.

She also used to bake cakes for sale, and I think all she got was about forty cents for one of those great big cakes. I was crazy about cakes. But I never did like the idea of my mother having to work at anything like washing and ironing and cooking and all that jive. I used to tell her that all the time, and one day I drew the picture of an automobile and showed it to her and said, "One of these days I'm going to get you a car just like that, and I'm going to stop you from working."

That was the first important thing I really wanted to do in life, and all of that was also what made me decide that I had to get out of Red Bank one day. That was my aim, and it never left my mind no matter where I went. Back during the days when I was playing and hanging around in all those old good-times joints and dives, in all those back alleys, I never forgot that promise I made my mother. Every time I got a few pennies ahead, I always sent a little something home to her.

Another thing about the snow in that backyard was the trail of tracks that I was always the first to make out there early every morning. Not to the clothesline but to that little outside office building out there where I transacted the first piece of urgent business of the day. Inside offices of that kind were very rare in those days. I can remember when one of our neighbors had one installed on the back porch. It had an overhead tank and chain and a much warmer enclosure. That was something else I promised myself that I was going to get for my mother.

In the summertime everybody used to ride the Shrewsbury riverboat. I remember how we used to take it up to the picnic grounds at Atlantic Highlands in August. It used to stop and pick up people at Fair Haven and let them off at Atlantic Highlands and continue on up to New York. To me it used to seem as if the trip from Fair Haven to Atlantic Highlands took hours. But then you were finally there, and the picnic would get under way, and it would have to end by four o'clock so everybody could get back down to the landing to catch the boat down coming back from New York.

I also used to go down to a little nearby beach on the Shrewsbury River. I would go wading, and there was also a dock down there where the commercial fishing boats used to come and dump clams and oysters. You could go down there and take a pailful home and nobody would mind, and sometimes I also used to go down with a chisel or some other piece of sharp

iron and scoop up a batch of them and sit down with them on a spread-out
newspaper right there on the dock and open them up and eat as many as
I wanted.

Another thing I like to remember about Red Bank back when I was a
boy is the way things used to be during the Christmas season. Sometimes I
see something that makes me remember how the streets used to look when
all the pines and fir trees and all the decorations were up, and all of the
Christmas merchandise was displayed out on the sidewalks. The soldiers
in town from Fort Monmouth used to walk up and down the streets during that time of year. I can remember the wraparound leggings they used to
wear in those days, and there were also a lot of sailors strolling along. I
guess a lot of different times run together in my head this many years
afterwards, so I can't fix any date on it, but I'm pretty sure that the part
about the soldiers and sailors happened during World War I.

There was also the way things used to smell during the Christmas season. First there were all the special fruits that you hardly ever saw in the
stores in those days until that time of year. Some fruits, like raisins and
dates, and some nuts, like almonds and filberts and Brazil nuts and English
walnuts, used to be so much a part of Christmas that you used to look
forward to finding some of it along with an assortment of hard candies in
your stocking or in your pile under the tree on Christmas morning just as
you could hardly wait to discover which toys you were going to find there.

But nothing was more special about the smell of Christmas than all of
the cooking spices that used to fill the house at that time. Most people did
their own baking in those days, and my mother loved to make cakes and
pies anyway; so there was all that nutmeg and vanilla and cinnamon and
chocolate in the air.

My mouth still waters when I remember those cakes and with all that
coconut icing and those jelly layer cakes and those potato pies and custard
pies. And all mixed in with all of that, you could also smell the celery and
the sage and black pepper in the chicken or turkey stuffing, and when my
mother baked ham, there were the cloves and the pineapple glaze.

＝

One thing I always wanted to do even before I even really thought about
being a musician was go on the road touring everywhere in the world of
show business with a troupe. When the carnivals used to come to Red
Bank, they used to set up in a big, empty lot on the corner down the street
from our house, and I always used to go down there and hang around
and frustrate the hell out of myself dreaming about leaving with them. My
whole damn being wanted to get with whatever show it was, and I used to
do anything I could just to be able to be as close as I could get to all of

that. I can still see the tents with all the colors and stripes and tassels and flaps and banners and signs and see the carnival wagons and the clowns and acrobats; and there were also the parade bands that played for the different acts and stunts. And then there were the merry-go-rounds and the Ferris wheels and the animal cages and the elephants. I used to help feed the animals, carry water, anything just to be there where all of that fantasy stuff was happening.

One time another carnival came and there was an accordion player that I liked to hear. They were there for about four days as I recall, and he would sit outside the tent in the open air every afternoon playing, and one day I went home and got a piece of cake and brought it to him, and he really played for me then. He also talked to me, and I told him how much I wanted to go off with a show. But he said I ought to stick in school, and when I finished, there would be plenty of time to think about joining a circus or minstrel or vaudeville or something like that. It was very good advice, but the truth is I just wanted to be on the road with a show so much so that I would have gone along just to be a water boy for the elephants if I could have.

School, I'm sorry to say, was not my thing. I learned to read and write and do some figuring and felt that was all you had to learn. I didn't really see any point in finishing school and all that jive. I was only interested in music and show business and traveling. That was the whole thing as far as I was concerned, and that was the worst mistake I ever made. I didn't see any connection between geography and history and things like that with traveling. I should have gone on and finished school just like that accordion player with that circus told me to do, but I just wanted to hurry up and get out of there and out of Red Bank and be going somewhere.

So I didn't go any higher than junior high school. I finally made it that far. But by that time about all I was really doing when I went was taking part in plays and playing piano or a program or something like that. Otherwise, I just wasn't interested in what school was about. It was just a drag as far as I was concerned, and I could hardly wait to get out of there. For me the end of summer was always the saddest time of the year, because that was when you had to go back to the everyday routine of school again.

I used to stay in one grade so long it was shameful. Kids would come into kindergarten and grow on up and catch up with me and then leave me sitting there in the same class. It got so bad that the teachers didn't even call on me to recite anymore. I would just go in and take my seat and sit there, and they would look out and see me, and that was about it. I could take any seat and nobody said anything, and I didn't pass in my homework or anything. I didn't take any tests. I didn't even have any report card anymore. It was ridiculous. I guess my parents must have said to hell with it.

It really got to be a pretty awful situation. The teacher would be up there trying to teach us something, and everybody else would be paying attention and trying to learn what they could except another old boy and me. We would be back there in the last row just fooling around doing something silly. Sometimes we'd be back there drumming under the desk knowing full well that we were making a nuisance of ourselves and keeping other students from concentrating. But we didn't care. We were just doing something. Anything.

Finally I just got tired of getting nowhere in school. So one day I just got up and walked on out of there and away from it, and Elmer Williams and I left town. Elmer was from Eatontown, which was only about three miles from Red Bank. I've forgotten how we first met. My guess is that we were hanging around the same poolroom or somewhere like that. But by the time we left school together, we had been pretty close friends for a while. We actually left school to go out and make it as musicians.

—

I knew that there was a war going on in Europe from the time that I was about ten years old until I was about fourteen. But it really didn't mean very much to me then. I heard people talking about Uncle Sam sending General Blackjack Pershing and the doughboys overseas to help the Frenchmen and Great Britain beat the kaiser and the Germans; and I saw the soldiers wearing those old olive-drab coats and wraparound leggings, and I never will forget those placards with a picture of Uncle Sam wearing his Yankee-Doodle hat and suit, pointing his finger and saying, "I Want You." But truthfully it wasn't until afterwards that I began to understand what it was all about.

While it was actually going on, people sometimes sat around talking German submarines loaded with torpedoes lying in wait for the troop transport ships crossing the Atlantic Ocean. And everybody also knew about going over the line and through the barbed-wire entanglements from the trenches, and you also knew about hand grenades and bayonets and gas masks just as you heard about the Argonne Forest and the Hindenburg line and the French gun called the Seventy-five and the longest-range German as Big Bertha. But nobody in my family was directly concerned with any of that, or if anybody was, I don't remember it. In fact, I don't remember knowing anybody that had to go in the army.

People didn't keep up with the news back during that part of my childhood like they started doing years later when the radio came in and started featuring the news every day. But there used to be some talk about the Spanish-American War, which Theodore Roosevelt and the Rough Riders had fought in down in Cuba back in 1898, and there was a lot of talk about how the Titanic, the greatest ship ever built, ran into an iceberg and sank on its maiden voyage. I was eight years old when it happened, in 1912, but not only did people talk about it for years afterward, there were also songs and sermons about it in church.

There was also a lot of talk about Jack Johnson. I was not quite six years old when the great Jack Johnson–Jim Jeffers fight took place in 1910, but when people talked about it, they always sounded as if they were talking about current news. Then when I was eleven, everybody was talking about it all over again because that was when he lost the championship to Jesse Willard down in Havana. Nobody I knew in Red Bank thought he really lost it fair. People said he let himself be knocked out because he had been forced to make a deal to give up the championship before the government agents would allow him to come back into the United States.

You knew some of the songs you heard and also sang in school during that time, such as "It's a Long Way to Tipperary," "Pack Up Your Troubles in an Old Kit Bag," "Keep the Home Fires Burning," and "Roses of Picardy." Then right along with other army songs like "Oh How I Hate to Get Up in the Morning" and "Over There," you also had "Poor Butterfly," "Dark Town Strutter's Ball," "Pretty Baby," "Indiana," "Me and My Gal," and "I'm Always Chasing Rainbows," and "Jada," and "Hindustan." But the army song that turned out to be the biggest for me was "The Bugle Call Rag," also known as "The Bugle Blues." I've gotten a whole lot of mileage out of that one over the years.

I guess show business got into my system very early. By all odds as far back as I can remember, my favorite place in Red Bank was the Palace moving-picture theater. I used to go down there and do chores for the manager every chance I got. I would help sweep out the auditorium and the lobby, polish the brass rails and fixtures, put up the extra seats and clean up the dressing room under the stage so that they would be ready for the vaudeville shows that used to play there on weekends. I also used to meet the entertainers when they arrived at the station and show them the way to the hotel.

That was the way I got to come into the theater free, and I would go strutting in front of the other kids, and when they said something smart about it, I'd just say, "Well, I work at the theater."

Then after I had been helping with cleaning for a while, I could also go up and help out in the projection booth. The men who worked up there was named George Ruth, and he showed me how to rewind the reels on the machine, which in those days had a crank handle; and before long I also learned how to help him when the time came to change back and forth between the projectors. So I got to see all the movies over and over.

I also learned to operate the spotlight for the acts during the weekends when the vaudeville used to be playing. I had to know how to hit the performers, how to track them, how to widen and close the spot as needed. They didn't have but one spotlight in that theater in those days, and that was what you had to do everything with, which was all the same to me as long as I was doing something connected with show business.

In those days of silent movies the Palace Theatre also used to have a house piano player who used to provide the musical background for what was happening on the screen. He used to come in from New York every day, but one day something happened and he didn't get there, and Mr. McNulty, who was the manager, couldn't find anybody to fill in. So I said I could do it. And I could. Not because I thought of myself as being a musician. Because I really don't think I did. But I had been taking piano lessons for a while by that time, and I knew how that kind of music went, because I had been hearing it over and over all that time, and I was also the type of guy who could hear something once and work it out on my own anyway.

I said I could play it, but Mr. McNulty just laughed at me and told me to go on up and tell George Ruth to put the picture on. Which I did. But once we got the carbons all lined up and the reels rolling, I made my way back downstairs to the pit and sat at the piano, and all you had to do was watch the screen and play something to go with what was happening in the story. Sometimes you got the cue from the captions. I had spent enough time down there watching the regular piano player to know what all of that was all about. So when there were cowboys and Indians, I knew what kind of things to play, and I knew what went with the action when somebody was sneaking in somewhere or when people were lively or when the caption read "That Night" or "The Next Day" or "Meanwhile in Town," and so on.

I played that matinee, and when it was over, Mr. McNulty told me to come back and play that evening show. I don't remember anything about what he paid me or even what he said about paying me. I just remember that I couldn't wait to tell all the kids, and when I did, they all wanted to come down to the Palace to see old Willie Basie play the piano for the movie. But of course, they couldn't get in. Not because they were under age or anything like that, but because they didn't have the price of admission. Kids didn't just happen to have spare change like that in their pockets in those days.

Then after I got home, Mrs. Reed came in and started talking to my mother. Mrs. Reed and her husband were rooming at our house at that time, and she used to go to the movies every day. She was talking to Mama about the picture as she often did, and then she said, "You know, one thing was kinda curious in there today. There was somebody different playing the piano, and it looked like Willie. Well, I couldn't really see him down in the dark and all, but it sounded just like him sitting down there at the piano."

"Well, it *was* me," I said.

"No, it wasn't," she said.

And then she said, "But it sure did sound a whole lot like him though."

As far as I can remember, we always had a piano. And I had taken piano lessons because my mother made me take them. She paid twenty-five cents a lesson, and that was that. And I learned how to play the exercises, and I could also just sit down and pick out things. That was my thing so far as the piano was concerned. I could pick out just about any song I heard. I liked ragtime. It was the big thing in those days, and all I had to do was have somebody else playing something and I could start right in and repeat it. That wasn't anything for me. And of course, in those days you also picked up things from player-piano rolls.

But I did take those lessons. So I learned how to spell out things too. I don't mean I learned how to read music like those kids coming up nowadays. They go to school, and they can sight-read almost anything you put in front of them. Just like that. Which I think is just remarkable. I never did spend a lot of time trying to learn to do anything like that. I just took a few lessons from a German lady, Miss Vandevere, and I could play things like "The Midnight Fire Alarm" and selections from *Rigoletto,* and finally I just weaned on away. Because by that time I could play the things I really wanted to play. I thought a little ragtime was all you needed.

I was attracted to trap drums very early. There was a drummer known as Chick Something who played for quite a few of the dances that my mother used to take me along to. So I got to know him, and he taught me a few little things, and before long he used to let me sit in on drums during intermissions. By that time, I was so wrapped up in drums that my father bought me a little trap set. It had a funny little snare drum and a bass, a hanging foot pedal, and both had cords on the side that you had to pull to tighten and tune the heads. I guess it really wasn't much of a set by professional standards, but it was all right for me at the time.

But before that happened, I had actually started to play drums along with a piano player whose name I've forgotten, and we picked up a little change from a few little jobs around town. In those days a lot of organizations giving a little dance used to just hire a piano player and a drummer. So in a little while I was beginning to play for a few dances with almost any piano player who could play dance music.

It was Sonny Greer, who later on went on to become one of the greatest and most famous drummers in the world with the Duke Ellington Orchestra, who got the notion of being a drummer out of my head once and for all. I would be playing on some little job somewhere around town, and every time Greer would happen to come in from Long Branch, which was only a few miles away, and you let him sit in on drums, that was it for me. A few times like that and I didn't want to play another lick. I had sense enough to know that I'd never be able to do what he did up there.

That's not to say that he ever really tried to do me in or anything like that. He was already so much better that he didn't even have to think about anything like that. He just liked to play, and he was already the sharpest thing anybody around that part of New Jersey ever heard. He didn't have the feeling that he was the big star. He was just being nice, because whenever he came in, everybody knew he was the champ. So he would sit in and do his thing, and I could see that playing drums was not going to be my gig.

He was very nice to everybody, and he was especially nice to me. He was a little older than I was. Not all that much older, but he was already playing as a professional with Chester Arthur's band, which used to come into Red Bank and play for the annual Firemen's Ball and other big events like that. That was how much of a pro he already was, and he knew he was the champ. But he was especially nice to me. For instance, one time there was a piano contest down in Asbury Park, and my mother went down with me, and when we got there, Greer was there, and he came over and said, "Hey, I'll play with you." And I won first place. And I think he was the reason. Because I don't really think I was that good. I think it also might have been something that they wanted to do for me because I was so young and strolled up there so cocky and started playing and flashing my hands all up in the air. I think it must have been something like that along with having Greer in back of me taking charge on drums. Because I heard some of the ones that came on before me, and they were really playing a lot of piano. There was one boy named Corky, and I was certain he could play more piano than I was playing at that time. But with old Greer with me I was the one they chose.

Before Sonny hit the road as a full-time professional drummer, we played on quite a few little gigs in Red Bank and thereabouts. We even did a three-day stand on the vaudeville stage of the Palace. They used to hold those amateur talent contests known as Opportunity Night, and my big pal, Raymond McGuire, won the vocal prize. So I asked Mr. McNulty about letting me get a group together for a weekend in there with Raymond, and he went for it. So I got Greer and Duffin on C-melody sax and Bill Robinson on violin, and that was really my introduction to show business. And it was just wonderful.

I also got to go out on a few jobs with Bill Robinson. He used me on piano at the beginning of the season, and then when the summer hit full swing, they brought in Freddy Tunstall because the music they were playing was a little too heavy for me. But Freddy, who as a stride man was right up there next to such champion keyboard ticklers as the Beetle, the Lion, and James P. Johnson, could read and play anything, and he also had a few fancy stage tricks that I began to pick up on.

So one day I decided that I was going to put on my own dance. So I printed up my own signs and had Pop get a night at the K & P Hall, and Mama made some sandwiches and Pop was the ticket seller. Then I went and got Bill Robinson and Duffin, and Cricket played the drums. It was a good thing that Pop got the K & P Hall free of charge, because when I paid the musicians, I don't think there was much money left. I didn't really know what the hell I was doing. I just wanted to give a dance, and I did.

—

At first Elmer Williams had just liked to come along with me on the little jobs in and around Red Bank just to listen. Then somewhere along the line he got a job as a chauffeur for a rich family, and he used to drive a woman around, and she was very nice to him. I mean, she really liked him, and she used to let him stop off in the poolroom and shoot a couple of games while she just sat out there in the car waiting for him to finish and come back out and drive her home.

So he could also get the car and drive around on his own, and he was only too glad to haul me and the musicians to the little jobs we used to get. And, evidently, that is when he decided to become a musician himself, because one day he came up with a mail-order catalog and said he was going to send off and get himself a horn to play. I just laughed at him. But he was serious, and when it came, it was a C-melody sax, and there was a little book that came with it, and he began to work that thing out all by himself, and before long he could carry a tune on it.

The first thing he learned to play was "The Wang Wang Blues," and he also learned "The Farewell Blues" and "Dardanella," and a tune called "The Yacka Hula Hicka Dula." So pretty soon he began to want to play with the little groups I got together, and when I got a job in Keansburg for a couple of Saturday nights, I let him play his four numbers. But when we got paid, I didn't cut him in. Because the real reason I was letting him play was to pay him back for furnishing the transportation. As a matter of fact, at that time he would have been glad to pay me for being so nice. But he kept with that thing and learned to play in different keys, and after a while he was really good enough to earn his cut.

The pay I used to get for jobs you used to pick up during that time was three or four dollars per night for each musician. But we also used to go out and work for whatever you collected when you passed the hat around. Sometimes we would go to the winter resort towns like Lakewood and play for the vacation people sitting out on the porches; and sometimes they could let us come into some of the hotels and play in the lobby and pass the hat, and most of the time we did all right by the standards of those days.

We used to play at a place on Springwood Avenue when the Harlem Renaissance basketball team used to come to Asbury Park. That was always a big event, and after the game there was always a dance. And there was a trumpet player named Cecil Benjamin who used to get us to play with him at some of the dinner dances that were held at the Coronet

Club in Red Bank. All of that was very important to me as a young
musician. I was always on the lookout for another gig. That was why I
had been going to school less and less and not doing anything but something silly when I did go. Every chance I got, I was hanging out down at
the pool hall, which was also the main place a lot of musicians used to go.

=

In those days you wore short pants, knee breeches, or sailor-boy pants
until you were in your teens. I don't remember exactly how old I was when
I got my first pair of long pants. But I was already playing some dances
while I was still in short pants. Sometimes we used to have to make up
some sort of excuse to get me into some of the places, because I was too
young. Back during the time when I was running around with Sonny
Greer, sometimes he used to let me help him carry part of his drum set so
I could get into the dance hall to play.

My first pair of long pants were sailor pants with the narrow hips and
the square-flap button placket and bell bottoms. I bought them and left
them around at Raymond McGuire's house on West Bergen Place. I
couldn't put them on at home because when I was growing up you were not
supposed to wear long pants until you came of age. I think you were supposed to be about sixteen or maybe eighteen. You started out in rompers,
and then you went into knickers that buttoned and bloused just above the
knee or just below them. Some guys used to wear them like baseball pants,
and if you could get away with letting them hang down, that was kind of
raunchy, and if you wore one leg up and one down, that was very sporty,
especially if you wore your cap cocked at a special angle or with the visor
flipped up or turned around to the back.

Grown folks used to call that being mannish, and when they said, "Well,
you mannish boy," that meant that you were in too much of a hurry to be
grown up and out from under the control of your parents, and what they
were signifying was that you were in too much of a hurry for your own
good. Once you started shaving, it was a different matter. If you were old
enough to shave, you were old enough to wear long pants. So, of course,
there were some guys who used to pretend that they had to shave before
they really had anything but a little fuzz on their chin. Your first pair of
long pants was a big deal back in those days.

The main reason Raymond McGuire's house was where I used to keep
my long pants stashed was all that skirt chasing I was already beginning to
do along with him. Actually old Raymond had a couple of years on me.
But we used to hit those joints together because he was a singer in those
days, and he used to take me around as his piano player; and that's how
I used to get inside those adult places and get next to all that upstairs
action.

I took my first drink of alcoholic beverage at a birthday party in Long Branch when I was about fifteen or sixteen years old, which means I was probably still wearing short pants. They were having a birthday party for a cat named Kid Nash, and they wanted me to play something on the piano, and I said no, and they kept on asking me, so I told them to get me a drink and I didn't mean fruit punch, and they brought me some gin and I played "The Japanese Sandman," which was a very new popular tune at that time and, by the way, is still a very good tune to this day.

I wouldn't say that I actually needed that drink in order to play "The Japanese Sandman" at Kid Nash's birthday party. I'd say I was just being kind of mannish and trying to show how grown up I was or something like that. But I can remember another time when I had to have a drink very quick because that was the only thing that could save me. That was the time when I first met a piano player named Donald Lambert. I don't remember which one of those little towns that was, but it was at a house, and a bunch of my friends from Red Bank took me up there to play against him one night. I was supposed to go in there and cut him, cut him a new suit and duster. So we went on up there to wherever it was and went on in. But as soon as I heard that cat start playing, I knew I was in bad trouble.

So I slipped on back into the kitchen and got myself two or three big dips out of that pot they were serving the juice in. And by the time Lambert was winding up and they came looking for me to take my turn, I was way into my act; and they said just exactly what I wanted to hear. As soon as they got there and saw that crooked look in my eyes and saw how I was holding onto things to try to steady myself, they said, "Old Bill Basie can't play, man. Look at him. He's drunk. He can't play."

But I wasn't drunk. I knew exactly what I was doing, and the more they talked, the drunker I acted. Hell, they didn't know whether I was going to be sick or be zonked out. So they took me out of there and put me in the car and headed back to Red Bank. And it was only after they got miles out of that town that I began to show any signs of sobering up. Then the closer we came to Red Bank the soberer I began to act, and by the time we got home I was just about sitting up straight in the car again.

That is how my first meeting with Don Lambert turned out. I had a very narrow escape. I don't think any of my good buddies were any wiser, but I wasn't about to let them get me all tangled up with the Lamb, because he had that hatchet even then. I didn't have to listen to but so many bars to realize that I didn't have any business messing with him.

I faked my way out of playing against the Lamb that night, but there were also quite a few other nights when I wasn't faking at all, and the fellows really had to take me all the way home; and sometimes they would all spend the night in my room, and if there were more than three, we used to have to sleep across the bed. But one night Raymond McGuire and somebody just left me on the stairway and left the lamp there. That's how my old man knew. I made it up the steps, but I left the lamp still burning. So naturally he checks me out.

"What's wrong with you, William?" he said, and all I could say was "I must have had too much soda, and it made me sick."

But he said, "It smells like gin to me."

Thinking back on it now I'd say that was pretty cool. So I also have to say that most likely he was just as hip about what I was getting into in those joints and other houses and out at those pig roasts in places like Reavytown and Pine Bottoms. I guess he must have decided not to waste his time trying to talk me out of all *that*.

—

At first there was only one theater in Red Bank, and that was the Palace. But some time later on there was also the Lyric, and the main reason I used to go down there was to listen to Mr. Henry La Ross play the organ. He was one of the professors at school, and he taught classes in music appreciation. I didn't find out until later on that he also played the organ and that he played for the shows. But when I did, I sometimes used to hang out around there two or three times every week just to hear him, no matter what the picture was.

All of my special interest in learning how to play the organ goes back to all those wonderful times I spent in the dark down there watching and listening to Henry La Ross playing at the Lyric Theatre. I never did get to take any organ lessons from him, but he was the one who made me aware of the organ, and there was something about it that I liked from the very first.

I never did get the chance to try to play that organ at the Lyric Theatre in Red Bank. But I feel as though it was my very first organ anyway. In those days the organist used to start playing before the lights would begin dimming for the first reel of the picture to start rolling. Sometimes Henry La Ross would play several numbers at that time, and I can still remember the way he used to play one special love song. I'm not sure about what the title of it was, but I will never forget how the tune went and how it sounded on that organ.

—

The one place where I could spend the night in Asbury Park in those days was Corky Williams's house. He had a room where you were welcome to flop until the next morning. But if more than two guys showed up, you would have to sleep crossways on the bed, and sometimes that could get to be a whole lot more overcrowded. One night as soon as I got there and looked around, I decided I'd better watch out for my money, and everybody knew I had just come from playing a gig. So before lying down, I slipped outside and hid my few little bills up in my shirt collar.

I just figured from the way those guys were casing me when I came in that they were going to try to roll me when I fell asleep. And I was right. We all were lying across the bed without clothes on, and after a while, when they thought I was snoring, I could feel someone's hand touching me up. They were pretty cool, but I had outsmarted them, and the next morning I just laughed at them, and I said, "Well, you guys didn't find what you were looking for last night, did you?" They tried to look all surprised like they didn't know what I was talking about, but they knew I had put one over on them.

Corky Williams didn't know anything about that. He was just a very nice guy, and you were always welcome to flop in that extra room. I'm sure he knew that you wouldn't even be there in the first place unless you were a little hard up at the moment. He was not running a bad place or anything like that. It just happened that sometimes the characters that you ran into around there couldn't be trusted.

—

My father had been trying to talk me into going into work with him cleaning up those houses and cutting the lawns on those big estates. I really couldn't see myself getting into that line of work. But I knew I had to do something, because he was getting tired of me hanging around home and always putting my feet under the table and not bringing in anything. It was time for me to start taking care of myself and paying for my keep. So one day Elmer Williams and I decided to get on the train and go down to Asbury Park and try it on our own. And we did.

But we picked the wrong time of year. We should have known better to go down there looking for work in the fall, but that is exactly what we did, and we soon found out that jobs were pretty scarce once the summer season was over. Of course, one big reason for going when we did was to get away from school. We hadn't been doing anything in class but waste time, because all we ever thought about was music and show business, so we decided to cut out.

I don't remember how we expected to live down there. Corky Williams still had that spare room around at his house, but you couldn't move in there, and I felt funny about turning up around there too often. So where we ended up sleeping was in the poolroom, where we also hung out most of the time. Truthfully, Joe Brown's poolroom on Springwood Avenue was really what we were heading for when we left Red Bank going to Asbury Park. We went down there to hang out at the poolroom with all the other musicians. That was like the main stem, and it was also where you found out about gigs.

Joe Brown was somebody I already knew, because I had met him on one of those trips I had made down there to work with Bill Robinson, the violin player. He was a very friendly guy, and he was nice enough to let us spend a few nights there. So wherever else we went during the day, we would make it back around to the poolroom by closing time, and after everybody else cleared out, Elmer Williams would take one of those benches, and I would grab myself another one, and that was our hotel room. Then we would cut out early the next morning and come back when everybody else began dropping in.

Then there was that little matter of getting something to eat. Since we couldn't find a job and our little money was running out, that was a problem right away. Actually, it got so bad that sometimes we used to take turns getting out to steal fresh rolls from those big old wicker baskets that the bakeries used to deliver to the restaurants. Back in those days they used to leave them outside on the sidewalk or the platform or the steps, along with the milk and the newspapers and those big pieces of ice, and I guess the restaurant people didn't really check those baskets very carefully, because Elmer and I used to lift a whole layer out of there, and evidently nobody ever go suspicious, because we never got caught. Of course, we didn't hit the same delivery ramp every day.

I did have one narrow escape, however. One morning at the Water Restaurant I was just about to pull my layer from one of those warm-smelling, mouth-watering wicker baskets, and I happened to look up and the cleaning man was coming outside. He just happened to be there early that day. All I could do was just look at him and smile, and I guess he must have thought I was working there, too; so he just went on doing what he was doing. But for a split second I really thought he had caught me in the act.

Then it also got to be more and more embarrassing to have to be sneaking in and out of the poolroom like that because we didn't want anybody else to find out how hard up we were. And it was also getting to be harder and harder to face Joe Brown after the first few nights. So after a week or so we gave it up and went on back and spent the rest of the fall and that winter in Red Bank.

—

When Elmer Williams and I went back to Asbury Park early that next season, I met a drummer named Harry Richardson, who had a nice little gig out on the outskirts of town at a roadhouse called the Hongkong Inn, and he hired us both, and he also had a violin player named Jimmy Hill. So things had started out much better for me down there when summer came that year. I even had a pretty nice place to stay. I was sleeping out at

Harry Richardson's house. That was a very good deal for me. It was convenient, and there was also always a lot of other musicians around. Not to mention the fact that it didn't cost very much.

The Hongkong Inn was run by a Chinese fellow and his family. I don't remember what his full name really was, if I ever knew what it was. But he was called Mr. Ah Kee. He was always very nice and friendly to me from the very outset. He started asking me all about my family, and I could tell that he was not just curious but really interested, and then one day he said he wanted to go up to Red Bank, and he and my father got along just fine. He went back up there several times.

He was a very fine man to work for. And I also got along just great with his two brothers. One was named Tommy, and the other was named Johnny. They were both always very nice, but I have a special reason for remembering Johnny—because of a present he gave me. I will never forget that. It was a pongee suit, and it was the sharpest thing I had ever had on in my life. That material was so fine you could roll the whole thing up and put it in your pocket, and all you had to do was just shake it out and put it on. I kept that pongee suit for years.

The Hongkong Inn was a roadhouse, but it was not just another joint. It was really a pretty classy place. But we did run into some excitement out there not too long after the season got under way. One night a bunch of sailors came in and began raising hell, and I guess somebody must have asked them to leave, because the next thing I knew they were all outside milling around saying they were all waiting to beat the hell out of everybody they could catch as the crowd came through the door.

I took them at their word because they looked as bad as they sounded, and as soon as we finished the last number, I cut out the back way and ran up the road and hid in some bushes up from the beach. I was not about to tangle with any of them. But they didn't scare Harry Richardson. He went right on out there and stood up to them. Of course, they beat him up pretty bad, but a lot of them got worked on pretty good in the process, and he stayed out there slugging and tussling with them until the last of them finally left.

After that, everything went along pretty smoothly out at the Hongkong Inn until about halfway through that summer. Then a little change took place. A piano player named Johnny Montague came down to Asbury Park from New York. He was around town for a while, and I heard him, and I knew how good he was. He could play some piano. He could play a whole lot of piano, and the word got around, and then when I got to work one night, he was already there at the piano, and I knew exactly what that meant. Nobody had to tell me a thing.

I don't think I even missed a beat. I just turned and went on into the office and told Mr. Ah Kee that I wanted to work outside parking cars.

That was the first time somebody just came in and took a piano gig away from me. And it wasn't the last time. It wasn't even the last time that summer. There were no hard feelings, because that was not considered dirty or underhanded back in those days. That is the way things were, and everybody knew it. If you were playing somewhere and another cat came in there and blew you out, he could take your gig.

Sometimes a guy would come in and you might let him sit in for a couple of numbers, and then he would cut on out and you would forget all about it. But when you came to work the next night, you'd find that everybody else was already there and the new cat is sitting in your chair. Everybody except you had been notified to get there an hour earlier. There were no unions and contracts back in those days. You were on your own, and if some cat cut you, what you had to do was go somewhere you could cut.

But when Johnny Montague took my job that summer at the Hongkong Inn, I went outside and started working in the parking lot. For some reason, which I've forgotten now, I know that was a good deal out there. I know I didn't want to go back to Red Bank, and I also liked working for Mr. Ah Kee and his brothers. But somehow or other I also already had the notion that things would work out very good for me out there. And I was right.

I went on out and started parking cars, and in a little while I was making more money doing that than anybody in the group was making for playing music. I had myself a good thing out there. I was meeting the cars as they pulled in, and I would let them out near the entrance, brush them down with a whisk broom, and then park the car and dust it off, and when they came back out, I would either get the car or escort them to it, and the tips were great.

And sometimes the fringe benefits were even better. When somebody came back out and couldn't quite make it to his car on his own because he had had too much to drink, I would support him all the way and then lay him in there.

Sometimes one customer like that was worth the whole night. I will not say how the money got out of his pocket and into mine, but somehow it always did, and he was feeling too good to miss it or need it, especially after I tapped him up a bit. When he woke up, he still had his wallet and watch and his jewelry. I didn't bother anything like that. But whatever amount of cash he still had in his pocket when he came back out by himself feeling too good to make it to his car was what my tip was for helping him.

That really was some gig. When Johnny Montague found out how good I was doing there, he offered to change jobs and park cars. But I said, "No, man, you play piano. This is my job now."

And that is also what I told Jimmy Hill. When he saw me with all those old, big greenbacks and quarters around at Harry Richardson's house every morning, Jimmy wanted to pack up his violin and come out and help me out. But I said, "No, thank you."

"I don't need no help, man. You play the music, and I will park the cars." And he got so hot in the collar that he wanted to fight. All those guys were outdone.

But I really couldn't stay away from the piano but for just so long, no matter how good the money was. Near the end of the summer I got a chance to go in and play with another little group in another club, and I took it and went over there. I've forgotten the name of that club, but it was a good job, and I was doing all right.

But at the end of the summer things really began to get slack down there again. So pretty soon Elmer Williams and I were back at Joe Brown's poolroom and taking turns rolling out early enough to pull that little raid on those restaurant deliveries every morning. We could have gone back around to Harry Richardson's house, but we didn't want to be in the way of the musicians he had with him at that time. He hadn't put us out, but after all he also had his family there. We just didn't feel right about being around at Harry Richardson's house without working. But the pool hall was another proposition. It was a little less embarrassing. But only for a while. Because after about a week we began to feel that we were getting to be a drag for Joe Brown too.

Then one afternoon while we were sitting out front just passing the time looking at the traffic and waiting for something to turn up, a big long Cadillac turned into that block and came cruising along and pulled up to the sidewalk a couple of doors away. There was a sharp guy sitting at the steering wheel, and he had two good-looking, and I mean good-looking, and hip-looking girls with him. I don't remember what they stopped for, but somehow I'm pretty sure that they were either on their way to the beach or on their way back home from the beach.

Anyway, they pulled up out there for whatever they had to pick up, and I was sitting there just blinking, and all of a sudden I heard Elmer Williams saying, "Hey, look. That's my Uncle Ralph."

I'm sure I didn't say anything at first. I just sat there looking at that sharp cat sitting in that fine automobile with those fabulous broads, but when Elmer nudged me and said it again, I said, "Your what?"

"My Uncle Ralph."

"Aw, come on, Elmer. Man, no it ain't."

"Yes, it is. Sure, that's my Uncle Ralph."

"Prove it," I said. "You got to prove that to me, Elmer. You got to prove that to me right now."

So Elmer just got up and walked on out to the car and said, "Hi, Uncle

Ralph," and when the man behind the wheel looked at him and smiled and stuck his hand out and said, "Elmer. Hello, Elmer," I couldn't believe my ears.

The man said something about what are you doing down here, and Elmer told him about us working around town as musicians, and his uncle said, "Well, good. That's fine." And they went on talking, and by that time I was standing there, too. So when Uncle Ralph said, "Where you fellows staying? You living around here somewhere? You got a place to stay?" I was ready.

As soon as Elmer said yes, I cut right in and said, "No, he ain't." I said, "Don't believe him. We ain't got no place to stay."

I wasn't about to let a big break like that get away, and I knew good and well that Elmer didn't want to go on sleeping on those benches in the poolroom any more than I did. I also told Uncle Ralph that we were not working at that time. Because I figured the least we might get was a little cash to help us out, and I was really hoping for more than that. The guy looked like he was loaded, and I knew damn well we were hurting.

And sure enough, the very next thing Uncle Ralph said was that if we were not staying anyplace in particular yet, there was plenty of room over at his place, so why didn't we just come on out and stay with him. And as soon as Elmer opened his mouth and said, "Well, we don't need. . . ," I cut him right off and said, "Yes we do too." And his Uncle Ralph said, "Well, just come on out. Go get your bags." And I said, "We ain't got no bags. We can just get right in the car now."

We had a few things, like a pair of pants and a pair of shoes and a couple of shirts or so and some underwear around at Harry Richardson's house. Elmer had his horn with him, of course. We didn't have much else at the pool hall, so we got in and circled by and picked up our things at Harry Richardson's place and went on out to stay at Elmer's Uncle Ralph's house, which was in another part of town. And that is where we were to stay for the rest of the time we were in Asbury Park.

It was a very big house with a lot of rooms. And it was also very well furnished. There was a big parlor with couches and chairs and a center table and also a piano, like most big houses used to have in those days—it was almost like a regular part of the furniture. Either a piano or a foot-pedal organ used mainly in religious homes for church music. There was also a big dining room, and beyond that was a kitchen that also had a door to the back porch and the backyard. I don't remember how many bedrooms that house had, but some were downstairs and more were upstairs, and there were also toilets upstairs as well as downstairs.

I won't say exactly what kind of business Uncle Ralph was in, but there was always a lot of very good-looking and very, very friendly female companions around, and there were a lot of visitors in and out of there all the time. And they were all so nice to us. So I said to myself, "Now, this is more like it." Uncle Ralph was really a smooth businessman, so every-thing was always cool. He liked us, and we got along just fine out there.

But what I couldn't get over was Elmer. There we were down there flopping at the pool hall and scrounging around before day trying to find something to eat, while he knew that he had a big-time uncle like that right over there in another part of the same town. That was bad enough, but even after his uncle turned up and invited us to his place, he would have turned it down if I hadn't jumped in. I said, "Man, you see what you almost did. We almost missed out on this."

I don't remember what kind of explanation he came up with, but truth-fully, nothing he could have said would have made any sense at all to me anyway. I don't know; I probably didn't let him say anything. I probably just gave him hell and just walked away for a while. I wasn't mad with him or anything like that; I was just exasperated.

The chance to go and stay out at Elmer Williams's uncle's house was really a big break for us, and we were hip enough to play it cool, and we made a lot of good friends out there and got a lot of experience that was very useful to a couple of youngsters starting out in the world of show business. But finding a place to stay was only a part of our problem. The main thing was to find a steady job playing somewhere. That is what we had come there from Red Bank to do, and we never gave up on it. We were musicians, and we didn't ever think about making a living doing anything except playing.

A few little gigs turned up around town every now and then, but there was nothing steady because by that time the season was really over and a lot of places were closing down. Our situation was a whole lot better than it had been the year before, but we were not really getting anywhere either, and we didn't even want to think about going back home again. Just the idea of going back to school was enough to keep us going in the other direction, regardless of how tough things got to be.

As far as both of us were concerned, we had left home and school and Red Bank for good. We were dead set on working our way into the world of professional entertainment so we could go places and see things and do things. We knew that we had a lot to learn about music and show busi-ness and also about people and life, but we were ready to learn. No more of that old, silly stuff we used to pull in the classroom. Once we left school, it was a different story.

We were also pretty game when it came to taking chances. I'd say we were pretty much willing to go just about anywhere and try a whole lot of things if it had something to do with music and entertainment. Not because we were so wild or anything like that. Sometimes we were just plain green about some things. But the thing about it was that you expected to run into some rough going. If you knew anything at all about the kind of life enter-tainers led, you started out by taking that for granted. I had been hanging around theaters and circuses talking to show people too long to be green about that. I don't think I ever came in contact with any rich entertainers when I was growing up. Money was not what it was about at all.

I liked playing music, and I liked the life. We both did, and I don't have any recollection of either one of us ever saying anything about giving up what we were trying to do. It never crossed my mind that I might have things easier or make a better living in another kind of work; and if Elmer ever had any second thoughts about making his living blowing his horn, I don't remember him ever mentioning it in my presence. Even when things got so rough that we had to go back to Red Bank that first fall, I'd say the farthest thing from my mind was giving up music. We just went back home to get ready to head out again.

Now, I wouldn't want to give the impression that Elmer Williams and I were all that high-minded about what we were so dead set on doing. I just wasn't interested in anything but music, and I figured that the time had come for me to get on out there and find out what I could do. What else can I say? I didn't want to go to school anymore, and I knew good and well you couldn't lie around home living off your parents. I had to get out of there and also out of Red Bank, and music was my ticket.

Actually, I don't remember that there was ever any question of me doing anything but playing music. The only question for me was where I was going to play next.

—

It was while Elmer Williams and I were living at his Uncle Ralph's house in Asbury Park that I met Willie Gant. When he came in town to work, he used to live right next door to us, and I also used to go around to all the places he used to work just to hear him, and I got to know him pretty well. He used to call everybody Mac, and we called him Gantie.

Then, sometime after I got to know Gant, Don Lambert also came down to Asbury Park to work in a place down there, and I remembered him, and we also got to be friendly. So one day I brought him by the house, and when he started fooling around at the piano, I went outside and called Gant and told him to come on over because there was a little cat over here think he can play some piano. So he put on his bathrobe and hopped over the fence and came over and said something like "Now, let's see what's happening" or something like that. Gant was always a pretty cool cat.

So Lamb was still fooling around a little bit there, doing little things, and Gant listened to him, and then he sat down and played a little something and kind of sparked things up. Then he got up, and Lamb sat back down again and lit up with either "Keep Off the Grass" or "Harlem Shout." I forget which one, but I think maybe it was "Harlem Shout."

Anyway, he tore it up. And Gant stood there listening, and then he turned to me and said, "Where'd you get him, Mac?" And I said I met him somewhere one night a few years ago, or something like that.

Then it was Gant's turn again, and he took out after him. I don't remember what he played, but it was like he was going on from where Lamb left off, and it was great. It was really a hell of a session they had in there that day, and when it was over, old Gant said, "Well, he's all right, Mac."

I don't remember what Lamb said about Gant. But the Lamb was on the loose, and he was walking all through town and walking through everybody. With that hatchet. He was something else. And years later he used to go all around Harlem looking for Art Tatum. He didn't back up from Art. He went looking for him. He was something else. He had a good right hand like Art, and a good left hand. Art said he himself had a right hand that didn't ever miss. They got to be great friends, and Art used to go to Newark and all around over there and find Lamb, and they used to hang out quite a bit. Then they'd come back to New York and find a place to play. (I guess you can say I learned something about playing the piano from Don Lambert. I learned not to mess with him. I learned to stay out of the way of the Lamb and that hatchet.)

Sometimes you got picked to go out on a little job at a club or maybe to play for a party, or somebody might recommend you for a gig because he was already tied up with something else at the same time and couldn't make it himself. But with more and more places closing down for the off-season, there was not very much going on for anybody anymore. The outlook was not very promising, but somehow or other we kept working enough to keep us going.

Then finally we sort of bumped into another little piece of good luck. One of the fellows we used to run a few racks with in Joe Brown's pool hall was a chef from Harlem named Smitty. He was working at one of the hotels for the season, and before long we had become friendly with him. He was crazy about music, and he used to see to it that we got to sample a lot of good things to eat just because we were musicians. He also liked to talk about all of the fabulous joints and showplaces in Harlem, and he made it sound so great that you couldn't help but dream about the day when you were good enough to work in such big-time places.

Which was exactly the effect he knew it would have. Because after he heard us play a few more times, he began encouraging us to think about going to New York. He didn't try to tell us that we were the greatest musicians in the world or anything like that, but he did say that we were already good enough to get a job playing in some of the places over there. Which we did start to think very seriously about. I remember that very well, because it was exactly when we really decided that we were going to New York that Elmer Williams really buckled down and started to learn how to play his horn in all the different keys. Me, since I could already play just about anything I heard, I figured I would pick up what I needed as I went along.

Our good friend Smitty was still there at the end of the summer when we started having a hard time finding work. The place where he was cooking was still open, and of course, Elmer Williams and I were still paying him those little visits in the kitchen to hear him tell about New York, and of course, the food was not bad, either. And then one day he really offered to do us a very special favor, which was just too big a break to turn down.

He said if we were really serious about trying our luck in New York, we were welcome to stay at his apartment for a while. He was going back home in a few days, and all we had to do was drop him a line and let him know when to expect us. Naturally we had some few doubts about being ready for a big-league city like New York, but I must say we were also pretty excited about all of the things we were going to have a chance to be around. The more we thought about it, the more we wanted to go. So we decided that the time had come and we had to make our big move.

There was one other little thing I remember doing before leaving Asbury Park. On the way to one of the places where I happened to be gigging off and on at that time, I had been looking at a little monkey-back suit in the window of a secondhand store. So I checked my little finances and found out that I had enough to spare for it, so I picked it up. I think the price I paid was four dollars. It had a few little darnings and hidden patches, but I had myself a monkey-back suit (which was also called the pinch-back and the jazz-back), and I figured I was pretty sharp. Of course, I still had the silk suit that Tommy Ah Kee had given me.

THE COLUMBIA WHEEL

Circa 1924 = Circa 1925

When we arrived in New York at the end of that summer, Smitty met us at the station and took us uptown. Our first address was 2150 Seventh Avenue, which was in the block between 127th and 128th streets in Harlem. The apartment was on the third floor, and for a few days we didn't go anywhere. Because we didn't know anywhere to go. Smitty had told us a lot about what a good town New York was for musicians, but the only address he had given us was his own.

It took us those few days to get our bearings, and the only place I remember going during that time was the Alhambra Theatre, which was only about a block away on the same side of Seventh Avenue, at the corner of 126th Street. Other than that, the main thing I recollect is how Elmer Williams and I used to come downstairs and out onto the porch where the other tenants used to sit chatting from around dusk dark until late into the night. I remember sitting out there on the railing and on the steps looking at the people strolling along the sidewalk and the traffic moving up and down Seventh Avenue.

The Alhambra Theatre was one of the main showplaces in that part of town in those days. Some of the biggest acts on the entertainment circuit used to play there just as they played the other big showcase theaters in other sections of Manhattan, Brooklyn, and Long Island. There was noth-

49

ing like it in Red Bank. Smitty took Elmer Williams and me there a day
or so after we came into New York, and that is where I first saw a show
band in the orchestra pit. I never will forget that. And I never will forget
the one particular number. It featured a sepia boy-and-girl dance team
that was really worth the price of the show so far as I was concerned. It
was called "Cut Yourself a Piece of Cake," which was also the name of a
very popular tune at that time. There was a great big cake on the stage
when the curtain opened for that part of the show, and when the spotlight
swung over onto it, that thing opened up and that boy-and-girl team came
out and started their routine and broke the place up!

That was the biggest stage show I had ever seen up to that time, and
Elmer Williams and I enjoyed it in spite of the fact that the only way you
could get in there was through the side entrance for colored people on
126th Street, and the only section you could sit in was the balcony. I hadn't
expected to find anything like that in Harlem, but that is the way it was,
and the Alhambra Theatre was not the only segregated place along that
part of Seventh Avenue in those days.

Actually, as you could see from just looking a block down the street,
the house where we were living was right on the southern edge of Harlem
as it was back then. Everything stopped at 126th Street. You didn't go
much further down than that. When you came to 125th Street, it was like
another part of town. You couldn't get into the Theresa Hotel in those
days, and the Apollo Theatre was a burlesque house known as Hurtig and
Seaman's Apollo. Frank's Chophouse was strictly lily-white, and so was
the Braddock Hotel over at the corner of 126th Street and Eighth Avenue,
where the New York Giants baseball team used to stay in those days. I
was not a big baseball fan at that time, but everybody knew about John J.
McGraw and the New York Giants, just as you grew up hearing about
Connie Mack and his Philadelphia Athletics. And so I also knew that the
Giants played their home games in a park known as the Polo Grounds at
Coogan's Bluff, which was about twenty-odd blocks up on Eighth Avenue
and beyond Sugar Hill.

—

The main thing I remember about those first few days in New York is that
we spent a lot of time out there on those steps and on the rails of that porch
just looking and listening. We didn't even go to any of the neighborhood
stores. We took all our meals right there in the apartment. Our friend
Smitty, being a chef, had made that a part of the invitation from the very
beginning. His pantry was always stacked with good things to eat. Elmer
Williams and I didn't really have any reason to go out to a restaurant for
a sandwich, which was just fine with us, because we had to make what
little money we had last as long as we could in the days to come.

We didn't know anything at all about anything below 125th Street yet. We didn't go sightseeing to look at all the people and tall buildings and traffic in midtown and down in lower Manhattan or anything else like that. You knew it was there, and every morning when you woke up and realized that you were in New York City you felt a big thrill just from being there. But I can't say that I actually thought about going downtown just to look around at that time. What Elmer Williams and I were really concerned about was where we were going to play music. The most important thing for us was making contact with the other musicians and people in show business. That was the problem we had to figure out first.

—

Then that next Sunday we decided to get out and go exploring in Harlem. So we checked our landmarks and started up Seventh Avenue. We passed the Lafayette Theatre between 131st and 132nd streets and went on beyond 135th Street and came to the Renaissance Casino at the corner of 138th Street, which was kitty-corner across Seventh Avenue from a section of houses knows as Strivers' Row. As I looked around, I figured we must be getting into the main part of Harlem, and later on I found out that I wasn't very far off.

A few more steps and we were at the corner of 140th Street, and that is where we turned right and walked over one block to Lenox Avenue, which was really the main stem of Harlem back then, and when we came to the corner we were at the Capitol Palace. There was a downstairs entrance, and on the sidewalk in front of it was one of those sandwich board signs like they used to put the restaurant bill of fare on years ago. But this one was an advertisement for the matinee going on that afternoon. The name of the band was the Washingtonians. And while we were standing there wondering who they were, I heard a familiar, kidding voice behind us.

"Hey, where you two farmers think you going?"

I looked around and saw Sonny Greer from Long Branch, of all people, coming up the steps from the entrance. He was dressed as sharp as usual, and as full of fun as always. Sonny was always Sonny.

"Hey, what you two country boys doing up here in the big city?" he said, and then he said, "Hey, Cousin, what you say, Cousin?"

I think that was the first time he actually called me that. But we always called each other Cuz from then on. It turned out that he was the drummer for the Washingtonians and that their regular gig was the Kentucky Club down in midtown, on Broadway at 49th Street.

Since I had last seen him in New Jersey, he had been on the road with Wilmer Gardner, a band of white musicians. It was while he was playing a date at a theater in Washington that he had met a piano player named Duke Ellington and a saxophone player named Otto Hardwick and had

decided to stay there and play with their group and pal around with them
for a while. They had come up to New York to join Wilber Sweatman and
had gotten stranded after a while, and Ellington had had to go back to
Washington. Now they were all back together again and they were beginning to make a reputation for themselves around town.

Sonny Greer had only come outside to catch the breeze for a few minutes during intermission. We stood there on the sidewalk swapping lies
about old times in New Jersey and bringing each other up to date. Then
when it was time for him to go on again, he took the two of us back down
there with him. So that was when I first met Duke Ellington. I think
Bubba Miley was on trumpet and Charlie Irvis was playing trombone at
that time, but I'm not really sure. I'm pretty sure that Hardwick was on
alto sax, but I'm not sure about Arthur Whetsol and Elmer Snowden.

Maybe it was later on that I found out that Elmer Snowden, a guitar
and banjo player from Baltimore, was the one who had gotten the Washingtonians into the Kentucky Club (which was first called the Hollywood
Club). I think they had reorganized with Duke Ellington in charge when
Sonny Greer took me and Elmer Williams downstairs and into the Capitol
Palace that Sunday afternoon. I'm not really sure. But I am very sure
about another musician I heard down there that day.

He was the house piano player in that club at that time, and his name
was Willie "the Lion" Smith. He was the Lion and the King, and when he
came on, they said the Lion was going to hold court, and that is exactly
what he did, and I mean he held it. Everybody knew that the Lion and
James P. Johnson were two of the very best piano players in a town full of
such other great ones as Beetle Henderson, Lippy Boyette, Willie Gant, and
Lucky Roberts, to name just a few. Anybody that came in there to play
piano had to come by him, and he didn't show anybody any mercy.

Another thing I remember about the matinee at the Capitol Palace that
Sunday afternoon is the new dance step one of the acts was featuring. It
was called the Charleston, and it was just catching on as a ballroom fad
because it had made a big hit in a Broadway musical called *Running Wild*.
But the undisputed champion Charleston dancer in Harlem was a cat
known as Brownie, whose act was called the Three Browns, and it was
them that I saw dancing in that floor show. By the way, all of the music
for *Running Wild*, including the piece called "The Charleston," was written
by James P. Johnson.

═

When we came back outside, it was around eight o'clock that evening, and
all the streetlights were on and all the Sunday night traffic was out. We
headed down Lenox Avenue toward the crosstown traffic on 135th Street,

talking about the show and about how well our old pal Sonny Greer was getting along in the big time. But I don't think we had walked more than a few blocks before we heard some more music coming from another downstairs place. We stopped and stood listening from the sidewalk, and then we went down the steps and came inside and sat down and ordered some ginger ale or whatever you were supposed to be served to stay down there at that time, and that was the beginning of a whole new thing for me and Elmer Williams as professional musicians.

I've forgotten how many pieces were in the combo playing down there that night. I'd say about four or five, not more than six, but I'm not really sure. I don't remember the name of the piano player. But I will never forget the trombone player. His name was Lou Henry, and he was the leader, and he was the one I went over and introduced myself to and started talking with when they finished the set and came offstage.

We talked awhile, and he seemed like a pretty nice fellow, so the first opening I got I made my move. I asked him if I could sit in with them for a couple of tunes. Because I had listened very carefully, and from what I heard I was pretty certain that I could take the piano player without any trouble at all. The idea was to get started, and after running into Sonny Greer, I could hardly wait to show somebody what I could do.

I had told Lou Henry that I played piano when I introduced myself to him, and when I asked him about sitting in, I told him that my friend Elmer Williams was a saxophone player. So he said okay, but that they were not due to go back on until awhile later, and he said both of us could play something if we came back at that time. Which was perfect, because Elmer didn't have his horn with him. I said we'd be there on the dot, and we found our way back to 2150 Seventh Avenue and got the saxophone and told Smitty what was happening, and when the time came, we were there waiting and Smitty was with us.

When Lou Henry saw us come back in, I could tell that he was surprised, and he said something like "Well, you actually did come back," or something like that, and I told him that we were ready anytime he was. And he said, "Okay, we'll see," or something like that. Then a few minutes later he came back from talking with the manager and told me we could go on and play something right away. Because it was time for the next set to begin and the other piano player, whoever he was, hadn't come back yet.

So Elmer Williams took his horn out of the case, and we followed Lou Henry on up there, and I adjusted the stool, and Elmer tuned up, and once we got into that first number, I went into my little act using some of Freddy Tunstall's tricks, making fancy runs and throwing my hands all up in the air and flashing my fingers. And every now and then I would also stand up and look all around without missing a beat. I had all of that down pat. Meantime, old Elmer Williams was doing all right for himself, too, and I could tell that the audience liked us, and I could also see the other musicians looking at each other as if to say, "Well, all right," and naturally Smitty was pleased.

That was how I got to play my first set in a New York club, and when we came off, Lou Henry asked us where we were working. I said, "Nowhere yet," and told him we had just arrived in town from Asbury Park. I told him we were just beginning to look around for something, and what he said then was just what I wanted to hear. He asked us if we wanted to travel. If we would like to go out with a big road show, and I said, "We sure would." And he gave me the address of a rehearsal hall on Lenox Avenue at 141st Street where the tryouts for a show he had an act in were being held that next week.

I can still remember where we went that next Wednesday, because it was upstairs in the same building where the Cotton Club opened later on. It was just diagonally across Lenox Avenue from the Capitol Palace. We didn't have any trouble finding our way back up there, and Lou Henry was pleased to see us, and I don't remember being nervous, although it was really my first audition for a show. I just went on up there and did my flashy little act again. I don't think I was worried about missing my big chance or anything like that. Maybe if I had known more about it I might have been concerned. But we had walked into it so fast that all I knew was that it was a chance to go on the road with an act in a road show.

Actually it was a job with an act in a burlesque show that was getting ready to go back out on tour on the Columbia Circuit, also known to performers as the Columbia Wheel. It was called *Hippity Hop*, and it played in the top burlesque theaters on the circuit. I didn't know very much about the Columbia Circuit and the Keith Circuit at that time. All I knew was that they took you to theaters in a lot of cities, and that was something that I had wanted to be a part of ever since I was a little kid hanging around the circus and McNulty's theater.

Everybody in charge of the audition seemed to like what we did, and when I saw that they were going to talk about taking us on, I told Elmer Williams to let me handle the negotiation, and he agreed, because I had always been the one to make the deals for the gigs we went on. Elmer didn't know anything about getting money out of people, and frankly, I don't think he really cared very much about the money angle in those days as long as he got a chance to play.

But I thought of myself as being a pretty slick talker and conniver when it came to financial wheeling and dealing, so I took over. And when Lou Henry said he wanted to tell us about how much the pay was going to be, I cut in before he could say anything else and told him we were not going anywhere unless we got forty dollars a week.

I could see that he was surprised, but I had expected that. So I told him again, and he just looked at me like he couldn't believe what he was hearing.

"Forty dollars a week," I said, "or we are not going anywhere."

I honestly don't know what I would have said next if he had named a lower figure and told us to take it or leave it. But I could tell that he was not annoyed with me. He seemed more surprised and amused than impatient with his little upstart trying to bluff him, and somehow I could sense that he was playing along with me, so I didn't back down, and he finally gave in.

He just looked at me and shook his head as if he was still trying to figure me out, and then he said he guessed that was what they were going to have to pay us, and when he turned his head the other way, I nudged Elmer Williams, and all he could do was look relieved and grin. But I really must say that I think he was so glad that we were going to be with a real road show that the money didn't really make any difference to him. And to tell the truth, it didn't really make all that big a difference to me either, but for some reason I just had to pull that hustle. I guess I must have thought that would give the impression that we had been around and were in demand. It never occurred to me that he might see right through me. Or if it did, I already figured he liked my spunk.

Anyway, we got the job and went into rehearsal, and that is how we became part of Katie Krippen's act that was known as "Katie Krippen and Her Kiddies." It was mainly her act. She sang and danced, and Lou Henry, who was her husband, played the trombone and was the unit manager and musical director. Mert Perry was the drummer, and there was Elmer Williams on saxophone. The trumpet player was Freddie Douglas, who was also from New Jersey.

One of the earlier piano players had been Fats Waller. I came in after the one who replaced him. Garvin Bushell, the all-around reedman, had also been with that act at one time. He was in it when Fats Waller joined it. In fact, Bushell says he once ran the act, which he says was known at that time as "Liza and Her Shuffling Sextet." Of course, I didn't know anything about any of that at that time, and I didn't meet Fats Waller until later, and I'm sure that I knew Fats for some time before I met Garvin Bushell. I don't know when the name of the act changed from "Liza" to "Katie Krippen," but that is what it was when I joined it, and I didn't realize that it had ever been known as anything but that.

Katie Krippen and Lou Henry rehearsed routines up there in the same hall where the tryouts had been held. I don't know where the rehearsals for the other parts of *Hippity Hop* were going on. But that didn't really concern us anyway. For all I know, everybody else might have had that time off in New York before going out on the road again. The main thing for Lou Henry and Katie Krippen was to get their own act together, and as I remember it, that really didn't take long. I don't remember having any trouble at all playing what they wanted. We all got along fine from the very start.

Meanwhile, the management let us draw some money in advance, and we shopped for things you had to have on the trip. One thing the newcomers had to get for the act was tuxedos. So we went down and took care of that at one of the tailor shops on 125th Street. I don't remember whether somebody in the management office made arrangements for us to go down there or not, but somebody must have done something or told us something, because we didn't know which one of those stores you were welcome in at that time.

Then, when the time came to leave for our first performance on the road with the whole show, we all came together on a pier on the Hudson River late that Sunday afternoon and took a boat to Fall River, Massachusetts, around eight o'clock. I don't remember anything else about the trip because I got seasick. I don't remember anything about leaving the Hudson River for the open sea or going past Long Island or anything like that. I just remember that we sailed all night, and that I felt better when I got back on land that next day. It was kind of embarrassing, but I got over it.

Hippity Hop opened its new season that same day, and our act, which came between the first and second half of the program, went over very well. So that was my initiation into real show business, which was my true ambition in those days. At that time, I didn't really think of myself as a jazz musician. I was a ragtime or stride piano player, to be sure, but I really thought of that as being an entertainer, in other words, just another way of being in show business.

Well, anyway, Katie Krippen and her boys were in for the tour. So then the road manager for the whole company called a meeting to command everybody and also to lay out a few rules on how he wanted everything to go while we were on the road. So we were all sitting there listening, and that is when he inserted one clause that sounded real underlined. He said there will be absolutely no mixing. He said if this sort of thing is caught, there will be an immediate dismissal of all parties concerned. Then he said something like "But other than that, this is going to be one great big happy family."

Now, I am not going to try to give anybody the impression that I didn't know anything about prejudice and discrimination up to that time, because truthfully I can't actually remember when I didn't know something about things like that, because the schools and things like that were not segregated in Red Bank, but that didn't mean that you were not aware of other things. But somehow or other, what that cat said in that meeting seemed like my first taste of that. It really sort of surprised you that they were hung up on something like that. I think all we did was just kind of look at each other, or something like that. I don't remember anybody saying anything.

We left Fall River by train, and that was the way we traveled everywhere from then on. The show had its own chartered Pullman cars, and believe me, that was my piece of cake. Most definitely. Because I have always been crazy about trains. I love the way they sound, whether they are close up or far away. I like the way the bell claps and also all the little ways they do things with the whistle. And I also like the way they feel when you are riding them and hearing them from the inside. When the show would come to the end of a stand after a few days or a week somewhere, they couldn't get through the last act fast enough, because I was so excited about getting back on the train. Then lots of times, instead of me getting into my bed, I used to sit and look out of the window most of the night as we rambled on from one place to another. That was music to me.

I don't remember how many people were in the *Hippity Hop* company, but there were quite a few. There was a big chorus line, and there was also a full-size show band. I've forgotten how many acts and skits there were, but I know there were two comedians, and they worked all through the show and I thought they were two of the funniest cats I ever saw. One was a little guy named Artie. I don't remember what the other one's name was, but they were a hell of a team.

There was also a prima donna. Every burlesque show had one of those. She was the center attraction. When people went to a burlesque, they were looking for a very special kind of entertainment. They expected a lot of singing and dancing and a lot of comedy, and some of the songs and jokes had to be kind of off-color and kind of racy and suggestive. There were also a lot of fancy sets and costumes, but I would say the main difference between the burlesque show and other vaudeville and variety shows was the way it featured striptease dancers. The prima donna of the burlesque show was the top stripper.

Our act, which was the only part of the show with sepia performers, was a special feature that used to be called the olio. We didn't have any connection with any of the skits and production numbers or anything like that. We came on and did our thing, and that was it. We would open up and bring Katie Krippen on, and she sang and danced. We also performed standing up, and all the little flashy-handed tricks I had picked up from Freddy Tunstall and a few others fitted right in. The only one who played sitting down was the drummer. By the way, Mert Perry was also a singing drummer like Sonny Greer used to be. Come to think of it, there were a lot of singing drummers in the old days.

Katie Krippen was a very good entertainer. You had to be a real pro with strong audience appeal to get your act in a big show like *Hippity Hop* and play the biggest houses on the Columbia Wheel. I hadn't heard of her before I joined the act. By the way, according to my co-writer, Katie had already become one of the first singers recorded by the famous Black Swan record company. Her first two sides were "Bird Man's Blues" and "Sing 'em for Mama, Play 'em for Me" (or "Play 'em for Mama, Sing 'em for Me," depending on which discography you use). Then, not long afterward, she did two more. One was "That's My Cup of Blues," and the other was "When It's Too Late You're Gonna Miss Me, Daddy." What was news to me was that the piano player on all those sides was Fletcher Henderson, and Garvin Bushell was also on the last two.

I'm not sure where we stopped next. It might have been Boston and a few places up that way, but I don't really remember. I'm not so sure about Boston on that trip, but I am sure that wherever we stopped we were on our way out into the Midwest. There was a long string of Columbia burlesque theaters on that route. You could start with the Casino in Philadelphia and go from there to the Gayety in Pittsburgh; the Court in Wheeling, West Virginia; the Grand Opera House in Canton, Ohio; the Columbia in Cleveland; the Empire in Toledo; the Lyric in Dayton; the Olympic in Cincinnati; the Capitol in Indianapolis; and also the Star and Garter in Chicago; the Gayety in St. Louis; the Gayety in Kansas City; and so on out as far as Omaha and then come back by way of the Gayety in Detroit, the Empire in Toronto, the Gayety in Buffalo, the Gayety in Rochester, the Colonial in Utica, and so on back into New York City.

I'm certain that I was with the show in a lot of those places. But that trip gets so tangled up with all of the other times I've been in and out of all those same towns during the last fifty years on the road that they all run together in my mind like those scenes in the movies when they show the train wheels rolling from signpost to signpost, arriving in different towns with different marquees with the pages on the calendar flipping from day to day to week to week and so on. Sometimes when I go back to one of those places and somebody reminds me of something that happened there back then, I can remember it, but otherwise it is like the way they show you how the boxer in the movies fights in all of those tank towns on his way to the big towns and his shot at the big time.

One of the towns I can remember very clearly, because we pulled in pretty early in the morning, was Omaha, Nebraska, and right away I got the impression that it was really a dreary and beat and dead place. But then, in those days, accommodations for sepia performers were pretty scarce everywhere. Sometimes you had to go all the way across to the other side of town to get a hotel that would take you in, and some other times there were no hotels or even rooming houses. When you came to a town like that, there were always some people who took in show business folks as transient roomers and sometimes also as boarders. You could usually count on getting their names from a list among the notices on the bulletin board backstage when you arrived at the theater. Also, sometimes people who took in entertainers and musicians as roomers and boarders used to be waiting at the station or at the theater when the company arrived. In some towns you could feel at home right away because the people who took you in had been in show business themselves at one time or another, and you got to meet more local people through them than you ever would when you had a room in a hotel. Of course, seasoned entertainers like Lou Henry and Katie Krippen, who had already been around the circuit a few times, had all kinds of contacts in a lot of towns, and they looked out for you, too.

I was recently shown the following article from *Billboard*, June 13, 1925. I think it is a pretty good sample of how information about accommodations was passed around.

Alberta Hunter and her boys had the distinction of being the first Negro act to play the Keith Theatre in Fairmont, West Virginia, and the act went over so favorably as to make colored acts popular with the local public. Miss Hunter recommends the house orchestra for its willingness to cooperate with the acts and the home of Mrs. Matthew Obie as a stopping place, declaring the meals at Mrs. Obie's to be "delicious." Norman and Bobbie, her boys, introduced the Charleston in the town and now the whole town is wild about the dance.

But they did have a little hotel in Omaha, and as soon as I walked in, I knew this was the place where the action was. You could tell because the atmosphere was great even at that time of day, when the only thing going on was what the cleanup people were doing. While we were checking in, I could see that there was a little cabaret in there, and there were also little secret gaming rooms back in there. So naturally all of us decided right away that we wanted to find out what all of that was all about after we finished the show downtown that night.

And sure enough, when we got back, things were popping. The good times were rolling, beginning right in the lobby and going right on into the cabaret. When we made our way on into where the main action was, we saw that there was a nice little combo playing, and there were also a lot of nice-looking girls all around, and of course, that really made everything even nicer. As far as I was concerned, that really made it. And of course, there was a little tasting going on.

We could also see that there were a lot of other show people hanging out in there, and when they recognized us, that was our chance to get up there and play something. So we did, and right away we were in. People were coming up to talk, and there were free drinks and all of that. I'll never forget that. It was just great.

After a little while, we sort of split up and started running around through the rest of the place, and that is when I happened to slide through one of those doors back there somewhere, where they had a dice game going. I knew what that was about. That was a part of the firsthand experience I was slipping around picking up back out in those wooded areas out in places like Pine Brook and Reavytown, New Jersey, back when I used to play at those pig roasts out there.

I never will forget that game in that back room in Omaha, because that was the first time in my life that I ever actually saw a silver dollar, and they had them stacked all around like they were poker chips. I never will forget that, and that's why I also remember what happened to the first silver dollar I ever held in my hand. While I was standing there watching, a lady next to me spoke to me.

"Boy, you don't want to just stand there and watch, do you?" she said. "Don't you want to take a chance?"

I really didn't know what to say, because I was really so surprised. It was like somebody had come up and caught me out there near those lanterns out among those trees near old man Reavy's joint.

"Well, I mean, I'm . . . I don't know."

That's about all I could get myself together enough to say. I really didn't know what else to say, but she did.

"Here," she said, "take this money. Go ahead and see what you can do with it."

And she handed me a handful of those heavy silver dollars. I don't recall how many it was exactly. Maybe five or six, or something like that.

"Go ahead," she said, "try your luck."

I'd say I've always sort of been on the left-hand side anyway as far as that sort of thing is concerned, and by that time I really figured I knew a little something about rolling bones. So I did.

But I really shouldn't have taken those silver dollars, because I dropped every one of them and also what little change of my own that I had in my pocket, and that was it. And so for the rest of the week I stayed the hell out of that particular little back room. But I certainly did have a ball playing at that little cabaret every night when we came back from the theater downtown. So that's how I remember my first trip to Omaha, Nebraska.

Another town I remember from that first trip out into the Midwest with the *Hippity Hop* show is St. Louis. We also stayed at a little hotel there. It was called the Booker T. Washington, and it was not far from the station. In fact, it was the hotel where the Pullman porters used to stay in those days. When you come out of the station, you just stroll about a block or so and you are there.

I had been hearing about St. Louis for a long time, so when I came back to the hotel after the show that night, I just had to get out and see what it was about, and I came back out and walked up the street. That's when I found that the part of town I was in was not only lively but also could get to be pretty rough and dangerous, and I mean detrimental to your health.

You could tell something like that right away, but I was still set on seeing some of St. Louis. So when I came to a place where the music sounded especially good, I decided to go inside and check it out. So I did, and there was a combo in there that was really firing that joint up. But before I could even get my bearing, somebody must have said something out of line to somebody, because all of a sudden there was a scuffle, and the crowd almost took that place down trying to get out of there. I just narrowly escaped getting run over and trampled to death. I still don't know how I actually got out of there, but I beat it back to the hotel, and I didn't see any more of St. Louis, other than the theater, while I was there that time.

From St. Louis we went to Kansas City on that first trip, and it really may have been after we left Kansas City that we went on out to Omaha. But that's not the way I remember it. Anyway, I didn't get to see very much of Kansas City on my first trip there either. We were working downtown at the local Columbia burlesque, which was another one of those known as the Gayety, but Elmer Williams and I were staying at a boardinghouse out on Twenty-second Street off Troost Avenue. I remember that place very well. It was run by Bob and Bessie Willis, and you could catch the streetcar right there on Troost, and it would take you right on downtown to Main Street, and that's just about all Elmer Williams and I saw of Kansas City that week, or whatever it was. Actually the main thing I remember about being in Kansas City that first time was how quiet Elmer Williams really was. That's when I realized that he really didn't talk very much. We would just come back across town after the show, and he would work on his shoes and clothes and fingernails and the keys on his horn and things like that, and then he would just be there in the room, but he never would say very much. There wasn't anything wrong. We got along fine. He just couldn't ever come up with any chitchat about anything.

I know I also went to Chicago on that trip. We played at the Star and Garter Theatre, which was downtown in the Loop district, and we stayed somewhere out on the South Side, and we rode the streetcar. But I didn't find out much about Chicago that first time, either, because I got sick there. I almost had pneumonia out there that time. I just could make it to those shows. So I didn't see anything but the Star and Garter Theatre and the streetcar that took you back and forth from work and the bed. I am pretty certain that by then it was wintertime, because that was why I thought I had pneumonia.

We also went up to Montreal in the wintertime with *Hippity Hop*. Most of that trip is vague, but the place where we roomed was on Antoine Street. I remember riding back up there from the theater in a sleigh because there was a heavy snow, and I don't think the streetcars were running. They had those heavy blankets, and there were several of us, me and Elmer and somebody, all snuggled up in there drinking White Horse ale or beer, or something like that, and it was fun. There were little bells on the sleigh going *ding-a-ling-a-ling*, and it was just beautiful.

It wasn't a hotel on Antoine Street. We were staying at another one of those private homes where they took in show people. I don't know where Lou Henry and Katie Krippen stayed, but three or four of us stayed over there.

I can't really recall how many times the *Hippity Hop* show came back into New York while I was with it. But I can remember several things that happened there, and it seems to me that they happened at different times. One time was when we were playing at the Gayety down on Broadway, right across Duffy Square from the Palace Theatre. That had to be September because that was where we were working when the Harry Wills–Luis Firpo fight took place. That was a very important fight because Harry Wills was the most important sepia contender to come on the scene since Jack Johnson gave up the championship to Jessie Willard. There was a lot of talk about him meeting Jack Dempsey, especially after he beat Firpo, but that fight never came off.

I also played at the Apollo Theatre on 125th Street while I was with the *Hippity Hop* show. That means that I had actually played at the Apollo some years before it became the top Harlem showcase theater that it is now remembered for being. Back during that time, the main showcase theaters for Harlem people were the Lafayette Theatre, on Seventh between 131st and 132nd streets, and the Lincoln, on 135th Street off Lenox Avenue. The Apollo was then known as Hurtig and Seaman's Apollo Burlesque House, and we were booked in there because it was a part of the Columbia Wheel, just like all those Gayety theaters across the country, and it was really a lily-white place. And so was 125th Street, as Elmer Williams and I had already found out before we left town. I don't remember whether any Harlem people used to go there in those days or not, but if they did, I imagine they had to sit in the balcony like in the Alhambra. I really don't remember much about that. But I do know that while we were working in there that time, we had to get a cab to take us to the theater and have it come back and pick us up after the show and take us back over to Lenox Avenue (which, by the way, means that whichever one of those trips back to New York this was we had already moved out of 2150; at that time I think we may have been bunking over in the apartment of a comedian named Billy Mitchell).

Another thing that I remember happening one of the times we were back in New York was the interview I had with Lou Henry when it was time to go back on the Columbia Wheel for the next season. Lou asked me what about it again, and that was when I found out that I had out-smarted myself on the first trip. He said he wanted to talk about money because he was not going to pay us forty dollars a week this time.

"I'm going to pay you what I should have paid you the other time," he said, and before I could get in a word edgewise, he went on. "I'm not going to pay you forty dollars a week; I'm going to pay you *eighty* dollars a week."

Naturally my mouth dropped open. I couldn't say anything. All I could do was just stand there and feel outdone and stupid. Lucky for me Elmer wasn't in that conference. Truthfully, I don't remember what I said when I told him about the new contract, but knowing the kind of jive I was into in those days, I'm pretty certain that I told him I finagled us a raise, and when he asked how much, I just sort of casually said that I had gotten them to double it.

We went back out into the Midwest again, and on my second visit to Chicago, Elmer Williams and I came across a roller-skating rink. I've forgotten how that happened, but it was an upstairs place, and that is where I learned to roller-skate. I had already known how to skate on ice since childhood. But this time in Chicago we spent a lot of our off time roller-skating. That's the main thing I remember about what I did in Chicago that time, and I still get a kick out of remembering how much fun that was.

On my second trip to St. Louis, I got a chance to drop in on a few of the joints because, in the meantime, I had become very friendly with Mert Perry. He was a real hip guy who had been out there on the circuits for years. For some reason he took an interest in me and used to come in smoking one of those big El Producto cigars, and he would look at me and tell me to come on and run with him so he could show me what life was all about. I never will forget him. I don't remember the names of the places he took me to in St. Louis. It was just several joints where you could have a nice time, and on a couple of nights when he wasn't tied up with something else, he let little old Base hang out with him, just for the experience.

He also used to like to try to play a little piano from time to time, and there was one special piece he always used to play. It had lyrics that started out: "Dirty hands, dirty face. . . ." He taught me that number, and I've never forgotten it, and every now and then I still find myself playing that number and remembering him and that trip to St. Louis. For a long time it was as if he and I were the only ones who knew that number. And then just several years ago I was in a nightclub somewhere and somebody started singing it, and I was shocked. I don't know where they found that old number after all those years. It really took me back.

Unfortunately it was also in St. Louis that Mert had a run-in with the management and had to leave the show. I am not going to get into any specific details about what that was about. I'll just say that it was a racial matter that the management regarded as a serious violation of its social policy. So anyway, Mert cut out just before we moved on from St. Louis to Kansas City, and Lou Henry had to send back to New York for another drummer.

That's how Steve Wright came into the group. Steve was known as one of the Wright Brothers because his brother was also a drummer. Steve's brother Herbert, as a matter of fact, had not only been the drummer in Jim Europe's famous Syncopated Orchestra; I'm sorry to say he was also the one who had stabbed Jim Europe to death during an argument one night in Boston four or five years before the time I'm writing about. Anyway, I remember that it took a few days for Steve Wright to catch up with us out there, so in the interim a wonderful local area drummer by the name of A. G. Godley was hired to fill in with us, and he was just great. I didn't know it at the time, but he was one of the top drummers in the Kansas City and southwest territory. Later he was with Alphonso Trent's band.

—

That second time in Kansas City was quite a different story so far as after hours was concerned. We went back into the Gayety, and we also stayed at the same place out on Twenty-second Street. But the thing about being out there that time was the night Elmer Williams and I took a walk down Troost Avenue.

We had been going downtown and playing at the theater and coming right on back to the rooming house just as we had done the other time and just as we did in most of those towns we played in. Then one night when we came back after the show, Elmer Williams and I decided to get out and look around. Because we really didn't know anything at all about what Kansas City was like, especially the section out there where we were rooming. So we started down Troost Avenue, and at first there didn't seem to be very much going on in the way of nightlife, but we kept on walking and looking because the trolley line ran along Troost and we figured it was leading to something.

We kept on going in the direction away from downtown, and then we came to the corner of Eighteenth Street and wham! Everything along that street was all lit up like klieg lights. It was one of the most fantastic sights I've ever seen in my life. We turned right there. We didn't figure that we needed to go any further on Troost. There were joints all lit up and going full blast on both sides of the street for several blocks. One of the first places I remember seeing was the Yellow Front Saloon. Another was the Sawdust Trail. And everywhere you went, there was at least a piano player and somebody singing, if not a combo or maybe a jam session.

There was so much going on that I couldn't believe my eyes or my ears, and neither could Elmer Williams. We hadn't had a chance to see very many joints in the short time we had spent in Harlem, so we didn't really know very much about what was back in New York. It took a little while to get to know some of those places back there, because this was during Prohibition and there were all those speakeasies and hideaways and private clubs, also known as key clubs, and you couldn't just go in places like that unless you knew somebody. But that was just the thing that was fantastic about what we found in Kansas City. All of those joints along that strip were wide open, and there were ambulances and police cars with sirens just sitting out there ready to roll.

We went back down there every night for the rest of our run at the Gayety. We would just walk on down there because it really wasn't that far from the rooming house. You just came on down Troost Avenue from Twenty-second to Eighteenth Street, and then I don't think we went any further over than Tracey. I didn't know the names of any of these streets then, but we didn't go more than two or three blocks. That was enough, and then, too, you had to know what you were doing in that part of town.

That was my second helping of Kansas City, and you could tell that there was a whole lot more in there to be tasted, and so far as Elmer Williams and I were concerned, that was the high point of the trip. It was fantastic, and it was so completely unexpected. There we were, way out there in the middle of nowhere, just looking around and hoping that we would find a little after-hours joint of some kind, and wham, we were coming into a scene where the action was greater than anything I'd ever heard of.

=

When we finally got back into New York, that was the end of my time on the Columbia burlesque wheel.

Katie Krippen and Lou Henry kept the group together, and Lou was able to get a few bookings in some of the smaller theaters and variety houses in the New York area. But that didn't go on very long, and it was not steady enough to depend on. So the act finally broke up. But Katie and Lou also had something else going for themselves, because they got the food concession in Barron's Exclusive Club. I can't report anything about that, because Barron's was not a place I was able to hang out in back during that time. It was very heavy over there. I did get a chance to go in there on a little gig, playing with a little pickup group one time. But I don't have any recollection of ever being in touch with Katie and Lou over there. However, I do know that Katie didn't really give up being an entertainer. She still did stage shows and also club dates from time to time.

Meanwhile the rest of the members of the act also stayed around New York catching what gigs we could, and that was when Elmer Williams and

I sort of went our separate ways for a while. We hadn't been bunking at the same address in Harlem since we moved away from 2150 Seventh Avenue. I've forgotten where he went when I was staying on Lenox.

We did run into each other in different places around Harlem from time to time, and I also remember that we went out on one more little job a year or so later, but that was it. We never did really run together anymore.

HARLEM STRIDE TIME

1925 = 1926

It was through my good buddy Freddie Douglas, the cornet player from Long Branch, that I got my first steady gig in a Harlem club. It was downstairs on the northeast corner of 135th Street and Fifth Avenue, and it was called Leroy's. Dougie got a job in there, and the man liked him, so he sneaked me in by using the same old trick that somebody always used to pull back in those days. He took me in with him one night, and he had told all the other musicians except the piano player to come early, and when the guy showed up at the regular time, the band was already playing and I was in his chair. That was his notice. He got the message and got his pay and cut on out.

The owner of Leroy's was Leroy Wilkins, the older brother of Barron Wilkins, one of the most important men in Harlem. Barron's Exclusive Club, known as Barron's, over on Seventh Avenue and 134th Street, the same club where Katie Krippen and Lou Henry had the food concession, was one of the top spots in Harlem. It was where a lot of downtown politicians, entertainers, and sporting-life people used to hang out uptown. Barron Wilkins was the first New York club owner to give the Washingtonians a break. It was from Barron's that Duke Ellington, Sonny Greer, and that band had moved downtown to the place on Forty-ninth Street and Broadway that became the Kentucky Club.

Barron Wilkins's career came to a sudden and shocking halt when he was murdered by some guy called Yellow Charleston. But that is another story. In fact, there were a lot of different stories about it. To some people it was a gangster story. All I can say is that I didn't know Barron Wilkins personally.

Leroy Wilkins had been in the nightclub business since before the war, and his place was a very special Harlem landmark. A lot of great piano players like Willie "the Lion" Smith and James P. Johnson and Willie Gant and Lucky Roberts and a few others, including Fats Waller, had played in there over the years and were still subject to drop by on any night. Somebody was always talking about the big piano battles they used to have in there.

It was mainly an uptown club for uptown people. You didn't see many, if any, downtown people and other tourists in there. A lot of celebrities used to be in there all the time, but they were mainly uptown celebrities.

It wasn't restricted to celebrities or anything like that, but it was not a hole-in-the-wall joint either. It had class, and they didn't tolerate any rowdy stuff in there. They featured first-rate music, and the prices were very reasonable, and people, including a lot of folks from show business, went in there to have a good time without having to worry about getting tangled up in a lot of trouble.

When I first started working in there, they had a big mirror up over the piano so you could see the dancers all around the room, and they were supposed to keep their hands up with those tips in sight. They used to sing and dance a chorus or two at each table out there, and they were getting a lot of tips, and they were supposed to keep the money between their fingers, and every time they brought their hands down, I was supposed to hit the piano, or Owen, the drummer, would hit the cymbal to make them bring their hands back up again so they couldn't hide that money in their bosom or some other place. All tips were supposed to go into the kitty to be shared by the musicians as well as the dancers.

After the dancers had done all of the tables, they would get out there on the floor and dance four or five choruses, and I mean they could cut it. They were some of the best dancers in Harlem, and they could also sing, but you had to keep your eye on their hands and all those tips. Because on a good night your share of the kitty might be more than your salary, and those girls had been around and had all kinds of ways of making money disappear before they got back there where they were supposed to dump that money in that box. And if one of the guys in the band was going with one of the girls, you really had to be alert every second.

There were about five or six pieces in that band, and we just sat down and played. We didn't have any music. The leader would call a number, and everybody knew it, and we'd play it. We played a lot of dance music and all the popular things that everybody else around town was playing.

You didn't think about what style you were playing or anything like that. You had your own way, and you just tried to play better than anybody else, because some cat could come in there and sit in and take your job.

—

I think I probably first actually met Fats Waller at Leroy's, because that was one of the spots he had been dropping in on and having piano sessions with James P. Johnson and the Lion way back before I ever even heard of the place. But we became friends at the Lincoln Theatre down at the other end of the block, on the south side of 135th Street near the corner of Lenox Avenue. He was playing organ for the movies in there. They had a ten-thousand-dollar Wurlitzer pipe organ, and I used to go in and sit right down on the very front row, right behind him. Fats was always a very friendly and outgoing type of fellow, and when he saw me there a couple of times, he started talking to me, and I began asking him questions about playing the organ.

That's how it all really started, and one day he told me to come on and sit over there with him. So I got under the rail, and he started showing and telling me about the stops and things like that, and the important things that made the organ different from the piano. He said he hadn't taken a lot of lessons on it but had figured it out for himself. I don't remember whether or not I knew anything about his reputation as a piano player at that time. But he had already been traveling around to rent parties and piano sessions in the company of James P. and the Lion, and you couldn't do any better than that in Harlem.

"With the organ," he said, "in the first place you got to start right down there with the feet."

I was sitting on a little rail that was up there, and he said, "Okay, now I'm going to play this song and you play the bass. You play with your feet just like you'd play the bass with the left hand on the piano." And I'd play the bass, making the changes down there. So I did that for a little while, like, say, a few days. And when I came back one day and we went up further and he said, "Okay, now you can play some songs," I said no. So he started up on top, and he said, "Take your foot and play the bass to the song," and he'd play something real slow again.

And when he saw me looking down, he'd say, "No, don't do that. You'll never play it if you look at it." And I finally got the picture in my mind, and I could play it by touch. Then he would switch on me and fool around awhile, and then he would play something else and say, "Now I'm going to play something, and I want you to just see if you can just feel out where I'm going to run and what changes I'm going to be making down in there. Just feel that out."

We were both sitting on the organ bench and he'd be playing, but he would be sitting over to one side and I would be sitting where I could reach two octaves of the bass. Then he showed me which was the accompaniment and which was the solo. It was a two-manual organ. Then he'd say, "Now, you figure where the bass is and the coloring and the stops and the different things for the solo." And then he'd say, "Now you just groove on these things, and sometime we can show you how these two things go together pretty good all the time, with the solo up here."

Then, after I'd been sitting in like that with him for a while, sometimes I'd get there early, and when the show would come on, he would say, "Now, sit over here," and he would ease over and say, "Now, don't try to play no song. Just play something. Think up a melody, and just make your chords down here and make your solo up here and just take it easy and play it. Play different things." And maybe I would do that every day for a week or so.

"Look at the picture on the screen," he also used to say. "Don't worry about the keyboard. When you see something up there in the story on the screen, just play something that comes into your mind. When you see something kind of lively, you play anything that will go with that. Or somebody might be sad, so you figure out a little something to suit that. And other times you have to play something jumping, and so on." That's how it was with me and Fats. That's the way he taught me, and those were the only organ lessons I ever had.

Old Fats used to play a lot of pinochle downstairs with the Lincoln stagehands, especially while the comedies and the short subjects were running, and I'd come in and go down there where they were, and sometimes he'd look up and look me over.

"Where you been? Come on here."

Then he used to send me up there to play until he finished the game. That really meant a lot to me. So naturally I was right there at the Lincoln every day that I could make it. I didn't actually get to play organ [on my own], however, until I went out to Kansas City with Gonzelle White, which was quite some time later on.

One guy I remember playing for during that time down at the Lincoln Theatre with Fats Waller is Cephus, who was known as Whistling Cephus. One time I was in there waiting for the show to come on and I decided to play a little something, and he started whistling, and everybody knew the special little phrase he used like a signature, and when he would come to that, the audience was right there with him. That went over pretty big, and Pip, the stage manager, liked it.

By the way, in those days, when it came to the live part of the show, the stage manager was the boss at the Lincoln. Nobody got their picture put up outside until after the first show. If your act went over you'd work all the weekend. If you didn't make it on that first show, that was it. Pip would fire you. A woman who was just known as Miss Downs was the owner of the Lincoln in those days, and she knew show business. But Pip could fire you without even checking with her. Of course, he also was responsible for giving a whole lot of people a big break that helped their careers, and I must say he was always very nice to me.

=

Before Smalls' Paradise opened over on Seventh Avenue between 134th and 135th streets, there was a Smalls' Sugar Cane Club a few blocks down Fifth Avenue from Leroy's. That is where I used to go to listen to a hell of a combo that June Clark had in there with the great Jimmy Harrison on trombone. I'm pretty sure that I first met June through Dougie, because both of them were cornet and trumpet players from Long Branch. Anyway, I used to go into Smalls' Sugar Cane quite often, and we got to know each other, and that's how I got to play in there with them from time to time.

I never did actually work in there on a regular basis because they had a piano player that they were just crazy about. His name was Smitty, and he was also known as Fat Smitty. He knew all the songs and all the keys and everything, and he played a lot of comp. No matter how much piano anybody else played, nobody could comp for June and Jimmy like Smitty could. So far as they were concerned, he was it. But he used to get sick a lot. I don't really know, but I think he had asthma. Or maybe something else. But anyway, June used to find me, and I would go on with them as Smitty's temporary replacement.

And of course, I knew that they didn't want anybody running all around all over the keyboard. That's not what you heard when you went down to Smalls' to listen to them. Smitty would just be there with that *oompa oompa oompa oompa* right there behind all those cats, laying it on heavy. *Oompa oompa oompa oompa.* That's what made Smitty so great. That's why those guys liked to play with Smitty so much. *Oompa oompa oompa oompa.* Beautiful. Just beautiful.

That kind of comping went out a few years ago. If you play that kind of comp behind somebody now, the cat will look back at you, as if to say, What the hell is this? But I learned a lot from what Fat Smitty used to lay down behind June and Jimmy, and so did a whole lot of other piano players around Harlem in those days. Of course, stride was the big thing. So that was my thing too. But as a show-band musician, knowing how to lay down a good comp came in very handy because playing behind those acts was a very important part of your job. You might get a chance to get in a stride chorus or so every now and then. But you were always comping for those acts.

I guess June must have heard me playing up at Leroy's because that first time he came up to me and said he was looking for me. That's how I got my big chance to go in there and sit in and play that gig with those two fabulous guys and that great little band. I forget the name of the boy who played banjo, and there was a saxophone player from Kentucky, which is also where Jimmy Harrison was from; and the drummer was called Jazz. His last name was Carson, and he was also known as Cripple Jazz because there was something wrong with his legs, but that didn't stop him from being a bitch of a drummer. He and I became pretty good friends, and later on we used to work on a few other gigs together.

Naturally I considered myself very lucky to have the chance to go in there and fill in with that band. Because you didn't just come down there and sit in and play along with those guys like you could do in a lot of other places. Those cats were too bad for that. You could get yourself very embarrassed trying to mess around with the kind of stuff they were playing. Most musicians just went in there to listen and learn something. Anybody that got up there with that pair better sure know what he was doing, because they didn't show anybody any mercy on the bandstand. The only guy I remember that used to come in the Sugar Cane and cut it along with June Clark and Jimmy Harrison in those days was Rex Stewart. Old Rex was still in his teens at that time, but he was already playing a lot of cornet.

June and Jimmy were known to be just about the hottest, toughest brass team in town. June was a first-rate cornet and trumpet man, and Jimmy Harrison was doing trumpet notes on the trombone that you couldn't believe until you heard him and saw him at the same time. Sometimes when he and June really got into something, it sounded like they had two trumpets in there. Most trombone players didn't tangle with him. They were no contest for him.

"Ain't no trombones going to come down in here and just fool around," he used to say. "They better be ready to play something when they come in here. I can't be bothered with no trombones. I only battle trumpets and cornets."

A lot of people seem to have forgotten what a hell of a musician Jimmy Harrison was. He was one of the most important trombone players that ever lived. I don't think anybody has had any more influence on other trombone players than Jimmy Harrison. Trombone players like Dickie Wells, Lawrence Brown, and Vic Dickinson all picked up things from Jimmie Harrison, and so did guys from downtown like Tommy Dorsey and Jack Teagarden. Nobody loved Jimmy Harrison more than Jack Teagarden. Jimmy was his main man. Every chance he got, he came uptown to hang out with Jimmy. He was in Harlem so much that it was like he was actually living up there.

Old Jimmy also used to like to vocalize a bit. You could tell by listening to him playing trombone that his main man was Louis Armstrong. That's why he sounded so much like a trumpet. But when it came to vocals, his big influence was the great comedian and novelty singer—the one and only Bert Williams. Jimmy knew all of Bert Williams's routines, and he always got a big kick out of doing them. I think a pretty good example of Jimmy doing one of his vocals like Bert Williams is the record of "Somebody Loves Me" that he did with Fletcher Henderson. But, of course, there was nothing like the way he used to do those Bert Williams routines in a club and at parties.

I got a chance to work with June again some time later on when he was working downtown on Fourteenth Street and Seventh Avenue at a place called the Dreamland or maybe it was Tango Gardens or some place like that. By that time, the Sugar Cane had closed, because Smalls had opened his big new place called Smalls' Paradise over on Seventh Avenue between 134th and 135th streets and was using a different kind of band because he was featuring floor shows and dancing, and it was another kind of thing over there. The Sugar Cane was one of those cozy downstairs neighborhood spots like Leroy's and the Nest and places like that. But Smalls' Paradise was in competition with places like Connie's Inn and the Cotton Club.

Anyway, June was working downtown, and I think he came and got me because Smitty was having another one of his attacks, and I was available because I was out of Leroy's for the time being. So I went down to the Dreamland. But that turned out to be a different scene in more ways than one. As far as playing with Jimmy and the group went, I was doing all right. But that wasn't all you had to do to make it down there. There were a lot of song publishers who used to come in there all the time, and they were always bringing the sheet music for their new things in there for you to play and give them a plug. That's one of the ways they used to promote their new tunes and songwriters in those days.

But the thing about it was that you had to take those things and read them and play them right off from the go. And that was a little rough for me because I still hadn't learned to sight-read yet. I could play it. I could play anything I could hear. I could listen to the first chorus and play it. Sometimes I could get by because I would figure out the first chorus and go on from there. But when they started modulating, and those mothers did modulate, that was a problem. As long as it was one of those stocks of just one sheet, everything was okay, because I could put my ear down on that, since all the changes were just about the same. But then they were beginning to make a lot of arrangements for combinations, and they started changing keys and using special choruses and special effects, like hitting chimes for the break. That tricked me.

So I came to work one night and June Clark told me that another piano player was going to work at it for a little while. And that is how I found out about Joe Turner, the fabulous piano player from Baltimore, Eubie Blake's hometown. He had just recently come to New York, and it wasn't long before a whole lot of piano players knew he was on the scene. Sight-reading those stock arrangements was no problem for him, and as far as I could tell, he didn't have any trouble with anything else either.

After a couple of days, June came by my apartment. I remember that I had bought a new suit and I was putting it on, and he sat there awhile, and I finally asked him what he was doing over here at that time, and that was when he told me. He said Joe Turner was coming into the group, and he gave me some money and said I didn't have to show up. Which meant I was fired. Joe Turner had taken the job.

Joe didn't stay down there very long. I think he went directly from that job over to Europe, and he's been living and working over there ever since. But I didn't get that job back. I'm not sure whether I went back into Leroy's again following the Dreamland, because I was sort of in and out of Leroy's a few times during those early years in New York, and I also worked in a few other places I've forgotten, because that's when I got my first taste of playing for singers in cabarets. I remember playing for the great singer and dancer Myra Johnson somewhere during that time. She was very nice to me, and later on, she got to work pretty steady with Fats, and she did a lot of theater things with him. She went to Europe with him. You may not hear much about her nowadays, but she was very well known for a long time.

In those days, I also moved in and out of a few different addresses. I stayed at Billy Mitchell's for a while, not very long; and then I went to live in a place on St. Nicholas Avenue right across from the 125th Street stop on the Eighth Avenue subway. My room was five flights up, and you had to walk it. They were building the Eighth Avenue subway line at that time, and they were in there digging, and you could hear all of that blasting and stuff over there. I remember a little park not far from there. I remember that very well, because sometimes during the hot weather I used to get a blanket and go out there and spend the night.

After I left there, I was also in and out of several other little apartments. One winter I was living on the third floor of a place where they had a way of turning your heat off if you got behind with your rent. It didn't cost any more than a few dollars a week in those days, but sometimes things got to be a little lean for me, and I was having a hell of a time trying to get that much together and also have a little something to eat on.

So I'd get a little behind and they would cut the heat off in my room. They wouldn't put you out, but you wouldn't get any heat or any hot water, and it was miserable. I mean, it was a bitch up there. And I would scuffle along and scuffle along. I remember sometimes I'd get a little change, say like fifty cents or something, and I would buy one of those great big hot dogs or a hamburger or something and take it with me and go on home and come up to that cold room and get in bed, reach out again and get that hot dog or whatever I had bought, and that was it for the day.

There was another time when things got pretty rough for me, and I used to have to scrounge some meals from Mr. Smalls for a while. He knew me and liked me from the times I used to work with June Clark and Jimmy Harrison and Jazz Carson and that band over at his place on Fifth Avenue. And I knew how generous he always was. So I knew exactly what time he always used to come to Miss Searcy's Restaurant, on the north side of 135th Street right across from the Lincoln Theatre, to eat his dinner, and I used to get there and stand in that alley by the theater until I saw him coming. Then I'd go over there and he'd see me, and he knew I was hungry and he'd tell me to come on in with him. He used to call everybody Baby, and he called me Baby Boy and would order his dinner and I'd sit there and eat with him. I never forgot him and the way he used to say, "Now, Baby Boy. Come on, Baby Boy. Eat some dinner."

By the way, that same alley where I used to wait across the street from Miss Searcy's for Mr. Smalls was where the steps leading up to where Marcus Garvey's office was, or used to be, or something like that. I don't know whether he himself was still in town at that time or not. I know I never saw him going up there if I ever saw him at all. Truthfully, I really didn't know anything about all those things Marcus Garvey was into. But of course everybody in Harlem knew about him because his people used to be in those parades. But my main thing in those days was show business and stumbling in and out of these joints, digging music, and trying to cop another gig.

—

The next traveling gig I was on was with Sonny Thompson's little band on the Keith vaudeville circuit. Somebody heard that there was an opening because the piano player was leaving. So I went over and got the job and began making trips out of New York again. We did a few weekend theater dates over in Brooklyn, but we did not play at any of the Keith theaters in Manhattan with that band, which was called the Jazz Hounds. A lot of combos used to call themselves the Jazz Hounds in those days. I don't know what made that name so popular. But Mamie Smith had her Jazz Hounds; Ma Rainey had hers.

Sonny Thompson himself was a drummer, and he had a singer named May something. There was a trombone player named Herb Gregory, and I forgot the name of the trumpet player, but I remember Bob Fuller, the alto player, because he knew a little too much music for me. He was always looking over my shoulder, and every time I made a mistake he would bump me with his horn. He was really a very good musician, and actually he was in charge of the music; and he was the one who had got me in there.

The Keith Circuit Theatres we played in were in a lot of towns in upstate New York. I'm sure we played in Saratoga, because Sonny Thompson had some relatives up there, and that was where he used to spend a lot of time when he was not working. And there was also one in New Haven, and we went into Massachusetts. It was while I was in Boston with Sonny Thompson that I saw *Shuffle Along*, and I remember seeing a young girl named Josephine Baker, then called Liza, tagging that line, and I mean she could tag it!

We also played some theaters on the Poli Circuit, and we went out into Pennsylvania to places like Scranton and Wilkes-Barre. I did that for a while, but I don't think that lasted more than a season if we made the whole season. Because it was not really steady work. We didn't have any long runs anywhere. We'd go out and do two or three days or a weekend and come back to New York, and sometimes it was a little while before something else turned up.

I don't know what Elmer Williams was doing all this time, but one day I just happened to run into him, and we decided to go back down to Asbury Park on a visit and see what was happening. So we went back to Uncle Ralph's house, and I began to check around for somewhere to play, and I got the idea of getting a few pieces together in a little group of my own for a while. I don't remember having any big urge to be a bandleader at that time. I didn't think anything about getting organized and rehearsing them to play any special music in any special way or anything like that. I just figured I would be the one to get a few gigs or something like that. I wouldn't say it was any more than that.

So I got Jazz Carson to come down and play drums because he wasn't doing anything. Because for some reason June Clark wasn't going back up to Saratoga that season as he usually had been doing. And the job I got us was in a place called the Smile Awhile. But we were not in there very long before Claude Hopkins and his band came into town. He was a piano player from Washington, and he was out barnstorming, and they had come from Philadelphia, I think, and were working their way into New York. So they stopped off to see what they could find to do in Asbury Park.

That's how they happened to come into the Smile Awhile one night, and Claude asked if they could play a number or two and got up there, and that was the end of our gig. They were out of our class at that time, and we knew it. As soon as they started, we knew we were in trouble.

They had a real band. They had been working together for a while, and they could play a lot of their own things, because Claude was also an arranger.

I came to work the next night, and the house manager called me into the office and said he wanted to find out how much I had drawn and how much I still had coming, or something like that. I told him, Don't worry about it, everything was cool. But then, all of a sudden, I felt a little strange, and my feeling was right, because then he said what I was afraid he was going to say.

"Oh, yes, we have to straighten it out and settle up the account because Claude Hopkins is going to take over."

That was the end of my first career as a bandleader, so I went back to New York and back to Leroy's with Dougie again. Because it just so happened that Dougie came down to see how I was making out, and he couldn't have picked a better time. So he rescued me, and when I asked him how he happened to come down there at that time, he said he was just wondering how I was getting along, and when he found out what had just happened, he talked to Magwood, the manager of Leroy's, and got him to let me come back to my old spot there.

—

Unless I'm mistaken, it was during the time that I was at Leroy's after I came back from Asbury Park that I got to know the Lion well enough for him to take me around to places with him sometimes. He took a liking to me, and he always treated me like I was one of his cubs, as he sometimes used to call the young piano players he liked. Fats was one of his favorites, and Duke was another. The Lion could get you a gig at a house-rent party from time to time. Sometimes he might carry one of his cubs along with him and let him sit in for him, just so he could come back in and wipe out anybody else who tried to cut in. The Lion was notorious for pulling little tricks like that. I personally never did get to do that with him. I heard about it, and I knew Lion well enough to believe it.

Maybe Fats had told him something about me, or he must have known about Fats and me and the organ at the Lincoln Theatre. I don't remember. But I do recall one place in particular that he took me to. One day he said come on, because he wanted me to hear some guy play, and we went up Lenox Avenue to the Douglass Theatre, another movie house up at 140th Street, and when we went in, there was a guy playing an organ. I remember the Lion listening, and then he hummed along, and he said the guy, whose name slips my mind, wasn't playing it right. The Lion prided himself on his ear. He was a hell of a musician, and you couldn't fool him on any instrument. He listened to everything, and he knew most of the good musicians around town, not just the piano players.

=

One of the main places a lot of musicians used to hang out at or in a café or bar somewhere near was the Rhythm Club, in the basement on 132nd Street off Seventh Avenue, right around from the Lafayette Theatre. If you were looking for the Lion or somebody like Fats or James P. or Willie Gant or the Beetle Henderson or almost any other musician around New York in those days, that was the best place to go. If he wasn't there, the chances were that somebody who was there knew where to find him. The Lion and Fats and Jimmy used to love the battles that used to go on at the Rhythm Club in those days. There was a good house band in there, but the thing about the Rhythm Club was that somebody was always sitting in. The piano and drums were already there, but a lot of other guys used to bring their instruments with them most of the time. Some musicians always used to do that just in case somebody came by there looking for somebody to go out on a job. Which happened quite often. So there were always some of them around, and then in the late morning and after midnight, when the other joints were closing, you'd see all those cats dropping in there on their way home from work, and most of them would be carrying their instruments too.

Sometimes those battles used to last until the middle of the next morning. The Rhythm Club sessions were a good way for a new musician to get himself some quick recognition if you were somebody with something special. And if you didn't and didn't have any better sense than to go in there and tangle with them cats, that was the quickest way to get yourself embarrassed. They didn't have any mercy on upstarts in there. Somebody was always talking about how many choruses guys like the Lion and James and Fats used to sit and run on any tune without ever repeating themselves.

The Lion was a few years older than I was. Maybe about seven years or so. That might not seem like a very big difference when you just look at it on paper. But out there in everyday life, it makes a whole lot of difference. When you meet somebody who has been a big-time pro for seven years at the time when you're just getting started, you feel like you belong to another generation, especially when you're still in your late teens and early twenties. As my co-writer points out, seven years was enough for the Lion to have gone into the Army and overseas to France, where he became a big war hero while I was still a schoolboy in knee pants. (Something, by the way, that I don't have any recollection of him ever saying anything about.) And he had already built himself a solid reputation as a piano player to be reckoned with well before the war.

James was a few years older than the Lion, but you always thought of them as being about the same age. They had been friends since before the war. I liked both of them, but I never had a chance to get close to James. The Lion was the one I got a chance to be closest to, because he was so outgoing. He liked to talk. He liked to have a little taste of the corn product, and he was also crazy about good cigars. Whenever you saw him, especially when he was playing, he always had a cigar in his mouth. He also had a thing about fine clothes, so he was always sharp, and he always sported a derby hat that he kind of cocked at a special angle and also wore while he played.

James also used to like to sport a big cigar in his mouth while he was playing, and he also wore very fine, tailor-made clothes. But he was not as sharp a dresser as the Lion, and he didn't keep his hat on at the piano as much as the Lion almost always did. I'm not saying that he wasn't a show man. He had his little things. All those cats had little things they used to do as a part of their stage act. I was already hip to that from watching Freddy Tunstall back in Asbury Park. I understand that Lucky Roberts also had a way of taking his fingers off the keys that was something to see. I never did get to see him play in those days, but not long ago I was talking about him and somebody was telling me that sometimes Lucky lifted his hands so high, it was like he was pulling the notes out on strings or something. I also understand that James had studied with Lucky years ago.

Fats had studied with James, so he was closer to him than he was to the Lion, and he played more like him; but sometimes he wore a derby as a part of his trademark, like the Lion did, and he was the biggest showman of them all. He was always jiving and making cracks and carrying on, especially when he was singing, and he became as famous for his singing as for his playing. When he started making records, a lot of people used to think of him as a vaudeville entertainer. Old Fats always liked to kid around, and he was always signifying and carrying on. That was the way he was when I first met him. But all the time he was having fun, he was playing a hell of a lot of piano, and I mean great piano, right up there with the Lion and James.

A lot of people are still slow about Fats as a musician. Fats could write his can off. He wrote two or three shows. People have forgotten that. But he penned them. Fats and James and those guys were not just piano players. They were composers. They could write. Fats wrote things for Broadway, and of course, James had things down there before Fats. He wrote *Running Wild*, and that was the next big show to come after *Shuffle Along*. Two numbers from *Running Wild* became standards. One was "The Charleston," and the other was "Old-Fashioned Love." I remember watching James rehearsing some big show down in Philadelphia once, and he was something. He did a show called *Plantation Days* that they took to Europe.

Everybody knows a number James wrote called "If I Could Be With You One Hour Tonight." That was probably his biggest popular number. And a lot of people also know that he wrote a great ragtime piece called "Carolina Shout." But James also wrote symphonic music and concertos and operas and suites, and it was all based on the kind of music that he and the Lion and Lucky and Fats were playing in Harlem. One time they had another big show down there on Broadway. I forgot the name of it, but there was a lot of stuff like "Rhapsody in Blue" and things like that in it, and they were looking for somebody to play it. Fats went on in there and played it. He just read it right off and played it.

People have been very green about a lot of things like that. They're talking about the things they're doing down on Broadway these days, like it's all something new. But I know for a fact that sepia performers were down there a long time ago *and ruled it*. Sissle and Blake also did a show called *The Chocolate Dandies*, and they were in one of those editions of Lew Leslie's *Blackbirds*. When I say they ruled it, I mean it. All you have to do is just name some names that were down there on Broadway shows back during that time. Florence Mills was in *Shuffle Along*, and so was Josephine Baker. Bill "Bojangles" Robinson, Ethel Waters, Buck and Bubbles, and Adelaide Hall were all in Lew Leslie's *Blackbirds*. And Bert Williams had already been a very big star in the *Ziegfeld Follies* long before that.

I didn't actually get to know Will Vodery, but I knew who he was, and I knew that he was a great musician. He was a composer and orchestrator and also a conductor, and I knew that he was one of the most important musicians connected with the *Ziegfeld Follies*, and later on he also became a staff arranger for one of the big Hollywood movie studios. People used to talk about him and Ziegfeld like they still talked about how Jim Europe helped to make Vernon and Irene Castle a famous dance team before he organized a military band called the Hellfighters and took them to France during the war. My co-writer was telling me not long ago that, as a matter of fact, Will Vodery also had a band over there. He was the lieutenant in charge of the 807th Pioneer Infantry Band. He also conducted the band for General Pershing's occupation army in Germany right after the war. One member of the 807th band, by the way, was Sam Wooding, who had his own band back over in Europe during the time when I was knocking around Harlem.

Another great composer and conductor that everybody in Harlem used to look up to when it came to putting music together for those big productions in those days was Will Marion Cook. I didn't really get to know him either. But I knew he was one of the great men, and so did everybody else. I really didn't know how much of a pioneer he was. I could tell that he represented something that went way back, but I didn't actually realize that he had had a musical comedy on Broadway back during the days of the cakewalk, six years before I was born. He was the first uptown composer to have something down there, and it was a hit.

Of course, everybody knew about Bert Williams and the famous Williams and Walker act, but I didn't realize that Will Marion Cook had collaborated with them on some of their most important shows long before Bert Wiliams went into the *Ziegfeld Follies*. I just knew that he was somebody who had been writing a lot of important music for a long time. One of his tunes that most people will probably recognize right away is "I'm Coming, Virginia," and I've been told that by the time I knew about him around Harlem there were high-school glee clubs down south that used a number by him called "Swing Along" as one of their standard recital features.

Maybe if I had been as interested in writing and arranging those big things as Fats and James were, I probably would have gotten to know him, and I would remember him, but I was always more interested in playing than in writing. I never was interested in longing to be a songwriter. I never really tried to write songs. But Fats and James knew all about him and things like that, and he was a pretty big influence on them and also on Duke.

By the way, Sonny Greer and Duke had already met Fats Waller down in Washington some time before Elmer Williams and I ran into Sonny that first Sunday afternoon outside the Capitol Palace. They had also met James down in Washington some time before they met Fats; and Duke was playing on the same matinee with the Lion the very day Sonny introduced me to him and the other Washingtonians.

A lot of important musicians from the old days before the war were still doing things around town while I was knocking around Harlem in those days. Ford Dabney was another famous leader and composer who had been around since the days of Jim Europe. He had worked on shows with Ziegfeld long before Ziegfeld started the *Follies*, which means he was in there before Will Vodery, and he wrote the music for the show for Miller and Lyles after James did *Running Wild*. I didn't see it. I don't even remember whether I was still in town or not. But you heard about things like that. It was called *Rang Tang*, and Mae Barnes was a hit in it.

Bill Robinson hadn't yet scored his big hit down on Broadway, but he was already a big headliner on the Keith vaudeville circuit. Playing in big houses like the Alhambra had been routine stuff for him for years. I don't remember when I first actually saw him, but you knew when he was in town because he used to make rounds to his favorite joints, and he also hung out at the Hoofers Club, which was where all the dancers used to hang out and work out in those days. Just like the musicians used to hang out and have sessions at the Rhythm Club.

Harlem was full of top-notch dancers in those days. The great Eddie
Rector, the king of the soft-shoe who was also something like the father
of the class act, was still in his prime, and so was U. S. Thompson, also
known as Slow Kid. He was Florence Mills's husband.

—

Meanwhile I was hitting the joints again. I used to go by a place on
133rd Street between Fifth and Lenox and listen to Tricky Sam Nanton
play trombone. A lot of those joints were downstairs in those days, but
this one was right off the street, and I used to go in there quite often, and
Tricky Sam and I got to be pretty good friends. And we used to have a lot
of fun together, jamming and also getting loaded together. This was a few
years before Tricky went with Duke. I think Charlie Irvis was still with
Duke at that time. I knew Charlie, and I also knew his brother. Charles
had a brother who was a very good piano player. I can't recall his first
name, but he used to work at a joint on Fifth Avenue, somewhere in there
between Leroy's and Edmund's.

Edmund's was another very famous uptown spot in those days. I've
been told that it was one of Ethel Waters's hangouts when she was in town,
but I don't know anything about that. I know I was never in there when
she was present. What I remember about the place was all the mirrors
they had in there, but I actually didn't go into Edmund's as a regular thing.
So I don't remember it like I remember Smalls' Sugar Cane and that place
where Tricky Sam Nanton was working. That was more like my speed at
that time.

Tricky's real name was Joe Nanton. I can remember when he joined
Duke's band. Somebody kept asking what he was going to do in Duke's
band with all the buckets and plungers and things. But Duke knew exactly
what he was doing. If Duke wanted you, he's got something in mind for
you; you don't have to worry about that. And sure enough, there it was, and
old Tricky was blowing like he was made for Duke. We were so happy for
him, and that's where he stayed for the next twenty-some years, right on
up to the end of his life.

Right across the street from where Tricky was playing back in those
early days, there was another joint that I used to go to quite often, too.
I can't remember that name either, but I'll never forget the place because
I almost got myself into some terrible trouble down there one night. I
got into a rumble down there. I got into an argument with some cat about
something. I don't even know what the argument was about, but it
couldn't have been about anything important. I was just in there to jam
and listen and get a little taste. I don't know what I said or anything. I
guess I must have been talking loud and woofing like everybody else in
there, and then all of a sudden there I was, facing this guy that I had never

seen before in my life, and everybody was looking, and I didn't even know why I was about to have to tangle with him.

It was crazy. Then, the next thing I knew, some little cat just kind of walked by and brushed against me and put something in my hand, and I looked down and there I was, holding a goddamn knife! That thing almost scared me to death. I didn't know what the hell was happening. I don't know how I got myself into all of that mess, and I don't know how I would have gotten myself out of there if it had not been for Carl Smith. Carl was in politics. He was a ward captain, or boss, or something like that at that time, and he always looked out for me, and he sure saved me that time. I don't remember how he happened to get interested in me, and we were not really close friends. He just sort of helped young Base out from time to time. I don't know whatever happened to Carl. The last thing I heard about him, he was managing some place down in the Nineties on the West Side.

—

Another member of Duke's crew that I got to know while I was knocking around in Harlem in those days was Otto Hardwick. Otto was also known as Toby, and he called himself Otoe and so did his close friends. I once played in a little group that Otoe had while the Washingtonians were sort of laying off. I don't remember exactly when this was, but I do know that whenever it was, that was the time that I got a chance to work down in Barron's.

I also know that this was while Bricktop was still working in Barron's, because that was where I first met her. In fact, it was probably through her that Otoe got that gig, because she had become friends with Duke and that whole bunch in Washington years before. I used to try to make Bricktop remember little Base down there. I used to tell her that I was one of the young sports who used to drink wine out of her slipper and buy her a new pair out of the tips.

It was while I was in Barron's club with Otoe's group that Duke got his band back together. I remember that very well. One night Sonny Greer and two or three other members of the bunch came in and had a drink and listened, and when we came off the stand, they called Otoe over and I could tell just by looking over there at them talking that something was up. So when Otoe came back, I asked him.

"You getting ready to go somewhere?"

"I think Duke's getting ready to do something," he said. "I don't know."

I keep thinking that the job that had come up had something to do with a show downtown. I'm not certain about the name of the show, and I can't even remember whether it ever actually got produced. But I do know that it was when some show job came up that those guys began to get back together, and the rest is history. People thought the Washingtonians had broken up for good. But I knew different. Because I was with Otoe. And I also remember Sonny coming back around there, sitting in with us. If Otoe was still alive, he could bear me out in this, because for years he used to get a kick out of reminding me of the times when I was his piano player.

=

There was so much going on all around in Harlem during those days. I wish I could get myself together about more of it. But I'll never be able to do justice to what it all meant to me. However, I can say I was there trying to get with it, and can also say that by the time I went on that gig with Otoe I had been around long enough and gotten into enough to call myself a New York musician. Maybe I wasn't raising any hell, but I was there, and in my mind I was one of them. So when I would get a chance to go on those little out-of-town dates that came up every now and then, I was not from Red Bank anymore. I was from New York.

TOBA

1926 = 1927

One night in Leroy's, a trumpet player by the name of Harry Smith told me about an opening for a piano player in a vaudeville act that he was with. He said they were getting ready to go back out on the circuit soon, and he thought I ought to try out for it. And I said okay, because I still wanted to be in show business and out on the road, traveling to different places and working in all of those different theaters as much as I ever did.

So the next day Harry Smith took me up to an apartment over on Seventh Avenue, and that is where I met Gonzelle White and had my audition. And I got the job. The act was called Gonzelle White and Her Jazz Band. I didn't know anything about Gonzelle White before Harry Smith told me about her, but she was a very big name on the vaudeville circuit, and she had already been a hit as a special added attraction, traveling and performing with big shows on the Keith burlesque circuit before that. She must have had the same kind of act that Katie Krippen had when we were with *Hippity Hop* on the Columbia burlesque wheel. Then she and her husband had left a burlesque show called *Ed Daly's Running Wild* and had taken the band into vaudeville on their own and had become a big headline act.

When she hired me, the band was still working as a special act. It was really a combo, although they didn't call them that in those days. Gonzelle

White herself played alto sax in a few numbers. Her husband, who was
the manager of the act, played C-melody sax. Harry Smith played trumpet,
and there was another trumpet player named O. C. Gary. The trombone
player was Jake Fraser. The drummer was Freddy Crump, who was also
known in those days by his show-biz name of Rastus the Drummer. I was
the replacement for the piano player who had already cut out before I
came in. There was no bass player when I joined.

That was the group Gonzelle and her husband and manager, whose
name was Ed Langford, took out on the first series of dates after I joined
her act. It was a stand-up act like "Katie Krippen" and a lot of other stage
bands in those days. Everybody played standing up except the drummer.
The upright piano was turned so that your side was to the audience, so I
played looking out over the footlights, and turned around and played
behind my back, and then I turned back around and stood on one foot,
and then the other, and put my leg all up on the piano and did all kinds
of fancy tricks with my arms and hands.

Harry Smith was a hell of a trumpet player, and he was also featured
in the act as a dancer. He could tap and do buck and wing, kicks, splits,
soft-shoe, all those steps. Freddy Crump was a top-notch drummer, and
he did all of the fancy things that show-band drummers used to, like throwing his sticks in the air and catching them like a juggler without losing a
beat. He was a whole little act by himself, especially when it came to taking
bows. He used to come dancing back in from the wings and hit the drum
as he slid into a split. He used to grab the curtain and ride up with it,
bowing and waving at the audience applauding. He was something else,
and another little thing I remember about him is how later on we realized
that he was always the first member of the band to get out of the theater.
We began to wonder about it. We couldn't figure out where he was always
in such a hurry to get away to. So one night Harry Smith, or O. C. Gary or
somebody, and I decided to follow him and find out. So we did, and when
we got outside and went around to the front of the theater, he was standing
where the people leaving the theater could see him, and every time somebody would say, "Isn't that the little drummer with the show?" he would
do his little bow. Whoever it was that was with me and I couldn't get over
it.

Of course, the star of the act was Miss Gonzelle White herself. She sang
and danced and did her number and encore on the alto sax, which was a
big novelty in those days. She was more of an entertainer than a musician,
but entertainment was what the act was really all about. She had a lot of
personality, and she knew just how to come out there and get that audience
with us. She was a real pro with a lot of class, and she was not hard to get
along with. It was just a great experience for me to be working with her.

I don't know how old she was at that time, but I'd say she must have
been in her late twenties or early thirties. She was very light-skinned, and

she had curly red hair and was very well put together. She was not a large woman. She was the kind of small, nice-looking woman that you think of as being very cute. And, of course, she always wore fine, stylish clothes and costumes, and she also sported a diamond in one of her front teeth. I don't remember what kind of rings she wore, but I'll never forget that diamond.

The first job I played with the act must have been in Brooklyn or somewhere out on Long Island, because Gonzelle was doing weekends and also some Wednesdays in the vaudeville theaters in the New York and New Jersey areas at that time. We didn't go out on the road for any long tours. We went down to Atlantic City on weekend gigs, but I don't remember going out any farther than that with the act as it was when I joined it.

As glad as I was to be back in show business, I don't remember my first performance with Gonzelle White's act as any big event. It is funny how you forget something that was so important to you at the time, but all I remember is just going out there, playing whatever it was that we were supposed to play, and taking our bows and curtain calls and getting on out of the way of the next act. We didn't use theme songs or anything like that in those days. They had the name of the act on a placard on the side of the stage, and when the curtain came down, they put up another one and turned the lights on it to announce what was coming on next.

There were usually about five acts, and when your turn came, you got the piano and drums and everybody all set up onstage, and when the curtain went up, you hit your big opening number and you went on. Then you went right on into whatever the next number was, and when that was over, we made a fast segue into whatever followed that; and that's the way it went for about ten or maybe fifteen minutes. When there was a comedian in the act, we would go right on into his music and then lay out and then pick right up as soon as he finished. There was no announcement at all between the numbers in the act.

One of the great comedians who worked with the act on a few dates during that time was Dusty Fletcher, who made a great comeback during World War II with one of his old things called "Open the Door, Richard." The number he used to do back during the early days on the vaudeville circuit with Gonzelle White was called "Whoa, Tillie, Take Your Time." He used to sing the hell out of that thing, with all the signifying verses, doing it to a shuffling dance step that looked like he was riding a horse or a mule or maybe something else. I can still hear him saying, "Whoa, Tillie, take your time; whoa, whoa, Tillie, take your time. Wait a minute, mule, is you losing your mind?" Or you making me lose my mind, or something like that.

Another comedian who was on one of those bills with us was Jazz Lips Richardson. He used to be very big in vaudeville around that time. I don't remember his act, but I'm sure he was on with us once, and I really think we worked together several times. We were on the same show with another comedian just one time. I don't remember his name, but I never will forget his act. We were playing at one of the Keith theaters somewhere out on Long Island, and they had one of those Opportunity Night segments, and this cat came out there and did a real classy recitation from Shakespeare, and I mean he had that audience *up there*. And then when he finished, he just stood there, waiting, and then he bowed real dignified and said, "And now you can kiss my ass," and walked off with his nose in the air! He killed them!

I guess we must have worked the weekend circuits for several months, and it was during that time that I began spending more and more time in and around places like Big John's over on Seventh Avenue. As a matter of fact, everything was beginning to move away from Fifth Avenue and over that way by then. Of course, Lenox Avenue was still jumping because the Savoy Ballroom was still brand-new, and the big heyday of the Cotton Club was yet to come. But Mr. Ed Smalls had closed the Sugar Cane on Fifth and opened his already famous Smalls' Paradise on Seventh between 134th and 135th streets.

I really don't know what was happening in Leroy's from then on, because so much was going on over on Seventh Avenue that I just didn't make it back over that way anymore. The Lincoln, over on 135th off Lenox, was still going pretty strong, so I used to get back over that way from time to time when something special was playing. But I would say that the Lafayette had become the main place for the big vaudeville shows. It was also a bigger theater than the Lincoln. It seated about two thouhand. The Lincoln seated only about half that many.

Big John's was right on the corner of Seventh Avenue and 132nd Street. It was not a club. It was a bar and restaurant with a piano in the back, and I had already been going in and out of there back while I was working at Leroy's and with Sonny Thompson. As a matter of fact, I'm pretty sure that it was in the back of Big John's that I heard James the first time. He sat down at the piano back there and said he had this new thing he had written, and he played it, and it was "One Hour Tonight," and he also sang it. *If I could be with you one hour tonight.* I'm pretty sure that had already happened before I heard him when he used to sit in at the Rhythm Club.

I had been going by Big John's ever since I first began to check out all of those joints over that way. The Rhythm Club was right around the corner on 132nd Street in those days, and right along in there was another little place I used to go to very often because that was where I used to get those hot dogs I used to take home and eat in bed (or save to eat for breakfast) when I was living in that place where they turned off the heat in your room when you got behind in your rent payments. There was also a famous Chicken Shack down on 133rd Street between Seventh and Lenox, but I didn't get in there too often in those days. That was a little heavy for my means.

Smalls' Paradise was only about a block or so away from Big John's Corner, but I didn't go in there very much either. Every now and then I used to get lucky and get a chance to go to one of those breakfast dances they used to have downstairs there, but I didn't get in there very often. It was pretty expensive over there. I never did work over there, and I never just went in there to catch the cabaret floor show with all the acts and all of that. I never heard the band that Charlie Johnson had in there. I didn't even know that Jimmy Harrison worked in there with Charlie Johnson for a while. Somebody told me about it later on. The next thing I heard about Jimmy Harrison after he was with June Clark in Mr. Smalls's old place over on Fifth Avenue was that he was with Fletcher Henderson's band. But I didn't hear Fletcher in person until a few years later. I'm pretty sure that Willie Gant also had a band in Smalls' Paradise for a while, because Mr. Smalls thought a lot of him, but I didn't actually hear that band in there either.

A lot of vaudeville people used to hang out in Big John's along with the musicians, and when I became a part of Gonzelle White's act, I began to meet a lot of them. That is where I actually met Dusty Fletcher, and there were dancers and comedians and other entertainers in there from Connie's Inn and Smalls', and I also remember Foxworth and Frances, who used to work in the club, under Hurtig and Seamans, that later became the Apollo rehearsal hall. And I also began to see old Fats again. For a while, I used to see him every Saturday night standing on the corner ready to go to work. He would have on his tuxedo and a new straw hat, and I never will forget how fine he looked and how good it felt just to be around him.

Gonzelle White and Ed Langford were old customers of Big John's, and they also were living somewhere on 132nd Street between Seventh and Eighth avenues, which was less than a block away. So the used to spend a lot of time in there, keeping in touch with who was around and what the other acts were doing and who was available to go out on those little week-end gigs when we needed a comedian or some other special number.

I didn't really get to know Big John very well during those early days. I got a chance to know him very well later on. But during the time I was working with Gonzelle White, I was really sort of like a young spectator, and it was a very great thrill for me just to be able to go in there and hang out around that crowd. I really can't say that I was a part of that scene at that time. I didn't even try to sit in on any of those great sessions they used to have in the back. That was dangerous. That could get you into the same kind of trouble you could get yourself in if you didn't know any better than to sit down on the piano stool in the Rhythm Club, a few doors away around the corner. There was no telling who was going to walk in there and wipe you out.

One time, while we were laying off and hanging out around Big John's, I sort of ran away from Gonzelle for about three weeks or a month, or something like that. I became interested in a singer whose name I won't call, and I followed her down to Baltimore and Washington. I won't go into that story. But while I was down there, I got a chance to make a little trip down to Virginia with Billy Ewing. Then one night I went cruising around Washington, and I just happened to be out in the alley by the stage door of the Howard Theatre when a singer named Linda something came out looking for a piano player.

I needed the work, so I went on up there, and that turned out to be a very special experience for me. There was a little band in the pit. I think it was made up of members of her family. But she wanted to do her special act with the piano player onstage with her. I would try anything in those days, and when I found out that there was no music to read, that was just fine. All you had to do was get the key she was singing in and just follow her and know where the breaks were. That was no problem. So we ran through a few tunes, and everything was okay for me so far.

So that night we went out there and played a couple of numbers, and I never will forget what happened next, because she decided that she wanted to walk off the stage for a few numbers to make a quick change or something, and she told me to play a number and walked on off and left me out there all by myself. I had never played a whole solo number on a vaudeville stage before, and it was pretty scary with the audience really waiting for her to come back out. I could hear some rowdy guys talking and carrying on and not really paying any attention.

But I knew I had to play something, and I began and I could still hear them talking, and then I started to stride a bit, and after a few bars I could hear somebody out there saying, *"Shhsh, shhsh. Hey, wait, listen."*

And it was like getting your first chance. I wasn't playing any particular tune; I was just striding, and whatever I did was with the help of God, I guess. Anyway, I kept on going, and I don't know how I got out of it. I must have been going out for about five minutes, trying to finish it up, and then I finally hit—bam—and made it; and afterwards the singer said, "What's your name?" And I said, "Basie," and she wanted to know what I was doing, and I said I was down there with the Billy Ewing show.

I think I also played the Bijou on Seventh Street while I was down in Washington that time. But I never did work in Washington with Gonzelle.

=

We worked the weekend and Wednesday-matinee events around New York and New Jersey for a while, and then Gonzelle and Ed Langford made some kind of deal with somebody to put together a big vaudeville show of her own, and she was supposed to start out by taking it down to Havana, Cuba. That is when she set up her own road company, and she called the show Gonzelle White and her Big Jazz Jamboree. That is when she brought in Crackshot and Hunter as a comedy team, and she hired a girl named Doris Rubottom as a featured singer, and talking about a beautiful singer— Doris Rubottom was it. She was not a blues singer or a jazz singer. She sang ballads and popular show songs like "Indian Love Call," "Somebody Loves Me," and with her great voice and stage personality she could break the house up every time. She was something else. She was also Crackshot's girlfriend.

There was also a chorus line of eight girls. They were the same kind of great dancers that used to play in Harlem clubs like Connie's Inn and Smalls' and the Cotton Club and all the big Broadway shows like *Shuffle Along, Hot Chocolates,* and *Blackbirds*; and they could also sing, and some of them could also act. They were all very fine-looking, and they also dressed fine and carried themselves with a lot of class. And, of course, Gonzelle had them performing in costumes that were a knockout.

Crackshot and Hunter were also two very good dancers. They did some skits, and they had their own dance routines, and sometimes they used to dance and make jokes at the same time, and there were also some numbers that featured them along with the chorus. There wasn't anything out of the ordinary for comedy teams to do things like that in those days. They didn't come out there just to tell jokes. Most of them were all-around entertainers like Miller and Lyles in *Shuffle Along* and *Running Wild*. They also performed in blackface like Miller and Lyles.

There were comedy skits, and there was also one dramatic skit that starred Gonzelle and Ed Langford. I don't remember what it was called, but Gonzelle played the part of Maude Wilson, and Ed was her husband, and his name was Ben Wilson, and he was a big, mean brute who was very cruel to her. Harry Smith was the good guy who really loved her, and he had to take on the big brute, and during the fight he would get knocked out and Maude would have to save him.

It was not really very long, but it was like a regular play about the girl, the villain, and the hero, and it called for some real heavy stage acting. I was very interested in everything about show business in those days, so I used to sit onstage and watch them rehearse, and I watched them play it over and over so many times that pretty soon I had memorized the whole thing myself.

The band didn't play onstage as a part of the act anymore. With the chorus line and all the other acts and skits in the Big Jamboree up there, the band played in the pit like a regular vaudeville orchestra. Gonzelle would do her alto number up there, and Ed Langford would join her, but the rest of the band stayed down there where it was.

I didn't know very much about the business details that Gonzelle and Ed Langford had worked out for the trip to Havana, but for some reason the deal fell through. I don't know who put up the money that was used to put that whole big show together, but we were all ready to go and then a storm or a hurricane or something like that came up all of a sudden, and the boat or plane or whatever it was that was supposed to pick us up got lost or was destroyed or something and didn't make it to New York, and they called the trip off.

So we didn't go down to Havana. But Gonzelle and Ed decided to keep the show together and take it out on the TOBA circuit. This was another new experience for me. The audiences in the theaters on the Columbia, Keith, Orpheum, and Poli circuits were either white or mixed. On the TOBA audiences were strictly colored, but sometimes there was a special little section for a few white people. Some TOBA theaters were owned by white people, but most were operated by colored people.

There were a lot of big vaudeville shows out there on the circuits in those days, and TOBA theaters were where they spent almost all of their time playing. They were really the same kind of houses as the Lincoln and the Lafayette in Harlem and the Howard in Washington, and a lot of them could seat as many as 1,200 or 1,500 people. Bessie Smith started out in the tent shows like Ma Rainey (*with* Ma Rainey as a matter of fact), and then she spent most of her career on the TOBA circuit; and so did Clara, Mamie, and Trixie Smith, and Ida Cox. Ethel Waters and Lucille Hegeman also spent time out on the circuit. Another act a lot of people think about as soon as you mention the old days of the TOBA houses is the husband-and-wife singing-and-dancing comedy team known as Butterbeans and Susie.

That Gonzelle White gang was a great bunch of musicians and entertainers to be with. It was just such a great atmosphere that we spent most of our time with each other. My oldest friend in the group was Harry Smith, the trumpet player and dancer. He could act straight parts, and he was also a very funny guy. He was always saying something funny, and he always gave somebody a nickname. His nickname for me was "Nuts." It was Harry Smith who first came up with the old saying that later used to be a name for one thing I did when I got my own band. The first I heard him say it was one time backstage between shows. After the first show, they used to put out a lot of cold cuts and sandwich meats and things like that, so we'd stay in and eat right there in the theater. You'd go up to the table and help yourself, and then everybody would spread out and eat. I was standing up there and Harry Smith came back and sat in the corner with his snack.

Then he looked at me and said, "Every tub. Every tub." Which was like saying, "Don't be asking me for nothing. You better look out for yourself. Don't depend on nobody else. Every tub got to sit on its own bottom."

So I went and got my cold cuts, too, and from then on, every time he saw me with something he'd say, "Hey, Nuts, what you got there?" And I'd say, "Every tub," and he'd laugh and say it again.

"Every tub, every tub, everee tub, everry *tub!*" If you came up to him when he had something, before you could even ask him what he had, he'd look down and say, "Every TUB." Like saying, "Man, I got mine." He was only joking, but he was also making a point that I have never forgotten.

Nuts was not the only nickname I had while I was with Gonzelle White. O. C. Gary, the other trumpet player, used to call me Bateman. At first he used to say "Base man," and then he kept playing around with that and changed it to "Bateman," and he would say, "Hey, Mr. Bateman, what you say, Mr. Bateman? We'll get it, Mr. Bateman."

When we were playing and it came my turn to take a chorus, he'd almost always whisper encouragement by saying, "We'll get it, Mr. Bateman!"

Some others used to call me Base; in fact, that is what a lot of my oldest and closest friends still call me. I don't remember who really started that, but it has stuck down through all these years. There was no "Count Basie" in those days.

As for going down into the Deep South for the first time, I've been asked about that many times, and some reporters have written up what *they* thought it *must* have been like, but truthfully, I didn't actually think about Jim Crow and things like that very much. I was just too happy to be with the show on the road to be concerned with that. Of course, we ran into strange things every now and then, but I didn't really pay that much attention to them because, hell, I had run into those situations long before we got down south. You ran into some of those same situations up north.

After all, Mechanic Street was in the across-the-tracks section of Red Bank. I wouldn't want anybody to get the impression that I didn't grow up knowing that. I don't remember when I realized it, but it must have been early, because I don't have any story about it. School was not segregated. But you couldn't miss the fact that ofays and souls went to different churches and some other things. I was very surprised when Elmer Williams and I arrived in Harlem, which we thought was the top sepia town, and found out things turned lily-white right at 125th Street, and that you couldn't use the main entrance and had to sit up in the peanut gallery at the Alhambra. But that didn't mean that I didn't know that Springwood Avenue was in the across-the-tracks section of Asbury Park, because that's where you lived and hung out, no matter what part of town you worked in.

So naturally, being down where we were, you knew that was there. But being so young and having such a good time, I just didn't pay that much attention. It just didn't matter that much, and I didn't feel restricted, because I was not aware of any big-time places I wanted to go to, no theaters or nightclubs and things anywhere down there that I really wanted to go to, or could afford to go to. The main thing was that you could have so much fun just traveling and living with the company.

I don't remember having any special problems about getting something to eat or finding a place to stay, because when it came to that, if we didn't already have rooms reserved in advance, all you had to do was get out and walk the streets until you came to somebody who looked like they might have a place, and you would just ask about rooms, and sometimes you could room and get meals at the same place and you had it made. In other towns the show issued meal tickets that you could use in certain restaurants in the area near the theater.

We traveled by train. I have forgotten where we went first. It might have been Philadelphia. I know we played at the Standard, on South Street in Philadelphia, on one of these early trips because that was when I first saw the comedy team called Sandy Burns and Ashes, two of the funniest sons of guns I ever saw in my life. And it was also where we ran into a little musical competition. They had a wonderful pit band down there at that time. They were very good. But one night during the late show we had to play the "Bugle Call Rag." I think that's what it was. And Harry Smith and Jake Fraser and O.C. and those guys went out there and played and almost tore that joint down, and those bad musicians in the pit were very, very surprised to find out that there was a bunch of vaudeville musicians that could play jazz like that. They thought we were just a bunch of jive show-biz musicians, but they found out different, and I don't think they forgot us.

I think we also went to Baltimore on that same trip, and then we went on down south, so we probably played in Richmond and I don't know how many other towns on the route down through Virginia, North Carolina, and South Carolina, and on down into Georgia. We played at the Douglas Theater in Macon, Georgia, and also at Bailey's 81 in Atlanta, where the director of the house band was a hell of a fine musician named Eddie Heywood. At that time his son Eddie Heywood, Jr., was just a little boy, and Big Eddie used to bring him down to the theater to play piano for us. Years later he became world-famous for his recordings of "Begin the Beguine" and "Canadian Sunset."

There was also another fine musician working in Bailey's 81 in Atlanta. We played there a couple of times at least, but the thing about it is that I really have forgotten whether I met him on the first trip south or the second time we were down there. But I do remember how it happened. I was backstage before the time to go on, and I heard the organ and it was just beautiful. I asked who that was out there playing all that great stuff, and somebody said it was a cat named Graham Jackson. And I said, "Hell, I know that cat from Asbury Park, but he wasn't playing no organ then."

So I went out to get a look at him, and the organ was in something like a special box off to the side of the stage, and they would put the spotlight on him from time to time, and you could see that so far as playing that instrument he owned that theater. I stood out of sight and listened and waited, and when I came off, he remembered me after all that time.

After Asbury Park he had come back down south by himself, and during that time he studied the organ and mastered it, and I think they put that big one in Bailey's 81 especially for him. He owned that town when it came to playing some organ, and later on he also became a famous accordion player and used to play for FDR down at the resort at Warm Springs, Georgia, and also at the White House.

Another southern town we played in as we worked our way on back up and on into the Midwest was Louisville, Kentucky. I don't know how many TOBA theaters we booked into between Georgia and Kentucky, but I remember Louisville because of a little incident on the day we left. We were staying at a hotel that was run by three brothers, and I became a sort of running buddy with one of the brothers. We hung out together all during the time the show was there, which was more than a week—maybe two or three weeks—and I spent what little change I had, and I had also gotten a few bills from him. So when the time came to check out, I owed for all my rent and I was flat broke.

It was really very embarrassing, and I was also very worried because everybody else was ready to pull out and it looked like they were going to have to leave me behind. I can still hear old Crackshot saying, "Well, let's see how old Nuts gets himself out of this."

They were all waiting to see what I was going to do. So I just went on down to the station and got on the train. And then, of course, we sat right there for about a half hour or maybe forty-five minutes or more than an hour. We sat there and sat there and sat there, and then they said somebody from the hotel was coming.

"Good-bye, Mr. Bateman."

But when he got there, he turned out to be the brother that I had been hanging out with, and he said everything was cool if I wanted to go, because he would take care of everything, and he also let me have a little cash to tide me over to our next gig. All old Crackshot and Harry and the rest of them could say was "Well, old Nuts got himself out of another mess. How'd you do it, Nuts?"

We also went to Chicago on that trip, and that is where I saw Louis Armstrong the first time. We were playing at the Monogram Theatre, and during a break between shows several of us went along with Harry Smith to a club where Louis Armstrong was playing in a band with his wife, Lil Hardin, on piano. I had never gotten to see Louis when he was in New York playing with Fletcher Henderson's band. I knew he was there. Everybody knew he was in town, but for one reason or another I never got to see and hear him in person. I didn't go to any of those places where Fletcher and his band were playing, and somehow or other I never did happen to catch him in any of the spits he used to visit in Harlem either. He was up there a lot. As luck would have it, I just missed him. He must have dropped by Smalls' Sugar Cane when June Clark and Jimmy Harrison were working in there, because they were crazy about him and so was Rex Stewart, and I understand that June and Rex used to hang out with him, or as near him as they could get, as often as possible. But I missed him all the while he was in New York.

But I went to see him in Chicago, and of course, he broke it up in there. Naturally, everybody already knew how he played, because you had heard him on records; but hearing him in person was something else. Those were the days when old Louis used to hit all of those high C's like he couldn't stop. They didn't call him the king for nothing. Nobody could touch him.

I think it was during that same time in Chicago that we went to hear Earl Hines playing with Jimmy Noone at the Apex Club. As a good friend of mine was pointing out to me not long ago, there was a lot happening in Chicago in those days. That's where a lot of very great musicians like King Oliver, Johnny Dodds, Baby Dodds, Kid Only, Zutty Singleton, Freddy Keppard, and too many others to mention were working most of the time. There were spots like the Dreamland on Thirty-fifth and State, the Plantation across the street, the Sunset Cafe on Thirty-fifth and Calumet, Lincoln Gardens, and the Savoy Ballroom, the Nest, and so on, and a lot of fantastic floor shows. There were also big-time bandleaders in Chicago back then. Carrol Dickenson was a big name during that time, and so were Doc Cook and his Doctors of Syncopation; Erskine Tate, who conducted a big twenty-piece orchestra in the pit at the Vendome Theatre; and Dave Peyton, who also had a great pit band that used to play for the shows at the Regal Theatre.

There was also a lot of recording being done in studios in and around Chicago in those days. I've heard that Louis did all of those records with those New Orleans groups called the Hot Five and the Hot Seven in those studios out there, and that's also where he did all those great sides with King Oliver. At this time he hadn't yet started making those things he did with Earl Hines, but that's where they were done. I have been told that Louis played on more than fifty record dates in Chicago in the first three years after he went back to Chicago from Fletcher Henderson's band in New York.

I didn't have any real connection with any of that during that time. I was just in town with the show, and I was all eyes and ears for what I could see and hear. But Crackshot and Hunter both lived in Chicago, and I lived in Crackshot's apartment, so through him I was able to find out more about what was happening around town than I had on my other short visits to Chicago on the Columbia burlesque wheel a few years before.

After a few days in Chicago I think we played in a few other tours out that way, and that is when we went to Indianapolis and Ed Langford got sick. We were out ballyhooing the show around town on a flat wagon, and a rainstorm started and Ed got soaked, came down with a bad cold, and I had to take over his part in the dramatic skit that he and Gonzelle and Harry Smith played in. When they realized that he was not going to be able to go onstage that night, they started wondering what to do about that part of the show, and I told them to let me try it. I told them I already knew the whole thing.

Which I did. But at first they just looked at me as if to say, "What's this?" And I told them to try me out because I had been watching them all that time, and Ed Langford's part was the very one that I knew best. I had been studying every move Ed Langford ever made on all those rehearsals and performances in all those towns since we left New York. I wouldn't say that I actually had thought about playing that part during all that time. I just paid special attention to Ed because I admired him very much, and I figured I could learn so much from him, both as a performer and as a person.

Anyway, they didn't want to cut that play out, because it was really like the pound cake of the whole show. So finally Harry Smith said, "Hell, maybe old Nuts can do it. Let old Nuts try it." And O. C. Gary was all for me, too, and he said, "Yeah, let Mr. Bateman do it. Go on up there and do it, Mr. Bateman. Sure, Mr. Bateman can do it. Get it, Mr. Bateman."

And I did. I can't talk worth a damn now, but I did lines in that show. Of course, I wanted to do everything as much like Ed Langford as possible, and I must have done all right, because they kept the skit in for the rest of the time the show was in Indianapolis.

I can still remember coming in there with my hat on, calling, "Maude, oh, Maude, you hear me calling? Where the devil are you? What the devil are you doing? Why you can't come when I call?"

And I go on like that because I was the bad guy. Then there was a big scene with Maude, and I would finally grab her; and then the good guy, which was the part Harry Smith played, would come running in to rescue her from me, because I was the mean husband.

So I would call him a young whippersnapper and a few other names, and we would fight, and I would finally knock him out. But then Maude would get a dagger and attack me, and when she was about to give me the final blow, she would say her punch line: "And the wages of sin is—" And then she would bring the dagger down and say, "DEATH."

And all the women in the audience would holler, "Yeah, yeah. Oh, yeah, yeah, yeah!"

Then we went back to Chicago. But Ed Langford didn't get any better. He got worse, and then he caught pneumonia and died in the hospital there. That was really a big blow to everybody. It happened so soon, you couldn't really believe it. But the show still had some bookings to fill, so the show didn't come to a standstill when Gonzelle left to take the body out to Kansas City for the funeral. We went on playing while she was away. One of the girls in the company did the part of Maude Wilson, and we still went over with the audience.

As I remember it, we did all right, in spite of what had happened. But Ed Langford was such a hell of a guy that you couldn't help worrying about how the show was going to get along without him now that he was gone for good. Because he was a good businessman, and he knew the circuits, and he was such a fine cat to work for. But Gonzelle White herself was a real pro, too, when it came to the business angles of show biz. Her husband had been the manager, but it was her show, and she knew as much about running things as he did. I don't know who she left in charge while she was on the trip to Kansas City, but when she came back after about a week we knew she still had every intention of keeping the show going.

She made a few changes, and we headed out on a tour that took us on the southern circuit again. She cut down on the chorus line and a few other things, but it was still a big show, and it was still called Gonzelle White and the Big Jazz Jamboree. I don't remember that she cut down on the number of acts in the show. I think it ran the same amount of time. I think she just cut down on the number of people. I'm pretty sure that it was at that time that Hunter left the show. I don't think Gonzelle wanted to lose him. I think he just decided to stay on in Chicago for a while and try something else. I don't really know what happened, but I do know that when we swung south on the TOBA circuit again, Crackshot was still with the show, and Gonzelle still needed another comedian.

I also know that she was still looking for one when we came back down to Macon, Georgia, and that is where she found Pigmeat Markham. He was not known as Pigmeat in those days. The name Pigmeat was already a part of the show when Gonzelle hired Markham as the new comedian. It was the name of a character in one of the comic skits. Markham took it with him when he left; and he is the one it stuck to, and he took it on up into the big time. Later on he was also famous for the line "Here come the judge!"

But during the days with Gonzelle White he used to do a song and dance and say, "I'm Sweet Papa Pigmeat. I got the Jordan River in my hips, and all the women is raving to be baptized!"

Crackshot Hackley was still our top comedian when Pigmeat came into the company. But after a while he left. I don't remember exactly when, but I'm pretty sure that when we played in Birmingham one of those times, we had a new comedian named Boots Hope, who used to be called the world's greatest liar. He could get out there and lie his butt off. I mean, he could tell them, and when he got going on something that was really just outrageous any way you tried to look at it, he always used to interrupt himself and look right at the audience with his eyes wide open and say the line that was his trademark.

"I ain't lying. I ain't lying. I ain't lying."

He was also one of the world's greatest New York Yankees fans. In those days before radio sportscasting some towns used to have those big billboard baseball charts where they used to post the box scores as they came in over the wire service. There was a big diagram of the diamond showing the lineup, and you could go there and follow the game inning by inning. Otherwise you had to wait for the newspaper the following day. That big billboard diagram was Boots Hope's thing. Anytime we were playing a matinee in a town where there was one of those big boards and there was a Yankee game on, Gonzelle knew that the show was going to be one comedian short. Evidently, old Boots had gotten that all squared away with her when she hired him. I don't know, and I can't say how the Yankees were making out when we went to Birmingham that time, but I do remember that as soon as we got there and he found that the game was going to be on the wire-service scoreboard, he made his usual announcement.

"Don't be looking for me at no matinee, because I ain't going to be there. I'm telling you. And I ain't lying! I ain't lying! I ain't lying!"

We also had another drummer when we went to Birmingham that time. Freddy Crump was gone. I don't remember where or why he decided to cut out, but the drummer we had when we were in Birmingham that time was Temple, because we ran into a little trouble and he was the one who took care of business. Some rowdy-acting local guys tried to come upstairs to the dressing room where the girls were, and Temple kept them off. He threw all kinds of stuff downstairs at those characters. He changed their minds. He was not the kind of guy to go around looking for trouble, but he wasn't scared of anybody, and when something came up, he was ready to get with it. Those guys didn't bother the girls anymore.

Temple and I became very good friends, and we stayed pretty close for the rest of the time we were in the Gonzelle White show, which was right on up to the end, and also afterwards.

When we got down to New Orleans, we had a pretty close call with another kind of trouble. We were playing at the Lyric Theatre, and a big rain started; it must have kept on coming down for a week. I think we were scheduled in the Lyric for two weeks. But it rained all during that first week, and then one day we came to the theater and found that the water was so high that the whole orchestra pit was washed out. We couldn't believe it. We went back to the rooming house, and by that time the whistles all over town were blowing because the water was rising so fast, and they were worried about the levees and things like that, and we realized that there wasn't going to be any more work.

So Gonzelle got tickets for us to get on the train and get out of New Orleans fast, and it turned out that we caught the last one to make it away from there. I can still remember just how tough that was. *We just did make it. Because the water was all the way up to the trestles and bridges. You could almost reach out of the window and touch it.* We just made it across the main bridge, and we headed up the Gulf Coast to Gulfport and Biloxi and Mobile. That was a very narrow escape because that flood was one of the worst they had ever had down there. When all those whistles started blowing it was time to get the hell out of there fast, and we almost didn't make it. A day or two later and no telling what would have happened to us.

I'm pretty sure we played in Mobile and a lot of other towns down that way. I don't remember what route we took to get back north and out west, but every so often over the years somebody will come up to me and ask me if I wasn't working somewhere with Gonzelle White and that show, and then they'll mention something that happened, and sometimes it comes back to my mind and I know I was there and that it had to be back during that time. Because whenever I remember who else was there, it turns out to be somebody who could have been there only when I was traveling with Gonzelle White.

We worked our way on back up north by way of the Bijou Theatre in Nashville and the Palace Theatre in Memphis and as many other theaters, mostly on the TOBA, as Gonzelle could line up, and then we went to St. Louis and from there to Kansas City.

The TOBA house in St. Louis was the Booker T. Washington Theatre, a pretty big theater on Market Street with about fifteen hundred seats. That was my third trip to St. Louis, and it was the third time that I stayed at the Booker T. Washington Hotel. But it was the first and only time that I played at the Booker T. Washington Theatre.

Later on, one of the biggest entertainment promoters in St. Louis was Jesse Johnson. I didn't get to meet him when I was there with Gonzelle White, and I don't know whether he had anything to do with booking the show in there at that time. But I do remember that he had a music-and-record shop at that time. I remember that very well, because it was on the street that ran behind the theater. It was just a very few steps from the backstage entrance to the Booker T. Washington Theatre, and I spent quite a bit of time in there listening to records.

—

On my first trip to Kansas City with Gonzelle White, we stayed at the Eastside Hotel on Eighteenth Street, and we played at the Lincoln Theatre on Eighteenth and Lydia. Our opening was reported in the Chicago *Defender* on July 16 by Charles O'Neal in his regular column, "In Old Kaysee," as follows:

Opening at the Lincoln Theatre July 4, the Gonzelle White Company held attention of those theatrically inclined with a group of 21 people. Being a holiday, every seat was filled and standing room was at a bargain. The show was far superior to the average we see from time to time, but as yet it cannot be compared with such companies as Irvin Miller's Tut and Whitney or the Whitman Sisters.

But at that Gonzelle White deserves credit, for as manager and owner and with all of the responsibility resting on her she is making good where a lot of wise, smart men fail. Her company is well talented and the staging and costuming is all that one could expect. The opening audience applauded the different bits and sketches of the show with the same profuse manner as an old maid hugging a country schoolboy.

It was during the time that the Gonzelle White show was playing at the Lincoln that I first met Piney Brown. There were all these girls in the show, and Piney was the man-about-town in Kansas City in those days, and by the way, he was the nicest guy you'd ever want to meet in the world. When you were with him, you never had to worry about anything, because he always took care of the bill.

I had already heard about him, and when he came by the theater and said he wanted to meet the show girls, I already knew who he was. So right away I said to myself, "I got to figure a way to get in on this action." Because I knew he had a little club down the street (Twelfth Street) that looked like it might be a little more expensive than I could afford. So I told him, "Why don't you invite us over to the club, and we'll come by there."

Then I went and told a couple of the girls.

"This rich gentleman out here would like to meet you." And they looked at me as if to say, "What's this?" And I said, "Oh, he is a very nice guy. Everybody knows him. His name is Piney Brown."

I think he also sent some little things backstage to them from the restaurant, and also a little taste, of course, a little something to sip. Then, after the show, he came and took them across the street, and I went along with them. That's how I got to meet him and began to get to know him, and he was definitely somebody worth knowing.

It was also during this time that I just met Ellis Burton. He was the one who ran the Yellow Front Saloon. Incidentally, I was actually the one who started calling him the Chief. But not at that time, because I didn't know him that well then. I met him because we were living at the Eastside Hotel, right across the street from the Lincoln, and his place was right down the street where Elmer Williams and I had discovered all that action when we were on the burlesque circuit. I used to go down there all the time. That was one of the first places in Kansas City where I got a chance to sit in on piano a few times.

There were a lot of joints right there in that same area, and I got a chance to play in several and meet some of the musicians around town. That was how I began meeting people like Baby Lovett, the drummer; and some people claim that I also played the organ in church a couple of Sundays. I don't actually remember playing organ in church at that time, but I know for certain that I did so later on.

The Eastside Hotel had a little restaurant on the street level, and the rooms were upstairs. The food in that restaurant was very good, and I also used to go to a Greek restaurant across the street. Another place I was introduced to during that time was Marie's on Hyde. It was right across the street corner from the stage door of the Lincoln. I remember that there was a little porch to that house, which I remember was next door to Watkin's Funeral Home. Marie had the best brew in town. When Prohibition went out, Marie's was one of the first places in that part of Kansas City to have a bar.

After we closed at the Lincoln, we cooled it around Kansas City for a while. Then we got a chance to go down to Tulsa, which was very exciting to me because at that time I had gotten it in my mind that Oklahoma was the wild West. I thought there would be a lot of cowboys and Indians like in the Western moving pictures that I remembered from all the way back to the time when I was working in Mr. McNulty's theater in Red Bank, and I was so excited about seeing all of that in real life that I stayed awake looking out of the train window all night.

I actually expected to see cowboys and Indians riding across the plains outside. I don't think I said anything to anybody else about any of that because I'm pretty sure that they would have made fun of me for still being such a kid. But actually, I sat awake looking out that window all night, and I was never as disappointed in all my life as I was when I finally nodded off and woke up. The train pulled into Tulsa, and I saw that great big city station. I was ready to turn around and go back to Kansas City. I didn't see any cowboys and Indians anywhere! There really wasn't all that much difference between Tulsa and Kansas City, or even St. Louis, so far as city streets and lights and automobiles were concerned.

I didn't really see very much of downtown Tulsa on that trip because when we got off the train we just headed directly on out to the soul section, where we found that the place where we were staying was right across the main street from the theater. I can remember the telegraph poles and lines along that street, and also the flivvers and delivery trucks and horse-drawn buggies and wagons, and I know that there was also some kind of public transportation that ran through that part of town to the outskirts, but I don't remember any streetcars coming along that particular street.

I really wasn't interested in going out sight-seeing and things like that anyway, so all I actually did for the rest of the day was just sit around the Red Wing Hotel, looking out of the window at what was happening along Greenwood Avenue. But I could tell that we were across the tracks in a section that was like a little Harlem. There were a couple of main streets, and that was where all the stores and shops and restaurants and entertainment establishments were. So that was where the action was as far as I was concerned.

But I could also see that as that section stretched on out farther it spread out a bit, and that's where the homes were. I didn't get very far out in that direction during the week or ten days that we were in Tulsa, but I did get far enough to see that colored people had some very nice homes out there.

=

It was while we were in Tulsa playing at the Dreamland Theatre that I woke up late one morning hearing the Blue Devils for the first time. And it was also while I was still in Tulsa that time that Seminole, that bad left-handed piano player from back east, came in and broke up a nice little thing I had going for myself in a great little back-alley joint. There was no battle or anything like that. They just brought him around there and invited him to sit in, and when I heard him, I knew I was out.

=

We didn't go directly from Tulsa to Oklahoma City. It must have taken us a week or so to work our way down there. One town we stopped in on the way was Muskogee, and that is where Pigmeat Markham left the company. One night after the show he and Harry Smith and I went out somewhere to find some juice and have ourselves a little fun, and while we were sitting in some joint drinking and talking, Pigmeat pulled out a telegram from one of his old road-show buddies inviting him to come and join a big carnival that was playing in Binghamton, New York.

He kept talking about it because he was having a lot of trouble trying to make up his mind about leaving Gonzelle short. So Harry Smith and I decided for him.

"Hell, man, go on," we told him. "This might be your big chance."

And when he kept on wondering what to do, we got him high on what-ever it was we were drinking that time and took him back to his room and packed his bag and checked him out and took him down to the station, got him his ticket for Binghamton, and put him on the next train going back east.

I don't mean to say that he was so drunk he didn't know what was really happening. We just got him high enough to listen to reason, and that is how he went on out of there and went on to become one of the big names in vaudeville. The next time I saw him, he was a headliner in New York, and he was killing those audiences on every show. He had kept the name Pigmeat, but he had worked up a lot of material to go with it that made it all his own stuff.

Another town we stopped in on the way to Oklahoma City was Wewoka, Oklahoma. I never will forget that town, because that was where I finally did get a quick glimpse of some real-life Indians. One night several of us went out and found one of those little districts where you could get bootleg booze of some kind. I think maybe it was bootleg beer or maybe Chock. I'm pretty certain it wasn't whiskey. Whatever it was, I remember that the whole little district wasn't more than a block or two and only one side of the street had paved sidewalks.

I forget who was along that night, but there were several of us, and we got our little juice in a little place that was really not a barroom, but just a bootleg joint. Then we came back outside and started home in the dark, and we were walking along, talking, and all of a sudden we heard a whole lot of hollering and some horses coming down the road, and we just had time to jump into the bushes.

And then we saw them, and it was a bunch of Indians whooping and hollering and riding bareback, and I mean they were tearing up that street. They went by us like a tornado or something. We didn't know what the hell was happening. It happened so goddamn fast, you couldn't believe it was real. It was like a dream. Talking about a nightmare! Wham! *Bookety-bookety-bookety-bookey!* All mixed up with all that whooping and yelling; and they were gone, and we were just rooted there for a few minutes, breathing the dust they kicked up.

Then that next morning I asked somebody and found out that there were about six of them, and that every now and then something like that would happen. A bunch of the young ones would come into town on those bareback horses, having fun. I guess maybe they would come into that district to get a little firewater and then they would leave. They didn't cause any real serious disturbance, because nobody tried to mess with them, and they didn't bother anybody either. They'd just ride across a few yards and up into a few doorways and split on back out to the reservation, or wherever they came from.

I don't really know where they went, because we left town before I could find out any more about them. I was very sorry about that because I didn't get a chance to see them up close and talk with them. That was something I really wanted to do, but the show pulled on out. I can't say for certain whether we went from there right on into Oklahoma City. But that is where we were heading, and it is where we had to stay for several weeks, and I got to meet the Blue Devils again when they came back home from touring out in their territory. And that is when I sat in with them that first time.

It was also while we were still laying off and waiting around in Oklahoma City that my good old drinking buddy Temple the drummer got himself into a real strange situation over a bowl of chili. I don't know what got into old Temp, but he could have ended up in some serious trouble or something even worse than that. But as it turned out, every time somebody mentioned it again, we got a few laughs out of it.

There was a restaurant right on the main drag, not far from the theater, just a couple of doors down the same block from Crip's place, and when we had the price, a bunch of us used to go in there and eat and hang out a little. On this particular night a group of us had been out somewhere doing something—I forget what—but anyway, we were coming back along that street, and when we got to that block, there was a whole bunch of people standing out in front of the restaurant.

I'm pretty sure that Harry Smith was the one who asked what the hell was going on, because everybody was just standing there on the sidewalk looking through the entrance, but nobody was saying anything.

"It's one of them show boys," somebody in the crowd said. "One of those big fellows. He shot into the restaurant."

"Shot right through the door," somebody else said.

Then one of the girls from the show, who was already there in the crowd when we came up, said it was Temple.

"He went up that way," she said, and I kind of halfway figured where he might be. So somebody and I went around an alley behind the place, and, sure enough, that's where he was. I think Harry was the one with me.

"Don't come in here," he said.

"What's the matter?" I asked. "What happened?"

"Well," he said, "I went into that joint and ordered some chili, and when I tasted it, I asked the waiter for some more beans, and they raised hell about it, and I raised hell back. So they threw me out of that joint, and I went home and got my pistol."

He had one of them little pop pistols. I don't remember whether it was a little derringer or not, but he came back to the door and pulled the trigger.

So they sent for the policeman and they came, and Harry (or whoever it was with me) and I talked Temple into coming on out of the alley to them. So they took him down to jail. But Gonzelle got with the restaurant people, and they went down and got old Temp out, and they all made it up so the guy didn't press any charges against him.

"What's the matter with you, Temp?" I asked him later on. "Man, what got into you?"

"Well, I didn't go in there to raise no hell," he said. "Now, you know if I wanted to shoot somebody I could have shot them, but I didn't intend to do that. I just shot in the place. Because I was so mad."

I had to laugh, and he did, too. He always could laugh at himself when something crazy happened.

"Hell, I just asked them for some more beans in my chili. That's all I wanted. What's wrong with that? Can't nobody tell me much about how no goddamn chili supposed to taste! I just said, 'What about some more beans,' and they tried to make something of it."

MOTEN SWING TERRITORY

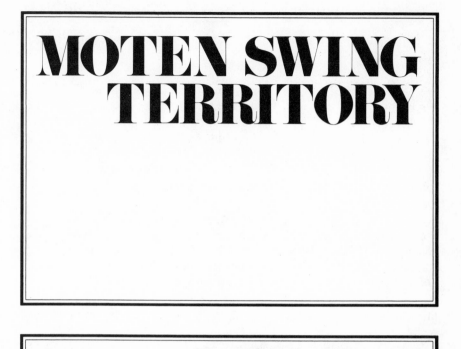

1929 = 1935

When I came back into Kansas City after spending the time I spent with the Blue Devils, I got my old job playing organ for the silent movies at the Eblon Theatre again, and it was during this time that I began to work and finagle my way into a few of the things that were going on around town.

I think I must have gone back to my little bunk at Temple's place back up in the alley off Eighteenth Street for a while, because I'm pretty certain that I had left a few of my belongings around there when I cut out for Oklahoma. Not that I had a lot of property to be leaving anywhere. I was traveling pretty light in those days. But that's where I left whatever I had to leave. And naturally, I also went back to all of that good home cooking old Temple used to do. I didn't ever live at the Eastside Hotel anymore.

But for a while I did used to go back over there and visit Gonzelle while she was still living there. I think that's where she had always lived in Kansas City. I think that must have been where she and Ed Langford had lived. Anyway, she was usually there, and she was just about always certain to be playing cards. She was a great whist player, and pinochle was also one of her games.

I would always go by and ask for Maude. Then I would also greet her

107

with the same old line from the skit: "Maude. Oh, Maude, where the devil are you, Maude?"

She always got a kick out of that. I would just visit with her, and we would talk about things. It was just a matter of keeping in touch, because she had always been so nice to me. She was just great to work for. I really thought a lot of her. But I don't know what finally happened to Gonzelle. I got all caught up in what was happening on the Kansas City music scene, and that friendship just sort of drifted and faded. Every now and then I would hear something about her putting another little jamboree together for a few days out on the road, but I really lost contact, and then I also lost track of her.

Meanwhile, without really being aware of the big change I was making, I was becoming more and more tied up with music itself and less and less concerned with show business and entertainment in general. Of course, it was all a part of the same world, but after playing with those Blue Devils, being a musician was where it was really at for me. I was still playing the organ at the Eblon, and that was still show biz, and as much as I still enjoyed it, the music scene was what Kansas City was really all about.

So I never did see Gonzelle White anymore, but I used to see her sister-in-law, Sis Langford, Ed Langford's sister. I used to see her all the time because she lived right on Paseo. But it's strange—she never did tell me any news about Gonzelle. I never heard anybody mention where she went. But one time, years later, I was playing somewhere with my own band, and somebody said she was in town. I think that was New Orleans. But I didn't get to see her wherever that was, and I never did catch up with her anywhere else. I think her home was St. Louis, or somewhere near there. So every time the band was playing there, I always hoped she would see the notices and come by. But that just never happened. I am really sorry that it didn't, because she was somebody I really loved and had a lot of respect for.

—

My next room after Temple's was in the Booker T. Washington Hotel, right across Eighteenth from the Eblon. It was right on the main drag then. It was only a few steps down the block to Jones Pool Hall, Lincoln Dance Hall, and the barbershop. The Subway Club was at Eighteenth and Vine. Piney Brown's place was at Eighteenth and Highland. Street's hotel was on the corner of Eighteenth and Paseo, and in the next several blocks beyond Paseo there were all those bars and restaurants and cabarets and other different joints that Elmer Williams and I had stumbled upon.

At first I didn't have nerve enough to go into the pool hall because that had seemed to be a bit out of my range ever since I used to sit and look out at it from the Eastside Hotel back before I worked up enough confidence to cross Paseo. Then I finally did start going into the pool hall, and then I also began to get hold of enough money to use the barbershop that was in the same building. Up to that time the barbershop I went to was the one right across the street from the Eastside Hotel, where Harry Smith had taken me.

Now, that's one of those little places I remember very well. There was a lady barber in there who was a very good friend of Harry's, and she used to fix him up, and he used to tell me I needed a haircut.

"Come on, Nuts, let's go get a haircut," he used to say. And he would take me in there and tell her to take care of me.

"Take care of my friend. Take care of Mr. Bateman."

There were matinees at the Eblon on Saturdays and Sundays. But during the week I used to go to work around six o'clock, and by ten-thirty the last show was over. So I was on my own, and there were all those wonderful joints and all that live music, and I used to go into a few of them. Not really a lot of them. The main one I actually remember hanging out in the most was the Yellow Front Saloon, which was run by Ellis Burton, also known later on as the Chief, who, as anybody who was there will tell you, was the greatest friend the musicians ever had in that town. He used to take care of musicians just like they were all members of a big family.

If you were out of work and showed up in his place and wanted to gig, he would give you a break. Because there was no regular house band, and he didn't book anybody for a definite period of time or anything like that. There was a good piano and a set of drums, and if you wanted to sit in and pick up a little change, it was pretty wide open.

The Yellow Front Saloon was at Eighteenth and Lydia, near the Phyllis Wheatley Memorial Hospital, and sometimes, when things were really jumping in the joints in that neighborhood, you could come in there and there would be musicians leaning out of the windows of the hospital, playing their horns. I'd never seen and heard anything like that in my life. Kansas City was a musicians' town, and there were good musicians everywhere you turned. Sometimes you just stayed at one place, and sometimes you might hit maybe two or three or more, but you could never get around to all the jumping places in that town in one night. There were just too many.

Sometimes I used to go by and listen to Joe Turner singing the blues. The first time I met Joe he was working down on Independence Avenue. He was the bartender down there in a basement joint where they used to serve whiskey by the dipper. Big Joe was the singing bartender. He would sing his numbers right behind the bar while he was mixing drinks. He'd be hollering the blues and dipping that good taste, and also taking special care of all the cats he knew. He was in charge of that whole basement down there.

Later on, he was working for Piney Brown at Piney Brown's Sunset on Twelfth Street with Pete Johnson, playing piano with Murl Johnson, and sometimes Baby Lovett on drums. And they were something. When I heard him that first time, I said to myself, Jesus, I *never* heard nothing like this guy. He was *the* blues singer in that town. Anybody who came to Kansas City talking about singing some blues had to go listen to *him*.

And Pete Johnson was the piano player. I liked Pete an awful lot. I was mostly interested in the blues, and Pete was really playing the blues and swinging the blues. He was really doing it. And another guy by the name of Everett Johnson was also playing the blues and singing. They were playing a lot of blues and boogie-woogie, and I really tried to get with it, and I really haven't gotten it yet. I still haven't gotten it like I really wanted to get into it. But those guys could really play it. Old Pete and Albert Ammons and those guys could get down with it.

I've been asked what I had going for me in a town with all those piano players like that around, and I say luck. That's what. And enough sense to stay out of the way of Pete and those guys.

I don't think I ever played up at the Lincoln Dance Hall. But sometimes I used to sit in at the Subway Club. I remember working down there with a drummer named Merle something, unless I'm confusing him with the Murl that used to play with Pete Johnson. But I didn't hang around there too often, because the Subway also used to be one of Mary Lou Williams's stopping-off places, and I always used to get out of her way. Anytime she was in the neighborhood, I used to find myself another little territory, because Mary Lou was tearing everybody up.

It was while I was working at the Eblon Theatre that second time and living at the Booker T. Washington Hotel that I got to meet the great Fletcher Henderson. When he came to town and worked at the Pla Mor Ballroom for about a week, he was also staying at the Booker T., and he used to come into a little candy stand near the theater. He heard me on the organ and wrote out a few little things he wanted me to play. I never will forget that. He said he had a little something for me to play down there, and he gave me an envelope with the music on it and went on to work. Then that night, when he came back to the hotel and saw me, he asked me about it.

"Did you play it?"

"I didn't," I said.

"Why not?"

"There were too many sharps in there," I said. I wasn't about to mess with all them sharps.

=

I remember another little caper I used to pull while I was living at the Booker T. Washington Hotel. Sometimes I used to sneak back into the Eblon and have a little after-hours party with a few of my friends. Somehow I found a way to get back in there after Jap Eblon had closed up. I used to wait until I was pretty sure he had plenty of time to get all the way across town to wherever he lived, and then I would take my little party in there and get my little quiet thing going.

But finally one night, there was a little surprise waiting for me. I don't know how many of us there were in there that night. Sometimes I'd take one other couple and sometimes maybe two, never a crowd or anything like that; and we would stay for about an hour or something like that. But when I started closing the organ up this particular night, a very familiar, very loud voice yelled out and shocked the hell out of me.

"What the hell are you stopping for?"

I knew exactly who it was, and all I could do was stand there thinking, Oh, Lord, I done lost my job.

"Ain't no use stopping now," he said, and then he said, "Come on up here."

He was way up in his office looking out through the window that opened out on the auditorium, and when I got up there, he called me a few little well-chosen names, and I just listened and waited. Then he smiled.

"You want a drink?"

I thanked him and took it.

"What did you stop for?"

I don't know what I answered.

"So you found a way to get in there? And you don't have to tell me how long you been doing it, because I been up here catching you for some time now."

=

During the time that I was at the Eblon, I also began to hear a lot of the territory bands. George E. Lee was a very important Kansas City bandleader at that time. He was a featured singer, and he also played reeds, and his sister Julia, who worked with him, was also a featured singer and a piano player. It didn't take very long for you to find out that George and Julia Lee were very big names in that territory. The band was billed as the George E. Lee Swing Novelty Orchestra, and it was just about tops for showmanship.

Of course, Andy Kirk and his Twelve Clouds of Joy were also around town. That was why Mary Lou Williams was there. She was the piano player in that band, and she also wrote a lot of the arrangements. At that time she was still married to John Williams, who played saxophone in that band and also wrote some of the arrangements. That was some band. They worked at the Pla Mor Ballroom for a long time. The star vocalist in that band was Pha Terrell, who later made a big hit with "Until the Real Thing Comes Along."

The orchestra leader that I got a chance to get closest to was Chauncey Downs. He was very nice to me. He was a piano player himself, but he used to let me sit in every now and then. He was very good about that, and it got so that whenever he was playing somewhere and I needed to pick up a little change, all I had to do was go by there and talk to him. All I had to say was something like "Why don't you stand up and direct for a little while? I'll take care of the piano for you."

Jesse Stone, Jap Allen, Clarence Love, and a lot of other territory bands were in and out of Kansas City back in those days, and they were all full of wonderful musicians. They used to play for dances at the El Torreon Ballroom at Thirty-first and Gillham, the Paseo Hall, and also at some of the hotel ballrooms in downtown Kansas City. And in the summer, there were places like Fairyland Park and a few others.

But the band that had the biggest reputation in the whole Kansas, Oklahoma, and Missouri territory in those days was the one led by Bennie Moten. I don't remember when I first heard about that band. I'm pretty sure I didn't hear about it while I was in Kansas City those two times on the burlesque circuit and that first time with Gonzelle White. But I don't know why I didn't hear about them while I was at the Eblon that first time. When I think about it now, I can't understand it. But I honestly don't remember anything about that band at that time. Maybe they were out in the territory most of that time. I have also been told that they left the territory for a long run in the East. And then another thing was that I didn't hang out around the big dance halls either. Unless I was playing. The only thing I can say is that I must have stuck pretty close to the Eblon and those few joints that I already knew. I guess the truth is that the only band that I was interested in at that time was the Blue Devils, who I had first heard in Tulsa and had played with a couple of times in Oklahoma City.

I do happen to remember something about Bennie and his band being down in Oklahoma City while I was there with the Blue Devils. I think they came there to play in the Park, and I even think I might have met a few of the musicians at that time. As a matter of fact, I think that is when I first met Buster Moten, also called Bus. Some say he was Bennie's cousin, and some say they were brothers. I really don't know which, but I do think that they were close relatives. Bus played accordion and sometimes he conducted and fronted the band, and sometimes he also played piano. I don't think we talked about anything in particular that first time. He was just one of the guys I talked to.

So far as I can recall, the Blue Devils never tangled with Bennie Moten in any battle of bands while I was with them. All I can say about any of the stories that anybody may have heard or read about the Blue Devils chopping Bennie's band in a contest is that I just can't figure out how I can have forgotten all about something as important as that. I don't think Walter Page would have forgotten, either. This is what he said in an interview some years ago: "I wanted to battle with Bennie Moten in the worst way because I knew I could beat him. He never would give me one, and we never did get the chance."

So much for the Blue Devils and Bennie Moten. But by the time I started to pick up on all of the talk about Bennie and his band that I was beginning to hear once I was settled back in Kansas City, the name was not really new to me. But then the more I heard, the more impressed I was. Then I also heard some of his records, and I found out he was the top recording band in that part of the country, and I was very impressed all over again. So then I really became very interested in what they were doing, and I can actually remember talking to somebody one day, and Bennie Moten's name came up, and I remember myself saying how much I liked that band. I said I would really like to play with that band, and whoever it was that I was talking to looked at me and asked me what I meant. I said I sure would like to play with that band. And he said, "What you talking about? *Bennie Moten himself is the piano player.*" Which was true. Bennie was a hell of a good piano player. He could play all kinds of stuff that I wasn't even about to try to tackle. But I have always been a conniver and began saying to myself, I got to see how I can connive my way into that band. I like that band. I got to play with that band.

I don't know why the fact that Bennie Moten himself was such a good piano player didn't faze me. All I know is that I just had to play with them, and I was going to do everything I could to get myself in there. I kept watching for my first chance.

Then, early one morning, I was standing on the corner around five o'clock, talking to somebody, and I happened to notice that there were a lot more people than I usually saw just standing around talking after the joints closed, and when I asked about them, somebody said that they were the wives and sweethearts and various other relatives and friends and followers waiting for the Bennie Moten band that was due back in town from a long tour out in the territory.

So right away I started thinking again about how I was going to connive my way into that band. So I waited along with the crowd, and it was kind of like standing around waiting for the hometown team to get back. By the way, Kansas City was also a hell of a great baseball town back in those days. All those other great teams at the time, like the Chicago American Giants, the Pittsburgh Crawfords, the Birmingham Black Barons, had to reckon with the Kansas City Monarchs. After all, the Monarchs had the great Satchel Paige pitching for them. Kansas City was a hell of a baseball team. As my co-writer likes to say, it wasn't just pure chance years later that when the big-league scouts started looking for a black player to break down the Jim Crow line in major-league baseball, they found Jackie Robinson (who had already been a great football star out on the West Coast) playing second base for the Kansas City Monarchs.

I stood there early that morning talking and waiting, and pretty soon the first car, carrying Bennie Moten himself, pulled in. I never will forget that. It was a Chrysler, and Bus Moten was driving. Then the other car, carrying the rest of the band, pulled in right behind him, and everybody crowded around, and that was when I got my chance to talk with Bus again. That next night I went to hear them play at a dance at Paseo Hall, and I really dug them. I came away more sold on them than ever. I wouldn't say that I thought that they could chop the Blue Devils or anything like that, because I still don't think they could do that. But they had a special kind of class, and they also looked like they had it made in some ways, while the Blue Devils were still out there struggling from gig to gig.

It was a solid band. Harlan Leonard was the lead man in the reed section. Woody Walder, sol called Hots, was playing alto and clarinet. Jack Washington was on alto and baritone. Thamon Hayes and Eddie Durham were on trombone, and Eddie doubled on guitar. Ed Lewis, Booker Washington, and Paul Webster were the trumpet section. The drummer was Willie McWashington, and the tuba player was Vernon Page. Leroy "Buster" Berry played guitar. Bennie was playing piano, and Bus was playing accordion and fronting with his baton.

I went to a couple of dances that they played in around town following that first night, and I met a few of the fellows, and I also got a chance to chat with Bennie himself. But the main contact I made was with Eddie Durham. That was a real piece of good luck. I think he and I must have turned up at a few of the same sessions, probably somewhere like the Subway or the Yellow Front or somewhere like that, and I got on more and more familiar terms with him. Then I found out from somebody that he could write music and that he was one of Bennie's arrangers, and that was when I saw my chance to make my first move.

The very next time I saw him, I asked him whether, if I played something on the piano, could he write it. He said sure. And it also turned out that he was always on the lookout for new things to arrange for the band. So we got together somewhere, and I began playing something on the piano that I wanted the band to play, and he wrote it down. I would play the parts for each section, and he would make the sheets for the trumpets and reeds and trombone and so on like that, and we worked up a couple of arrangements. I knew exactly how I wanted the band to sound, and Eddie picked right up on it. So I was ready for my next move.

I got Eddie to take me and the sheets along with him to Bennie's next rehearsal. I sat there and listened and then, when Eddie got a chance, he had them run down our two things, and both of them sparked old Bennie up a bit. It's a peculiar thing, but for the life of me I can't remember the names of those two charts. I don't think they were originals; I think they were something we did on a couple of standards or something like that.

But anyway, Bennie liked the way they went down and said he wanted to talk to me, and he asked me a few little things and then said the very thing I had been waiting to hear. He asked me if I would like to go along on the trip that the band was getting ready to make out to Wichita for a few days. He wanted me to listen to the band and work with Eddie on some more arrangements. And right away I said I'd love to go down there with them, and I said we had already been thinking about some more things we'd like to work up for the book.

So Bennie said okay, and I went and told Jap Eblon, and I went to Wichita on my first trip with Bennie Moten. I went along as a staff arranger, and I couldn't have written a tune on my own or worked up a chart if my life depended on it. But the understanding was that I was to be working with Eddie. So everything was fine, because the main thing for me was that I was getting that much closer to actually playing with that band. That was what I was conniving for, and I got a chance to sit in that very first trip.

Maybe Bennie had heard me playing. I don't really remember much about that. But I probably sat in on the piano at some point while the band was rehearsing the two numbers that Eddie and I had brought in, or something like that. Or maybe he just took Eddie's word for it. Anyway, after a couple of sets at that dance in Wichita, he wanted to take a break to look into some business matters, and he called me and told me to come on up and sit in for him. That's how I got my chance to perform with that band, and right then I could tell that he liked the way I sounded in there. Because he took his time about coming back, and when he did, he just played a few things and turned it back over to me again until just before the last number.

Naturally I had myself a ball, and I told him how much I enjoyed getting the chance to sit in like that, and I also told him I sure would like to run with him as his second piano player for a while. He just listened and said, "We'll see what happens," or something like that. But I was pretty sure that he was going to think about it, because I could tell that he was really listening to some of the little things that I was doing that were different. I figured he must have liked how those little things made the band sound; otherwise he wouldn't have taken those arrangements that I had worked out with Eddie.

We didn't stay out on that trip very long, but by the time we came back into Kansas City, he was already letting me sit in at least half of the time just about every night, and I had to work in a makeshift uniform. At that time the band was performing in gray tuxedos. So I took a little gray suit

I had and went by a tailor shop and had some satin put on the lapels and down the side of the trousers, and that is what I played in until they ordered me a regular uniform from whatever costume company supplied the band.

I was still not a regular member of the band yet, but when Bennie took me aside to explain what they could do about money, I said not to worry about that, because I was just so happy to be in there with those guys on any basis. But he went on and told me what they had decided. Everybody was going to chip in a dollar a week, and Bennie himself was going to round it off to fifteen. So that was what I was drawing at first, and it was all right with me because it was another one of those times when I was getting a chance to do something I wanted to do more than anything else.

That didn't mean that I didn't still love the Blue Devils. But Bennie Moten's outfit was number one throughout that part of the country. Everybody knew that. When you were with Bennie Moten, you got to play most of the choice gigs in Kansas City. And he also kept us pretty busy out in the territory. I don't think we ever played in St. Louis while I was with that band. I guess somebody else had that all tied up—somebody like Fate Marable or like the Jeter-Pillars band later on. I really don't know, because I wasn't too concerned about anything like that in those days. But I do know that St. Joseph was a different story. We played there, and sometimes we also went on out of our regular territory and on up through Iowa and into Minnesota. I must say, we didn't make very much of a dent up there, however, because Lawrence Welk already had that all locked up. Even way back in those days.

But Bennie Moten was something else. I mean, really something special. There was something about that whole operation that made you feel like you were playing in a bigger league than the Blue Devils. And the difference was not so much the music either. Because although the Devils didn't have as many different arrangements and stocks, they didn't really have to back up off of anybody. You felt you were closer to the big time when you were in Bennie's outfit, not only because he was a hell of a musician and musical leader with a lot more experience in the band business than anybody in the Blue Devils, but also to a great extent because he had so many more big-time connections and so much political pull.

No matter how much you liked somebody else, you had to be impressed by Bennie Moten. He was always making something happen, and he always seemed to have plans for something bigger. When you became one of his musicians, that meant that you were *in* so far as Kansas City was concerned, and you also felt that you were a part of something that was going somewhere. What Bennie Moten had in mind was not just to be the best band in the territory but one that would be in the same big-league class with Fletcher Henderson, Duke Ellington, Chick Webb, Claude Hopkins, and McKinney's Cotton Pickers.

That was Bennie's goal, and when you remember that during the very same time that Bennie was thinking along these lines Earl Hines in Chicago, Jimmie Lunceford down in Memphis, and Andy Kirk right there in Kansas City were just getting their bands together, maybe you can begin to realize how open the field still was in those days, and how good we felt our chances were of making a big enough hit to get the kind of backing and promotion that would get us into the top clubs and dance halls, especially in New York and Chicago, and get us on the big coast-to-coast radio hookups.

Bennie Moten was already pretty familiar to a lot of people outside the territory because his records already reached a fairly wide distribution and had really sold pretty good. Then, not long after I connived my way into the band as his second piano player, he was able to make a big new deal with the Victor Record Company, and we really began reworking and building the band's book. Ordinarily they didn't rehearse every day. The only time they rehearsed was when they used to get new stocks. But we really wanted to be ready for those recordings, and we worked pretty hard and steady to get all that material in the shape we wanted.

Then we made the trip to the Victor studio in Chicago. We didn't have a vocalist at that time. So with me taking turns with Bennie himself on the piano, that meant that there were thirteen musicians in the band at that time. Bus Moten could also play the piano, but he was spending more and more time on the accordion. On trumpet and sometimes cornet we had Ed Lewis and Booker Washington. The trombone players were Thamon Hayes and Eddie Durham, and Eddie also doubled on guitar. There were theree men in the reed section. Harlan Leonard played alto and doubled on clarinet. Woody Walden played tenor and doubled on clarinet. And Jack Washington played baritone and doubled on alto. "Buster" Berry played banjo and guitar. Vernon Page was on bass horn at that time, and the drummer was Willie McWashington, sometimes called Mack Washington and sometimes Willie Mac. By the way, Willie Mac was a singing drummer.

We stayed in Chicago three days and worked two sessions and cut ten sides. That was where we recorded "Jones Law Blues," "Small Black," "Everyday Blues," "Band Box Shuffle," "Rhumba Negro," "Boot It," "Mary Lee," "Rit-Tit Day," "Sweethearts of Yesterday," and "New Vine Street Blues"; and Bennie let me have quite a bit of space on those records considering how new I was in the band at that time, and also considering that it was my very first record date. But that was just the kind of beautiful guy he was. He was always more concerned about the band as a whole than he was about featuring himself as a performer.

Of course, I was tickled to death because I was getting such a break, but when I think back on all of that now, it's pretty hard to believe. But it is a fact. He started giving me all that space from the very first. Right away he would just open up playing a few numbers because he knew the people wanted to see Bennie Moten in person. That was advertised. But then he would turn it over to me, and most of the time he would come back on the stand just before the closing number, just like that first night in Wichita.

We also played a dance in the Ritz Ballroom while we were in Chicago that time. But the thing that stands out in my mind is what happened on the Sunday we spent there. We were staying in a hotel over the Grand Terrace Ballroom, and that Sunday afternoon Bus Moten and I got out and walked up South Park way until we come to the Regal Theatre, which was on Forty-eighth. I remember us standing there looking at the publicity pictures and announcements out front and seeing that there was a big stage show with Dave Peyton's big orchestra in the pit, and Sammy Lewis was featured on the organ and with the sing-along.

I remember telling Bus Moten that I sure would like to hear that guy play that organ in there. So we bought tickets and went in, and the theater was so full that we had to go up to the balcony. We found seats, and I sat there looking around. It was fabulous in there with all of those chandeliers and boxes and draperies. And then the lights went down and that great big orchestra came rising up in the pit playing a *symphonic overture* down there.

"Jesus!" I said.

I had never heard anything more beautiful in my life. Something like that in a theater, and it was an all-colored orchestra to boot! Then the curtain opened and there was that big, fantastic stage production, and I could hardly believe that either. The show that Elmer Williams and I had seen in the Jim Crow balcony at the Alhambra up on Seventh Avenue at 126th Street one night shortly after we arrived in Harlem from Asbury Park didn't have anything on this. It was almost as if I had never seen a big show before.

I just sat there looking and listening, and I don't know what made me do what I did next. I nudged Bus.

"You know one thing, Bus? Boy, one of these days I'm going to be down there onstage with my own band."

The funny thing about it is that I can't remember ever thinking about anything like that before in my life. I had never thought of myself as a future bandleader, even when I organized that dance in Red Bank, or even when I took that combo down to the Smile Awhile in Asbury Park and got stranded down there that time.

But that is what I said. I don't know why. I just said it.

"One of these days."

And Bus just sat there looking at me for a minute, and then he leaned over and whispered back at me, "Did you bring that bottle up here with you?" We always kept a little half-pint flask of something to sip on in our room. So he sat there looking at me as if to see if I really had been drinking or maybe really had snuck it along. All I could do was just move to the other side of my seat and slide down and prop my legs against the seat in front of us.

"All right, man," I said. "All right. All right. Just let me look at the goddamn show."

So he didn't say anything else then. But old Bus never forgot that, and years later, when I actually did come into the Regal Theatre with my own band, it just so happened that he was playing downstairs at the Blue Note. And we got together and were sitting in a bar or coffee shop or something like that, talking, and all of a sudden he looked at me and grinned.

"You know something, Base?"

"What?"

"You son of a gun. You *said* you were going to play that theater with your own band one day, didn't you?"

"Aw, come on, Bus," I said. "When did I say that?"

But I know very well what he was talking about. And all through the years I have never played on that stage without remembering that balcony and Dave Peyton conducting that pit band.

=

When we got back to Kansas City from that trip to Chicago, we were booked into the El Torreon Ballroom on Troost Avenue, and by that time we were also being picked up on Tuesdays, Thursdays, and Saturdays by KMBC, the local Columbia-chain radio station. Of course, we still worked out in the territory from time to time too.

To the best of my recollection, it was during that same summer that a band known as the Alabamians out of Chicago were booked into the El Torreon Ballroom for a couple of months, and that's when I met a hell of a great guy and struck up a very special friendship that has continued right on up to the present day. His name is Cab Calloway.

Cab was fronting that band, and he wanted me in there. We used to sit on the corner talking about things. The band had come out to Kansas City from Chicago, but after the El Torreon it was going to work its way through Ohio to Pittsburgh, and then they were hired up for the Savoy Ballroom in Harlem.

"Man, wouldn't you like to go to New York with us?" he kept asking me every time we got together. He was very excited about that. He had never been there before.

"Man, you know I'd like to do that," I said. And he really was trying to get me into the Alabamians. I think he almost lost his friendship with some of the fellows in that band because they saw that he was trying to bring me in. But Cab didn't give a damn. It didn't work out, but he really was for me.

In the meanwhile, Eddie Durham and I had something going in the Bennie Moten band, and by that same fall we were able to make a very important addition to the lineup. We brought in Jimmy Rushing to be our featured singer. I don't know whether Jimmy had already cut out from the Blue Devils before that. I think he had. I think he was just doing a few little things around Oklahoma City on his own, because I don't think the Devils were doing too much at that time. Anyway, Bennie got in touch with him, and he came up to Kansas City and joined the band.

This was great for me personally, because old Rush and I were a pretty tight pair of old running buddies. So as soon as he hit town, he and I began making the rounds to a lot of joints and houses in Kansas City just as we used to hit those good old back alleys when we pulled into another town traveling with the Blue Devils. Anywhere they had a piano, you might find me playing and old Rush singing. We used to go around from house to house having a ball all day long.

Then after Jimmy had been in the band for a little while, he and Eddie Durham and I started a little more larceny, working to influence Bennie to get Lips Page in that trumpet section. We wanted somebody in there to play the kind of get-off stuff that we felt we needed for the new things we were adding to the book. Of course, before Eddie and I began bringing in our arrangements, the band had its original Kansas City stomp style. It had a special beat, and it really had something going, and I could understand what was happening, because it was a very happy band.

I really don't know how you would define stomp in strict musical terms. But it was a real thing. What I would say is if you were on the first floor, and the dance hall was upstairs, that was what you would hear, that steady *rump, rump, rump, rump* in that medium tempo. It was never fast. And you could also feel it. Of course, the band used to have to play other kinds of things too. Sometimes we'd be playing somewhere and there would be those little cardboard signs that somebody would put up on a rack by the bandstand to announce that the next dance would be a one-step, fox-trot, waltz, and those other little steps that called for different rhythms and tempos. When we were playing that kind of dance, most likely Bennie himself would take over at the piano. Naturally, he could play the stomps too, because that was the band's thing. But anytime they played anything, the floor was full of dancers. *That* told you something.

But it was not the kind of jump band or swing band that the Blue Devils band was. The Blue Devils' style was snappier. They were two different things, and we wanted some of that bluesy hot stuff in there too. So we needed Lips, and Bennie brought him in for us. We didn't get rid of anybody to bring him in. Eddie wrote special parts for him.

Here are a few bars that Eddie ran down for my co-writer about what was happening musicwise: "When some of the guys in the band heard that Lips was coming, they came and asked me whose place he was taking and what notes he was going to play. 'I'm playing second and so-and-so is playing lead and what's his name is playing third on the trombone.' So I said, 'I'll find a note for him. I'll add another part to the harmony.' Because they were just playing three-part harmony all the time. And when Lips came, I started writing four-part harmony, and I added a sixth tone in there. And I found out that those guys couldn't play a sixth. They couldn't hear a sixth. It would hurt their ears. So I gave it to Lips because he was a hot man, and he was hitting them sixes as solo work.

"Now, the way all that got started was with the things that Basie was playing for me to work up arrangements on. I told him, 'Man, this stuff you got here will stand four- and five-part harmony. The way you're carrying this, let's get away from all these triads and add another man.' So he said, 'Get Lips.' That's the way it was, and then I was writing ninth chords, which is a five-part harmony, and they could hear the ninth a little better than the sixth. I gave that to Lips. They didn't know how to blend it. So that's how Basie and I got it going. The others thought it was out of tune. But Bennie went along with us, and when the rest of them heard it on the next records, they began to understand what was happening."

—

Sometime during the early part of that next year, Bennie got us a deal as the house band in the ballroom at Fairyland Park, out on Seventy-fifth and Parkway in the country club district. That meant a whole lot to everybody. It was such a special thing that Bennie ordered new outfits for us, and by the way, that was when I finally got to wear a regular band uniform like everybody else. I was already working a regular salary for quite a few months before that, but all during that time I was performing in my make-do tuxedo and whatever else I had that was close enough to the band's other uniforms not to be too noticeable.

The Fairyland Park job was a seasonal thing. The ballroom was open only when the park was going full swing for outdoor recreation. For the record I would just like to say that it was lily-white out there in those days so far as the customers went, but I don't remember that we ran into any trouble during those several seasons that we worked out there. I don't know what some of the other musicians out there during that time might have to say about it, but I don't know any stories about anybody giving any of our guys a hard time out there. I don't know of anything that came up, but I'm pretty sure that if it had Bennie Moten would have taken care of it pretty quick. You can bet that Bennie had checked all that out before he took us out there. When I say Bennie Moten stood for something and was respected in Kansas City, I mean all over Kansas City.

So along with all of the new things Eddie and I were working up to make the band swing more, we also played a lot of stock arrangements of pop tunes for the customers out there. Of course, Eddie and I did our thing on a lot of pops too. But Bennie also used to buy a few of those big stocks from somewhere, and some of them were kind of out of my reading range, but Bennie would just take over and run them down with no trouble at all.

I think I had already talked him into using two pianos sometime before the Fairyland gig came up. But it was while we were out there that we actually used them on a regular basis. But even then he didn't come onstage any more than he had to, and of course when we played most other places, working with two pianos was out of the question.

So sometimes we would double-head and play four-handed piano, which was really still two-handed piano a lot of times, because one of us would just play the left hand while the other would take the treble, which was something that I already knew a little something about because Fats Waller and I had done some of it on that organ in the Lincoln Theatre.

But that was such a wonderful learning experience for me because it put me so close to Bennie himself and the way he handled the band from the piano. That's not what I had in mind when I came up with the idea of two pianos. That was just a little something extra that turned out to be one of the most important experiences a future bandleader could ever have had. I don't think you can get that kind of experience in any conservatory. But then, after a while, we just kinda forgot about two pianos, and he spent more and more of his time taking care of business matters. Of course, he was still running the band, although he still let Bus front it with the baton.

One radio broadcast we used to pick up on a crystal set all through the territory was Earl Hines from the Grand Terrace. I can still hear that band coming on with that theme song "Deep Forest," with that cat saying, "Fatha Hines, Fatha Hines," and of course, a few years later there was his famous "Boogie Woogie on the St. Louis Blues," with another cat saying, "Play it till 1951!" He really thought he was saying something. Nineteen fifty-one sounded like a long way off then. Now it is actually a hell of a long time ago.

Another reason I bring up Earl is that he was such a great stylist. He changed the whole style of the piano, and I certainly picked up things from him.

All those stocks and pops Bennie used to buy were also pretty important to his long-range plans for the band. Because he wanted an all-around band that could go on and play for any occasion anywhere in the country. Naturally, he wanted a band that could battle all those other dance bands in the territory, but he also had it in his mind to go after some of that action that the big hotel bands were into. A lot of people seem to have forgotten how important big hotel and casino bands used to be, but back in those days every time you turned on the radio, you used to get those bands playing the pop and stocks on classics, right along with the jazz that the networks used to pick up from the bands in the nightclubs.

One reason it was so easy for Eddie and me to get Bennie to bring Jimmy in when we did was that ballads were really Jimmy's thing in those days, and that fit in so beautifully with Bennie's plans. Later on, Jimmy gained recognition all over the world as one of the great blues singers, but he started out doing the same kind of tunes as George E. Lee and Pha Terrell and a lot of other band singers during that time. He had made one blues recording with the Blue Devils not long before he left them, but when he and I were running together he did most of his blues singing in those alley joints he and I used to go out looking for as soon as we hit another town.

We had another big recording session that next fall. But we didn't have to make the trip back to Chicago, because Victor brought the equipment to Kansas City and rented a local studio. And the crew stayed around there for about a week, I guess, and we had four sessions and cut thirteen sides. According to the discographies, that was when we recorded "Oh Eddie," "That To-do," "Here Comes Marjorie," "The Count," "Liza Lee," "Get Going," "Professor Hot Stuff," "When I'm Alone," "New Moten Stomp," "As Long As I Love You," "Somebody Stole My Gal," "Now That I Need You," and "Bouncing Around."

These were the first records that Lips and Jimmy made with Bennie Moten. It was not the very first time either one of them had made records, however, because Vocalion had come out to Kansas City and recorded the Blue Devils playing "Squabblin'" and "Blue Devil Blues" a few weeks after the Moten date in Chicago. Which reminds me of another date I was on around that same time. One day while I was hanging out at Bennie Moten's record shop, a singer from St. Louis by the name of Edith Johnson, the wife of Jesse Johnson the promoter, came in looking for a piano player to play behind her on a couple of records, and right away I jumped up. "That's me," I said. And I asked her if she had some music. I don't know what I asked that for, because that was the last thing I wanted to see. I probably wouldn't have known what to do with it if she had had some. But she said, "No. Just follow me." She also asked if I could play some blues. So we did a little song. I never will forget the title: "Live and Love Tonight." Then we did another song, and I tried a couple of stride choruses in there, just piano. She has kept that record all these years, and every time I see her when we play St. Louis, she tells me she still has it. Then she tells whoever is with her, "That's my piano player."

And I say, "Yeah, that's right."

II

Even before we finished that first session out at Fairyland Park, Bennie was already busy trying to get some plans working to take us on some tours out of the territory. He really wanted to see if we could work our way east and try to break into some of that big-time action that you had to have if you were going to get national recognition. That was his goal, and the band was doing so great with the recordings and all that, he was pretty certain that we were ready. So he made his move.

That was when he brought in Maceo Birch to work with him as our advance man. Maceo was a local businessman and promoter. He had quite a bit of show-biz experience, first as a member of the dance team of Maceo and Red Groves and also as the manager of a theater on Elizabeth Street. His job was to go out on the road and sell the band to local promoters and theater managers in as many towns as he could line up, and feed the information back so that Bennie could lay out the itinerary.

Sometimes Maceo and Bennie would go out on the road at the same time. Sometimes they would take different routes and meet somewhere, and sometimes they would go out together. I think the reason for that was that sometimes it was just a matter of lining up dates in different towns, but other times, when he wouldn't work out anything else, Bennie would rent a hall or a club somewhere and sponsor the dance himself. Because the band needed the work, and the exposure. I already knew about that from some of the dances the Blue Devils used to run from time to time. Maceo and Bennie would set up the whole thing, and then they would take care of the admission, and the band would play, with somebody also keeping a pretty close lookout on how things were going, because sometimes the musicians also had to function as the bouncers. If something started happening out on the floor, the band would get up and come down off that stage like a football team, and if they had to break up a fight and throw somebody out, they did it and went on back onstage and started playing again.

When the band was on the road like that in those days, we didn't work on a straight salary anymore. We operated on the same kind of commonwealth basis that I already knew about from my time with the Blue Devils. The take would be counted and Bennie would take the expense money off the top, and the rest would be divided in equal parts. A lot of territory bands used to do that. But so far as I know, there was nobody made it work any better than Bennie. When things used to get a little tight out there, you always figured that he was going to come up with something, and he always did.

Before the end of that winter, he and Maceo Birch had lined up a series of one-nighters that took us across Missouri, Illinois, Indiana, and

Ohio, and by the end of February we were working our way into Pennsylvania, and from there we were going to try to make it into New York City. That was our ultimate destination. In the meanwhile, things were really going pretty good for us, and I think everybody in the band felt like we were really on our way up in the world. We were already beginning to read notices about the band in the Pittsburgh *Courier,* an outstanding weekly paper that had a nationwide circulation like the Chicago *Defender,* the Baltimore *Afro-American,* and the Norfolk *Journal and Guide.*

As early as February 14, the *Courier* ran the following article:

Bennie Moten Coming with Great Orchestra. Famous Victor Recording Orchestra to Make Tour of This Section On Way East. Bennie Moten— if you please—and his great Victor Recording Orchestra, admitted by press and public alike as one of the truly big-time orchestras of the century and as the rage out St. Louis and Kansas City way, where music is the all important thing, is coming to Pittsburgh!

This announcement was released by Wednesday evening, after the contract for his appearance here had been received. Moten, whose work on records and on the air has made him a worthy rival of McKinney's Cotton Pickers and Duke Ellington and who had jumped into the public spotlight rating. His records rank with the best Victor sells, and his appearance here will be in the nature of a real treat. Moten's orchestra played on the same platform with Noble Sissle upon the occasion of the latter's appearance in Kansas City. The Orchestra will tour this section for a week before going East.

Knowing what I know now about promotion, I would not be surprised to find out that everything in that article came right off the release material that Maceo and Bennie either worked up themselves or had somebody work up for them. But any way you look at it, things were going in our favor. A follow-up article came out in the *Courier* of that next week.

Naturally, we didn't feel as famous as newspaper articles pictured us to be. But we did go into that Pythian Temple and do our thing, and we knocked them out. It was a fabulous place, and there was a wonderful crowd, and they really went for us, and we laid it on them. It was only a one-night stand, but we left there feeling that things were getting better and better all the time.

So then, after playing those other places in Pennsylvania, we moved on to our next big step, which was Philadelphia, and that was where we had to do something a little different from what we had been doing up to then. We were booked into the Pearl Theatre for about a week. That sounded just great, but I don't think a lot of us realized what it meant until we pulled up at Twenty-second and Ridge and saw all of those lights and displays on the marquee. We were billed as one of the next attractions, and we were supposed to go in there as part of a big fantastic stage show that also featured singers, comedy teams, dance teams, and a big line of chorus girls.

And to top it off, the band that we were supposed to follow in there was Fletcher Henderson, with Rex Stewart, Bobby Stark, and Russell Smith on trumpets; Coleman Hawkins, Russell Procope, and Harvey Boone on reeds; Claude Jones and Benny Milton, trombone; Walter Johnson, drums; John Kirby, bass; Clarence Holliday, guitar; and Fletcher himself and his brother Horace on piano. That made us all stop and think a little bit, and Bennie decided that we needed some special things to take in there.

So he told me and Eddie Durham to start working on something, and then at rehearsal we found out that one of the big features that we were going to have to play for on the show was Ristina Banks and her famous Number One Chorus, one of the greatest lines of chorus girls in show business at that time. They were in the same class, but not as famous, as the girls in places like the Cotton Club, Connie's Inn, and in such Broadway musicals as *Chocolate Dandies* and Lew Leslie's *Blackbirds*. They had also been used to doing their routines to the kind of stock arrangements used in Broadway musicals and cabaret floor shows. That was what all the other bands had been playing behind them, even Fletcher Henderson.

One of the numbers they were featuring at that time was "Honeysuckle Rose." As I remember it, there was also a team of two dancers that did a soft-shoe routine in there after the lyrics, and then the line of girls came on and danced two choruses. Then there was something else they did, and the thing they rehearsed by was thirty-two bars. So we went home that night after rehearsal and figured out a couple of our own ensembles, one for "Honeysuckle Rose" and one for something else, and then Eddie and I also made up some special choruses of our own because Bennie also wanted some real hot things for encores.

Now another thing about all of that was the way all of those fine girls treated us when we came there for that first rehearsal. I guess they must have decided that they were not going to have anything to do with the guys in this little old country band. After all, they had been used to associating with well-known musicians in all of the top bands in the country. Fletcher Henderson, Duke Ellington, McKinney's Cotton Pickers, Claude Hopkins, were in and out of Philadelphia all the time, so who was this bunch of guys that nobody ever heard of, coming in there from out in the sticks somewhere? Anyway, they looked at us as if to say, "Where did they get those guys from, and what can this band do?"

But when the show started, it was a different story. They came out and did the first chorus by the stocks, and I never will forget what happened next, because that's when we laid them ensembles on them. They didn't know what hit them. But they started to move. I'm pretty sure they'd never moved like that before in their lives. And that is when we really went to work on them. And the audience loved it. I don't want to take any special credit or anything like that, but backing up acts was right down my alley. I had had a lot of experience doing that during all that time I had spent with Gonzelle White on the vaudeville circuit.

We were doing our thing on all those acts in that show, and they all sparked up as if to say, "Looka here. What's this?" and they all got some extra applause from the audience, and then, when we got down to the finale, we laid our "Nagasaki" on them, and what can I say? After the encores, the girls came backstage asking what was all that, and from then on we got along just fine. That was a classy bunch of girls with very high standards, and if you didn't measure up, they just didn't pay any attention to you.

It was during the week we spent playing on that big stage show at the Pearl that Eddie Durham and I came up with the number that went into the book as "Moten Swing." It started out as our thing on a great pop tune called "You're Driving Me Crazy," but we were not trying to work that up into anything. It was just something to take off from. Because Bennie said we needed some more instrumentals for the next show, and he sat in at the piano and let me and Eddie off to work out something new.

So we went down to the piano in the basement there, and I came up with a little something that Eddie liked, and while he was working on it, I slipped out and got myself a little taste and to see if I could connect with something pretty or willing. When I came back, he was ready to work out the channel. We played over what he had put down, and then I just went on and tried something, and he picked up on that, and I said, "You got it." I cut back out to have another little nip because I knew he knew where it went from there.

That's how we came up with that one, and we had to name it something, so we just said, "Hell, call it 'Moten Swing,' " because it really was for the band, and it turned out to be the most famous number associated with that band, and to this day, when you play "Moten Swing," right away everybody knows that it has something to do with that band and those good old times back in Kansas City. It was copyrighted in the name of Bennie and Buster Moten, but Eddie Durham and I were the ones who wrote it out together. They didn't steal it or anything like that; we just turned it in, and it became a part of the book. That was our job as staff arrangers, and we didn't think anything about taking credit as composers. To us it was just our end of the business. We didn't know anything about royalties for something you worked up like that. If you sold somebody a piece of music or he hired you to write something for him, he could copyright it in his name since it was his property along with the band.

(And then too, as my co-writer has reminded me, staff arrangers did not hesitate to use all kinds of little things that other sidemen had been contributing to the overall sound and personality of the band as solo licks, riffs and those wonderful little call and shout things. As a matter of fact there is, as he has also pointed out, a very familiar figure that everybody associates with Moten Swing; also sounds like a passage from a tune we had already recorded for Victor in Kansas City back in October. That was something that Bus and Eddie had worked up, and they called it, get this, "Oh, Eddie." No telling who actually brought figure into the band!)

When we got to New York, we went into the Lafayette Theatre for a week as a part of a big vaudeville production called "Rhythm Bound," which included the great dance team of Wells, Mordecai, and Taylor and also had a great singer by the name of Minto Cato. Her great number was "Memories of You," which Eubie Blake and Andy Razaf had written especially for her as a feature in Lew Leslie's *Blackbirds* of 1930. There was also a comedienne then billed as Jackie Mabley and later known as the famous Moms Mabley. In all I guess there were about fifty or more musicians, singers, dancers, and comedians in that show, and the movie that week was *Body and Soul* starring Charles Farrell and Elissa Landi.

We laid "Moten Swing" on Wells, Modecai, and Taylor. They had a routine called hitting the bottle. That was their big number at that time. It was something they had worked out at the Cotton Club for a tune by Harold Arlen. They would get out there and do a fantastic number of steps, each one getting closer and closer to a bottle on the floor without actually hitting it. It was something else, and the tune they did it to was called "Hitting the Bottle." But we worked those "Moten Swing" ensembles in there on them, and that lit an extra spark under them just as we had gotten to Ristina Banks's Number One Chorus. Another big number on that Lafayette gig was Jimmy singing "Old Rocking Chair," with Lips needling him on with that trumpet. And the audience also loved the way Bus riffed on that accordion.

We also played at the Savoy Ballroom on that trip. That was the first time I went in there to play. The other time was when somebody took me up there back when it first opened, and I had been so impressed with the place itself that I really didn't pay any attention to the music or the musicians. I remember that Fess Williams had one of the two bands in there that night, and Vernon Andrade had the other, and that's just about all. I don't remember what they played or how they sounded. What I remember are those colorful lights and spotlights and the biggest dance floor I had ever seen. And off the floor itself there were all those thick carpets and cabaret tables and padded booths and overstuffed chairs.

All of that along with all of those glamorous hostesses got all of my attention that first time. But this time I went in there to help Bennie Moten take care of business. Not many people around New York knew anything about that band when we went into the Savoy. But we were a big hit in there. When we laid that "Moten Swing" on them, it was shocking. They couldn't understand it, but they knew they could pat their feet and dance to it. So we laid the rest of our things on them, and we had Jimmy Rushing sing ballads and blues, and we had Bus Moten and his accordion.

Of course, you had to be ready when you went in there, because the house band was Chick Webb, and his chief arranger at that time was Benny Carter. He had Louis Bacon, Shelton Hemphill, and Louis Hunt on trumpets. Benny Carter was playing alto and clarinet and leading the reed section, and there was Hilton Jefferson on alto, and according to some documents, the tenor man was none other than Elmer Williams, my oldest musical buddy! The rhythm section had Don Kirkpatrick on piano, Elmer James on bass, and John Trueheart on banjo, and then there was Chick himself, one of the all-time great drummers. Our drummer, Willie Mc-Washington, was thrilled to death just to have a chance to see Chick Webb in person.

They didn't really try to run us out of there or anything like that, but they didn't go light on us either. They were like the hometown team, and we were in their ballpark. We did all right for ourselves because we had something that was a little different, and we knew it, because every time I came off the stand, somebody would come up and say something. Everybody wanted to know where we had been and where we were going and things like that.

But that Elmer Williams—I still haven't gotten over what happened when I ran into him on Seventh Avenue. I had forgotten how little we had actually talked to each other during those years we had spent running around together. He was standing right outside of Big John's. It was a chilly day, and he was wearing a blue chesterfield overcoat, a derby, and gloves, and he was carrying a cane. It must have been five years since I had last seen him, but when I called out to him and went over and grabbed him, he just stood there and nodded his head and grinned back at me like I had just been out of town for a few days or a week or something like that.

"Whutcha know, man?"

That's all he said. Not a word about what you been up to since I last saw you that many years ago, or anything like that. And when I asked about himself, he just said something about trying to make it or something like that, and we just stood there looking out across Seventh Avenue for about another half-hour before he said anything else.

"When you been home?"

"I just called down there," I said. "I figure I might go down there next week."

Then we just stood there looking at the traffic before he spoke again. "Say, where you gonna be?"

"I'm going to be right around here," I said, because the Lafayette Theatre was right there in the same short, busy block.

"Okay. Then I'll see you," he said, and cut out, just as he used to do before we left Red Bank and we knew just about where each other would be every day. That is really the only thing I can remember about seeing Elmer on that trip back to New York.

I also made a few rounds and dropped in on some of the old familiar places such as the Rhythm Club and Big John's, but I must say that I felt more like I was one of Bennie Moten's guys from Kansas City than like somebody coming back home.

I also went over to Red Bank to visit my parents for the first time in five years, as I told Elmer I would, and that was when I found out that my father was not living at home anymore. That was a very big shock. I definitely was not prepared for anything like that. I just couldn't believe it. But there it was, and to this day I still don't know what led up to it. Neither one of them ever told me. It was something about not seeing things eye to eye anymore, or something like that.

Naturally I had to try to do what I could to get them back together. But I didn't get anywhere with my mother because she just didn't want to talk to me about it. So I went to talk to my father, and he just told me that it was their business and not mine. That's exactly what he told me. Naturally I said it was. But that didn't get me anywhere. So I didn't bother my mother about it anymore, because I knew I was going to take care of her the best way I could, and that was that. I had been sending a little money home whenever I wasn't broke, ever since I earned my first real money out on the burlesque circuit. Now that I had found out what the situation really was, I knew I was going to have to do what I could to scrape up a little more. There were some bad months in there from time to time, but whenever my luck changed, I sent her something.

Meanwhile, every time I was back in Red Bank from then on, I would try to talk my father into patching things up. I remember one time in particular.

"Let's just straighten this thing out," I said, and he just looked at me like I was still a little boy in knee pants. "If you all don't straighten this thing out, I just feel like I don't ever want to come back down here no more."

"Well," he said, "if that's the way you're going about it, that's the way it'll have to be. Because, after all, she's your mother, and I know you love her, but she was my sweetheart and my wife."

He still kept in touch with her, and he also used to go by there from time to time, but they never did get back together, and I never did get any more information, and that's where I'm going to leave it.

⸺

When we left New York, we went down to Baltimore and played at the Royal Theatre on Pennsylvania Avenue for a week. Then by the middle of May we were back in Kansas City in plenty of time for our gig out at Fairyland Park when it opened for the season. So we spent all that summer right at our home base. Which was okay for a change because you didn't have to go to work until around eighty-thirty, and that left you all that time on your own just to hang out at the Yellow Front Saloon and the Subway Club and all of those other places if you wanted to; you were back in town by midnight, and those places stayed open until morning.

⸺

That turned out to be a very busy year for us, especially for me. While we were working out at Fairyland Park that summer, I got myself my first automobile, and I also got married. Then that fall we went back out on another barnstorming tour, and we went back to New York several more times and played at the Lafayette Theatre two more times. We also went back into the Savoy Ballroom for a night.

Fairyland Park was out on South Parkway at Seventy-fifth Street, and after a few weeks I began to realize that some of the fellows were beginning to get their own rolling stock to drive out there. So I said, "Hey, what's going on here? I need me some wheels, too." And I did a little checking around and managed to find out what the deal was. So I just went to the nice lady in the finance company and talked her into letting me get a down payment, and I got a Pontiac.

I haven't thought about that car in years, but I do remember that it was a roadster and it had a rumble seat, and the speedometer went up to sixty miles per hour. That was the limit, but that was pretty fast in those days because most roads were only about two lanes wide, and they didn't have a yellow strip down the middle because most of them were covered with gravel or macadam. Once you passed city limits, you didn't see a lot of concrete and asphalt anymore in those days. I can still remember that very well, and I can also remember those road crews, and a lot of them were still using mules and horses to pull the earth-moving equipment. And when you got on those back roads, as we often did, you never knew when you were going to find yourself bouncing into the next mudhole.

I went and got married right around the same time that I got my first car. Frankly, I'd just as soon skip that part of the story. It didn't turn out so good. It was a mistake. In fact, that was the biggest mistake I had ever made up to that time. The young lady's name was Vivian Wynn. She was a Kansas City girl, and she made an impression on me. I was dating her more regularly than I was dating anybody else when the band was in town. So we got married. Some of the other fellows in the band were getting married that summer, so I went ahead and did likewise.

Eddie Durham says he and Jack Washington and I all got married the
same day. Could be. But I really don't have enough curiosity about it to
check it out. I honestly can't remember the date, and as far as I'm concerned, it can stay forgotten.

However, I do seem to remember that some of us had our wives and
automobiles with us for at least part of the trip when Bennie and Maceo
took the band back out on another eastern tour right after Fairyland Park
closed down for the fall and winter. I know that Vivian was out there
with me for part of the time. But I don't remember how long she stayed
and when she went back to Kansas City, and which town she went back
from.

The main thing that comes to mind about Vivian being on that trip
is the time the band was laying off in New York for a while. I think this
had to be during the first part of October, and we were waiting around
while the transactions were under way for us to be a part of a very special
package deal produced by some outfit Bennie got hooked up with called
Associated Colored Orchestras.

There is one thing I knew for certain that Vivian and I did while the
band was waiting around New York, whenever that was. We took a little
trip over to Red Bank, and she met my mother and also my father. I do
remember that. But for the life of me I can't figure out where and how
she left the tour and went back home. She could have gone by train, but
I think maybe one of the other wives drove and whoever else went along
rode in that car.

I know for certain that they didn't drive my car back out there, because Eddie Durham and I drove it from New York to Philadelphia on
the way down to Baltimore. But we couldn't find our way out of Philadelphia. We couldn't find our way out of some park down there. We must
have driven around in that park for an hour trying to get out of town.
Then we got disgusted and put the car in a garage and went and caught
the next bus for Baltimore.

That was the last I ever saw or heard of that Pontiac roadster. I guess
the finance people must have found it where I left it. Because they were
looking for me and it anyway, and I didn't get any more notices about the
back payments that I had missed. Anyway, that was the end of my first
automobile, and I spent the rest of the tour riding in the bus like I was
used to doing before.

The special tour that Associated Colored Orchestras concern had set up
was advertised as a "Battle of Music." It featured five big dance orchestras
playing against each other on the same bill. The other four were Chick
Webb, representing New York; Blanche Calloway, representing Washington; Zack Whyte from Cincinnati; and Johnson's Happy Pals from down
in Richmond, Virginia. We were supposed to begin in Philadelphia. Then
after Baltimore we were to go to Richmond and come back to Washington;

Harrisburg; Pittsburgh; Orange, New Jersey; Wheeling, West Virginia; and then on out to Cincinnati.

I don't know how many of these towns we actually hit, but those five bands created a lot of excitement and got us some good newspaper publicity, especially when we played in Pittsburgh. This was very important because, as my co-writer reminds me, the Pittsburgh *Courier* was not just a local paper like the old New York *Age* and the *Amsterdam News*; it was a national publication like the Chicago *Defender*, the Baltimore *Afro-American*, and the Norfolk *Journal and Guide*. So when they printed something about you in the *Courier*, people read about you all over the country.

They really liked the Bennie Moten band in Pittsburgh. The *Courier* gave us big headlines on the entertainment page and ran a big picture of the whole band onstage to announce that the Battle of Music was a coming event at the Knights of Pythias Temple in October. Then, a few weeks later, the same picture was printed again to announce that we were coming back for a one-night stand, and that was also when the *Courier* said that Bennie Moten's band had won the Battle of Music at the Pythias temple the week before by popular applause.

By the first week in November, we came back into New York and went into the Lafeyette Theatre for the second time that year. The stage show that we were a part of was called *Music and Laughter*, and the headline singer was Alice Harris, who was very well known in vaudeville, and the other star was Garbage Rogers, a top comedian from Chicago. He was a very funny guy. We liked one of his skits so much that we stole it and tried to use it later on.

Old Garbage used to come onstage in a full-dress outfit, top hat, cane, gloves, and everything. The scene would be a restaurant, and he would come in with a lot of high-class airs and carefully remove his hat and gloves and then remove his chesterfield overcoat and white silk scarf and hang his things on the coat rack in the corner and then walk around as if he were picking out the best table in the house. Then he would walk right over and pick up a towel and start waiting tables! That tickled the hell out of us. So not long after, when we left New York and went down to Wilmington, Delaware, we got booked into some little theater and found out that we were supposed to do a whole show. So Bus Moten was Garbage, and I was his straight man. We put the burnt cork on and everything, and we were up there walking around doing Garbage's act, and the people in the audience were looking at each other as if to say, "Where did they get those guys? Where the hell did they come from?" But nobody was laughing or anything. Nobody. That audience couldn't believe it. Somebody told the man he ought to be ashamed of himself. I don't know what Bennie got for that date. Probably about fifty dollars so we could get out of town.

Some of the other acts on the show during the week we spent at the Lafayette with Garbage and Alice Harris were the Four Bobs, the Alabama Tin Band, and Ted Blackmon's Chorus. The movie running in there that week was *Bought*, starring Constance Bennett. It was recently brought to my attention that some of the other movies playing in Harlem that same week were *A Free Soul*, starring Norma Shearer; *This Modern Age*, starring Joan Crawford; and Maurice Chevalier in *The Smiling Lieutenant*.

Which also reminds me how close stage shows and screen shows used to be in those days. All of the big showcase theaters presented live entertainment along with first-run screen attractions. The title movie following us into the Lafayette also brings back memories, or maybe I should say feelings. It was called *Sob Sister*. I don't remember anything about the story, but that title certainly takes you back. It was a pretty popular catchphrase for a while.

I think it might have been while we were laying off in New York for a few days that November that I ran into Fletcher Henderson at Big John's, and he took me down to Roseland Ballroom. I think that was probably the first time I was ever in Roseland. Anyway, I was sitting on a little step right on the side of the bandstand, listening to Coleman Hawkins, and all those cats. After a while, Fletcher looked down at me and beckoned.

"I got to run out of here for a few minutes. Come on up and sit in here for me until I get back. I'll be right back."

I said, "What? Who, me?" or something like that, because I knew good and well that music was a litle beyond my range. But he came on down where I was and gave me a little shove up toward the bandstand.

"Go on and play," he said again, and he walked away.

I got up there and looked at the sheet music on the piano *and everything I saw was in D or B- natural or something like that*!

So I just got right back down and sat on those little steps where I had been in the first place. Then I realized that Fletcher could see every move I had made because he was looking out through the window of a little room that must have been used as a control booth during broadcasts and he was laughing his can off. That band played some hard keys. I guess that's why it sounded so good. But I didn't fool around up there because I knew that pretty soon there was going to be a piano solo in one of those hard keys, and something like that was the last thing I wanted to get tangled up with. I just sat right there on those steps as if nothing had happened.

We got back down to the Pearl in Philadelphia and the Howard down in Washington, and a few other places during the weeks after we finished that run at the Lafayette with Alice Harris and Garbage Rogers. Then we worked our way back up to New York again, and the next time we played at the Lafayette was around the middle of December. Bennie and Maceo had us hooked up with the famous Whitman Sisters for that one. Now that was really the big time. The Whitman Sisters had a show that was second to none in show business. They had a top company for years.

The show we were on with them was supposed to be their greatest revue. They advertised it as having a cast of fifty, including us. In their own cast, they had Alice and Bert Whitman; two kid dancers named Pops and Louis; Princess Pee Wee (a midget); Sam and Scram; Willie Tootsweet, who later on became more famous as Willie Bryant, the emcee all-around entertainer and bandleader; Eloise Bennett; the same Doris Rubottom that I knew from the time when we were both working for Gonzelle White; and the Three Snakehips Queens plus the great Shelton Brooks.

The four Whitman Sisters were named May, Essie, Alberta (or Bert), and Alice. Pops, the kid dancer, was Alice's son. By this time May wasn't performing anymore. She mostly took care of the business deals and rehearsed and taught the dancers. I don't really remember much about Essie. Actually I don't know whether she was there at that time, but I know she could sing and do comic skits. Bert was the one who dressed like a man. She wore her hair short and danced the male parts in duets. Alice was the baby sister, and she was one of the greatest tap dancers around.

But the most important thing for me about being on that program with the great Whitman Sisters was that I saw a very beautiful girl who a few years later became my second and permanent wife. Her name was Catherine Morgan, and she was one of the three Snakehips Queens. That was the first time I saw her. I didn't actually meet her then, because she wouldn't even speak to me. I tried to meet her, but she just went on doing whatever she was doing. Of course, she was only sixteen years old at that time, and the Whitman Sisters were very, very strict on the juveniles in their show. But I never will forget seeing Katy that first time.

—

Our main hangout in Harlem during the time when we were laying off between gigs that fall and winter was good old Big John's bar. As I had already known ever since the days when I was stumbling around between those trips out on the vaudeville circuit, Big John was always very generous to musicians and entertainers, and by the time I came back into town with Bennie Moten, he had added something special. Sometime after the Big Depression came on, he had started putting on a big stewpot on certain days, and if things were not going too well for you, you could get a free meal in there to kind of help you along. That stewpot and those beans and ham hocks and whatever else he cooked up that day, like maybe some greens and corn bread, sure became famous among musicians and entertainers during that time. A lot of people have a lot of stories about Big John's and those meals. I don't know whether Horace Henderson named his tune "Big John's Special" for those meals, but they sure were special.

I never will forget how good those meals were, especially one day when things were really getting pretty tight, and Big John helped us out by putting on the stewpot for the whole Bennie Moten band. It was just good old plain solid food, but it was fantastic. And then one cat, whose name I won't give, had to go and scandalize everybody else in the band. There we were with all that free stuff on our plates, and he called out to the bartender and said something like "Hey, man, give me a glass of water over here to go with this, will you?" Everybody just stopped eating and just looked at him. As much as to say, "Damn, man, this is a bar. The least you can do is buy a bottle of beer."

—

By the first part of the next year Bennie was beginning to make a few more changes in the lineup. That was when Big 'Un joined. So we had Walter Page on bass instead of Vernon Page. Naturally Eddie Durham and I were all for having him in there, because that meant one more Blue Devil, and that made the band sound more like we wanted it to sound. Of course, Bennie was for it because Walter had worked for him before Eddie and I had ever heard of him and the Blue Devils.

What made Big 'Un decide to change his mind and come when he did is something that I really didn't know a whole lot about. But I do know that it was not just a matter of him walking out on the Blue Devils. As I understand it, he had to give up the Blue Devils because he was having some trouble with the union about some misunderstanding about hiring some cat in Des Moines, so he turned them over to somebody else and got himself a little combo and was having a tough time trying to gig around Oklahoma City area when I got Bennie to make him an offer he couldn't refuse.

I think the next big event following that was the trip we made back to Chicago. Maceo and Bennie got us booked into a theater on the north side for a week. It was the kind of job that Bennie was always on the lookout for because he wanted the band to have as much of that kind of exposure as it could get. It was a big show and the master of ceremonies was Ralph Cooper, and our big number was supposed to be a special arrangement of "Rhapsody in Blue" by Bob Sylvester. But to tell the truth, I honestly don't think we did a good job on that. I must say, we got a lot of encouragement from Ralph, and we hung in there for a week, but we just did squeeze through.

Then we also did a couple of other little gigs around town. But things just didn't really go so good. It was tough to get into things around Chicago. In fact, our financial situation got so bad that we almost had to give up the bus. But Bennie maneuvered. Bennie always had a way of getting around things and getting something done. He always had an ace in the hole. So we didn't actually get stranded, and when we came back, we brought two new reed men along with us.

The first one was Ben Webster. He was hitchhiking his way back home to Kansas City from Philadelphia after touring with a band fronted by Blanche Calloway. The other one was Eddie Barefield. Ben Webster just happened to bump into him in the lobby of the Trenier Hotel one day. They already knew each other from the territory. So Ben brought him to a jam session we were playing, and when Bennie Moten heard him, he invited him to come on back to Kansas City with us too.

So when we got back, Ben Webster came in and replaced Woodie Walder, and Eddie Barefield got Harlan Leonard's chair. Joe Keys was also brought in for Booker Washington on trumpet. Then Ed Lewis left the trumpet section and Thamon Hayes quit the trombone section, and that's when Dee Stewart came in.

So the new lineup then was Lips Page, Dee Stewart, and Joe Keys on trumpet; Ben Webster, tenor; Eddie Barefield, alto and clarinet; Jack Washington, baritone; Eddie Durham, guitar and also trombone, along with Dan Minor; Walter Page, bass; Buster Berry, guitar; Willie McWashington, drums; and me and Bennie on piano and Bus on accordion.

That was some time in February, and we spent about a month just rehearsing, and then we did a few things in Kansas City and in the territory, but we were really getting ready for another tour east. I don't know why we didn't go back out to Fairyland Park that next summer. Meanwhile, since the band wasn't really working steady, some of the guys went out on other gigs from time to time. But that was just to pick up a little extra change. Nobody quit the band during that time.

Eddie Barefield and Ed Lewis say that was the summer that we lost the battle of the bands during the annual musicians' union benefit dance at Paseo Hall. That was when all of the top bands around the area came on and played one after the other and the crowd picked their favorite. Every year there were bands like George E. Lee, Paul Banks, Andy Kirk, and George Wilkerson participating, and Bennie always came out on top. But according to Barefield and Ed Lewis, things turned out a little different that year because Thamon Hayes was there with the Kansas City Rockets, a new band he had built around the musicians that Bennie had let go.

Eddie Barefield, who was in there with us, says, "They had all these bands over there and all the fine girls were out and everything, and Bennie Moten's band was going to play last because he was considered to be the king around Kansas City. So we go over to the hall, and everybody's playing. But of course, most of the crowd is waiting for Bennie's band. They're the big shots. So we are there, but we are not really paying any attention to anybody else. We're too busy socializing, but then just before the time for us to go on, Thamon Hayes went on, and Big Ed Lewis and those guys took off, and they were knocking the back out of that place, and they really were going over big with the crowd.

"Meanwhile, with all that socializing, when the time came for us to go up there and wipe everybody out, just about everybody in Bennie's band was drunk. We couldn't get ourselves together to save our lives that night. Eddie Durham was sick. Jack Washington was sick. Ben Webster was drunk. Basie was drunk. Lips was drunk. The whole brass section was drunk, and of course, Joe Keys was completely cut. We went up there on that stage and stumbled through something, but Thamon and those cats tore us up that night."

The funny thing about all of that is that I can't remember it. I guess I must have been pretty drunk. But I've just got to say that in all those years I was with him, I don't ever remember Bennie Moten's band ever being too drunk to play. The only time I remember anybody chopping Bennie Moten when I was in that band was when Don Redman and McKinney's Cotton Pickers came to Kansas City. That was while we were playing out at Fairyland Park, probably the summer before that.

They were out in Denver and they were scheduled to come to Kansas City for one night, so Don Redman, who was McKinney's musical director, came into town a day or so ahead of the band to hear us and see what we were doing so they would know what to lay on us. I remember meeting and talking with him in town somewhere, and he came out to Fairyland Park. And later on in the years, we got to talking about that, me and old Don, God bless the dead. I asked him about it.

"Yeah," he said, "I came out there to see what you cats were doing, and when I heard that first set, I got on the phone and called Denver and told McKinney, 'Don't worry about nothing.' "

I honestly don't remember Harlan and Thamon and those guys chopping us or tricking us or anything, although I don't say that they couldn't or didn't make things hot for us if that battle took place. But we got stepped on that night when Don Redman and McKinney and those Cotton Pickers came there, and we hurried up and got on out of that hall as quick as possible, because we played first. Then Don came up to the stand and said, "Okay, we got it from now on." And they lit in and that was it. I couldn't even stand to stay around and listen to the rest of it.

Chopping other bands was our thing. When I was with Bennie Moten, we were always looking for that kind of action. I'm not saying that Thamon didn't have a great band. He had a hell of a band. He had Jesse Stone as the musical director, and Jesse Stone, as everybody knows, was one of the best arrangers in Kansas City. Later on he wrote great stuff for all kinds of big-time outfits, including Earl Hines; and he was also a wonderful piano player. Baby Lovett and Vic Dickinson were in that band, and so was Herman Walder, Woodie Walder's brother. So Thamon played second trombone, and he had Vic Dickinson on first. He had Ed Lewis, Booker Washington, and Rick Smith on first, second, and third trumpets. In the reed section, he had Woodie Walder on clarinet and tenor; Herman Walder on alto; and Harlan Leonard on clarinet, alto, and baritone. In the rhythm section with Jesse Stone and Baby Vernon Page on bass.

They had a band that was good enough to make it tough for anyone. But whatever happened that night at the union hall, let's not forget that the band we're talking about is the same great band that Bennie brought east that year. Except for Joe Keys, who didn't come out on that tour and was replaced by Dee Stewart, that's the band you hear on "Moten Swing," "Toby," and "Prince of Wales."

The band we had when we headed east that next time was something else. Big 'Un in there on bass made things a lot different in the rhythm section, and naturally that changed the whole band and made it even more like the Blue Devils. With Eddie Barefield playing lead on alto, we had a man who could set riffs in the reed section like we had in the trumpet section, and he was also a real swinging solo man. And so was Ben Webster. The Frog, as we called him, was definitely one of the best tenorsax men I ever heard anywhere. Everybody in that territory knew what he could do.

The trombone section was also better than ever. Dan Minor was an old Blue Devils member like Eddie Durham. And being the kind of arranger he was, Eddie also set a lot of riffs, and he was a good solo man on guitar as well as trombone. Then there was also Bus. He knew what was happening, and he could really swing on that accordion.

But as great as that band was and as big as Bennie Moten's name was getting to be, that trip turned out to be rough going all the way. We came pretty close to being stranded in just about every town we played in. In one of those towns in Ohio, we hooked up with a fellow named Ross Conway who had been a big-time football player, and he started booking the band into a lot of different places. So we worked out of that town from night to night, and it was during that time that we swung down into the South, because I can just vaguely remember being down in Vicksburg, Mississippi, working for a local promoter named Sam something who had a red brick place. He was crazy about Bennie's band. I'm pretty sure we were down there for two or three days. Then we came back up into Ohio.

I never will forget what happened to me in one of those towns in Ohio on one of those tours with Bennie Moten. I'm not really sure whether it was Toledo or some other place in Ohio. But wherever it was and whenever it was, I still remember what happened to little old smart-ass Basie.

We stopped off there and went into a bar where you could get sandwiches and cigarettes and candy and things like that, and they had a good piano in there. That's the part I will never forget, because I made the mistake of sitting down at that piano, and that's when I got my personal introduction to a keyboard monster by the name of Art Tatum. That's how I met him. I remember that part only too well.

I don't know why I sat down at that piano. We were all in there to get a little taste and a little snack, and the piano was there. But it was just sitting there. It wasn't bothering anybody. I just don't know what made me do what I went and did. I went over there and started bothering that piano. I just started fooling around with it, and then I started playing and messing around. And what did I do that for? That was just asking for trouble, and that's just exactly what I got. Because somebody went out and found Art.

That was his *hangout*. He was just off somewhere waiting for somebody to come in there and start messing with that piano. Someone dumb enough to do something like that, somebody like Basie in there showing off because there were a couple of good-looking girls in the place or something like that. Oh, boy. They brought him in there, and I can still see him and that way he had of walking on his toes with his head kind of tilted.

This was several years before Joe Louis came on the boxing scene and wiped out all of the heavyweight prizefighters, but what happened was just like when a cocky boxer in the gyms shows off, sparring around, and when he looked up, he saw Joe coming through the ropes. Because I'm pretty sure I had already heard a lot of tales about old Art. But when I went over there and hopped on that innocent-looking piano, I didn't have any idea I was on his stomping ground.

"I could have told you," one of the girls at the bar said.

"Why didn't you, baby?" I asked. "Why didn't you?"

——

We were back in Ohio by the middle of that October because Conway (I think) swung some kind of a deal for us to go to Columbus as a special added attraction at the big football game between Ohio State and the University of Michigan. Then, one night during the week after that, we played some kind of very special dance in an auditorium that was supposed to be the biggest in the area. The other band in there that night was led by a guy named Paul Tremaine who was pretty well known in that part of the country in those days. But I think we took care of that business. It was Tremaine's territory, but the crowd went for us right away, and their special favorite was old Lips Page. That was his town that night.

I don't actually know how many towns we hit during the next five or six weeks of that trip as we barnstormed our way east again. But we got stranded in quite a few of them. That didn't mean that we were not having a ball or anything like that. It just means that we'd come into a town and play a great gig and then we wouldn't know where the hell we were going next. So we'd have to stay there until Bennie and the advance man came up with another arrangement somewhere. Then we would pack up and roll again. Of course, we were not eating a lot of steak and chicken dinners during those times. It was more like hot dogs, sardines and crackers, or cheese and crackers, and soda pop and bootleg whiskey, things like that. Meanwhile we also made a lot of friends in those places. You were always meeting people during those dances we played, and when you had to stick around for a few days afterwards, you had a chance to get to know them better. A lot of long-lasting friendships began like that.

Sometimes we stayed at a hotel or in a rooming house, but a lot of times maybe one or maybe two or three of us would have a room with a private family, just like when Elmer Williams and I first went on the road with the burlesque show. When you got stuck in a situation like that in one of those places where you were rooming with a private family, it could get to be very embarrassing. But not always. Because people who took in traveling musicians and entertainers were usually pretty reasonable about things like that, especially when they were old show-biz people themselves. But things could still get uncomfortable if you were still in there when another band or another show came into town with some money.

Along with all those financial ups and downs, however, the band was playing better and better all the time, and when we finally made it to Philadelphia by the middle of that December and went back into the Pearl Theatre for the third time, we were completely certain that we could take care of just about any break that opened up for us.

The gig at the Pearl was our first big theater date of that tour, and it was also the first time since we left Kansas City we were scheduled into a job where we had a whole week's salary coming. That was very good for morale, and we went in there jumping. And we also had ourselves a ball all that week, playing those shows and wining, dining, and partying the chorus girls. We really lived it up.

Then as soon as we closed, we found out that some of us had splurged ourselves into trouble. Quite a few of us had run up tabs at the hotel and couldn't come across with the cash and ended up getting kicked out of the hotel and having to spend that weekend sleeping in the bus while waiting to draw our pay that next Monday. I don't remember what the explanation for the delay on the pay call was at the time, but there we were—or at least a lot of us—the big headliners of last week out there sleeping in the goddamn bus!

So then that morning we parked the bus a few blocks down the street from the theater and came on up there to draw our pay, only to find out that we didn't have any money coming to us. And that was not all. The bus was also going to be confiscated. We had been working to pay back money that had been borrowed from Sam Steiffel to buy the new uniforms we had used on those shows with the Whitman Sisters the year before. So there we were, stranded again with not even the bus to sleep in anymore.

Naturally the fellows were pretty upset about the mess we were in. But it was pretty clear to everybody that Bennie Moten hadn't brought us into the Pearl Theatre on that kind of deal. He never would have taken his band in there just to have all the money to go to pay off a debt. Anybody who ever worked for Bennie would know that he just didn't do things like that. There was no way that he would have made any kind of deal like that without telling the band up front and having us vote on it, and I can't imagine him asking all of the new guys in there to work for nothing. But that's the way it turned out, and there was nothing we could do about it.

Everybody could see that Bennie was just as shocked as the rest of us. But the band didn't break up, which just goes to show how much the guys loved and respected him. And as usual, old Bennie came up with something that saved the day. I don't really remember what we did about our hotel bills. I think a few fellows must have pawned some things. Eddie Barefield, for one, who played alto and doubled on clarinet, says he hocked his clarinet and borrowed Jack Washington's, since Jack was concentrating more and more on baritone anyway.

But Bennie got us out of that spot somehow or other, and then he came up with some local cat named Archie Robinson, who was some kind of promoter and businessman, and they got us a recording date, and Archie got a bus from somewhere, and that's how we went from Philadelphia to the Victor recording studio in Camden, New Jersey, and made one of the best batches of records any of Bennie's bands ever made.

Archie Robinson was really a great friend of that band, and he helped us in all kinds of ways. He was the one responsible for that pool-table feast a lot of people have been hearing and reading about over the years. When we got to Camden, we hadn't eaten a real meal in quite a while, but we went on into that studio and made all of those records that turned out to be the ones that most people remember Bennie Moten by. They were "Toby," "Moten Swing," "Blue Room," "Imagination," "New Orleans," "The Only Girl I Ever Loved," "Milenburg Joys," "Lafayette," and "Prince of Wales."

I don't actually remember if that's the order we made them in, but I do know that we cut them all in that one long session. Then when we got off around six o'clock, old Archie had gone somewhere and rounded up something for us to eat, and he took us into a pool hall, and there was a big pot of rabbit stew and a pot of beans and hocks and a big old pan of corn bread all spread out on that pool table. So we all gathered around and ate. I can still taste how good it was.

Everybody was there except Jimmy Rushing and Ben Webster. Those two low-down dirty dogs has sneaked off to a restaurant around the corner somewhere. They always kept one or two dollars stashed away somehow or other. I think Ben's folks were always sending him cash from home, and I'm pretty sure that Jimmy still had some of the same dollars he had when we were in the Blue Devils together. I don't think Jimmy was ever hard up for something to eat. He was always saving for hard times.

Ben Webster and I used to sit next to each other on the bus, and he was always running out of cigarettes and borrowing one from me. I remember one time we were somewhere and I didn't have any. So he said, "Come, Basie, I'm going to buy you some cigarettes." And he bought me a pack and himself one. Then when we got back on the bus, every time I'd light up a cigarette, he'd reach over and take it and smoke it up. He smoked up all my cigarettes. Then when I asked him to give me one of his, he looked at me as if he was scandalized.

"Hell, Basie, I just bought you a whole package and here you come asking me for mine."

I think it was after that session in Camden that we swung down into the South again. I'm not clear about which route we took and where we stopped along the way. But if I'm not mistaken, that's when we went down into Virginia and out to Newport News, which most of us were old enough to remember as a place that had been a big name in the news back during the war. It was a very important seaport town that had been the most famous port of embarkation for the doughboys of the AEF (American Expeditionary Forces) heading across the Atlantic to Brest, which was the port of debarkation on the coast of France. The war didn't mean all that much to me while it was going on, but names like Newport News along with tales about German submarines laying in wait to torpedo troop-transport ships stick with you.

I'm not sure about which route we took out of Newport News either. But we headed back west, and we probably came back through Zanesville, Ohio, because we were back in Columbus just before the beginning of the Christmas season. And that's where a lot of the fellows began to get restless, because they wanted to be back in Kansas City with their families for the holidays. They were getting letters and telegrams and long-distance calls, and things were getting to be a little strained, and some of them started to cut out for home. Ben Webster was probably the first to go, because, although he was not married, he was very close to his relatives. He was always ready to head back home.

He and several others left from Columbus. So when we got back to Cincinnati, the band was dwindling. Eddie Barefield was the only man left in the reed section. We still had the rhythm section, although I'm not sure whether Buster Berry stuck around or not. I think we might have still had two trumpets, and I think Eddie Durham was there with his trombone and guitar. We had a theater date Christmas Day, and we played our same arrangements and actually it all turned out pretty good.

The people in the hotel gave us a Christmas dinner and a party, and we stayed in Cincinnati through the holidays because we had another theater date on New Year's Eve. I think Eddie Barefield had cut out in the meantime. I think the only ones we had left by that time was Willie McWashington on drums, Big 'Un on bass, Lips on trumpet, and me on piano. Maybe Bus Moten was still there, too. But I'm pretty sure about the others.

When it was the first of the year and we headed back to Kansas City, I think we still had the bus, such as it was. I think just about everybody who had left had gone by railroad. Of course, some of them had to wire home for money. I don't remember what route we took out of Cincinnati, but Bennie got us out of there somehow and we tried to pick up a little change on the way. But things were really rough in all of those little towns across Indiana and Missouri, and when we finally did make it back into Kansas City, we were pretty raggedy.

None of those guys who had cut out had actually quit the band. They just left because they didn't want to be away from home at Christmastime. But there really weren't enough steady gigs around town to keep a band like that together. There were all of those wonderful joints, and most of them featured live music, but what most of them used were combos, duets, trios, and there were also a lot of places where they just had a house piano player. Everybody talks about how great the jam sessions used to be in those days. But you couldn't live on jam sessions, and that wasn't band work anyway.

We did lose a couple of very important members of the team during that time, however. I think Eddie Barefield went first. He went to Columbus, Ohio, and joined Zack Whyte's band, and later on I found out that he also went with McKinney's Cotton Pickers for a while and then went on to Cab Calloway's band. Then Eddie Durham pulled out and went to New York to join Willie Bryant's band at Connie's Inn for a while, and then Paul Webster and Eddie Tompkins, two of his old Kansas City buddies, got him to join them in Jimmie Lunceford's band for a while. Ben Webster stayed on for a while longer.

We didn't have our regular thing out at Fairyland Park to look forward to anymore. Thamon Hayes was out there that year. I'd say we still got

1. Harvey Lee Basie of Red Bank, New Jersey. (Basie Collection)

2. Lillian Ann Chiles Basie of Red Bank, New Jersey. (Basie Collection)

3. Harry Richardson's Kings of Syncopation with whom a very young and thin Willie Basie worked as a piano player from time to time. Harry was the percussionist. (Basie Collection)

1

2

3

4. Katie Krippen and Her Kiddies on the Columbia Burlesque Circuit. Left to right: Basie; Steve Wright, drums; Freddy Douglas, trumpet; Katie, Elmer Williams, sax, and Lou Henry, trombone and manager.

5. June Clark, trumpet and Jimmy Harrison, trombone, with Fat Smitty comping on piano at Smalls' Sugar Cane. (Frank Driggs Collection)

4

5

6

7

8

6. Seventh Avenue in Harlem, uptown side between 131st and 132nd streets. Also nearby: Connie's Inn, Big John's and The Rhythm Club. Beyond the billiards sign was Harris' Corner, which became Count Basie's club in 1958. (Driggs Collection)

7. Gonzelle White, star of The Big Jazz Jamboree. (Basie Collection)

8. Gonzelle White's piano player and trumpet man, O.C. Gary on TOBA, 1926–27. (Basie Collection).

9. Walter Page, center; Jimmy Rushing, extreme left; Hot Lips Page, second from extreme right. (Driggs Collection)

WALTER PAGE *and his Famous Blue Devils*

9

10

11

10. Staff arranger Basie checking a score with
Bennie Moten as co-arranger Eddie Durham, who
actually wrote it down, looks on from directly
above Basie. Standing left to right: Hot Lips Page,
Willie McWashington, Ed Lewis, Thamon Hayes,
Woody Walder, Durham, Jimmy Rushing, Buster
Berry, Harlan Leonard, Vernon Page, Booker
Washington, Jack Washington and Bus Moten.
(Driggs Collection)

11. Two very hip Benny Moten sidemen: Bus
Moten, accordion player and front man, and the
co-piano player and co-staff arranger.
(Driggs Collection)

12. Catherine Morgan, the future Mrs. Count Basie,
performing as a featured single after an
apprenticeship with the Whitman Sisters.

13

14

15

13. At the Apollo, January 1939. Left to right front: Dan Minor, Dicky Wells, Benny Morton, Herschel Evans, Jack Washington, Lester Young. Rear: Harry Edison, Shad Collins, Ed Lewis, Buck Clayton, Jo Jones, Freddy Green and Walter Page. (Driggs Collection)

14. John Hammond as he looked when the band began recording under his supervision for Columbia Records in 1939. (Driggs Collection)

15. Jimmy Rushing sings the blues on Treasure Island during San Francisco World's Fair 1939. (Tuggle photo, Basie Collection)

16. Name Band in lights on the Big Track.

17

17. Herschel doing a get-off at The Famous Door, with Lester snapping his fingers and getting ready to follow him and wrap it up for the outchorus. (Hess photo, Driggs copy)

18. Running down a new chart with arranger Jimmy Mundy. (Driggs Collection)

19. Arranger Andy Gibson between trumpet men Sweets and Buck. After Eddie Durham left in 1938, Buck had become the chief sideman-arranger. (Driggs Collection)

20. Kate and Diane in the LaGuardia apartment on Fifth Avenue. (Allure Magazine Photo. Basie Collection)

18

19

20

21. Helen Humes and the band of the early 1940's. Buddy Tate has succeeded Herschel on tenor, Tad Smith's alto has been added. Don Byas has come in on the other tenor during Lester's extended absence (1940–43) and Al Killian has the chair between Sweets and Ed Lewis in the trumpet section. (Duncan Schiedt photo. Institute for Jazz Studies)

22. In the Blue Room at Lincoln Hotel in New York 1943. Lester is back. Jimmy Powell has replaced Tab Smith. Rudy Rutherford is Jack Washington's wartime replacement on baritone alto and clarinet. Eli Robinson and Lewis Taylor have replaced Dan Minor and Benny Morton on trombone. Buck Clayton is in the Army band at Fort Dix, N.J. (Driggs Collection)

23. With Artie Shaw, Buddy Rich and Tommy Dorsey, 1945. (Charlie Mihn photo. Driggs Collection)

21

22

23

24. The Mainstream.
View from the bandstand.
(Sylvester Brosier
photo, Basie Collection)

25. The Mainstream.
View from backstage,
off stage and elsewhere
border and coast to coast.

24

our share of the big dances, and there was still some work in a few of the
nearby places out in the territory from time to time. But all in all, things
were a little slow for us. Sometimes there was such a big gap between dates
that some of the guys used to go out on jobs with other bands. But they
were always ready to come back whenever something came through for
Bennie.

III

What used to be the old Eblon Theatre, where I played the organ for the
silent movies, was remodeled and reopened in the spring as a real classy
nightclub. I don't know how all of that came about, but I did know that
old Jap Eblon was no longer running it. Somebody from across town had
taken over, probably while we were out on the road. As a matter of fact,
after all these years I can't really say for sure whether the Eblon went out
with silent pictures, because, truthfully, once I got to be a part of the
Bennie Moten band, I really wasn't very interested in a lot of the other
things anymore.

Anyway, the new club at 1822 Vine Street was called the Cherry
Blossom, and it was designed to look like an Oriental spot. All of the
decorations were Japanese, including a Buddha on the stage, and the
waitresses wore costumes that made them look like they were Japanese.
That was about as far as that went. You couldn't get any Japanese meals
in there or anything like that.

As I already mentioned, we were spending a lot of time going out into
the territory again, so I really was not very close to what was happening
during those last weeks just before they opened for business. But I do
remember that George E. Lee was the first band to play in there, and if
I'm not mistaken, they opened around the same time in April when we
came back in town for the third annual Musicians Ball, sponsored by the
Musicians' Protective Union, Local 625, at Paseo Hall. As a matter of fact,
one of the extra added attractions at the Local 625 ball was from the
floor show at the brand new Cherry Blossom.

George was in there for a couple of months, or something like that.
Then I think we must have been next, because we went in that summer. I
don't know what kind of transaction Bennie made to get the band in there,
but after we had been in there for a while, he didn't like the way things
were going. Things had been pretty slow for a while, but Bennie still had a
lot of big plans for that band, and something was not going right at the
Cherry Blossom, and there was some dissatisfaction among some of the
musicians. I won't go into all of that. But what it all came down to was
that he wanted to pull the band out and try to get into something else. I
think he had something cooking with George E. Lee that he wanted to
bring the band in on. But it seemed like a lot of the guys wanted to stay put.

So Bennie called a meeting to find out how things stood, and that led to one of the hardest and saddest decisions I ever had to make in my life. Because then it all got to the point where the main question was Bennie himself, and they wanted to take a vote to see whether or not they were going to keep him as the leader. So Bennie said something like, "Well, if that's the way you feel and you're positive that's what you want to do, okay." And he just walked on out so they could vote their honest opinion.

They went on talking and then somebody called on me, and I had to go down front, and I wondered, Why me? because I was not one of the ones doing the complaining. But they said they wanted to know what I was going to do. That really put me on the spot, because I dearly loved Bennie, and I really hated to have to make that decision against him, but I said I would go along with whatever the band decided. So they decided to stay, and they voted Bennie out. I couldn't believe it.

"Damn," I said to whoever was sitting next to me. "What's happening?"

Then the next thing. They had to decide who they wanted to be the new leader. Now, that was something that I had never thought anything about. I can truthfully say that when I went in there to that meeting, I didn't have any idea at all that Bennie Moten himself was going to be the one getting fired. I knew it was a commonwealth band, so the members could vote on anything if enough of them wanted to. But it never crossed my mind that things were going that far. Then before I could get over that, they had picked me to take his place.

Then I was really on the spot. I went to Bennie and told him what had happened, and I said I was just keeping the band together until he came back, because nobody could really replace him. But I must admit that I was also ambitious enough to try to prove that I could make it as a leader. I meant what I said to him, because I didn't do anything to get elected, and I was ready to step down as soon as he came back, which I was pretty sure was what was going to happen sooner or later.

Meanwhile the band was now called Count Basie and His Cherry Blossom Orchestra.

That was the first time I was actually billed as Count Basie. But it was not the first time I was called Count Basie. I know about all of those newspaper and magazine stories about a Kansas City radio announcer just happening to give me the name Count to fit in with titles like Duke Ellington, King Oliver, Earl Hines, and Baron Lee, and so on. According to those stories, that was supposed to have happened while I was broadcasting from the Reno Club—which wasn't until about four years after the band that was in the Cherry Blossom. But as I've already said, the truth is that I named myself Count Basie back when the Cherry Blossom was still the Eblon Theatre.

The news story that came out in the Kansas City *Call* about what had happened at the Cherry Blossom mentioned that the band had gotten a new leader, the piano player "who calls himself Count." That was about three years before that cat is supposed to have hung that name on me on radio. Because I didn't start broadcasting until after I had been at the Reno for a while. As of this writing, my main man in the research department hasn't been able to turn up that article, because the files of the Kansas City *Call* for that year are incomplete. But he did find issues using Count Basie in articles about the Cherry Blossom and also in the ads for it.

My old buddy Eddie Durham also gave my co-writer a few bars on me and the name Count. "When Bennie used to come looking for Basie and Basie wasn't there, he'd say, 'Aw, that guy ain't no 'count.' Basie and I were supposed to be making up new arrangements, but as soon as Basie would hit on something and get me started on the scoring, he would slip on off somewhere, looking for something to drink and some fun. He never got tired of partying. So Bennie would come in and say, 'Where is that no 'count rascal?' Every time he'd come and Basie had slipped off somewhere again, that's what he used to say. So I even wrote a tune and gave it to Bennie, and everybody knew that it was about Basie. I've heard that he had called himself the Count before that. I didn't know about that, and I'm pretty sure that Bennie didn't know about it, either. He just called him no 'count, as the old expression goes."

Bennie went on over to Club Harlem, which was once on Fifteenth and Paseo, in the same building that used to be the old Paseo Ballroom. He got together with George E. Lee on some kind of special deal over there, and of course, some of the fellows stuck with him. If I remember correctly, Jack Washington, Willie McWashington, and Dan Minor went. I think Ben Webster stayed on for a while, and then he cut out and joined Andy Kirk. But it really is very hard for me to remember who went where and did what at that time.

I don't remember when Herschel Evans came to Kansas City, and I can't say for sure that he was the one we brought in as Ben Webster's replacement on tenor. But sometime later on during that same year, he worked with us at the Cherry Blossom. And it was during the time that Herschel was there that Lester Young came into town. I have been told that Lester had been with the Blue Devils for a year or so, and they had gone east and got stranded, and he had made his way out west to Kansas City. If I knew about all that at the time, I've forgotten it. I don't even remember knowing that the first band he joined in Kansas City was the one Bennie Moten and George E. Lee had over at Club Harlem. As strange as it sounds, in view of what happened later, I cannot pinpoint the first time I became aware of him.

But I certainly can remember already knowing that he was on the scene making the jam sessions at places like the Subway, along with Herschel and Ben Webster and a few other top-notch local tenors at least for several months, maybe more, before the famous battle of the saxes that took place in the Cherry Blossom when the great Coleman Hawkins came to Kansas City with Fletcher Henderson's band that next fall. I'd say most musicians around town already knew him very well. I mean, they knew very, very well what he could do on that horn.

Now about that so-called famous battle of the saxes. I really don't remember that anybody thought it was such a big deal at the time. I was there. But I don't remember it the way a lot of people seem to and in all honesty I must also say that some of the stories I have heard over the years about what happened that night and afterwards just don't ring any bells for me. I'm not saying that none of those stories are true. I'm just saying that I remember it the way I remember it.

The way some who claim to have been in the Cherry Blossom that night tell it, a bunch of local tenor players gave Hawkins such a rough time that he overstayed his time in Kansas City and he was still up there blowing when Fletcher and the band pulled out for their next gig in St. Louis or someplace. So then when Hawk finally did get out of there, he almost burned his car up trying to get to St. Louis in time, or wherever it was. According to just about everybody who tells that story, the main reason Hawkins got hung up was Lester Young. According to that story, Herschel and all of the other tenors were all big fans of Hawkins, and they were blowing to show him how much they had learned from him. All except Lester. He had his own style, and the way they tell it, he kept blowing chorus after chorus, and that challenged Hawk, and Hawk had to dig in, but he still couldn't make Lester give in. So there was also supposed to have been some cool feelings between Herschel and Lester from then on over that.

I don't remember it like that. I was there that night, at least for a while, and I remember that Herschel and Ben Webster and Lester and a few others were up there jamming, and Hawkins came by and decided to get his horn. Somebody kept asking him to play, so he finally went across the street to the hotel, and when he came back in with his horn, I was sitting at a table with John Kirby and some friends, and John thought that was something unusual.

"I ain't never seen that happen before," he said.

"I ain't, either," I said. Because that was something that Hawk didn't do in those days. Nobody had ever seen Hawk bring his horn in somewhere to get in a jam session.

That's the main thing I remember about that night. Because it was so strange. All of those other saxophone players were up there calling for their favorite tunes, and then Hawk went up there, and he knew all of the tunes, and he started calling for all of those hard keys, like E-flat and B-natural. That took care of quite a few local characters right away. Not many piano players were too eager to mess with that stuff. I knew I wasn't going up there. I don't actually remember Mary-Lou Williams being in there that night, but there is a story about Ben Webster going and getting her out of bed to come down and sit in on piano. Maybe I had left by that time (which should tell you something), but I will say that if they were looking for somebody who could play in all of them badass keys Hawk was calling for, Mary-Lou was the one to get.

I don't know anything about anybody challenging Hawkins in the Cherry Blossom that night. Maybe that is what some of those guys up there had on their minds. But the way I remember it, Hawk just went on up there and played around with them for a while, and then when he got warmed up, he started calling for them bad keys. That's the main thing I remember. I don't know anything about any cool feelings between Herschel and Lester over whatever happened that night. But I do know that Herschel and Lester were not working together in my band at that time. Herschel was still with me, and Lester was still with Bennie Moten and George E. Lee. Then later on they exchanged jobs and Lester came over to me and Herschel went to Bennie. But they didn't start working together until several years later in that band I had in the Reno Club.

That's how Lester happened to be in the band that I took from the Cherry Blossom down to Little Rock that next spring. We went down there to work for Sam Baker. Sam had a hotel down there, and he had had some dealings with the band before that. The details are very vague in my mind. But I think he had booked the band on a few short trips out into the territory, because I can just dimly remember him coming back to Kansas City with me when I was living over on Eleventh and Paseo.

Anyway, the band went down to Little Rock to play in Sam Baker's hotel, and that is where we were when Lester got a wire from Fletcher Henderson inviting him to come to Detroit and join his band as Coleman Hawkins's replacement. Hawk had left to go to England. So Lester cut out, and the tenor player we got to replace him was a fellow by the name of Buddy Tate. He was from Texas, and he had played with some of the top bands in that territory, such as Troy Floyd and T. Holder, and he was also an old pal of Herschel Evans.

Other members of the band at that time were Lips Page, Joe Keys, and Dee Stewart in the trumpet section; Dan Minor, trombone; Buster Smith, alto; and Lester on reeds; Claude McTear, guitar; Walter Page, bass; Jo Jones, drums; with me on piano. Jo had come into the band at the Cherry Blossom in December. According to him, he didn't feel that he had enough experience as a drummer to work with the band and finally gave in because Ben Webster, Herschel, and Walter put so much pressure on him. Up to that time he had thought of himself as being a piano player who could also sing and dance. He says he had come into Kansas City from Omaha with the Tommy Douglas band.

So when Lester left to join Fletcher Henderson, Buddy Tate, who was already in town from Texas with a group that had just broken up, came in on tenor. But the band didn't last very long after that. Some of the guys like Lips Page and Jimmy Rushing went back to Kansas City to join Bennie; others like Joe Keys and Buster Smith went with Buddy to join Nat Towles in Dallas. So pretty soon Jo Jones and I were the last two left down there, and for a while, we had to sleep in my car and we spent most of our days hanging out in Jones Pool Hall. We had to get out of Sam Baker's hotel because he needed the rooms. He brought a big crack band out of St. Louis in there. The leader was a piano player named Eddie Johnson, and there was this wonderful saxophone player with him named Tab Smith.

I wasn't ready to go back to Kansas City yet. So Jo and I stayed. We made a few friends who were very nice to us. There was a guy named Sweets Davis who was especially nice to us. He had a little joint we could slip into and play a little music every now and then and pick up a few tips. Then there was also another very nice guy down there. They called him Black Mack. He had a little rooming house, and he let me have lodgings in there, and he let me have meals when I couldn't hustle them gigging around. He was a hell of a swell guy.

And so was a tailor I met and used to hang out with. Somehow I'm always running into guys like that. One day he told me to come on by the shop, because he had a suit in there that he thought would fit me. So he laid that on me and saved me from being put in jail for indecent exposure. I was in pretty bad shape down there for a while. Talking about hard up. I must have had some more clothes back in Kansas City, but the suit pants I was wearing got so worn that when I went down the sidewalk, I had to stay close to the wall to keep my raggedy seat out of sight.

All in all I think I hung around down in Little Rock for a couple of months or something like that. We went down there sometime in March, and I'm pretty sure that Jo and I stayed down there until after Easter. Then Jo went to Omaha and Minneapolis, and I got together enough scratch for bus fare back to Kansas City. So I came on back and went over to Brooklyn Avenue to a place I used to call my second home.

My landlady was known as Aunt Lucy. Her name was Lucy Smith, and her husband's name was Howard Smith, and he worked for one of the big political bosses downtown. She was the most wonderful little lady. I had stayed at her place ever since Vivian and I had separated, some-

time before I went to Little Rock. By the way, that was one reason why
I was not in any big hurry to come back from down there. It was not the
only reason, because the main reason I took that band down there was
that not much was going on for us in Kansas City at that time.

I came up the steps and knocked on Aunt Lucy's door, and she looked
out and saw me.

"Somebody is in your room," she said.

"That's all right," I said. "I'll just sleep out here in the swing."

"Come on in here," she said. "I been looking for you all along."

I went on in and followed her into the kitchen and sat down at the
table.

"So here you are," she said. "I knew you weren't going to be away but
for so long."

Nobody could make you feel more at home than Aunt Lucy, God bless
her.

So I got busy trying to see what I could get back into around town.
Later I rested up for a day or so. Business hadn't been too good for bands
for a while, but that didn't mean that all of those great joints were not
still alive. They were still very much alive. There was always something
happening around those spots. Of course, my main standby was the
Yellow Front. The chief didn't care too much about hiring anybody per-
manently up there. But the piano was still there, and he still had his old
wide-open policy for anybody who wanted to sit in.

I wasn't too worried about having to pay rent, and as far as your meals
were concerned, if you really got pressed, you could always count on
getting enough for that in one joint or another. But I never was really
hard-pressed. Because in those days you could get a top meal for twenty-
five cents, and for thirty-five cents you could get a super top meal with
dessert and everything, and an extra order of rolls or biscuits. So picking
up enough change to get something to eat wasn't really any big problem
at all. The main reason you went to all those different spots and played
was that you just wanted to play.

During that time, when I was just knocking around town after coming
back to Kansas City from Little Rock, I also used to go in and play the
organ in the Baptist church on Nineteenth and Centennial Avenue. I had
become very friendly with Roy Dorsey, who was Harry Smith's brother
or half-brother, I think, and I guess he must have been a member of that
church, because he used to ask me if I would go around there and play.

It was Reverend Mackie's church, and they had a nice big organ in
there which I used to love to play. So I used to get myself together and
do a little churchgoing from time to time, and so did Jimmy Rushing.
Jimmy used to sing during Sunday-morning services. He used to sing
"Rose in the Bud," I think it was, and a couple of other church songs.
Jimmy was right at home with those church folks, and they just loved

him in there. They appreciated what both of us were doing. I guess it showed that we hadn't forgotten our upbringing in spite of all the joints we hung out in.

There wasn't anything all that special about musicians going to church, of course. I wouldn't want to give that impression, because it just so happens that Reverend Mackie had a son who was a drummer. I got to know him pretty well too, and he used to carry his drums into the church during the week. We used to steal in there and open that organ and play it. We'd have it shouting in there. Nothing sacrilegious. We'd just have it shouting like when the whole congregation was feeling the spirit.

——

Downtown Kansas City didn't really mean anything to me in those days. It's strange when I think about it now, but I never did go down there. As far as I was concerned, there was nothing down there for me. Everything that I was really interested in was in all those places either on Eighteenth or Twelfth streets or somewhere nearby. Naturally I knew that there were clubs and theaters and a whole big entertainment district down there because I had played down there with the burlesque on my first and second trips into Kansas City. Duke and Fletcher and all those big headliners also used to play down there. But they hung out in our part of town.

Meanwhile Bennie Moten was reorganizing and making plans to hit the road again, and as soon as I found out that I had a chance to go back and work for him again, I took it, even though he couldn't pay me a regular salary and had to take up a collection from each musician, just as he had done when I first joined the band about six years before. I was glad to be back, and he couldn't have made me feel more welcome. Which just goes to show what a prince of a guy he was.

It was a good band, and Bennie and Maceo had high hopes and a lot of plans for it. But it was not really the same band that split up at the Cherry Blossom. Of course, Eddie Durham and Eddie Barefield had gone before the Cherry Blossom, and by this time Ben Webster was probably in New York with Fletcher Henderson. But Jack Washington, Lips Page, Dan Minor, Bus Moten, and Jimmy Rushing were all there, and so was Buster Smith. I don't remember when Herschel Evans cut out. I think Lester was up in Minneapolis, and I think that was when Walter Page was in St. Louis with Jeter-Pillars, and in his place Bennie had Bill Hadnot. Bill Saunders and Pimpy were in the reed section. McTear was playing guitar. I was back on piano.

I am not really together on what gigs we played during the rest of that year and on up into that next spring. But there is one little thing that happened while the band was still over at Club Harlem that I have to mention. I can't pin down the date on it, but whenever it was, it was the second time I crossed paths with Catherine Morgan.

She must have been about twenty by this time, and since I had last seen her as a chorus girl with the Whitman Sisters she had become a fan dancer and was working as a featured single. Later on I found out that she had gone to the Chicago World's Fair the year before that and picked up pointers on fan dancing from Sally Rand herself.

The ad in the Kansas City *Call* for the Local 627 Big Labor Day Stomp billed her as Katherine Scott. Later on she used other stage and screen names, especially Princess Aloha. But the point of this story is that when I saw her at Club Harlem, that was the second time that I *didn't* meet her. In fact, she almost got me fired and even arrested.

I was backstage and her dressing-room door was open, and I thought I would go in and try to say something to her, like maybe mention something about when we worked on the same program at the Lafayette Theatre when she was with the Whitman Sisters. But she saw me looking in there, and before I could say anything she started blowing the whistle on old Basie.

"Hey, somebody come here. That piano player with Bennie Moten's band—I caught him trying to peep behind my fans!"

I wasn't doing any such thing, and she knew damn well I wasn't. But I got the hell out of there fast, and when I used to bring that up after we finally got together and got married, she would just pull my leg by reminding me that she was already a star while I was still just Bennie Moten's alternate piano player.

—

Jo Jones says that he just happened to come back through Kansas City with a traveling show while Bennie was reorganizing, and Bennie asked him to come in. But first he had to go down to Oklahoma with the show for a while and then came back to join us. According to him, that was how he happened to be with the band that next spring when we went out to Denver.

We were booked into the Rainbow Gardens out there for a week. But Bennie didn't go with the band to Denver. He and Maceo had been very busy lining up the next tour. So he stayed behind in Kansas City to work on that and also because he had to have his tonsils taken out. I don't remember him being bothered by tonsillitis or anything like that before, but I guess he must have been having some kind of little trouble. But when we pulled out, I just had the impression that it was like a little nuisance that he wanted to get cleared up before he hit the road for a long trip. I don't think he was supposed to come out to Denver. I think he was planning to catch up with us somewhere else.

Denver was all squared away. Bus Moten could handle that. What

Bennie was really getting ready for was the trip after that and a deal that would bring us back across to Chicago and into the Grand Terrace. I don't know where he had planned to meet us. But we left him at home, and the next thing we heard he was dead. He had died during the operation.

We were at a rehearsal when the word came. The Rainbow Gardens ballroom was in another part of town, and when we came back into the hotel, Bus got the message. We had come back to the hotel to get dressed to go back for our opening that night, and there it was. It was so shocking you couldn't really believe it. Everybody just stood there. Then we just split up, and everybody went off to different places for a while and came back and let Bus know that we were all going to help him carry on.

Then we had to go on and open on that very same night, and we couldn't get back to Kansas City for the funeral because we were booked into Rainbow Gardens for a solid week. Only Bus went back. That was rough, because Bennie was not just a guy you loved, because when you worked for him you were like a member of the family. So we played that whole week, and we did all right because we were not about to do anything that wouldn't reflect credit on his name.

That's about what I remember about that. I wasn't in Kansas City, so I don't really know what happened there, and I don't want to get into all of the different stories and speculations about it. It was all such a shock that people said a lot of things. He was supposed to have just a little routine operation to remove his tonsils. But he bled to death right on the operating table. So naturally a lot of people wanted to blame the doctor. But Dr. Bruce was one of Bennie's best buddies. They were together all the time. Nobody loved Bennie more than Dr. Bruce, and he was also a top doctor, and I understand that he was the chief surgeon at the Wheatley Provident Hospital.

I don't know just what happened. It was just something that happened, and nobody was hurt more than Dr. Bruce. He left town right after that. It was really rough for him.

People near and far were very upset, because Bennie was so well liked. Then there was also Bennie's family. They had their feelings, and you really can't take their feelings away from them either. How his wife, Crable, and his daughter, Zella Mae, eight years old, felt about the whole thing was a very important part of the situation too.

The funeral was held at Centenniel M.E. Church at Nineteenth and Woodland Avenue, and according to the old-timers on hand, it was the biggest they had witnessed in Kansas City in the last twenty years. The church was crowded of course, and when the procession to the burial out in Highland Cemetery came slowly along Nineteenth Street, there were lines of people on both sidewalks. That's the way it was on Vine and on

Eighteenth and into Woodland. And according to the accounts I heard, most of those people were in tears.

I'm just going to have to leave it at that. I am not even going to try to express what a loss it was to me personally. I'll just say it took a while for me to accept the fact that I had seen him for the last time.

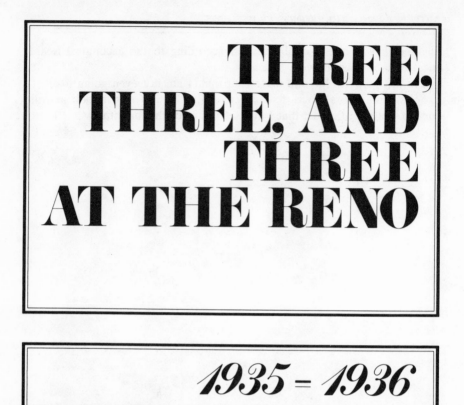

THREE, THREE, AND THREE AT THE RENO

1935 = 1936

At the end of that week at the Rainbow Ballroom in Denver, the band came straight back to Kansas City, and our next job was in a club out on Troost Avenue somewhere between Thirty-fourth and Thirty-fifth streets. It seems to me that we were supposed to be in there for two or three weeks, and we were also already lined up for a few other gigs. But I left during the second week. We were still doing all right, but with Bennie Moten himself gone, it just was not the same anymore.

So I started looking around and checking what was happening in the joints. Because, to tell the truth, by that time I also wanted to see what I could do out there on my own again. That's what I told Bus Moten when we got together to talk things over, and he was one hundred percent for me to go ahead. Bus and I had always been good friends ever since I first came into the band, and all I really had to say was that I thought I had a little something in the works for myself, and he said that was great.

As a matter of fact I didn't really have anything I could actually count on, but I did have my eye on a couple of little possibilities. I didn't have any notions of reorganizing a big band or anything like that at that time. I had picked up that little experience as a bandleader in the Cherry Blossom and down in Little Rock before we got stranded down there, but what I had on my mind was a spot in one of those little joints, maybe with a

156

little combo or something like that. I really didn't have anything definite. I just wanted to see what I could do.

That's how I happened to be the first one to cut out after Bennie Moten's death, and that's why I wasn't there when the band finally broke up for good a few weeks later. I checked around quite a few of the joints. One after-hours joint that Jo Jones and I used to hang out in was a place called Pretty Nell's. But, of course, my main standby was the Yellow Front Saloon. I could always go by there and check Ellis Burton if I really needed a little change real bad.

Then I got my chance to go into the Reno Club all the way downtown at Twelfth and Cherry, and I guess I stole that one. Somebody else was playing there, and he wanted to go somewhere for a few days on another job and asked me if I'd like to fill in for him, and it was just one of those things. I went in there and stayed. The guy's name was Art something. If I ever did know his last name I've forgotten it, but I might have just known him as Art. Anyway, he wanted to get away on another little deal for maybe about a week, I guess, and it sounded like it would be a pretty good gig for me. So I went down there to see what everything was all about.

Because as long as I had been around Kansas City, I actually didn't know anything about that part of town. I had spent most of my time either on Eighteenth Street or Twelfth Street or down through in there. I never did go below Troost. So far as I was concerned, there was nothing down below that. Downtown Kansas City didn't mean anything to me. All of the real action was right where I already was.

So when I went on down to Twelfth and Cherry to see what was happening, and they had a drummer and a couple of horns, but the only name I remember now is Slim Freeman. He was playing tenor, and he was also calling the numbers. I hadn't played with any of those guys before, but the gig looked okay, and I told Art I would do it for him. Of course, I also needed the job, and by that time I was also curious about what it would be like to work in that part of town for a change. And the pay was eighteen dollars a week.

The Reno was not one of those big fancy places where you go in and go downstairs and all that. It was like a club off the street. But once you got inside, it was a cabaret, with a little bandstand and a little space for a floor show, and with a bar up front, and there was also a little balcony in there. There were also girls available as dancing partners. It was a good place to work. I liked the atmosphere down there. There was always a lot of action because there were at least four other cabarets right there on that same block, and they all had live music and stayed open late.

The manager of the Reno was a little short fellow named Sol Steibold, and we got along just fine from the very beginning. For some reason he seemed to take a special interest in me right away. When I'd come off the bandstand between sets, he always had a drink waiting for me at the bar, and sometimes we'd just stand there and sip and chat for a while. And he would always come over and say something to make you feel welcome when you came back to work the next night.

That was the way things started out at the Reno Club. Then, after I had been substituting in there for about a week, Sol and I were standing at the bar between sets one night, and he asked me if I would like to have the job on a permanent basis. I knew he liked me, but that took me by surprise, and when I asked him what about Art, he just shrugged his shoulders.

"It's your job if you want it."

So when Art came back to town, I went to see him and told him, and he looked more relieved than surprised.

"Oh, hell, if you want to gig, go ahead. I ain't worried about that. I got some other things I want to do anyway."

So I took over his chair, and to tell the truth, I really was hoping things would turn out like that. I didn't have any special plans in my mind at that time. I mean, I don't remember thinking that this was my big chance to get somewhere or anything like that. I just needed something to do, and I liked it down there, and the boss was already in my corner. It was just one of those things that happens sometimes, and one thing just leads to another, and before you realize it, you are into something bigger than anything you would have asked anybody for a shot at.

One night while Sol and I were standing at the bar, he asked me why I didn't take the band over, and I said I thought it belonged to Slim Freeman. But he said that it was my job, so the band was working for me, and that I would get an automatic raise from eighteen to twenty-one dollars, as well as those tips being sent up to the piano all night, and also a kitty. I hadn't expected anything like that either, but this time that little bulb up there lit up, and the wheels started turning. So I told him okay, and that was the beginning of my next move; because right then was when I started thinking about a few changes I wanted to make in the lineup.

I just let things ride for a while, and then, when I figured Sol and I were close enough for me to talk him into laying out some more money, I told him I wanted to add a couple of new men. Sol really was a very nice guy, and he went along with what I wanted, and that was actually how I started getting my own band together, and I have been a bandleader ever since.

Somebody is always claiming that I took over Bennie Moten's band after he died, but that's just not what happened. Not at all. Sol Steibold gave me some money to make a few additions and changes in the group he had put me in charge of at the Reno. So I went down to Oklahoma City and talked Jack Washington and Big 'Un into coming in with me, and then I went on down to Dallas and got Buster Smith and Joe Keys to join me. Because by that time the Bennie Moten band had broken up, and the rest of the musicians were scattered all around. Jo Jones had gone back to Omaha or Minneapolis or somewhere shortly after I cut out. I didn't take anybody out of that band while Bus still had it. And anyway, some of the guys that finally joined me were not in that last Bennie Moten band. Walter Page wasn't a member of that band. Neither was Lester, and I think Herschel Evans must have gone to California around the time that I was down in Little Rock, because he was gone when I rejoined Bennie.

Lips Page and Jimmy Rushing had stayed in Kansas City, but when they came down to the Reno, they came as singles. I don't remember which one came first, but I know that Lips was also the master of ceremonies and entertainer, and he would sit in with the band, but he was not a regular member of the trumpet section, and he didn't work with me. Jimmy Rushing didn't come in there to join me, either. He got a job as a regular single feature and as a part of the floor show, and he was such a hit that he could have stayed in there as long as there was a Reno Club.

When Sol put me in charge and gave me the go-ahead on a few additions, I started bringing some of my old bandmates in there, and that meant those other guys had to go. I guess there was a little dirty work in there on that score, but since it was my band, naturally I wanted some guys down there that I was already used to playing with and who I also thought were the greatest. And that is what I had thought of Big 'Un and Prof ever since I first heard the Blue Devils, which I was crazy about for quite awhile before I got interested in Bennie Moten.

In a way, I guess what happened at the Reno was a little like what Eddie Durham and I did once I got settled in Bennie Moten's band. I started trying to bring some Blue Devils in there, and after a while, I had three trumpets, three reeds, and three rhythms. So we called it Three, Three, and Three. There was no trombone in there at first. I couldn't afford one at that time. As a matter of fact I actually didn't have but two trumpets, because Lips Page made it three. The other two trumpets were Joe Keys, who had been in Bennie's band, and Carl Smith, better known as Tatti, who had once been with the great Alphonso Trent band out of Dallas, Texas. I think Big 'Un and Jack Washington put me in touch with him in Oklahoma City.

I don't remember how many different drummers I had in the rhythm section with me and Walter Page before Jo Jones came in. But it seems to me that Jesse Price was in there at one time, and I also got Willie McWashington to sit in with us for a while. Now, Willie Mac had been Bennie Moten's drummer for most of the time I was in that band, but he wasn't in the band when Bennie died. Jo Jones was. So he wasn't in the band when it broke up. Actually I don't think Willie Mac was very well at that time. That may have been one reason why we got in touch with Jo when we did. He was in St. Louis playing in the Jeter-Pillars band at the Plantation Club by that time, and he came right away.

But for a while we thought we had gotten into some trouble with the people in St. Louis about that because Jo had come without giving them any notice. We were very concerned because there were some pretty tough people with interests in that club, and they could get pretty mean if somebody was trying to steal their musicians and entertainers. I don't know what all Jo Jones was into, and I don't know what happened. I don't know whether some of Sol Steibold's friends fixed it up or something like that. But somehow it all got straightened out. They just let it go, and Jo was free to stay at the Reno with us. So he took over from Willie McWashington, and that's when that band really started swinging.

Meanwhile I had also lucked into another little deal in downtown Kansas City. I had become more familiar with that part of town, and I used to like to go down to Jenkins's music store and, then I found out that you could go down there and just practice on the organ. That was right down my alley, and that's how I met one of the VIP's at WHB radio station. He heard me playing and came over and asked me if I would like to have a little organ program on radio in the afternoons, and of course, I said that would be beautiful, or something like that, and that was how I started broadcasting as a single.

The studio was right there in the same building where Jenkins's music store was. It was upstairs, and there was a Wicks organ in there. I'm pretty sure that it was another Wicks they had up there. Anyway, that program was a big thrill for me. It was about fifteen minutes every day during the week in the middle of the afternoon, and the only tough thing about it was to figure out what I was actually going to set myself up to do day after day. So I found myself composing every day. Sometimes I'd think about it before I went down there, but sometimes I'd just go in there and just start playing something and just go on from there. They didn't have to announce the numbers or anything like that, and that was a good thing for me. I had a ball in there.

Then it was not very long before the band started broadcasting from the Reno. That was over W9XBY, another local radio station. They used to bring a pickup in there at least a couple of times a week, and people used to hear us from as far away as Minneapolis and Chicago and the East and all the way down to the Gulf Coast states. That's how Lester Young heard us up in Minneapolis and got in touch with me and came down and replaced Slim Freeman on tenor. There also used to be a pickup in Piney Brown's Sunset Club. That was where Joe Turner and Pete Johnson used to broadcast from.

W9XBY used to catch us pretty regularly on the weekends, but they also came back in there at other times. You wouldn't actually know when you were going to be on. I guess they just liked to catch you when every-thing was just like it was. In those days it was no problem for them to put you on the air, because you didn't have to program anything ahead of time. They'd just come in there and pick you up, and you might be on for an hour or so any night. It was always late at night. There was no contract or anything like that. It was all arranged through the Reno, and we were just happy to be doing it, because it was a good advertisement for the club and for us too. Years later, people in towns in the Midwest and down into the South used to come up and say they first heard us when we were broadcasting from the Reno. Roy Eldridge once told me he used to catch that program when he was in Chicago with Fletcher Henderson, and Fletcher himself also used to listen, and he sent me some arrangements.

When Lester came in there on tenor, I figured I had just about what I needed for what we were doing in the Reno. We didn't have very much room on that bandstand anyway. But what I also mean is that I had a hell of a reed section. With Lester in there with Prof and Jack Washington we were cooking with gas, lots of gas. We all liked to hear Lester play. As for his tone, truthfully I never did really think about it. I mean, I didn't think there was anything odd about it or anything like that. I knew it was special, but everything he did was special. I just liked the sound he got on his horn. It sounded right for what I wanted in there. It just sounded natural to me. After all, he had been in the Blue Devils.

Prof Smith was the lead man in the reed section, and every now and then he would put a couple of little things together for us. But most of the things that we were playing at the Reno were heads. Prof wrote a few things when he felt like it, and when he was in a good mood he would really put something together for you. He could put something together for you, and he could play for you, too. He was great. And I also loved it when he'd start playing that stick. He could play some clarinet, and of course, there was nobody like him on alto. He had a style that was different from everybody.

Then there was Jack Washington in there on baritone, and he would also play alto and clarinet. But his thing was that baritone. He gave us all that rich bottom in that section, and he could also solo in there right along with Buster and Lester. Almost everybody in that Three, Three, and Three band in the Reno took solos. That's the kind of band it was, espe-cially with all those head arrangements. That little cat would take care of business, and he always did.

I didn't really have any big plans for that band at that time. I mean, I wasn't really thinking about taking it on the road or anything like that. I just took that chance to get a group of guys together and work in a place like that and have some fun. I really didn't think all that much about the airtime we were getting. It never did dawn on me how important that was. I realized it later on after all those things started happening for us.

But at the time it was just another thing that went with the club, and it was good for business. So we didn't worry about what we were going to play. We never made up any program, and you didn't have to clear anything or get any release anyway.

Sometimes I would just start playing. We might be on the air playing for an hour and a half and run out of tunes, and when the announcer used to say what are you going to play next, I'd just start off something and pick any kind of title. We did that a lot of times. We worked up one of our all-time standard numbers like that. One night we were on the air and we had about ten more minutes to go, and the announcer asked what we were going to do, and I said I didn't know. We were talking off the mike because there wasn't but one microphone in there anyway in those days, and that was the one the announcer was on. I said, "I'm just going to start playing," and he said, "What is this?" and I saw how many minutes to one o'clock it was getting to be, so I said, "Call it the 'One O'Clock Jump.' " And we hit it with the rhythm section and went into the riffs, and the riffs just stuck. We set the thing up front in D-flat, and then we just went on playing in F.

One of the things I talked Sol Steibold into letting me put on after I had been in the Reno for a while was the breakfast dance. That was something I remembered from years ago, back in New York. I told him about it, and he went along with the suggestion. I had some invitations made up that read something like "You are hereby summoned to a Spook Breakfast Party at the Reno Club at Twelfth and Cherry," and so forth and so on. Spook was an *in* jive word among entertainers in those days. It didn't really have anything to do with color or ghosts directly. It was something that entertainers used to call themselves. I don't really know where that came from. Maybe it had something to do with being mostly nighttime people. So we kept late hours, spooky hours. The hours when the spooks came out.

That was really the idea. Other entertainers and people in show business were the main ones we sent invitations to, and of course we knew that if they came, a lot of other people were going to come along with them. You could always count on that. We made it a Sunday-night after-hours thing. It didn't start until after most of the other joints were closed. Right around three o'clock, bingo. Everybody began falling into the Reno, and the party would go on until around six or seven o'clock in the morning, which was Monday morning, and we didn't go to work on Sunday night until around twelve o'clock, so whiskey could be legal. I don't know how they did this, because, come to think of it, on Saturday night they just ran on through, and they didn't stop selling whiskey at midnight. I don't know what the deal was, but nobody bothered them.

During the week, we used to go to work around nine o'clock every night, and we would get off around three or four the next morning. There was a floor show with acts, and we also played dance sets. One of my favorite female performers in there was Hattie Noels. And of course, Jimmy Rushing was a part of that show, and old Lips Page kept things moving as the emcee, and then he would come and join Joe Keys and Tatti Smith in the trumpet section and set some more of those fine brass riffs he could always come up with. He used a glass for a mute, and when he put that glass up there, I'm *sorry*. He was *something*!

—

Piney Brown was somebody I had connived my way into meeting way back when I came to Kansas City with Gonzelle White the first time the Big Jamboree played there. But I didn't actually get to be a close-enough friend to hang out with him regularly until all those little things started happening for me at the Reno. Of course, all during those years in between I used to see him all the time, because he ran the Sunset, and I used to go there quite often. I don't know anything about the business connections he had downtown, but so far as musicians and entertainers were concerned, he was one of the main men in our part of town, and he was the most popular playboy of that time.

I just began to get a little closer to him when I came back from Little Rock, because there was a piano around at Aunt Lucy's and he used to come in there from time to time with some of his friends. Then, after I got my own thing going at the Reno, we really got to be pretty tight friends. He used to like to come down there. And sometimes when he used to come in late, there would be a whole bunch in there waiting for him, because they knew they were always in for a good time for the rest of the night if he wanted them to run with him.

Sometimes we'd end up bringing them back by Aunt Lucy's, and we'd carry on all the next morning. He was famous for that kind of action. Everybody wanted to be able to hang out with Piney Brown in those days. By the way, it was during the time that I was at the Reno that he started calling me Count, and he called himself Duke.

"Hello, Countee," he always used to say when he called me on the phone. "Say, Countee? This is Dukee." Then he would jive around a little, and then he would say where the action was going to be that night or whenever it was.

I finally moved back over to the Booker T., where most of the musicians had to hang out in those days. I can't pin down the date on that. I think it must have been sometime around the end of that last summer in Kansas City. I know it wasn't until some time after June, because I was still living over at Aunt Lucy's when the great Joe Louis–Max Schmeling fight took place.

We were all there listening to the radio broadcast, and when things

began to get stranger and stranger for Joe, I couldn't stand to listen to it
anymore, so I just went on outside and got into the hammock, and that's
where I was when Aunt Lucy came out and told me that Joe had gotten
knocked out.

—

I don't remember exactly how long we had been in the Reno when Fats
Waller came down there. But he came in there to see me one night, and he
just flipped out over that band. He sent back to the hotel to get Ed Kirkeby
to come down there and listen to those cats. Kirkeby was his personal
manager at that time. Fats was *crazy* about that band. He was in there
every night while he was in town. I think he was either on his way out to
the Coast from New York and Chicago, or on his way back east, because
he did something in the movies out in Hollywood around that time.

He was working in some theater downtown, I think, and as soon as his
show was over, he was right back down there at the Reno. He'd come in
there and sit down, and he was there for the evening.

"*That's* what I want," he told Kirkeby.

He said he wanted to fire his band and take mine on the road with him.
He didn't mean that he wanted to take it away from me or anything like
that. He just wanted that band to have a break. He kept saying we ought
to come on the road with him.

I don't mean to pat myself on the back, but that band was strutting,
really strutting. It was still pretty new when Fats heard it, but we already
had all of those heads together. I don't think we had over four or five
sheets of music up there at that time. But we had our own thing, and we
could always play some more blues and call it something, and we did our
thing on the old standards and the current pops. We had a ball every night
in there.

It must have been at some point during that time that I got Sol Steibold
to put an elevated band shell in the Reno. I suggested it to him, and he
thought it was a good idea. So I told him that I knew the guys who had
built the one in the Cherry Blossom, and that's who did the job in the
Reno. That showed the band off very nicely, but it was pretty crowded up
there, too, because they also brought a baby grand in there. And we also
forgot that the tuba player couldn't quite fit in there, either. So old Big
'Un used to have to go outside and reach in through the window. He'd
leave the horn inside, but he was outside, sitting on a stool or something
if he wanted. But he didn't mind that at all, because he had his little
action going on out there. He could take his little nips. He had a ball out
there. But of course, when we used the bass fiddle, he was inside, right
next to the piano. It was pretty tight in there. But when we really got into

those broadcasts, I'm pretty sure we were beginning to use the fiddle most of the time. I think that's what most people remember on those broadcasts—not the tuba—and he was walking on that thing, too, you can bet that.

That band went on like that in there for quite awhile. Then I began to get little messages from a fellow in New York named John Hammond. They were not letters or telegrams or phone calls or anything like that. He was writing articles for *Down Beat*, or some magazine like that, and he would put little things in there about picking up our broadcast on the shortwave-radio set he had in his automobile.

Somebody would always let you know when there was something about you in the papers and magazines, and I'm pretty sure somebody also let me see some of those articles mentioning how much John Hammond liked the band, and I thought that was just great, but I really didn't think about it anymore. Even when he mentioned something about how he would like to hear from me and said I should drop him a line or something like that, I didn't really pay much attention. I really didn't know what to think about what he was writing.

Then, in another article, he said he was wondering why I hadn't responded. I think he must have mentioned something about that more than once, because I seem to remember something like "I don't see why Count Basie doesn't answer his correspondence," or something like that. So that's when I finally got together with a friend of mine and wrote to him, and that's when John got word back to me that he was coming out to Kansas City to hear us. But I didn't think about that very much either, because I didn't think he was really coming all the way out there just to hear us. I really didn't know what to make of it. I guess the thing about it was that I really wasn't actually shooting for the top at that time. I was just interested in having something sounding good there in the Reno.

But he did come, and we hit it off all right immediately, and we've been friends ever since. He came in there that night and sat right on the piano bench with me.

It was a Sunday night and we were on the air, and this very young cat just came right on up there and sat on the bench beside me. I didn't pay much attention to him at first, because actually that was something that used to happen very often, especially at the Reno. I was also busy trying to figure out what we were going to do for our next number so I could tell the announcer while we were still playing. After I did that, I looked around, and that's when I saw that the young fellow sitting there was a complete stranger to me.

"Hi," he said with a big, wide grin. "I'm John Hammond."

At that time I was a pretty good gin drinker, and he ordered me a little taste, and we had a ball all through that set, and he stayed through all the shows. And the band played exceptionally well that night too. I don't know, but all of a sudden it just sounded like the guys turned on another button or something. I don't think it was because John was there either, because nobody knew who John Hammond was. It was just one of those good nights when the band was solidly in the groove and could go on and on swinging like that forever. We didn't know that anybody was coming to check us out, but the way those guys played that night surely was a good example of what we were about and what we could do.

And this young fellow really dug it. He stuck around to talk some more after we finished our last number, and we went out to some other spots that were still open, and that was a ball, too. He liked what I liked. He liked the blues. So we took him by the Sunset to hear Pete Johnson and Big Joe Turner, which, of course, he had already heard about; and those two cats damn near killed him because they were swinging so much. He just sat there shaking his head and slapping his hands.

We also went to a couple of more places that he was curious about, and then we had breakfast at Eleanor's and I introduced him to some fried corn and ham and some beautiful biscuits that I think he still remembers.

I was very impressed with all of the musicians that this very young cat was familiar with. He started dropping all kinds of names on me. I mean, there were some names of musicians and names of joints, too, in there that people right up in Harlem and right out in that part of Kansas City probably wouldn't pick up on right away, and some they wouldn't recognize unless they happened to come from a certain neighborhood.

But here was this cat asking about guys and joints in places I had almost forgotten existed. He even told me about what was going on when he first saw me with Bennie Moten at the Lafayette and had actually spoken with me at the bar in Covan's Morocco Club back when he was still just a little schoolkid from down on Fifth Avenue running around up in Harlem and hanging out wherever they would let him in. He was something else.

He must have stayed around for another day or so, because I know we also went downtown to studio KMBC, where some kind of reception or something was going on, and I did a little session on the organ with a couple of cats, and I think he came back to the Reno at least one more time before he left. But I already knew that he was all for us.

So he made his report back to New York, and that sort of started a lot of things for us. It was through him that Willard Alexander at MCA, which was booking Benny Goodman, who was a very big hit at that time, became interested in us. John was also connected with that in some way. As a matter of fact he says that it was while he was in Chicago with Benny Goodman that he happened to go out to the parking lot and turn on the shortwave set in his car and pick us up that first time.

I think John must have come back out to Kansas City at least two more times that year. That first time was in the spring. Then he came back in the summer. But before he got back that second time, Dave Kapp from Decca Records came out there and told me that he was a friend of John's and said that John had been telling him all about us and so he had come out to hear us, and he offered me a contract to make twenty-four sides a year for three years.

That was how I came to sign my first recording contract, and I really made a very big mistake on that one. He said something about how Decca was going to provide us with transportation for the band to go to Chicago to record, and at that time that sounded like the biggest deal I'd ever heard of, and I asked him again, and he said, "Oh, yes." And I was ready to go. So I told the guys the good news, and the part about transportation made a big impression on most of them too.

I never will forget what Lester said when I took him aside and told him about that. I think I must have passed the word on to the other fellows before Lester got to the Reno that night. So when he came in, I called him over, got us a couple of nips, and we went and stood outside the doorway to the back alley, where we usually went when we wanted to have a little private sip and a little personal chat.

"Well," I said, "I got some great news. I think we'll take a Pullman into Chicago and do some recording for Decca."

And all he did was just sort of stand there looking into space like he hadn't heard what I said because he was listening to something else or thinking about something else. Then he looked at me again.

"What did I hear you say? Did I hear you?"

"Yes," I said. "We're going to Chicago to make some records for Decca."

And he just stood there and looked at me and looked away and then looked at me again. Then he went into his sweet-talk thing.

"Listen, Lady B, you all right?"

"Oh, yes," I said. "Everything's okay. I got me this contract with Decca."

And he just stood there nodding his head, thinking about it, and then the next thing he said was like he was talking to himself.

"Well, okay. So now we'll find out what happens."

Then he finished his shot and looked at me and mumbled and went back into his sweet-jive thing again.

"Hey, look. I tell you what, Lady B. Let's go back in there and get us another little taste, and maybe you'll tell me that again."

When John came back out there a short time later and saw that contract, he hit the ceiling. Without realizing what I was doing, I had agreed to record twelve records a year for $750 a year outright, no royalties! I didn't know anything about royalties. John couldn't believe it. He couldn't get us out of that contract, but he was able to get Decca to raise the musicians' pay up to minimum scale. I don't think I had ever heard of minimum scale before that, and if I had, I had never paid any attention to it. I guess I just had to learn some things the hard way.

The thing about the whole situation was that the very reason that John had come back out to Kansas City at that time was to tell me about a deal he had in the works for me with Brunswick Records. Naturally it was a much better deal, and John had set it up just because he liked us and wanted people to hear us on records. There was no money at all in it for him.

Joe Glaser, another big-time promoter, also came out to Kansas City sometime during that summer. He was the head man at Associated Booking Corporation. I don't know whether he came out to listen to us or to listen to Lips Page or what it was. But what I do know is this much: I know that he decided that he wanted a package with Lips heading it. The night Glaser caught the show, Lips was sensational. No question about it. So Lips was the one he talked to, and he got him to sign with him. Then Lips came back and told me about it.

"Listen," he said, "I'm going with Joe Glaser."

"Is that so?" I said.

"Yeah," he said. "I'm going to New York, and I want you all to come along, too. I need you all with me."

"What do you mean, 'come along too'?" I asked.

"I'll be in front of the band, but it will still be yours."

"I know that," I responded, "but we ain't ready to go yet. You go."

"This is a big deal, man," he responded. "This is our big chance at the big time."

"I know. So you go ahead. I'll see you there later."

I also remember sitting in the booth with Joe Glaser later on that night. I guess he must have sent for me. Anyway, I was sitting there listening to him, and he could talk pretty good. But when he got to the part where he said he was going to put Lips out in front of the band, I said, "Wait a minute," and I told him that I had something else that I was expecting to come through for me, or something like that, and he saw that he was not going to get us on that particular package. Actually I had just recently got word from John Hammond again, and he said he was coming back out to try to help arrange a few things for us to get into Chicago and New York.

By the way, here's a little something that I don't think is generally known. During the same time that John Hammond began his thing, somebody else was trying to get in touch with me about coming east. It's funny how things can get mixed up. There was a time when promoters used to give the impression that Benny Goodman was the one who discovered us out in the sticks and opened the way for us. Now, Benny and John were close, and I don't know what went on between them regarding me, but it just so happens that the name bandleader who actually offered to sponsor us was Charlie Barnet. Charlie sent me a telegram from the Glen Island Casino saying that all I had to do was just drop him a line.

But when John came out to see me and we got along so well, that decided it for me, and I didn't even answer Charlie's wire, which I think I still have somewhere among my souvenirs. Every time I remember that, I feel like apologizing to Charlie for not acknowledging his message, because later on we became very good friends, and he has always been one of the most wonderful people I've ever met.

John Hammond says that he felt that Willard Alexander was probably the only topflight booking agent in the country at that time who would understand why he was so excited about our band. I didn't know anything about all of that at that time, either, but I do know that once John got Willard involved we had to start making plans for a different scene, and that's when I started building the band up to the standard dance-band size.

Actually John liked the band just the way it was when he first heard it. But Willard said the booking possibilities were too limited for a group that size. So I think the first thing we started on was the trombone section, when we got Hunt, also called Rabbit. Then later we added Dan Minor. Those two trombones were all we had in that section for the rest of the time we were in Kansas City.

Then Herschel Evans came back from California, and that was the beginning of the two tenors. Herschel and Lester had been pretty close friends ever since the days when I was at the Cherry Blossom, and they used to swap gigs back and forth between the band I had in there and the one Bennie Moten and George E. Lee had over at Club Harlem. Now, with two bad soloists like that in the same reed section, we really had something special. But I actually didn't begin to realize how special that was until a little later on.

Herschel also brought Buck Clayton into the band. He and Buck had come in from Los Angeles around the same time. So when Herschel found out that we needed somebody else in the trumpet section because Lips Page was leaving to go out under the management of Joe Glaser, he said he had a cat named Buck Clayton who played a lot of trumpet, and he brought him in. Buck had been in China with a band, and he had also had his own band in Los Angeles for a while. When Herschel brought him in, he was in town because he was from Parsons, Kansas, and he was stopping off on his way east to join Willie Bryant's band in New York. But when he came into the Reno and sat in with us, he changed his mind about going on to New York at that time. That's how Buck came in, and then one night long after he got there, I remember somebody coming into the club and saying, "Hey, look, they have a green-eyed trumpet player back there."

Herschel and Buck also found us a new alto player when Buster Smith decided to cut out on us. I guess Prof didn't really think we were going to make it into the big time. I don't know. But when Claude Hopkins came through Kansas City and offered him a job in his band, Prof went with him. So Herschel and Buck got in touch with Couchy Roberts back in Los Angeles, and he came and joined us. Couchy had been in Buck's band in China, so all Buck and Herschel had to do was say the word and he came.

By the time we first started getting that band together at the Reno, I already had some pretty clear ideas about how I wanted a band to sound like. I knew how I wanted each section to sound. So I also knew what each one of the guys should sound like. I knew what I wanted them there for. Even back when I was dictating those arrangements to Eddie Durham for Bennie Moten's band, I could actually hear the band playing those passages while we were working on them. And that's the way Eddie wrote. We could write just like I heard it. He could voice each section just the way I wanted it.

I have my own little ideas about how to get certain guys into certain numbers and how to get them out. I had my own way of opening the door for them to let them come in and sit around awhile. Then I would exit them. And that has really been the formula of the band all down through the years. It's been more or less the same patterns, and all of our arrangers know what I like to hear and how I like to do things.

Just recently somebody was asking me if I thought playing the organ had anything to do with me being able to make arrangements for big bands like Bennie Moten's and the one I was getting together at the Reno. Whoever it was said he was wondering if the sort of ensemble-like sounds you get on the organ had any influence on the way I use sections and ensembles in the big band. I guess so. I could think like that, but I couldn't really actually play like that. Not like Wild Bill Davis, a guy John Hammond took me by Smalls' to hear one Easter Sunday years later. Wild Bill is the master. He *is* an orchestra. He can actually do it all on the organ. And you can hear that background of the brass playing down under whatever he is playing and the solos and everything. He is a past master of all that. I could sit and listen to him all night.

But to get back to the band. Sometimes I like to play loud. And fast too. Sometimes you need to do it with a little volume, and I hear some numbers with the tempo way up. But I also like the band when the guys are just swinging their cans off down easy, like a number called "Softly, With Feeling." Then I also like to bust it out when we have to. That's the sort of thing I already hear in my head before the band plays it. I always did hear things like that. And of course, I always did like good shouting brass.

Shouting brass choruses. And we used to do it. And I'm gradually getting back to that a little bit. Good shouting brass choruses, boy . . . that's something. When you have a good shouting brass section, you got yourself something.

When we started working out the arrangements for the full-size band I was getting ready at the Reno, I knew just where I wanted those two tenors. After certain modulations and certain breaks, I knew exactly which one I wanted to come in, and sometimes it would be one and sometimes the other. Because each one had his own thing. But it was not really in my mind to battle them. Not at first. It was just a matter of using two different styles to the best advantage of the band.

The band was called the Barons of Rhythm. So we were advertised as Count Basie and His Barons of Rhythm. That was the name somebody thought up as a gimmick for those radio broadcasts over W9XBY. So the announcer could say, "And now here is Count Basie and his fourteen Barons of Rhythm." Something like that. I don't know, maybe that is what somebody got mixed up with how I got the name Count Basie. But as I have said before, I was already billed as Count Basie a few years before those broadcasts. There were no Barons of Rhythm before those broadcasts, but there was Count Basie.

We finally decided to take the band out of the Reno because I needed a more comfortable place and more time to work out some things we thought we ought to have ready for the bookings that Willard Alexander was lining up through MCA for the eastern trip John Hammond wanted us to make. So we laid off and rehearsed and got some new things together, and we also got a chance to pick up some experience in different spots by going out on the road. I got Maceo Birch to come in and work on those kinds of details for us. Maceo was probably the best contact man in Kansas City in those days.

And that was also when we got our first bus. I went and talked the local Greyhound people into letting us have one of their models, and we did a few things down in Oklahoma. I think that band played in places like Tulsa, Muskogee, Okmulgee, Oklahoma City, and I think we also went to Wichita and Omaha. All of these were dance-hall gigs. So they were mostly one-nighters. We didn't play any clubs and theater dates on these little trips. But those gigs were very important because the band was getting some travel experience.

Which reminds me of a little practice we used to have in that band even before we came out of the Reno. I used to have a little book that we used to call the draw book. That was what we used to keep a record of the money the guys used to draw against the pay they had coming. It was really just a little thing for a few small conveniences they wanted or needed from time to time. One cat used to draw seventy-five cents, and another would want thirty-five and another some other amount. Lester always used to get either fifty-five or sixty cents. You couldn't draw over a buck and a quarter, though. That was the limit. But you could get quite a few little things for a few cents in those days. You could get a full-course meal for thirty-five cents. A whole pack of cigarettes didn't cost but a dime, and you could buy loose cigarettes for a penny a piece. A ten-cent cigar used to be a big deal.

Jack Washington used to be the bookkeeper, and those little entries told a very important story. I kept that first little book for years. I used to just look at it from time to time. Then I lost it somewhere. I don't know what became of it.

All of this was what was going on from the end of that summer on into the fall. In September we were one of the five bands that played for the Musicians' Labor Day Ball sponsored by Musicians' Local 627 AF of M at the Labor Temple on Fourteenth Street and Woodlawn. The other Kansas City bands were Andy Kirk's Twelve Clouds of Joy, Harlan Leonard's Rockets, Bus Moten's combo, and Pete Johnson's band, and there were also two guest bands—Clarence Love, who was probably working out of Indianapolis at that time, and Jerome Carrington. There was also a big floor show.

By this time we had also become a local standby for the union, so we got a chance to go on and play first, or we would alternate during intermission when out-of-town bands were booked into Kansas City. This kind of deal was not booked as a battle of bands, but sometimes things used to get pretty warm in there. Naturally the Kansas City cats were not about to let anybody come into town and show them up too bad. So they always went in there ready to blow, and they could really make things pretty hot for a name band or anybody else. But of course, it was a different story when Fletcher and his band came to town. Those cats just came on in there and played. They walked all over you like you were a carpet.

—

The next big shot to come out to Kansas City from New York to hear us was Joe Belford. He was the manager of Roseland Ballroom at that time, and he had been hearing so much about us from John and Willard that he had finally decided to come all the way out there and check us out for himself. He sent us a wire telling us when to pick him up.

So we arranged to use Street's Blue Room, which was a downstairs club in Street's hotel building, and that's where he heard us that afternoon. Street's was a better place for that kind of audition than the Reno would have been. The bandstand was better for that size band. There was more privacy, and the location was also more convenient because it was just a short walking distance from where most of us were living at that time.

Naturally I was a little nervous, but the band was really in shape for

Joe Belford that afternoon. And the atmosphere was just great because he was such a nice guy and everything was relaxed and friendly. He just sat in the back and listened to everything we wanted to play for him, and he kept nodding his head and smiling. By the way, he was a great fan of Fletcher Henderson's band. He was the main reason why Fletcher was in and out of the Roseland so much over the years.

"That sounds pretty good. That sounds very good. That's all right."

And we just went on playing and having a good time. What we played was just our regular thing. We didn't work out anything special just for the audition. We just played all the flag-wavers we could.

Then, while we were taking a little break and having a little nip together, he kept on saying how much he liked all the numbers and how different it was from anything he had ever heard before. Which made me feel pretty good, and I took another little nip, and we went on talking. And I never will forget what he said next.

"Count Basie," he said, "now, what about one of your tangos?"

I am pretty sure—in fact, I am damn sure—my mouth dropped open, and I can still remember that funny feeling in my stomach.

"Tangos," I said, or maybe I just gulped.

"Yes, tangos," he said. "I haven't heard you play a tango yet. Don't you have any tangos in your book?"

I just about went through the floor. At that time I don't think we even had a waltz in the book. I just knew that was the end of the deal, because I don't think I even knew what a goddamn tango was. I am pretty sure that I could have recognized that particular rhythm from the radio and movies and things like that, but I couldn't have said this is a tango and that is a samba, or anything like that. It was just music from south of the border.

"The tango is very important at the Roseland these days," he said.

All I could do was just stand there, and I just looked in another direction because I didn't know what to say. But when I turned around to look at him again, he was cracking up, which eased me up a bit. Then he eased me up a lot.

"Don't worry about it," he said. "You can get ahold of it a little later. Now let's go somewhere where we can have another little nip."

We went down to a joint on the corner and sat around talking for all the rest of that afternoon, and I had a very good time and so did he. He really was a wonderful man. He really was. But he didn't make any definite promises or anything like that. He just took his report back to New York, and he told them that it was all right to book the band into the Roseland. I don't remember whether they set the date at that time, but we were notified that we had made it. I'm pretty sure that we got our information from MCA through Willard Alexander, because he was the one who was working out the booking details for our tour. Anyway, we knew that we were not scheduled into the Roseland until a few months later. Meanwhile Willard and MCA were trying to get us into the Grand Terrace in Chicago.

There was also another very important thing that happened while we were trying to get the band together to head east to the Big Apple and the big time. The Chief passed away. The very next year after the loss of Bennie Moten, Ellis Burton got sick. He had been so helpful to me in so many ways in all those years in Kansas City, and he was doing everything he could to back me up in what I was trying to do with the new band. I mean, in every way he could.

Actually he was the one I had gone to talk to when Sol first offered me the job as leader down at the Reno; and I remember exactly what he said.

"This could be your chance. Why don't you do it?"

I already knew I wanted to do it, because, to tell the truth, I had been hoping for it and also working at it, trying to steal it, really. But now that I was about to get it, I needed to talk to somebody. So I said okay.

"You're right," I told him. "But I got to run it like you would."

"Well, ain't nothing I can say about that," he said. "Just do it like you think is right, but do it right, and don't let nobody row with you."

And I had been going back to discuss things with him whenever I felt the need, and he always did what he could. And then, right at the time when it seemed that things were just about to open up for us, wham. I found out that he was very sick, and when I got to where he was, they were not letting anybody in to see him.

But I slipped past them and went in there. There was a screen up around him, which meant that only the doctor and nurses were allowed back there. But I looked back there and saw him lying there, and I had to let him know I was there.

"Chief," I said. "Hi, Chief. Don't worry about nothing. Somebody'll be coming to see you pretty soon. Don't you worry about that."

"Well," he said in a very weak voice. "Tell them they'd better hurry up."

Then I heard the nurse outside.

"Somebody slipped back in that room," she said. "Get him out of there."

And that was the last time I saw him alive. And the thing about it all was that it seemed like a pretty good deal was just about to open up for him too. And one of the last things we talked about was how the band would always have a home base when backing for a new and bigger club finally came through; it seemed that it was likely to do so before long.

It was also during the time that we were laying off to get the band ready for the tour that I got my second car. It didn't have anything to do with any money the band was making, because we were not really working steady enough to be making very much at that time. We would go out on something in the territory, and other than that, the guys were just gigging around on their own. But we would still get together and rehearse from

time to time. So what happened was that this big piece of good luck came
around and I paid down on a Buick. That was something which was strictly
my own private affair. But right away somebody tried to make something
of it. Jo Jones remembers that story very well because he and I were hanging out together a lot at that time, and he knew exactly where the money
came from. In fact he was the one who called me on the phone and said,
"You better come on over here." Which I did, and he and I were sitting
on Nineteenth Street when the president of the union came up and started
asking questions.

"Say, Basie," he said, "everybody wants to know—"

"What do you want to know?" I asked.

"Where did you manage to get this car from?"

"That ain't your business, now is it?" I replied.

"They tell me this summer one of the people in New York sent you
something for the band and the boys. Sent you some advance money to get
the band some new uniforms and instruments and transportation. Is that a
fact?"

"Hell no, it ain't a fact."

That was all I told him, and Jo Jones and I just sat there and looked at
each other.

That was the car I let Maceo Birch use to drive Lester out to Los
Angeles. That's where Lester's family had settled, and there was an emergency out there. I have forgotten exactly what it was, but I think there was
a death in the family. Whatever it was, Lester had to go, so I let Maceo
have the car and they drove on out there, and since the band was not
doing very much right then, they stayed out there a few days and made a
few contacts and then drove back.

Jo Jones and I also took a little trip to Chicago in that car. Another
personal matter came up, and things got a little complicated for me, and
I thought the best thing for me to do was cool out of there for a while. So
Jo said, "Hell, let's go to Chicago." And we just got in the car and took
a little drive up there for a few days and took in some shows. We went to
the Grand Terrace and caught Fletcher Henderson, and when Fletcher
asked me if I wanted to sit in for a few numbers, Jo told him we would
just wait our turn with our own band. We also took in a few other spots.
That's how we found Claude Williams. He was playing guitar and violin
in one of those places, and I decided that we could use him in the band if
things worked out and we came into the Grand Terrace. I couldn't hire
him then because the band was still waiting for the word from MCA.

We stayed in Chicago for just a day or so, and on the way back we
stopped in St. Louis and told Dan Minor to get ready to give his notice
to Jeter-Pillars because we wanted him to join us in Kansas City as soon
as Willard Alexander finally notified us that the first date under our contract with MCA was all set, which happened not long afterward. We were

booked into the Grand Terrace for a month beginning the second week in November. That was what we had been waiting around for. But before we hit the road, we played two more dates in Kansas City.

The first was a Halloween dance at Paseo Hall that last Saturday night. We advertised it as our farewell dance. They always did like farewells and homecomings in Kansas City, so we called this our farewell thing. But actually we went right back into Paseo Hall that very next Monday night and played our last gig as the local union band. The big headline attraction that night was Duke Ellington, who had just made a sensational hit at the Texas Centennial in Dallas. It was a very special night for everybody, because Duke had been coming to Kansas City for at least several years by that time, but this was the first time he was coming to play a dance at Paseo Hall. All the other times he had been booked into the big theaters downtown.

I remember when he came during the time when I was working in the Cherry Blossom, because one of the guys who ran the club took me over to where he was playing, and we stood right down in front of the bandstand. I never will forget that, because my friend from the Cherry Blossom turned to me and said, "You know something? I've been watching this guy. He leads that band with his head." And I said, "Yeah." And them cats in the band were *there*. I said, "Boy, they're something. Boy, just look at them."

As far as I'm concerned, Duke was always so interesting to look at along with all that music he played. I mean, to watch him you could understand where the music was coming from and how he was walking around the stage bringing it out. He was a picture. Something to see as well as to listen to. He directed that band strangely, and then when he sat down at the piano, it meant something. And the minute he played that little bit, he got right up from there and started walking again. He was something. He was colorful. Oh, I love him. He was the man. Oh, he was some kind of man. All down through the years, I used to go and listen to him, and I knew just exactly where he was, because I could *feel* him.

Ellington played a different kind of music, a special kind of music. He played music that was never offensive. He played music that you could always listen to. It was music that was never too loud. And when it was— when he played something loud and played something fast—it still wouldn't be loud, and it would not be that fast. But it was, and it all meant something. It all had a story. Each thing that was done was like a story-book, with a story built behind each soloist. He was a remarkable man.

But I didn't get to hear him that last night in Kansas City, because we went on first, and we couldn't stay for the main event because we were scheduled to leave for Chicago that very same Monday night. In fact our bus was parked outside, ready to pull out as soon as we finished our set and loaded our instruments. Our suitcases were already on board. My bags were in my Buick, which Maceo Birch was taking, but I was riding in the bus with the fellows.

We went on early, and of course, we did our best to liven things up in there, and we always did. But then when Duke's famous musicians began arriving, the crowd couldn't help showing how excited it was about having them there. So as many friends and well-wishers as we knew we had in Kansas City, I don't think there were many more than about a dozen people who came outside to see us off.

But Duke himself came out, and he was very nice. I hadn't yet had a chance to get to know him personally at that time. Of course, Sonny Greer and I were old country cousins from New Jersey, and I already knew Tricky Sam from the time when he was playing on 133rd Street between Lenox and Fifth Avenue, and I also knew Otto Hardwick from Barron's; and of course, old Sonny and I had always gotten together a little bit when they came to town. I hadn't even tried to get to Duke, because there was always so much going on around him. I think he might have come into the Cherry Blossom, and I might have spoken to him then, and he was always so nice, but I still didn't really get to know him back during that time.

But that last night he made it his business to come outside of Paseo Hall and give us his congratulations and wish us good luck, and he gave me a few words of encouragement and a big pat on the shoulder just before I got on the bus. He was beautiful.

"Go ahead," he said. "You can make it."

That meant a lot to me. Nothing anybody else could have said would have meant that much to me. Because he was the boss. He was in a class by himself.

EAST TO THE APPLE AND THE WOODSIDE

1936 = 1937

Some of us stayed awake just about all night that night. I can still remember the fellows talking and laughing and having a little taste and carrying on while the bus was rolling on across Missouri toward St. Louis. I don't actually recall any one thing that anybody in particular said that night, but I remember the sound of the voices in the dark and the sound of the bus, and I also remember how strange I was beginning to feel now that the first leg of the trip back east with my own band was finally under way.

I wouldn't say that I was uneasy about anything in particular at that time, because I think I have always been pretty good at taking things as they come. But there was something about what was happening this time that was different. It was not my first trip as a bandleader, because I had taken that band from the Cherry Blossom out on a few trips. But this was my first experience as a leader taking a band outside the territory. That was a different thing, and somehow or other I also must have known that I was really pulling out of Kansas City for good after being out there for nine fantastic years, which I wouldn't trade with anybody.

When we crossed the Mississippi River bridge going out of St. Louis, we were in the state of Illinois, and we headed north to Chicago by way of Springfield. That was the most direct route in those days, and we didn't stop anywhere any longer than it took to get the bus serviced and to take

178

care of a couple little urgent needs of nature. The main thing was to make time, because we were supposed to be at the Grand Terrace to rehearse with the new floor show a few times before we were due to open. Of course, all of us also wanted to hurry up and get there so we could get on with it and see what was going to happen.

I didn't really begin to worry about anything until we arrived in Chicago and I realized what we were actually getting into. I already knew that the band we were following was the great Fletcher Henderson bunch that Jo Jones and I had seen in there during that little trip he and I made up to Chicago a few weeks earlier. But it wasn't until we checked into our rooms and I went back into the Terrace that night and dug how smoothly Fletcher and Horace and all those great cats were cracking that show down and wrapping up the last few nights of that gig that I began to get nervous. I said, "Oh, Christ!"

Then the trouble really started. We went in there for the rehearsal that next day, and I found out that the music we were supposed to play for the big number was a special arrangement of the Poet and Peasant Overture. All I had to do was just get one quick look at that thing—and talking about scared. I said *sheeoot,* they better send to the union or somewhere and get somebody to play that, because damn if I can. So they finally sent and got some lady, and she came in there and played it.

But that was just the beginning. We caught hell trying to play that show, because pretty soon there was some tension in the band. I think maybe a couple of guys had made up their minds that they were not even going to try to play those special arrangements. I mean, it was not the kind of show they thought they were coming up there to play for, and they just didn't want to do it. That wasn't everybody. But it was enough to throw the band off. We just didn't get it right.

Then there was another very special little problem. There were some lines they wanted me to speak, and I never did have a lot of words. Hell, I still don't have but so many right now. And this was right at the beginning of the show too. I was standing back there, and the chorus girls danced the first number and then they formed two lines, and I was supposed to go down that corridor to the footlights and say something.

So then the announcer was saying, "And here is Count Basie." It was like he was sending me to the electric chair. And I finally made it on down front and saw all those people looking up, smiling, and waiting, and I guess I must have said *abba, abba, abba*—something, something, something—and I got back up to the bandstand and stomped the first number off as quick as I could.

Of course, you always have problems on opening night. Nobody really expects everything to come out right on the very first performance. But I don't see how any show could ever have been played worse than we did that one that night. And one of the write-ups that came out in one of the downtown Chicago papers didn't pull any punches either. The reporter said something about the band being a top attraction in Kansas City, and he said, "By the time you read this they will be on their way back to Kansas City."

All of the big acts in the show just went ahead and did the best they could on opening night. But after a few more nights of struggling with us, they began to complain. Some of them would come over and look at us and say, "Christ, what is this? Oh, God!" And you could hear the middle acts up there grumbling during the performance, saying, "My God! What the hell are they *playing*?" And the boss would just look at us and shake his head and throw up his hands and walk away.

The only part of the show we really got along fine with was some of the dancers. Especially Alma Smith and Elmer Turner. I never will forget them.

"Don't you worry," Alma said from the very first. "Just play something behind me."

She was one of the big stars of the show, and I heard her talking to one of the bosses about us.

"Why don't you just lay off?" she said. "Take it easy. These are just a nice group of country boys. They just came to town. This is all new to them. My God, one of these days you might be trying like hell to get them back in here. Just wait and see. And I hope to God I'm still living to see them turn you down."

I will always remember her. She was so very nice to me.

"Come on and go with me and meet a friend of mine," she told me one night. "We're going to take you out."

And she introduced me to the maître d', and they took me out on the town, and we ended up at Club Delisa, and that was the first time I ever saw a real hopping show that went on all night long. And I mean it was swinging every minute.

Alma Smith was just wonderful to us. "You just play," she said. "Just follow me."

I could do that because I had played for all those different people in vaudeville during those years on the circuits. When you were playing for stage shows back in those days, they were used to working with different musicians all the time. That was the way it was. So the acts would come to rehearsal and hum the routine for you, and all you had to do was hit some kind of introduction, and you went into something. Playing for singers and dancers was no trouble at all for me. That was my shtick.

John Hammond came out to Chicago to be with us during that opening week, and of course, he was pulling for us, and it was during that first week that I made those first records for John and Vocalion. We didn't record under my name, and we didn't use the whole band because the

Count Basie band was tied up in that contract that I had signed with Decca. We didn't even use the Three, Three, and Three group.

We used Tatti Smith on trumpet, Lester on tenor, Big 'Un on bass, Jo on drums, Jimmie on vocals, and me on piano and called it Jones, Smith Incorporated. That was the day we recorded "Shoe Shine Boy," "Evening," "Boogie Woogie" and "Oh, Lady Be Good." John had wanted to use Buck on trumpet, but he had a sore lip that day. From all that overwork he was doing to try to cover for the guys in the trumpet section, because he could read that score better than the others. By the way, the date of this session is given as October 9 on all of the discographies I've seen. I don't know how that got started, but we didn't leave Kansas City until the end of October. When we came into Chicago, it was already November.

That was a very easy session. John was very pleased, and as for somebody shipping us back to Kansas City, he and Williard Alexander were not about to let that happen. I mean, they really wanted us to have a fair chance. Willard says he figured all the band needed was more experience. Luckily for us, he made allowances for the fact that the full fourteen-piece band had only been together for a couple of months or so. I never will forget how John stuck with us during those first days, and Willard was already busy lining up dates for us to work our way to New York and the Roseland Ballroom.

We also got some very favorable write-ups in the Chicago *Defender*. At that time there was a reporter named Jack Ellis writing a regular weekly column on orchestras for the entertainment section, and he was in our corner all the way. I guess he must have heard some of our broadcasts from the Reno, because even the week before we arrived in Chicago he gave us a nice little headline article and said, "The unique style of syncopation played by this aggregation has placed it among the top notchers." He was nice to us all during our stay there, calling me the Kansas City Swing King and saying that our music was something new.

Another thing about playing at the Grand Terrace was that you also had to play a radio broadcast every night. One of the reasons that the Grand Terrace was such a famous place was that people all over the country were used to hearing Earl Hines and his Grand Terrace Orchestra or the great Fletcher Henderson and his band broadcasting from there, just as they used to listen to Duke and then Cab Calloway broadcasting from the Cotton Club. We knew that was part of the deal, and I think we got with it without too much trouble, although they had us playing a lot of stock arrangements on popular tunes. We probably played as many, and sometimes more, of those stocks than our own things.

That was part of the deal, too. I mean, plugging those new pop tunes was a standard procedure on a lot of radio programs in those days. So we didn't get a chance to play as many of our own things as we would have liked, but I don't remember those stocks giving us any real problems, and those broadcasts were good for our reputation.

I really felt that we also did all right with the audiences at the Grand Terrace. Our big problem was that show and those entertainers. The people out front were really pulling for the band, even during the show. I could see it in their faces. They came in smiling and pleasant and very friendly. They were not acting like we were a killer-diller or anything like that, because we were not really killing them, but you could tell that they were trying to be with us. Then when we played our dance set, you could see that we were really getting to them.

Actually the one in our number who came off best at the Grand Terrace during that run was Jimmy Rushing. Jimmy wasn't used in the floor show. He just worked with the band during our dance set, and he went over just fine. Actually he sort of broke them up because he always did know how to sing the blues and shout those other numbers we played for him, although he still really thought of himself as a ballad singer.

After about a week or so a lot of the entertainers in the other acts began to warm up and come around and get together with the guys in the band. Because they really were a nice bunch of fellows. I guess somebody must have decided that we were just a bunch of nice, poor country boys trying to make it out of the sticks. That made the situation a lot better. Of course, in the meantime the guys had been in and out of Chicago three or four times before. So it wasn't as though nobody knew how to get around.

One thing a bunch of them had been doing from the first night on was hanging out with Roy Eldridge. Almost every night Roy would come by and pick them up and hit the joints. Jo Jones was the main contact for that. Jo and I had been in touch with Roy and Fletcher when we had that little trip up to Chicago in September, but when we got back with the band, Roy had gone into the Three Deuces, leading a little group of his own with Zutty Singleton on drums. I think Scoops Carry was also in that group. Which reminds me that it was when we came to Chicago that time that I saw Elmer Williams again. And just about the same thing happened out there that had happened on the sidewalk in front of Big John's in Harlem. This time we were in a bar not far from the Grand Terrace.

"Hey, Elmer. How you doing, old pardner?"

"What say, Basie? You looking good."

Then something about when have you been home, when have you heard from home, how are they getting along down there. Then something about things not being too bad and about sticking in there or something like that, and then nothing. We just sat there having a nip, and I'm just waiting to see just how long this cat can go before saying anything else. So what happens? When he finally finishes his drink, he just stands up and starts brushing the little wrinkles out of his sharp suit.

"Well, I guess I ought to be getting on along."

I just looked at him and shook my head and laughed.

"Yeah. You might as well, because you damn sure ain't saying nothing. Go ahead."

All he could do was laugh at himself, because the thing about it was not that our friendship had really cooled off or anything like that. There was no strain. That was just simply the way he was. He was the same old Elmer. He was still sharp, and he was still crazy about keeping his fingernails neat. But he didn't have anything much to say.

Speaking of people in Chicago, that's also where I finally got to meet the fabulous Earl "Fatha" Hines in person. He had been out on a road tour, and he pulled back into Chicago while we were still there, and he came into the club one night, and naturally they didn't have to introduce him, because he was back home. They just presented him, and of course, the house broke up when he took his bow.

Earl went through a little speech and introduced a new singer he had found in Pittsburgh. Her name was Ida James, and he played one for her, which was wonderful. Then he sat back down and played one on his own, which was just about the last thing I needed at a time like that. It was terrible to have to sit down at the same piano behind the stuff Earl was laying down—just terrible.

But personally Earl was very nice to me. He really didn't have to be, but he was. He could have just cut on out of there with his fans, but he went out of his way to encourage me. I never will forget that.

My band was getting better and better with experience. But our book was not really big enough yet, and most of the things we had were heads. So we began working out a few new things, and that was also when Henry Snodgrass gave us a few more arrangements from Smack's book. We already had a couple that he had sent us while we were in the Reno. That was a big help.

We picked up some more publicity when the *Defender* invited us to play at the annual Bud Billiken pre-Thanksgiving party for children. That was a very big matinee event at the Regal Theatre. Some of the big acts from the Grand Terrace Revue also performed that Saturday afternoon, but our band was singled out for special mention. "Count Basie is this week receiving congratulations on the very fine manner in which he dished out that new style of jazz at the *Chicago Defender*, Bud Billiken Club's Pre-Thanksgiving party at the Regal Theatre. You can bet your life that the Count won't forget that party soon. The kiddies gave him a wonderful send-off."

After we closed at the Grand Terrace, we headed east doing a string of one-nighters, and I think we went to Buffalo. That's when we ran into Mal Hallett and his orchestra and had our first battle of music. We were booked in somewhere with him, and we sat out there and listened to him playing a dance set, and we didn't figure that was going to be too much of a problem.

But the next set he went into his show, and he had his ax out then, and he chopped heads. It was murder. It was just the same as if he had a shotgun along with that ax. He ran us out of there. He opened them double barrels, and I'll never forget that. He had his thing together, and it was an entirely different band up there when he went into their thing. We heard them play that first set, and we got up there and played a little thing or two, and that's when they came back up there and pulled all the stops out. And that was it. As far as show business was concerned, he had one of the greatest bands going. I'll never forget that experience.

I don't know how many other one-nighters we played during the following weeks, but by Christmas Eve we had worked our way to New York. That was the date we were due to open in the Roseland Ballroom. We all felt good about that, but as Jo Jones and I stood on Broadway and Fifty-second Street with all that midtown action around us and I saw "COUNT BASIE AND HIS ORCHESTRA" up there along with all those other bright lights, I was also kind of nervous. That was going to be my first time to play at the Roseland. The only other time I had been in there was the time I had gone down there with Fletcher Henderson and he tried to trick me into sitting in, and I looked up there and saw all of those things written in all of those hard keys.

They had given us quite a buildup. They had ads and placards, and they had also printed up some handouts and mailing fliers saying something like "Yes, there is a Santa Claus, and he is bringing you Count Basie at the Roseland Ballroom for Christmas." That's how we were billed. "The biggest Christmas present you can get. We know there is a Santa Claus." With all that big promotion, people in New York had to know we had come to town.

But we didn't raise any hell in there either. It was not as bad as the Grand Terrace, which was the worst. But we were definitely not a hit in the Roseland either, and the one review I remember sure didn't have any mercy on us at all. The cat said something about "We caught the great Count Basie band which is supposed to be so hot he was going to come in here and set the Roseland on fire. Well, the Roseland is still standing."

Then he said something like "I'll say this much; if you don't believe the band is out of tune, just listen to the reed section. If you don't believe the reed section is out of tune, just listen to the brass section. And if you don't believe that, just listen to the band."

Another new band was also in the Roseland. It was led by a young guy named Woody Herman. That's where I first met Woody, and he was very nice. He and his guys had been in there a few weeks before we got there. So they knew what it was all about, and they were playing their things

cool. They were real cool. They knew how to play all of those old things
and a lot of standards for a place like that. They had it down.

They knew exactly what they were doing, and Woody was very helpful,
very generous. He gave me my first waltz arrangement. I think it was
Number 63. "Just take it easy," he said, "and just relax if you can, and
everything is going to be all right. Just don't worry about it too much."

I never will forget that, and I never will forget that guitar player he had
at that time, either. That cat used to grab me every time I used to come off
the stage, and every time I would be sweating like hell, and we'd have to
walk right past him and he'd say something about it.

"Hey, what the hell you sweating for, man?"

Every time we came by he'd kid me.

"You did it again," he'd say. "Stop working so hard, man. What you
working so hard for?"

I wanted to kill him. But, hell, we just thought we'd go in there and
play our behind off, lay on them, play hard. That's how we'd do it. But the
people didn't know what the hell we were doing. It was a bitch. There was
a wall back there where all the cats would come and stand and listen, and
when they heard two or three minutes of it, they would ease away from
that wall and say, "Oh, man, let's get out of here." Some few people did
like to stand in front of the band platform and just try to dig what was
happening, but the management wanted everybody moving and dancing.

That was a trip in there, a real trip. No matter how many other ballrooms you had played, the Roseland was different. As a matter of fact it's
the same way right now. You go to the Roseland right now, and it's a
different thing. All you have to do is just go in there any night and listen to
how the bands play when they're in there. It's always another thing when
you play in there.

We were booked in there for the whole Christmas holiday season, and I
must say Joe Belford really stuck with us all the way. He turned out to be
just as nice to work for as he was during the afternoon when we were
auditioning for him in Street's Blue Room back in Kansas City. He kept
telling me we were doing okay. One day he came by while we were rehearsing and took me to his office.

"Let's have a drink," he said.

He poured us a little nip, and we had a couple. He said not to worry
about anything. Just take it easy. Just go ahead. And then when I was
walking out the door, he called after me.

"And don't forget the tangos."

Of course, John Hammond was there, and he was doing everything he
could to help. He was always bringing somebody in there to hear us, and
there were also a few things he wanted us to hear. That's John. He always
had something he wanted somebody to hear. To this day. So anyway, while

we were in the Roseland, John told me something about a young guitarist. He said he thought this guy would be good for the band, and he'd like for me to meet him, and if I'd like, after one of the breaks he'd like for me to hear him play.

That seemed kind of funny. He wanted me to audition a guitarist. I hadn't been used to a guitar in the band except when Fiddler would put his violin down and strum the guitar. I'd always been used to hearing a banjo. Like Buster Berry in Bennie Moten's band, and Reuben Roddy in the Blue Devils, and the other little groups that were around all had banjos. So this was something that was a little strange to me at the time.

I don't know why the hell I didn't remember Cliff McTear, who played guitar in the band I had in the Cherry Blossom and took down to Little Rock, Arkansas, because Cliff was a hell of a guitar player. But for some reason that must have slipped my mind, and I'm talking about the same Cliff McTear that I just heard in Oklahoma City in the same show with Roy Eldridge.

Anyway, when John Hammond brought him in there, I said, "Why don't we just play," and we just played maybe one song with a couple of choruses, and when I heard that much, I knew that was all that was necessary. There wasn't any need for anything else. Because if I was going to use a guitar, that would be it, because that would be just what I would want to hear. And that is how I met Freddie Greene.

Freddie was working in a club called the Black Cat and, although I didn't know it at the time, so was a very good-looking dancer named Catherine Morgan, who had first caught my eye back when I was working with Bennie Moten and we played on the same bill with the Whitman Sisters. Anyway, I hired Freddie when we came out of the Roseland, and he went to Pittsburgh with us. By the way, I don't think that addition hurt Fiddler any at all. First of all, Fiddler didn't give a darn anyhow. He wanted to leave anyway, and the guitar wasn't what he wanted to play. He wasn't getting enough work. He really wasn't used to being tied down to just playing the guitar in a band. He only used to play the guitar now and then. The fiddle was his instrument. We got together on that, Fiddler and I, and what is why we have always stayed good friends right on up to this day. He really wanted his own thing, and there was no problem about him getting a gig. He went back to the Midwest or anywhere else and got a gig. I don't remember exactly when he cut out, but I did know that he was still in the band when we went to Pittsburgh, because he's on the air checks of those broadcasts we made during the time we were there. Those are his violin solos on "Lady Be Good" and "St. Louis Blues."

Our gig at the Roseland lasted on into the New Year, and it was in January that we had our first recording sessions for Decca. That was when we made "Honeysuckle Rose," "Pennies From Heaven," "Swinging at the Daisy Chain," and "Roseland Shuffle," which we also used to call "Count and Lester." Fiddler was also on those recordings. I really can't recall anything about any other little gigs we might have played in or around New York right after we came out of the Roseland, but I couldn't possibly forget our next big job. That was the one that took us to Pittsburgh.

Willard Alexander had booked us into the Chatterbox in the William Penn Hotel. That was a very special deal, and as my co-writer has reminded me, the Pittsburgh *Courier* was quick to take note of it. This is what was printed in the box under a big picture of me on the entertainment page: "Count Basie's band entered upon an engagement in the Chatterbox at the William Penn Hotel, Pittsburgh's swank hostelry, last week. This is the first time a Negro band has played this spot. The band sprang into the spotlight when heard nightly from the Grand Terrace in Chicago a few months ago. In Pittsburgh the 'newest of swing sensations' broadcasts nightly over radio station WCAE."

We had our trouble with that engagement in the Chatterbox, too. Because I don't think the people were quite ready yet for what we were doing. I think we were kind of disturbing to them when we first went in there. Willard had us marching in there in line like soldiers, and all you could hear was the sound of knives and forks just barely touching the plates. I can still see that room. When we sat down, they were still eating. Then we stomped off, and when I think of that, I almost start shaking all over again.

I didn't start so many numbers on the piano in those days. We just stomped off and hit it right on the nose. We went in there that night and opened up with "I Found a New Baby." The people were sitting in there eating dinner. *Clink . . . clink . . . clink . . . clink*, and we hit, and *WHAM!* And everything froze right in place just like in the movies. The waiters came to a cold stop right wherever they were and whatever they were doing. I could see the expressions on their faces.

"Oh, hell," I said to myself. "This ain't right."

Everybody was just sitting there frozen, and that's the way they sat right through the whole set. They didn't go back to their plates until we finished and marched right on out of there like soldiers.

It was a damn good thing that the radio broadcast didn't begin until around eleven o'clock, when dinner was over and the people had had a chance to have a few nips. Those cocktails helped the situation a lot. So when we came back in, the atmosphere in there was a little different, and I guess we didn't sound so shocking to them. But I knew we had to make some adjustments if we didn't want to get kicked out of there. People couldn't eat dinner while we were up there taking off like we did on that first set. What the hell did we know about playing for dinner? We'd never even been in a room like that, let alone knowing how to play in there.

The waiters were looking at us as if to say, "Where did they get *these* guys?" But of course, John Hammond was there with us, and he was still smiling through the whole thing just like he smiled all through what happened to us in Chicago. He stuck it out. He would not let our chance get away.

He got with us, and we sort of worked things out after a couple of rehearsals and some suggestions. First of all, we played softer. Then we also began to play a lot of things that we could just work up easy, just have somebody do a solo on. We'd play some oldies and some pop tunes that everybody knew. Then, when the mood was right, we could get down to the nitty-gritty and pick up the tempo a little bit. It was a wonderful experience, and by the time we got ready to leave there, by the end of the engagement, we had it pretty well down, and it was fairly nice because the damage had been done right at the beginning, and from then on we were getting with it.

But it was a big relief to get out of there, though. I was just as happy when it was over as I was about the Grand Terrace and the Roseland. I think we might have done a few little one-nighters or something after we left Pittsburgh, but I don't think anything special happened. We did make a couple of changes.

Our next big thing back in New York was in the Apollo Theatre. But before that, right after we checked back in at the Woodside, John Hammond came by and told me there was a singer he wanted me to hear. So we went to Clark Monroe's downstairs place on 134th Street and Seventh Avenue, the same old place that used to be Barron's back when I gigged in there with Otoe Hardwick when Bricktop was singing in there, and that's when I heard Billie Holiday the first time.

And she was something. I was really turned on by her. She knocked me out. I thought she was so pretty. A very, very attractive lady. And when she sang, it was an altogether different style. I hadn't heard anything like it, and I was all for it, and I told John I sure would like to have her come and work with the band if it could be arranged. And naturally John agreed, because he already had the same idea before he took me to hear her. So he arranged it. I've forgotten what the terms were, but he and Willard Alexander worked it out, and she came with us.

And she did so very well that everybody immediately fell in love with her. Of course, she wasn't entirely a stranger to everybody. She and Lester already knew each other because he had met her when he left that band I had in Little Rock that time and came to New York to join Smack. So naturally they were very tight, and later on she and Lester and Freddie Green became real close road buddies.

Before we opened at the Apollo, we went back out to do a few more one-nighters, and Billie's first gig with the band was in some kind of park up in Binghamton. It was called Enna Jettick Park. For some reason every time one of our trips takes us anywhere near that part of Connecticut, I remember how Billie used to sound and how she looked when she first came into the band.

There is no way that I'm ever going to forget that first time at the Apollo. In those days you started out with your band in the pit, and you had to play a first number like an overture before the stage show came on. Then you played that part of the program from the pit. So we came on playing "I May Be Wrong, But I Think You're Wonderful," which was the Apollo theme, and we did very well on that tune too, if I do say so myself. Then we were supposed to play for the stage acts. That was the procedure, and the musical director for all the shows at the Apollo at that time was Tom Whaley, God bless him. He would rehearse the music the band had to play for each of the numbers. It was his responsibility to see to it that the whole production was synchronized, and of course, he was an expert at all of that. But he was always nervous on opening day, and he would be running around worrying about every little thing that might go wrong.

Poor Tom. We came out there and almost blew his mind. We switched tunes on him. We played the number for the first big act like we had rehearsed it. But then for those little middle numbers, like the soft-shoe and the things the girls did before the next big number, we put *our own* arrangements in there. Like if they were supposed to be doing something to "Honeysuckle Rose," we would hit something with the same amount of bars but with our own little twist to it. And old Tom couldn't believe his ears. You can imagine the look on his face. And then he burst out, and I'm sure the people out there in the first couple of rows down front could hear him.

"What the fuck are y'all playing? What the fuck is this? What the fuck is going on here?"

But there was nothing he could do, because that band was tooting a little down in that pit by that time. Jo Jones was playing his can off. He wasn't juggling his sticks. He wasn't doing any fancy stuff at all, just playing, just laying down all that stuff. And the band was right *there*. We were *on* it, and the dancers picked up on it right away, and so did the audience. And when they finished and moved off, they found that they had to encore. I don't mind patting myself on the back for the way we pulled that off.

So far so good. But then you had to go up onstage for the second half of the show. That was when they featured the band that was the headline attraction for the week. That was the real test. So we took a break while the movie was on (by the way, it was James Cagney in *Great Guy*), and then while the short subjects and the trailers announcing the coming attractions were running and the band was getting set on the stage and I'm standing there in the wings, this mean old bastard working back there starts signifying at me.

I'm standing there shaking already, and this son of a gun is back there working on a line or cable or something and talking loud so I can't help hearing him.

"Now here's the great Count Basie back here. The great Count Basie! Well, I want to *hear* this. The great Count Basie. Now we'll find out what he's going to do in *New York*! Hell, I wouldn't miss this for anything. The great Count Basie! I sure want to *see* this."

I looked at this cat, and he didn't even pause. He got worse.

"Hey, what's he looking over here at me for? I'm just standing here waiting to see what happens when the great Count Basie gets out there. Go on out there. Don't be looking at me. *Okay, everybody, all on!* Now we'll see what the great Count Basie can do at the *Apollo*. Now we see in *New York City!* All on. Curtain time. *All on. All on.*"

That was the damnest thing I ever heard backstage in my life. Then I went out there, and they had a microphone that came up out of the floor. You were not supposed to touch that particular mike. But I went out there and grabbed hold of that son of a bitch, and it went *down!* And it was full of grease! That was my first time on a stage like that. The bandstand we were set up on was really a car that was controlled from backstage. When you came on playing your band number, they moved you down toward the footlights. Then I was supposed to introduce the next number from the mike, and I messed that up because I never was any good as an emcee. And then when I turned around to stomp the intro for the tune, I saw the bandstand moving *away?* So I just stopped and ran back to catch it, and the people out in the audience just fell all out in the aisles laughing. They were hollering.

I was actually running to catch that thing. One of the hardest jobs I ever had was to go out there to the mike and then come back and get on that damned band car. And after that first time I never did let it get away from me anymore either. Anytime that thing started going back, I was on it! I just stepped out there and took my bows and—bam!—went right on into another number. Actually all you had to do was introduce the singer or dancer or couple or whatever it was, and the bandstand would roll back to make room. And when you got through saying, "Now, here's Moke and Poke," or somebody, you could just walk on back to where the car had stopped. But that first day I was out there running to catch that son of a bitch like I thought it was going right on through the wall!

Billie Holiday sure was a great help to us on that program. The entertainment reporter for the New York *Age* called her the sensation of the show. He liked the band too. He said we were a wow, and he also said that Jimmy Rushing hung them from the rafters. He said Jimmy had a voice that won't wait and a getaway that is encore-ensured. Billie's name was not listed on the newspaper ads for the show, but the New York *Age* reporter gave her more attention than he gave Jeni Le Gon, one of the most popular single acts around at that time. He went for the way Billie sang "I Cried for You," "My Last Affair," and "One Never Knows." She also sang "Them There Eyes" and a couple of other things, "Swing, Brother, Swing" and "I Can't Get Started."

One of those nights, Fats Waller came by the Apollo to check us out, and he rescued me from a little situation that came up. He was sitting over in a box seat enjoying the show, and just as I was about to start the next number, somebody out in the audience hollered out.

"Jam session. Jam session."

And that got me. I didn't know what to do. I was scared to death up there, because right away everybody was asking for a jam session. I just stood there holding up my hand. Then I finally got nerve enough to introduce Fats and ask him to come on up on the stage.

So he jumped over the railing and came on and called a couple of other guys up there. We introduced them, and everybody was still hollering, clapping, and stomping, and when they kept on, old Fats held up his hands and stretched his big eyes at them. "Hey, wait a minute. You said you wanted a jam session, didn't you?"

And they said yes.

And he said, "Well, get quiet then so you can hear it."

Then he sat down at the piano, and he and those guys tore it up in there, and that was the only thing that saved me. Old Fats. That's the kind of man he was. He could take charge of the situation.

Cab Calloway also came by and checked us out, and he invited me down to catch his show at the Cotton Club. He invited me as his guest and told me to bring whoever I wanted along with me. So I got a few of the fellows together and we went. The Cotton Club had moved from 142nd Street downtown to Forty-eighth Street and Broadway by that time. He had reserved a choice table for us, and between sets he came over and we chatted. Then when we got ready to leave, I told him how much we enjoyed the show, and he took me aside for a minute.

"Look, I wish you all the success in the world, and if at any time you get into any trouble here, let me be the first one you see before you see anyone else."

I'll never forget that. He was one of the most popular names in show business at that time, and he was still just as much for me as he had been back when I first met him, when he came to Kansas City fronting a band out of Chicago called the Alabamians.

"No matter what happens. If you make it or you don't. Whatever happens, if you need anything, *see me first*."

After we closed at the Apollo, we went out on another string of one-nighters that took us out to Ohio. That's where we found Earl Warren. We were looking for a new alto player because Couchie Roberts was getting ready to go back to L.A. Earl was playing in the band alternating with us at the Cincinnati Cotton Club, but I didn't hear him until Herschel told me about him. Herschel thought Earl would be just what we needed to replace Couchie, and he was right.

Which reminds me of something. I can't think of anybody that I have actually found and hired for my band since I brought Big 'Un and Jack Washington and Prof Smith into the Reno that night. Somebody always suggested that I hire them. The guys were always bringing somebody around. I don't remember who got me to send for Ed Lewis when Joe Keys had to cut out. Of course, I already knew Ed from our time together in Bennie Moten's band, but I'm pretty sure it was somebody else who reminded me to get in touch with him again, and naturally I agreed, because I knew what he could do. You couldn't get a better guy to play first trumpet. Jo found out about Bobby Moore through John Hammond, and that's how he happened to be the one to come in as Tatti Smith's replacement.

Earl actually started playing with the band in Philadelphia in the middle of April. We were booked into the Nixon Grand Theatre, on Broad Street at Montgomery Avenue, along with a big stage show. We were the headliners, but when we got there, the sign read COUNT BASIE AND HIS ORCHESTRA, THE BAND DISCOVERED BY BENNY GOODMAN. I don't know who thought that one up, but the Philadelphia *Tribune* picked up on it and repeated it in a box under my picture when we were booked into the Knights of Pythias Hall that next month. "This is the band Benny Goodman discovered in the West and brought East."

We went down to Baltimore and Washington, and unless I'm confusing the other part of that trip with the time we heard Earl Warren in Cincinnati, where he was playing with Al Sears, we swung back out through Ohio and Indiana, and while we were around Indianapolis, we picked up a few arrangements from a young fellow named Skip Martin. Somebody recommended him because we needed some numbers to level the book off and cool us down a bit. We didn't want to run into any more situations like we got caught in at the Chatterbox.

Skip was a very young cat at that time, but he did some nice little things for us, and a lot of other bands used his arrangements. He also played sax in bands like Jan Savitt, Gus Arnheim, Glenn Miller, and Benny Goodman. Charlie Barnet stole him, so he worked as Charlie's staff arranger for a while. Then he went with Les Brown. The big hit recording that Les made of "I've Got My Love to Keep Me Warm" is one of Skip's things.

Come to think of it, we made quite a few little changes during those first five or six months of that year. At the time it was just a matter of taking care of little things as they came up, but now it seems like a lot of adjustments in a very short space of time. It didn't have anything to do with changing the kind of band we had. John Hammond would have been one hundred percent against that. It was really a matter of being better prepared to go into the kind of jobs that MCA was getting for us.

One of the most important things we did was to bring Eddie Durham into the trombone section, because that also meant that I had somebody who was just the kind of arranger the band needed. I don't think I had seen him since he cut out from Bennie Moten and went to New York to join Willie Bryant's band. But John Hammond had been in touch with him, and John knew all about the arrangements Eddie and I used to work out for Bennie Moten's band, so we decided to bring Eddie in, which also gave us another guitar, because Eddie was one of the pioneers on the guitar. He may have been the first jazz musician to experiment with the electric guitar, and he was a hell of a soloist on the guitar, too.

According to Eddie, John Hammond came to talk with him while he was playing with Jimmie Lunceford at the Larchmont Casino, and Eddie promised to come and work with us for a year. I'm not clear about how all that was worked out, but I do know what happened on the night he actually joined us. We went up to Hartford, and we knew that another band was also supposed to play, but we didn't know who it was and I didn't even think about it. We just went on up there, and our band boy got our stands all set up early, and we were just sitting around killing time when this big bus pulled in, and it was the great Jimmie Lunceford band, which was going under the name of the Harlem Express at that time.

We hadn't known that we had been set up to play a battle with Jimmie Lunceford, but somebody at the Pittsburgh *Courier* got that idea, I think, and there were some people who came up from New York to see us get chopped. I looked up and saw that big fancy bus pulling in and I said, "What is this?" They took their things inside, and their band boy just went right on up there and moved our little stuff right on over to one side of the stage and set their stands up. I'll never forget that.

Then their fan club had set up a big banquet table over on the floor beyond their side of the stage, and we were sitting on our side, and nobody said anything about coming over or anything. Eddie Durham was the only guy that came over to where we were. That was his last gig with Lunceford. He had already given his notice, and he was all set to come with us when it was over.

When things got under way, that great Lunceford band was fantastic. They had all those arrangements, and they were doing those trios and glee clubs and all kinds of things, and they were together. Oh, man. That was a bigtime band. I think they had just recently come back from a big tour of Europe, and we were still just a few months out of the sticks. By that time we were beginning to get a little publicity, but we still didn't have much more than a dozen arrangements. Everything else we played was heads.

But I guess I can say our guys were swinging pretty nice in there, and

Jo Jones was something else that night, too. He was on fire. Jo and Big 'Un were driving all the way. Considering what we were up against, I think we did pretty good. At least we didn't get chopped too bad. Of course, our guys didn't think we got chopped at all. Jo Jones, for one, still feels that our head things gave us the edge, especially when Lunceford would bring out a big arrangement on something and we had something like it that we played without any music at all. Eddie Durham also thinks we did all right. He told my co-writer that it was a matter of two different styles. He said Lunceford's band was smoother and had more musical variety and great show-band novelties, but that there was something about the way we did our things that made us sound more down with it. Eddie says Lunceford had about three hundred arrangements in his repertory at that time, and I can believe it. It would have seemed like at least that many to me at that time if it had been just fifty or seventy-five.

The biggest puzzle I have about that trip is Billie Holiday. I can't remember what she did on that trip. She was in the band before that, and she stayed with us for about a year, so she should have been there. But maybe she stayed in New York that time.

=

Eddie says the first thing he did for us was "Topsy." He says he wrote it on the train going up to Albany, New York. The band made the trip by bus. He says we sent him up by Pullman so he would have those hours by himself to write something, and he came to rehearsal at one o'clock that afternoon with the lead sheet for "Topsy." He says we were booked into some park up there, and that was where we already were set up and rehearsing when he got there.

We ran it down and everybody liked it, and we put it right in the book, and we recorded it a few weeks later. By that time Eddie had also had another tune. He came up with "Time Out," and he and I had worked out "Good Morning, Blues" for Jimmy Rushing, which we also recorded on the same date. Then, not long after that, Eddie wrote "Out the Window," which he named for the "go in and out the window" phrase that Bennie Moten plays at the beginning of his trombone solo.

It was also sometime during those first months after we came east that our two tenors became a very important feature of the band, along with the rhythm section. People picked up on the rhythm section right away. Even the cat at *Metronome* that thought the band was out of tune in the Roseland liked the rhythm section, and so did reporters on the *Defender*, the *Courier*, the New York *Age*, and the *Amsterdam News*. As I have said so many times before, it was not really in my mind at first to battle those tenors. I just liked the idea of two tenors, and I knew where I wanted them placed. After certain modulations and certain breaks I knew I wanted

Lester in there, and after certain other modulations and breaks it would be Herschel's turn. Sometimes one would come first, and sometimes it would be the other one. That was the way it started out back in the Reno, and using two different styles like that became a regular thing in the band. I just knew that it was something different and that it worked.

Then one night in New York, Benny Payne, Cab Calloway's piano player, asked me about it. He wanted to know why I battled the tenors. He asked me if I thought that was good show business, and I just looked at him and said, "What do you mean?" Because I hadn't really thought about it like that. I remember exactly where I was when Benny asked me that. I was sitting in Mom Baker's between shows, eating, and I was surprised.

But then I did begin to think about it, and from then on it was a set-up thing. I used to dictate the arrangements to Eddie Durham, and we would fix things so people really thought there was a feud going on between them, and after awhile there was. And I used to do things to keep them fired up. I used to tell Herschel that Lester had said something about his solo, and then tell Lester that Herschel had said something like "You know, that cat really thinks he really got me on that last go-round." And it was on. They would both be just raring to go.

Deep down inside they were still very close friends. I mean they really loved each other, but once they came to work, they had that thing. And when Herschel led off, he really gave Lester something to shoot at, and Lester did the same thing. It got so that whenever somebody brought a new arrangement to rehearsal, if there was something in there for one, the other had to have something, too, or he'd have to have the next one.

It really was a very special kind of battle, because when they were on the same arrangement they didn't argue about who came first, and they didn't even complain about one having more bars than the other. On that first recording session for Decca, Herschel had the solo in "Swinging at the Daisy Chain," and Lester had it on "Roseland Shuffle." When we recorded "One O'Clock Jump" a few months later, Herschel led off and Lester followed, but when we were using "Moten Swing" as our radio theme, it was Lester who led off, and most of the time all we played was just a few bars and then faded on out or segued right on into the opening number.

I wouldn't say that either one of them was really trying to be the star of the band or anything like that. It never was something that got out of line. They never got so carried away that they forgot about the rest of the band. That's not the kind of thing it was. It was not like a hand-to-hand battle like in chase choruses. That's not the way the arrangements were set up. We would build up to one. Then we used to just drop in a few bars and an interlude in there, and then drop another tenor solo in there, and it was another atmosphere, another feeling right from the word go. No matter how much the first one broke it up, the other one came on in there and did his thing and got the crowd excited all over again. They were good for each other because they made each other play better all the time.

Those two tenors created a lot of interest in what was going to happen on those numbers, and pretty soon Herschel had his fans, and they would all be bunched down in front of the side of the bandstand where his chair was, and Lester's would gather out in front of him. Herschel sat on the end of the reed section next to the piano, and Lester sat all the way down at the other end beyond Jack Washington.

The first time I noticed the fans dividing up around the bandstand like that was in Baltimore. Herschel and Lester were really big in that town. People down there really looked forward to those two. As soon as we used to hit town, some of them would come around and even be sitting around during rehearsals. Baltimore was something. There were people in that crowd who just about knew who was going to be in there on that first solo as soon as they heard the type of tune we were kicking off.

Before long, there were fans following Lester and Herschel like that in most of the different places and ballrooms we played. It just got started and then there it was, and we were the first to do it. To me it just seemed like it was something that was intended, and the great thing about the whole thing was it was two different styles, different tones and everything. Herschel had a heavy tone and he was so melodic and soulful, and he could really get off. So could Lester, and he was different from everybody. He also liked to play slow and play those beautiful ballads, but he always played them in his own style. Nobody had ever had two tenors like that before.

—

But to get back to that first spring in New York. Our home base was the Woodside Hotel. That's where we were when we were not out on the road doing those one-nighters. We really didn't go anywhere in the neighborhood during those first months in Harlem. We'd do those little gigs or go out on those tours and come back and have our little balling parties right there in the hotel. There would be those little balls going on from room to room.

Talking about jumping at the Woodside, that was our thing. But I also have to say that it was at the Woodside that I finally began to feel, and I mean really get a deep feeling, about the big difference that fate had made in my life. It was right up there in that little room that it came to me that I really wasn't William Basie or Bill Basie the piano player from Red Bank anymore. From now on and for better or worse I was Count Basie, the bandleader out of Kansas City, back in New York.

One day not long after we came to town, I woke up and was just sitting by myself in my room, looking down along that part of Seventh Avenue from 140th Street, and suddenly all of that hit me. I was back in New York City with my own band, and I had already worked on the big track. Of course, we didn't really raise any hell down there, but *Count Basie* was now a name that had been put up in lights as a featured attraction on Broadway.

I hadn't really thought too much about things until all of a sudden this light turned on, and my goodness—this was really something. It was unbelievable, but there it was. I was actually under contract to MCA, one of the biggest talent-promotion agencies in the world, and I was also all set to make two dozen records for Decca. As I've already mentioned, that was not a good deal moneywise. But still it did mean that there would be Count Basie records, and they would be coming out on one of the top labels in the business.

The more I thought about all of that, the more I realized how much my personal situation had already changed since we left Kansas City. It was not just the matter of being the boss. There never was any doubt about that from the time I took over from that other cat at the Reno. What it was about was the personality of a band that was becoming another name band.

When I saw my name up in lights and in the newspapers and magazines in New York, it was a different thing from what it was back when it was Count Basie and the Cherry Blossom Orchestra, and Count Basie and the Barons of Rhythm. *What that name stood for now was me and the band as the same thing*, and that's what made it a different ball game. Because it was not just a matter of a promotion gimmick to get people interested; what I am trying to get at is what people were going to expect when they came to hear you.

I am not trying to say that I sat there in that room and tried to figure all this out, because I didn't. Because what I actually did was get the hell out of there and find somebody to have a few nips with, which I was doing quite often in those days.

Which reminds me of another thing I want to mention that used to happen at the Apollo. There was an old boyhood friend from Red Bank who turned up backstage one night and we chatted for a few minutes, and then he asked me if I had a little time between shows, and I told him I wasn't going back on until after the movie, and that's when he said his famous words.

"Oh, I just thought maybe we could go down the street here and throw our heads back a little bit."

So that's exactly what we went down the block and did; and the next time he came to the stage door and asked for me, he told the doorman he just wanted to find out if I had time to throw my head back. So that's the

way it went, and it got so that whenever he would show up, somebody
would recognize him and announce him.

"Hey, Count. Here's Throw-Your-Head-Back. Hey, somebody tell
Count that Throw-Your-Head-Back is here."

And that reminds me of the good times I also used to have with Henry
Armstrong, the triple crown boxing champ, another one of my old buddies
that I used to hang out with whenever the band was in the Apollo in the
old days. Old Hammering Hank and I were great friends, and sometimes
we'd just sit around backstage between shows, and sometimes we'd go to
a nearby joint or maybe over to the Theresa. Boy, that's been a long
time, but it was always so much fun to be with him in those days.

—

I really wasn't interested in going out a lot during those first months at the
Woodside, and I didn't know anything about that part of Seventh Avenue
anyway. Even over on Lenox it was a different life from what it had been
back in those days when the Lion used to take me up to the Douglass
Theatre to hear Cecil Scott on the organ. I mean, it was a different ballpark altogether when I came back to Harlem after being away that long.
When I left town with Gonzelle White's Big Jamboree, most of the action
was around in the neighborhood of the Lafayette, Connie's Inn, and
Smalls', and that was where it still was when I came back into town on
those tours with Bennie Moten. Everything was still above 125th Street.
But by the time I came back with my band, the corner of Seventh Avenue
and 125th Street was getting to be the main stem that it was when Joe Louis
was in his prime. I think the Theresa Hotel changed from being lily-white
just as Joe Louis was coming up, and pretty soon the Theresa Bar was the
main place. The rolling stock used to be two-deep in front of that joint,
and nobody bothered them.

But during those first months I stuck pretty close to the Woodside.
Every now and then we'd get another little trip somewhere, but there were
very few of those. Willard was still trying to get us some heavy and steady
bookings, and I imagine that was quite a job, because we were still very
new and still not very well known in booking circles.

We didn't have to go hungry. I must say whenever we did work, pretty
nearly all the guys were pretty sensible. I mean, they were not wasters or
anything like that. Then, if they needed anything, John Hammond wouldn't
let anybody want for something you really had to have. And Willard would
also help out if we were having a little financial trouble. Most of the guys
didn't have to worry too much. I was about the only one who never did
have anything. I used to drink a bit in those days, and we also used to do
little strange things in the alley back of the hotel, little things called
sevens and elevens and nines and sixes and snake eyes. But of course,

that was always after I had sent a little something home to my mother. I didn't ever forget to do that and I always stayed in touch by phone.

Anyway, we had an awful lot of time to rehearse, and that was what we did, right down there in the basement at the Woodside. We got together down there at least three times a week, and we made some great head arrangements down there during those sessions, and those guys in each section remembered everything. I don't know how the hell they did it, but they really did. So by the time we got through with a tune, it was an arrangement. People thought it was written out.

It was like the Blue Devils. We always had somebody in those sections who was a leader, who could start something and get those ensembles going. I mean, while somebody would be soloing in the reed section, the brasses would have something going in the background, and the reed section would have something to go with that. And while the brass section had something going, somebody in the reed section might be playing a solo. When a trumpet player would have something going, the band would have something. While he's playing the first chorus, they'd be getting something going down there in the reeds. That's all they needed, and the next chorus just followed.

That's where we were at. That's the way it went down. Those guys knew just where to come in and they came in. And the thing about it that was so fantastic was this: *Once those guys played something, they could damn near play it exactly the same the next night.* That's what really happened. Of course, I'm sitting there at the piano catching notes and all, and I knew just how I wanted to use the different things they used to come up with. So I'd say something like "Okay, take that one a half tone down; go ahead down with it and then go for something." We'd do that, and they would remember their notes, and a lot of times the heads that we made down there in that basement were a lot better than things that were written out.

There's no telling how many things we worked out during those sessions, because this went on for two or three years, and we didn't just do originals. We also worked up our own thing on a lot of standards and current pops. Two of the first originals we did down there were things like "Shout and Feel It" and "John's Idea," and later on, of course, there was "Jumping at the Woodside," which is still a featured item in the current book.

We named "John's Idea" for John Hammond, who was down there at those sessions as often as he could make it. I mean, he was right in there from the very beginning, sitting back there listening and smiling and doing whatever he could to help things along. He got a big kick out of just seeing how the band was coming along. We recorded "John's Idea" for Decca in July on the same date that we made "One O'Clock Jump," but by that fall Eddie Durham and I had changed it into the version we used on those broadcasts from the Meadowbrook.

Billie Holiday didn't hang out down there in the basement of the Wood-side with us very much. I think she might have come by there a few times, but not very often. I don't know of Billie hanging out anyplace much. She lived at home with her mother, and she still had connections at Monroe's, and she also had her own recording contract. That was the reason she never did record with us. She recorded with her own little combos that John Hammond helped her to get together from time to time. As a matter of fact Billie had already been recording using combos with top musicians like Teddy Wilson, Benny Goodman, John Kirby, Ben Webster, Cozy Cole, and a lot of others for about a year.

We all knew about that because we had heard the records. Because sometimes while we were out on tour, some of us used to get together up in her room, and she used to play all of the numbers that she had made with those different combos up to that time. She did quite a bit of touring with us, making those one-nighters and theater dates, but during the times when we were back in New York just hanging around the Woodside, she had her own little things going.

Actually some of the fellows from my band had already started record-ing with her right after we arrived in New York to play the Roseland. Lester, Freddie, Buck, Big 'Un, and Jo Jones were on a session with her, along with Teddy Wilson and Benny Goodman in January before Freddie went with us to Pittsburgh. And after that, Lester, Buck, and Jo and a few others backed her on quite a few records over the years.

When she rehearsed with the band, it was really just a matter of getting her tunes like she wanted them. Because she knew how she wanted to sound, and you couldn't tell her what to do. You wouldn't know what to tell her. She had her own style, and it was to remain that way. Sometimes she would bring in new things and she would dictate the way she'd like them done. That's how she got her book with us. She never left her own style. Nobody sounded like her.

Every now and then somebody asks me something about how I felt and how we came out in a big battle of bands with Benny Goodman at the Adams Theatre in Newark that spring. I really don't have any recollection of that gig as a battle. I'm pretty sure that what happened was that we came on first because Benny was the star. He was the top drawing band in the country at that time, so people were really there to hear him as the main attraction. We were in the house-band spot just to set things up, and I think what we did was just play our set and get the hell out of there and come on back to New York. I don't remember anything about being in any battle. Maybe they advertised it as a battle. But I wouldn't call it that, not as I remember it. I don't think we even heard Benny that night.

We were booked back into the Apollo during the first week in June, and I think everything must have gone all right in there, because our next thing in New York was the Savoy Ballroom. Which meant we were booked as headliners into the two top showcase spots in Harlem during the same month. That was a very important break for us, because for me the Apollo was the greatest schooling for playing theaters. The experience you got from being in there set you up for a lot of things. In those days you had the Nixon Grand in Philadelphia, the Howard in Washington, and a lot of others that were big-time theaters, but the Apollo was the one you had to get by.

Likewise, when it came to ballrooms, there was the Savoy. I had already seen my name up on the marquee on Broadway when we were in the Roseland. But when you came across Seventh Avenue from the Woodside to Lenox and saw your name up there in front of the Savoy, there was a special thrill. It was also a chill. Because the Savoy was something else. It had its own special thing, and all the top swing bands in the country really wanted to come in there and see how they could make out with those dancers and that audience.

Which reminds me of something very strange. It wasn't until I was getting ready to go into the Savoy with my own band that I finally realized how cool we all were when I went in there with the Bennie Moten band on that first trip to New York seven years earlier. I don't mean that we were not excited, but we just went on in there and played.

I guess we were too crazy to be worried about it. We were so busy that we really didn't know what was happening. Bennie got us in there, and we just went on in and did it, and I don't remember thinking that much about it until many years afterwards. If we had actually thought about where we were at that time, we probably wouldn't have been able to hit a note.

The main thing I was concerned about when I went in there that first time with my own band was getting those tempos together. Because no matter what you were playing, the tempo meant everything so far as getting those dancers together out there. A lot of people also used to stand up in front of the bandstand because they just wanted to listen, and sometimes you didn't know whether to play for them or the dancers out on the floor. But actually that wasn't really a problem. Sometimes you played something slow but still swinging, and everybody liked that, and then when the dancers really wanted to get away, they'd ask you to bring the tempo on up. And that was when the rug cutting started and those circles formed around certain couples or pairs of couples and so on.

We really had a ball in the Savoy. That was one of the grandest times the band had ever had up to then. We really enjoyed each date in there from then on, because it was just so wonderful. The Roseland was the top ballroom in the country so far as all of the different kinds of standard dance steps went. They did a lot of serious dancing down there. When it came to waltzes and fox-trots and one-steps and two-steps and congas and things like that, the Roseland was noted for that. I didn't see very much jitterbugging down there. But the Savoy was just what the title said. It was the Home of the Happy Feet. People who came in there to dance were out to swing.

After the first couple of nights in there, we had ourselves pulled together and things really settled down, and people began to come up and say hello, and pretty soon we were making a lot of new friends. And the great thing was the policy. Anything you wanted to play you could just go ahead and play. Nobody from the office ever came to tell you what you had to play. You never had to worry about the manager telling you that you were playing too fast or too slow or could you bring it down a little. When you worked at the Savoy, you played what you played. That was what they hired you for. That made a big difference, and you felt that you were really at home.

And those dancers were right there waiting for whatever you wanted to play. At first they were standing around out there, just listening and waiting to find out where you were, and then they got on it. Meanwhile Big 'Un and I were feeling them out too. It was sort of like playing checkers. Getting on to the dancers is a very important part of being a bandleader. I had learned a lot about that from Bennie Moten back when we were playing those ballrooms out in the territory. So it wasn't really so hard for me, because Bennie was a master of tempos.

The only recordings of Billie Holiday with my band were made from air checks of one of the radio broadcasts we played late just about every night while we were in the Savoy that time. She did two numbers on that particular program. One was "They Can't Take That Away From Me," which we took in a medium tempo, and the other was "Swing Brother, Swing," which we played up a little higher and swung a little harder. Jimmy Rushing also sang two numbers on that broadcast, and both of them were ballads—"The Me and You That Used to Be" and "When My Dreamboat Comes Home."

We also did "Bugle Blues" on that same broadcast. We had "Ole Miss" on the end of "Bugle Blues," just straight, very straight—it wasn't jazzed at all—and then some jazz in there and out with the blues. At the time of that broadcast, we were still using "Moten Swing" as our theme. We used to come on with it and sign off with it. We had the solos up front right after the vamp, before the ensembles.

In August we went into the Ritz Carlton in Boston. That was another one of those very choice deals, and it was a very important date for us. But for a while things were a little strange in there, but it wasn't really the music that was the problem this time. I knew something was not quite right, but I couldn't really figure it out. There was something about the atmosphere that was not really comfortable, and it was not really the audience.

I began to feel it right after we had been in there a couple of days. You'd come to work and it was a hell of a feeling, because there were all of those people taking care of us, like having newspapers there and bringing sandwiches in between sets and all kinds of little things like that, but it seemed like everybody would find a way not to have that smile that you look for when everything is fine. It was very strange.

And it was also sort of strange out front because I could see the waiters with their pencils and order pads looking up at the bandstand and then putting on their little act and pretending that they couldn't hear what was being ordered. I had never run into anything like that before, and it really puzzled me. There was a chill in the atmosphere, and when Willard came up there, he saw that something was not happening like it should, and he started asking around about how the band was doing.

Then we found out. We didn't know that we were supposed to lay something down for all that deluxe service. That was the whole problem. We were in trouble with the help because the fellows in the band were picking up those newspapers and not dropping anything off. I guess we must have thought that everything was fine. We didn't know we were supposed to be coming across. We never thought that meant so much. But it did. So a lot of ends had to be closed up. Everybody had to be satisfied. You had to go along with the help and everybody around there, because they could give you a boost. Even the elevator boys. When Willard came in there and asked a couple of them how Basie was doing, he could tell right away that something was wrong.

But we got together on it. We hadn't ever been exposed to anything like that before, so we just didn't know. What would we know about tipping with folding money? When I found out what was wrong, I told the guys, "Looks like they think we're kinda cheap." And the guys said, "Why the hell didn't somebody say something?" They said, "Ain't nobody said nothing to us." And I said, "I know ain't nobody said nothing to us, and that's why it's been so cold."

So we learned something from that. When you jump into the pool or the ocean where the water is deep, you got to know how to swim. Whatever it is, you ought to know what it's all about. A lot of times you go somewhere and whatever you do you just do it, and that's all there is to it. But other times you can out-cheap yourself in certain places.

Which is what we almost did. But when we got that little matter straightened out, the Ritz Carlton was a beautiful gig. John Hammond came up there to catch me, and of course, he always liked us from the

very beginning. He was always very nice to me. Which is something else
that could have had something to do with us not realizing that we were
supposed to take care of the staff with those tips.

Billie Holiday was in the band when we went up to the Ritz Carlton
that first time, and that was also a big plus for us because her repertoire
and her style were just great for a place like that, and she just had so much
personality as a performer. She was something. She was something else.
And those college students from up at Harvard and those places were
crazy about her. They also liked Jimmy Rushing up there. They loved
Jimmy Rushing.

Billie had a room in the Ritz Carlton and so did I. That was supposed
to be a very big deal back in those days, but I spent most of my time out at
a place called Mother's Lunch. That was a restaurant on Tremont Avenue
with rooms upstairs, and that was where the band stayed. There were two
great places out that way. The other one, farther on out toward Roxbury,
was called Chicken Lane, a real swinging place in those days. A lot of fine
beautiful people used to hang out in there.

Eddie Durham has a funny little tale he tells about me up there in
Boston that time. Eddie claims that I was more interested in having him
up there so we could hang out in some of the joints he had found out
about on trips up there with Lunceford and those other bands than having
him as my staff arranger and collaborator. He says his understanding with
John Hammond was that he and I were going to work up a batch of new
things by the time John came up from New York. But according to him, I
kept telling him that we had earned the right to have a little fun after all
the work we had done when we were buddies in the Bennie Moten band.
And he says I told him we were already covered on the new arrangements
because we had already bought a batch of eight or ten from some guy in
New York.

According to Eddie's talks with my co-writer, he tried to tell me that
we were not going to be able to get away with that, and we didn't. As soon
as John heard the first few bars of the second one I brought out at rehearsal, he knew that somebody else had done them. That's Eddie's story,
and some of it sounds kind of familiar. So I'm not saying that it didn't
happen. But I don't remember all of it. I do remember the part about
having a good time, and John Hammond says he remembers the part about
those arrangements.

I do remember one other little question about music that was brought
up while we were in the Ritz Carlton that time, however. One night Willard
Alexander came in, and I saw him out on the floor dancing, and when the
set was over, he invited me over to his table, and we talked and had a
little sip and then when I was getting ready to go back up to the bandstand, he took me aside.

"By the way," he said, "what was that tune you were playing while I was dancing?"

I told him so he would know what to ask for when he was in that mood again. But I missed the point of the question.

"Well," he said, "don't play that one anymore, for Christ's sake."

The band was really in pretty good shape for the Ritz Carlton. Earl Warren was settling very nicely into the reed section with Lester, Herschel, and Jack Washington, and we also used him on a few ballads. Freddie Greene had fit right into the rhythm section with me and Jo and Big 'Un from the first number we ran down together. But we had made a few changes in the brasses before going up there. We had added Eddie Durham to the trombone section, and then George Hunt left and went to Fletcher Henderson, and we replaced him with Bennie Morton, who had once been with Fletcher, Chick Webb, and Don Redman. We also had to find a replacement for young Bobby Moore in the trumpet section sometime during that summer, but I don't remember exactly when it was that Bobby got sick, but I do know that we brought Bobby Hicks in and he was with us for a few months.

After the Ritz Carlton we went back out on the road playing one-nighters. We played quite a few dance halls and also some college-campus hops when school opened that fall. There is a record made from an air shot of a broadcast we did from the Meadowbrook, a club in Cedar Grove, New Jersey, but I don't actually recall anything that happened on that gig. Some books give the date of that broadcast as the third of September, and some give the third of November. They both come as a surprise to me because I've been under the impression that Frank Dailey didn't start using Harlem bands in the Meadowbrook until later on. So I'd say it must have been in late October, because it must have been during the off-season.

The most important thing about that air shot is that it has Billie Holiday singing "I Can't Get Started" with the band, and truthfully there is nothing really special about that, because *I Can't Get Started* was one of her regular numbers when she was with the band. As a matter of fact, you would have heard practically everything on that program in the Savoy, the Apollo and a lot of these places during that year. But as far as hearing Billie with us, that is the third track that I know about. There is also a tune by Eddie Durham called *A Study in Brown* which I don't think we ever recorded in a studio.

We were booked into the Apollo for the third time on the fifth of November, and then we went back down to the Howard Theatre in Washington one more time for another week. Then after that we worked our way into the midwest doing another string of one-nighters, and in December we went into the Fox Theatre in Detroit for a week.

Actually, I didn't think too much of that engagement. As Billie Holiday has already mentioned in her book, *Lady Sings the Blues,* somebody out there in Detroit had some pretty screwed-up notions about blackface minstrels and things like that. I'm not going into all of that. But I must say, that was our introduction to a big production theater. Of course, we had been well schooled by those times in the Apollo, and the Nixon Grand and the Howard were also very important. But in those days the shows they put on at the Fox Theatre in Detroit were right up there next to Radio City and the Rockettes. In fact I think the chorus line they featured out there was trained by the same woman who trained the Rockettes. Her name was Gay Foster, and I think she was one of the main ones who wanted us on that gig, and later on she also helped to get us into the Roxy in New York. The Fox and the Roxy were the two top big-production theaters we played.

When we came out of the Fox Theatre, we headed back east again, doing dance dates on the way. According to the *Courier,* we were booked back into the Nixon Grand, but I really can't say that I remember anything special about that particular Christmas season after we left Detroit. Except maybe one little thing. If I'm not mistaken, it was somewhere on the last leg of that trip back to New York that Billie Holiday won almost all of everybody's money in a little game that somebody was always starting back in the back of the bus in those days. There have been many tales over the years about how Billie cleaned the cats out back there.

And it was really a case of beginner's luck, because she actually didn't know the first thing about that little game of galloping dots, and everybody else had been playing for years. But she made every point that anybody called. If somebody called the wrong point, she didn't know the difference, so she'd make that one too, and still won. She ended up winning so much money that she had to lend some of the guys a little change to get them through the rest of the Christmas season.

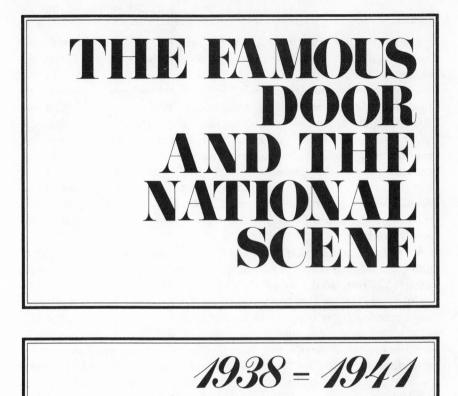

THE FAMOUS DOOR AND THE NATIONAL SCENE

1938 = 1941

The first big thing that the band was booked into during the beginning of that second year in New York was a battle of music with the great Chick Webb at the Savoy Ballroom one Sunday in the middle of January. Actually some of us made two gigs or at least a gig and a half, because that was also the very same Sunday that Benny Goodman played his first concert at Carnegie Hall, and John Hammond had arranged for me, Buck, Lester, Freddie, and Big 'Un to go down there and join Johnny Hodges, Cootie Williams, and Harry Carney from Duke's band and jam a couple of things in a session with Benny and a few of the fellows from his band. Then we zipped straight from there uptown to our thing with Chick.

The Savoy was a big sellout that night because of all of the buildup; and the gig itself also brought us a lot of favorable publicity, because when it was over, it was also written up just as if my band had been battling Chick for the championship. That made more people curious about us than ever before. It helped us to get bigger and better bookings, and it didn't hurt our record sales any either. By this time, "One O'Clock Jump" was already beginning to catch on. A lot of other bands, including Benny Goodman's, were beginning to add it to their books. As a matter of fact, Benny, who was probably selling more records than anybody at that time, made a record of it that very next month.

The reporter for the *Amsterdam News* described what happened at the Savoy exactly like a sportswriter telling about a boxing match. And, by the way, so did the same *Metronome* reporter who had given us so much hell when we made our famous debut in Roseland Ballroom. "Throughout the fight, which never let down in its intensity during the whole fray, Chick took the aggressive, with the Count playing along easily and, on the whole, more musically scientifically. Undismayed by Chick's forceful drum beating, which sent the audience into shouts of encouragement and appreciation and caused beads of perspiration to drop from Chick's brow onto the brass cymbals, the Count maintained an attitude of poise and self-assurance. He constantly parried Chick's thundering haymakers with tantalizing runs and arpeggios which teased more and more force from his adversary."

A whole lot of people said a lot of pretty nice things about us, and quite a few of them voted for us when they passed by the ballot box on the way out. In fact, according to Billy Rowe in the *Courier*, the outcome was so close that the fans were just about evenly divided. But of course, Billy himself was on our side as usual: "From our perch we saw Basie as the close winner. But ours is the opinion of but one man, one not well-versed in the arts of sharps and flats. *On the other hand, one cannot take too seriously the decision of the Savoy 'cats,' for that is Webb's home, and one cannot expect an outsider to beat him doing anything though he might be a shade better. In view of the divided opinion of the masses, I for one would enjoy a repetition of this history-making battle of swing between two of the greatest swing bands in the country held some place outside of New York and the Savoy Ballroom. Then and only then can we bestow the title of swing on the musical head of Basie or Webb.*"

Metronome was in our corner all the way. Its headline was "Basie's Brilliant Band Conquers Chicks: Newspapermen Give Decision to Count Over Webb in Savoy Battle . . . Solid Swings to Body Triumph Over Sensational Blows to Head."

And how about this? "*Metronome, usually proud of its predictions, completed a complete turn-about-face that eve, and right now goes publicly into print with apologies to backers of the band who have been singing its potential praises for many months now, but with whom Metronome, unimpressed until Basie's recent upheaval, could never bring itself to agree.*"

Nobody was in there plugging for us any harder than Billy Rowe in those days. But to tell the truth, as far as I was concerned, Chick Webb was fantastic, and he had one hell of a band. That band had a houseful of great arrangements. They had Edgar Sampson and Charlie Dixon, and Van Alexander, and all those guys writing for them, and they were playing flutes and toots and boots, and just doing the hell out of everything. With Chick sitting up there on drums and Ella taking care of the vocals.

The Savoy was really their turf. So they were set up on the main band-stand, and we had the small one, and the Little Giant took charge over there. And I mean he really took charge. It was something else, and when I wasn't on the stand, I just went somewhere and found me a place so I could sit or stand and listen. If you never got a chance to hear that band live, you really missed something. They had three or four arrangements on just about everything, and Chick kept them all together with those drums.

The only thing that sort of helped us out a little was the sound system. They had the main bandstand where all of the best equipment was, but something happened, and their microphone wouldn't work for them. That was one break in our favor, because we were over there on that tight little second bandstand, but our mike was okay. So we were able to get Billie Holiday out there, and she went over great, and every time Ella Fitzgerald came on with Chick, she had trouble with that main mike they had over there. They never did get that thing to work right, and that was very lucky for us, because Ella was the hottest singer in town at that time. She didn't record "A Tisket, A Tasket," her big nationwide best-seller, until a few months later, but she already had her thing then, and she still has it to this day.

Of course, I'm only remembering some of the things I myself was feeling. But I also have to say that I guess the guys in my band must have been too crazy or too green or something to be as scared as we all really should have been. Those cats were up there acting like they didn't think *anything* about being up there playing against the great Chick Webb. They were actually raring to go; I can still remember hearing somebody saying, "Come on, what we waiting for? Let's play!"

And they did. They really did. I mean, they went on and played. I knew what the hell they were really doing. So I was sitting in there playing and listening, and they were really carrying on. I was really surprised at them and at myself too, because it really turned out to be a wonderful experience for us. At least we didn't get run out of there, but I'm still glad and thankful that we didn't have to run up against those babies anymore.

They could put stuff on you like Edgar Sampson's "Stomping at the Savoy, "Don't Be That Way" and "Blue Lou," three of the biggest instru-mentals in the country at that time, which nobody could cut them on. They also had another great number by Edgar called "If Dreams Come True," which is played as much as an instrumental as they played it for vocalists. Chick himself had his own things like "Let's Get Together" and "Spinning the Webb," and later on Benny Carter wrote an arrangement on "Liza" featuring him, Bobby Stark and Taft Jordan, one of his star trumpet players and also a good vocalist. They also had a great medium-tempo thing on old Fats Waller's "Squeeze Me," which featured Chick and Taft.

After the Savoy we made a shortcut to a little town called Potswell in Pennsylvania, and then our next important date was back in New York at Loew's State for a week beginning the following Thursday. That was our first job playing in a big Broadway movie house. That kind of booking didn't do our reputation any harm, either. The only thing that got criticized was the stage design. *Metronome* magazine came out with an article raising Cain because the set didn't showcase us with any kind of class treatment that the featured bands were getting at that time. Other than that, I don't remember having any problems at Loew's State. The band was really doing all right, and of course, Billie and Jimmy went over big.

Then we hit the road and went down to Washington and Harrisburg, Pennsylvania, and then one night during the first week in February we went down to Baltimore for a battle of music at the Armory with Lucky Millinder's band. There was also a pretty big buildup for that one, and it turned out to be another one of those near wipe-ups. It was advertised as a battle, and that's exactly what we had on our hands.

We went on first, and I guess we must have been playing for about fifteen or twenty minutes before Lucky and his band showed up. I thought we were playing very well, so we just went on; and when we finished that first set, I moved on back into one of the corners and started talking with somebody while they were getting set up. Then the next thing I knew, Lucky had come in and jumped up on that little box he used to stand on, and when the band hit, everybody stopped talking, and I looked up and saw the whole crowd moving across the dance floor toward the bandstand. Lucky and those guys turned it on! Boy, did they turn it on. Whew!

It was a rough night. Lucky had a lot of top-notch musicians in that band. He had Billy Kyle on piano. He had Tab Smith on alto and Don Byas on tenor. He had Carl "Bama" Warwick in that trumpet section and also Harry Edison, and I think he had Walter Johnson in there on drums at that time. And I'm also pretty sure that he had Andy Gibson writing arrangements for that band at that time, but I'm not too sure that he was also in the trumpet section. Lucky himself didn't play any instruments. He just fronted the band, but he was one of the best front men in the business, right up there giving Cab Calloway and Willie Bryant some real competition.

The Pittsburgh *Courier* and a few other papers gave us a little edge in that battle too. I'm not going to make any claims, because I just thought it was very close, but we did win one thing from Lucky as a result of that night, and that was Sweets Edison. Jo Jones and Big 'Un had played with him in the Jeter-Pillars band back in St. Louis, so they talked him into coming with us, and he fit right in with Buck Clayton and Ed Lewis right away. I don't remember how soon after that night in Baltimore he joined us, but by the middle of that same month we were featuring him on trumpet on our recordings of "Every Tub," "Swinging the Blues," and "Sent For You Yesterday." Sweets is a guy that gets an awful lot of humor in all of his playing. A lot of humor. I mean, it's alive. There's a lot of life to it, and he can swing his butt off, with a mute or not. And he's a great guy with a derby fan.

There was also another important change in our lineup during that February. Lady Day decided to leave, and she cut out before we went back into the Apollo for a week that ran on into the first couple of days in March. The *Amsterdam News* ran a picture of Billie and me in the entertainment section under a two-column headline: "Count Basie Eliminates Billie Holiday's Singing."

According to the story, I had let her go because I felt that it would be easier to work without a girl singer. But I think Billie left because she got a chance to make more money than we could afford to pay at that time. As far as me not wanting a girl singer, how could that be true when we replaced Billie with Helen Humes as fast as we could? And we hung on to Helen for as long as we could, which was for four years!

I had first heard Helen during one of those trips we made out to Cincinnati. At that time she was working in the local Cotton Club in the Ferguson Hotel with a little band led by Al Sears, a sax man who was then known as Prince Albert (and who years later was Ben Webster's replacement with Duke). She came to New York with Al, and the two of them were working with Vernon Andrade at the Renaissance Ballroom. That's probably where John Hammond heard her and arranged to get her on the Wednesday night amateur show at the Apollo while we were there, and not long after that, we maneuvered her into the band. Meanwhile Billie had joined Artie Shaw's band, which was booked into the Roseland State Ballroom in Boston for a three-month engagement.

The big-name feature on the program with us at the Apollo that time was Louise Beavers from Hollywood. She was playing in a lot of movies in those years. She and Freddie Washington had already made *Imitation of Life,* one of her biggest pictures, a couple of years before that. So she was a very popular box-office attraction. The movie that week was Ricardo Cortez in *City Girl,* and the stage show also had comedy acts, singers, dancers, and the Apollo chorus girls known as the Harperettes.

When we came out of the Apollo that next week, we went up to Wellesley College in Massachusetts and back to Washington and then back up into New England again; and then we came back into Harlem for another week at the Savoy Ballroom. I'm pretty sure that Chick and Ella were on tour when we went in there that time, and unless I'm mistaken, the house band was those bad Savoy Sultans, with guys like Rudy Williams on alto, Sam Massenberg on trumpet, Grachan Moncur, bass, and Razz Mitchell on drums. They had about nine pieces, and the leader was Al Cooper, who played alto and clarinet, and they ran the hell out of us. I don't ever want to see them cats no more. Every time we came down off the bandstand, they were right back up there swinging.

By the way, that's a hopping little band right now with Panama Francis. He wasn't in the original band, but he got a group together for a reunion program during the New York Newport Jazz Festival a few years ago, and they've been doing a few things together. Somebody told me that they went over to London not long ago and tore that son of a bitch up! Norman Granz heard them over there, and when he got back, he came to me.

"I got to get a tour together. I think it would be a gas if we get the Sultans in front, and then you bring up the rear."

"Go screw yourself," I said. "I won't do it. You're not going to get me up on no stage with those crazy sons of bitches."

He looked at me and laughed.

"*Sheet,* don't put that stuff on me."

"What do you mean?" he asked.

"Just what I said."

"You scared of them?"

"Yep, yeah, I ain't scuffling with them cats."

I've got to the place now that I want to be relaxing and playing. If somebody's cutting me now, they're going to be cutting me relaxing. Those Sultans will out-swing anybody right now. Right now. Somebody told me they got a few old cats in there, and they're playing like they did years ago, playing their cans off.

I never will forget Al Cooper and those Sultans back in the old days. Every time we'd turn that mike loose they'd grab it. And oh, man!

—

I think Helen Humes actually joined us when we came out of the Savoy and headed out through Pennsylvania and West Virginia on the longest string of one-nighters that had been lined up for us up to that time. We started out in Harrisburg around the third week in March, and we were out there on the road until almost the middle of May. We really covered some territory on that one.

We spent the rest of March playing in a different town every night. From Harrisburg we went to Wheeling, West Virginia, and then on out to Akron, Ohio, and down to Lexington, Kentucky; then back up to the Cotton Club in Dayton, and from there to the Vanity Fair in Huntington, West Virginia, and after that to Mount Hope, Bluefield, and Charleston, West Virginia; and on the last day of the month we played the Armory in Louisville, which was Helen's hometown.

She didn't have any time to get around town very much on that trip, however, because we had to be down in Memphis that very next day. Then the day after that we went on down to Birmingham, which was Jo Jones's hometown, or at least one of the places he claims as his hometown. We played at the Masonic Temple on Saturday night, and I think we also played a dance in another part of town that Monday night. I do know that our next gig was in Chattanooga, and then we were supposed to drop down to the Sunset Casino in Atlanta. I don't remember whether we actually made it down there that time or not, but I do know where we were headed when we left the Southeast. Our destination was Kansas City, and we went by way of Bowling Green and St. Louis.

We stopped off in Kansas City that Saturday night and went on to Omaha for a dance that Sunday. Then we were back in Kansas City for our big homecoming celebration at the New Municipal Auditorium that Monday night. According to the report that came out in the Chicago *Defender* a couple of weeks later, there were four thousand people in there that night.

It was some turnout all right. I guess just about everybody came. There were so many of my old friends there that I'm not even going to try to name all of them. Actually I was kept so busy celebrating that it is a wonder that I can remember anything at all about that wild weekend. But naturally my man Piney Brown was on the scene taking care of business as usual, and so was Sol Steibold from the Reno, and the announcer for the occasion was Jerry Burns from station WHB.

There was also one other guy there that night. I don't remember his name, and I don't want to remember it. I remember what he looked like, and I never will forget our little encounter that night. I'm walking across the floor during intermission, and people are waving and I'm blowing kisses back to the crowd all around the edge of the dance area and up in the balconies, and I look back and see this son of a bitch walking behind me. I don't even have time to think anything, because by that time I was just reaching the middle of the floor, and that's where he caught me and did his thing.

I see him pull something out of his inside coat pocket, and when he handed it to me, I saw that it was a summons for something I owed around there. I don't remember what it was. He just walked me right across to the middle of the floor in all my glory and gave me a goddamn summons. I said, "You dirty son of a bitch." But all I could do was keep on smiling.

Everybody knew what it was, because everybody knew that son of a bitch, so they knew it couldn't have been but one thing. So I just took it and held it up and said, "Yeah, I got it." That's all I could do. I couldn't hide it. I just kept on waving and bowing until I got to the other side of the dance floor. I remember that very well, but I don't recall whatever came of it.

We pulled out of Kansas City that very next day and headed for Texas by way of Topeka and Wichita, Tulsa, Muskogee, and Oklahoma City. Which means that most of us were back in the territory of the old Blue

Devils and Bennie Moten days one more time. Just about the only ones who hadn't worked that route in one band or the other were Freddie Green and Helen Humes. Benny Morten had been through there with Fletcher Henderson, and when Sweets Edison was with the Jeter-Pillars band, he was based in St. Louis.

After Fort Worth, which was the first stop we made in Texas on that trip, we circled back over to Louisiana and hit Shreveport, but we spent the rest of April in Texas playing one-nighters in Waco, San Antonio, Houston, Port Arthur, Galveston, Beaumont, Houston again, Dallas, and then we cut back up to Fort Worth at the beginning of May.

Then we headed back east by way of Little Rock, St. Louis, Evanston, Louisville, and Lexington, Kentucky. Then, on the last leg of the trip back to New York, we played in Charleston, West Virginia, down in Durham, North Carolina, and got into Harlem and laid off for a couple of days before going into the Apollo for the third week in May.

There was a nice little buildup in the *Courier* for that one too. The headline story in the May 7 issue was "COUNT BASIE IS IN DEMAND IN NEW YORK": NEW YORK . . . *Count Basie and his men of fascinating swing music are out of town, but far from forgotten. With reports filtering in from out of town that Basie and his Orch are a decided hit on tour and one of the few traveling outfits dance promoters can make money or break even on, his following here is voicing the belief that it's time for him to come this way again.*

"With his last return engagement at the Apollo Theatre still hot in the minds of swing cats throughout the city, the management of that house is at present billing the Count for a May 13 appearance. The pending run of the new swing sensation at the Harlem Theatre [*sic*] will mark the fifth time he has played a return date there since making his debut late last year."

The other acts on the program with us that time featured Avon Long, who had played the part of Sportin' Life in *Porgy and Bess*; a couple of funny guys known as Moke and Poke; another comedy team called Mason, LaRue, and Vigol; and of course, they always had the Apollo chorus line called the Harperettes.

After that week at the Apollo we went down to Atlantic City on Friday and on down to Philadelphia on Saturday, and then came back and went into the Savoy for a week that Sunday. Then that next Sunday we went over to Asbury Park to play in a Carnival of Swing. That was my first time back on that scene as a headliner. So it was really another homecoming for me, especially with all those people from Red Bank there, too.

We went from Asbury Park to Trenton and then on down to Washington and when we came back to New York, we recorded three more numbers for Decca. One was a little novelty tune for Jimmie called "Mama Don't Want No Peas and Rice and Coconut Oil." The other two were

"Blue and Sentimental" and "Doggin' Around," two instrumentals. Herschel had most of the meat on "Blue and Sentimental." He had two tenor solos, but of course, Lester got his little taste, too, which he played on the clarinet that Benny Goodman gave him.

Herschel got the first tenor solo on "Doggin' Around," and then after Buck, Jack, and I take our little turns, Lester gets his. Both of those cats really took care of business on that one. "Doggin' Around" is a very good example of what Lester had to shoot at when he was in the follow-up position, just as "Every Tub" shows what Herschel had to hit when Lester led off. It was a battle, but it was beautiful because they were so good for each other. One couldn't let down because the other wouldn't. "Doggin' Around" is also a very good example of how those two different styles and tones and everything added up for us. But now we don't want to forget that Earl and Buck and Jack and Jo take care of business very nicely on that record, too, and we had all that wonderful brass in there on those ensemble riffs and that outchorus.

By the way, we used "Blue and Sentimental" as our theme for a while. I've lost track of exactly when that was, but I do know that it had been in the book ever since the Ritz Carlton, which was almost a year before we recorded it. Maybe somebody somewhere has an air check of us using it. We didn't use it for a long time, but we did use it for a while before we finally settled on "One O'Clock Jump."

—

I could be a little mixed up about this, but I think it must have been some time while we were back in town from one of those trips before the middle of that summer that I moved out of the Woodside and started living at an apartment over at 120 West 138th Street. That building was right by the Renaissance Ballroom and Abyssinian Baptist Church, and it was also right across Seventh Avenue from the Red Rooster. But that was a big-time joint, so I didn't ever hang out there. Hell, I don't think I ever went in there in those days.

Chick Webb was also living at 120 West 138th when I moved in there, and so was Jimmy Mundy. As things turned out, that was where I was to stay for at least a couple of years. Then I finally had to move out because my mother had a pretty bad accident. She fell down the stairs and broke her neck, and when I brought her from the hospital, I had to get a bigger place so she could live with me from then on.

That's when I moved up to 555 Edgecombe, and I also had to hire nurses to take care of her around the clock, even after she could get up and about again. Actually she never did recover. She still had to wear a collar brace thing because her neck kept on bothering her from time to time. She had one nurse for the day and another one for the night, and when she felt well enough, anytime she wanted to go back down to Red Bank and spend some time visiting her old friends, she also had a chauffeur and everything.

That was a hell of a thing to have happen to your mother, but thank God it didn't happen until I was able to provide for her properly and that she was still able to enjoy some of the good things that were beginning to come my way.

Whenever it was that I moved down to 138th Street, I'm pretty sure I was already living there when the second Joe Louis–Max Schmeling fight took place, because I distinctly remember stopping by the Woodside to join the celebration on the way home from Yankee Stadium.

Here's my litle story on that famous fight: John Hammond took me along as his guest, and he had ringside tickets. So what happens? We're getting settled in our seats just as the fight is about to begin, and I dropped my goddamn straw hat and it's rolling around down by my feet and I'm trying to pick it up. I'm bending down there looking for my hat so I can settle back in my seat and watch Joe take that cat apart, and everybody started jumping to their feet, hollering, and I looked up and the goddamn fight was all over.

—

At the beginning of July the one-year term that Eddie Durham had agreed to come and work with us was over, and he decided to cut out and try something else for a while. So he left us, and that was when he started arranging for Glenn Miller. I don't know how many arrangements Eddie did for Glenn, but I do know that he reworked the thing we had done on "Nagasaki" back when we were with Bennie Moten and called it "Slip Horn Jive." The version of "Nagasaki" that we were playing at the time is the one on the air check of a broadcast from the Famous Door in August of that year. Of course, we also played it in other tempos, depending on what was happening with the audience.

The replacement for Eddie Durham in the trombone section was the one and only Mr. Wells. Brother Dicky Wells, and he was a great jazz man and a wonderful soloist. Just great. Right away he fit in just beautifully. He hadn't been with us for more than just a few weeks when we recorded "Texas Shuffle," and there he is right in there smoking with Prez and Herschel like he was a member of the family all the time. He got two solos on that one, and he also got a little taste of "Jumping at the Woodside," which we did on that same date. Of course, Dicky was not really a stranger to us. Some of us had met him back when I was working in the Cherry Blossom and he came out to Kansas City in Fletcher Henderson's band. He had grown up in Louisville, home of the great trombone player Jimmy Harrison, who was his idol, and by the time he hooked up with us, he'd been with Charlie Johnson before he was with Fletcher and also with Benny Carter, and a few others; and he had been over to Europe in Teddy Hill's band.

=

It was not long after Dicky Wells came into the band that we got a gig that turned out to be our biggest break. We got booked into the Famous Door. John Hammond and Willard Alexander found a little club down in midtown at 66 West Fifty-second Street that was run by Jerry Brooks and Al Felshin. And when they began trying to talk them into putting a full band in there, Jerry and Al thought that was the most ridiculous thing they ever heard. I guess it did sound pretty ridiculous for a little place like that, where they had only had singers and combos and little acts before. But John and Willard worked very hard on that thing and they got us in there.

I don't know what the deal was, but I do think that one part of it was that John and Willard would help them get air-conditioning put in there. I don't really know whether that actually was the deal. But they did wind up getting air-conditioning, and that made it possible to bring enough people into a little place that size to justify a fourteen-piece band and two vocalists. It was a pretty tight squeeze just to get everybody on the bandstand. It was even tighter than the bandstand at the Reno back in Kansas City.

The other part of the deal that John and Willard worked out with Al and Jerry was what really did it for us. John and Willard arranged to bring in a CBS-radio-network wire so that we would be getting airtime out of there several nights a week. That was the very best thing that could happen for the band, because we had excellent airtime, and that was when radio was it. People used to tell us about how they would go out and drive through Central Park listening to us on their radios in their cars, and those jitney cab drivers out in Chicago used to run up and down South Parkway digging us on their radios, too, and when we got back out there, they used to tell us about it.

The write-up in *Billboard* magazine reported how things went our first week:

Count Basie went into the Famous Door for his first engagement in a midtown nightspot last week, and the way he was received would seem to indicate a prolonged tenancy there. His fourteen men haven't too much elbow room, but it doesn't seem to interfere with their swinging, and led by the Count's superior piano playing, they do a great job. There's no reason why Basie shouldn't prove to be as popular here as Louis Prima.

Half-hour floor show is headed by Jerry Kruger, fresh from singing with Gene Krupa's new combo. The gal handles the emceeing in addition, and does all right, but her warbling is the main thing. "I'm Gonna Lock My Heart" and Irving Berlin's torch tune from As Thousands Cheer, "Harlem on My Mind," are delivered in no uncertain terms, but the roof-raiser is "Old Man River." Miss Kruger offers it 'with all due respect to Jerome Kern and Oscar Hammerstein' but that's not necessary since neither they nor anybody else could recognize it. But the little lady is in the upper brackets when it comes to real swing singing.

Jimmy Rushing, sepia and rotund, opens the show with a Louis Armstrong rendition of "St. Louis Blue" and a current pop tune, minus trumpet but with the same listener appeal. Jerry Wither follows with a well-executed tap which is all the more remarkable because of the little space she has to work in. Shavo Sherman has some good stuff in his mimicry of Durante, Ted Lewis and Hugh Herbert, managing somehow not only to sound like them but to look like them as well. Basie, of course, is the main attraction, but the surrounding entertainment is also good, a lot better, for that matter, than in a few more pretentious spots. Added to the place's virtues is a cooling system which really cooks, making it one of the most pleasant oases around town despite its box-like dimension and over-crowded atmosphere.

We got a lot of good write-ups like that while we were in the Famous Door, and with those broadcasts going out over a coast-to-coast hookup, we could finally really begin to feel that we were making it into the big time. But we still didn't realize how big a reputation we were building up until we went back out on the road and out to places like Cleveland, Dayton, and Cincinnati again.

Naturally things around New York picked up for us right away, and of course, the Apollo was the place, but when you went out to all those other towns and everywhere you went there were all those people who knew about you from those broadcasts and your records and were just waiting to see the band live, especially Jimmy Rushing and Prez and Herschel and Jo Jones and Big 'Un, that was really something, too. That was very important for the band and also for MCA. Because there were a lot of very good bands that couldn't get work in many places outside of New York.

By the way, it was on one of those radio broadcasts from the Famous Door that Sweets Edison started a little something that everybody began to look for back during those days. I would be taking a piano chorus on something, and suddenly in the background there would be this high, keen voice calling my name. *"Count Basie!"*

That would be old Sweets up there in the trumpet section making his voice sound like a girl, just like he sounds in the background during my solos on those two records of "Indiana" that were made from the air check in September and October of that year (and released years later on a Jazz Archives LP [JA 41] called *Count Basie at the Famous Door*).

"Count Basie. Yeah, Count Basie. Play it, Count Basie."

Sweets made a regular thing out of that, and people picked it up from the radio, and when we started playing theaters again, everywhere we went that's what somebody or maybe a whole lot of people out in the audience would say as soon as we would come on, with me doing an intro with the rhythm section in the background.

"Count Basie. Yeah, Count Basie. Play it, Count Basie."

—

We stayed at the Famous Door all the way up to just about the middle of November. In the meantime we also cut a few more records for Decca and took part in a swing festival organized by Martin Block out on Randall's Island on the afternoon of the first of September. Martin Block was one of the top radio announcers of that time. He came on over station WNEW, and I guess he must have been one of the first disc jockeys. I'm pretty sure that he had already held another swing festival out on Randall's Island back at the end of May, but we had missed that one.

One of those recording sessions was in August. That was when we cut two instrumentals, "Jumping at the Woodside" and "Texas Shuffle," and also two novelties for Jimmie: "Stop Beating Around the Mulberry Bush" and "London Bridge Is Falling Down." Lester takes the tenor solo on "Woodside," and Herschel took to the clarinet with those ensembles in the out chorus. Buck and Dicky get a nice piece of that one, too. "Texas Shuffle" was Herschel's tune, but he let Lester go first on clarinet on that one, and he followed on tenor after Dicky. That's another example of how those two guys actually felt about each other.

During the first part of November, I recorded "How Long Blues," "The Dirty Dozens," "Hey Lawdy Mama," "The Fives," and "Boogie Woogie," using just the piano and the rhythm section. Then that next week we went back in the studio with the whole band and cut three vocals and two instrumentals. We did one vocal with Helen Humes called "Dark Rapture." That was Helen's first record session with the band. We did two vocals with Jimmy on that date, a novelty called "Do You Want to Jump, Children," and a blues called "The Blues I Like to Hear," which old Prof Smith, Buster Smith, came by and laid on us.

That was one of the greatest arrangements I ever heard. Old Prof brought it in as an instrumental blues in D. I think Jimmy added those lyrics for his two vocal choruses on the record. But it was really just an instrumental at first, and it was just great. It was a plain blues, and I've been after him to write that same arrangement again just exactly the same, if he can remember. Because it was just a plain blues and I don't think it will ever get webby. Because I don't think blues ever gets old anyway. I think a blues is the same no matter how long it's been around, no matter how many years. Of course, there are a lot of ways you can treat the blues, but it will still be the blues. Ellington can take the blues and make classics out of them. You split them many ways, and that's what he did, and it still will always be the blues.

The two instrumentals we did on that date the second week in November were "Shorty George" and "Panassié Stomp." We named "Panassié Stomp" for Hugues-Panassié, one of the top French jazz critics. He had written a very important book about jazz a few years before that. He was one of the first writers to treat jazz as being not just for entertainment but as serious music. The name of the book was *Hot Jazz: A Guide to Swing Music*, and it had come out before we came east, but it did have something about Bennie Moten's band in it, and he had given me a special mention as a member of the rhythm section on those recordings of "Toby," "Lafayette," "New Orleans," and "Moten Swing" that we did for Victor in Camden.

Evidently he had been keeping up with the progress of my band from the records we'd been making, and I'm pretty sure John Hammond had been working on him, too. So he came over from Paris and dug us at the Famous Door, and I mean, he really dug us. So we cooked up a little something to express our appreciation and called it "Panassié Stomp," just as we had named "John's Idea" for John Hammond. And of course, he was very pleased. But he was not a jive cat. So that didn't mean that he was too flattered to analyze it in his next book. When *The Real Jazz* came out about four years later, he said a lot of very nice things about us, especially about "Topsy," "Out the Window," "One O'Clock Jump," "Honeysuckle Rose," "Baby Don't Tell On Me"; and then talking about how you always have to have "perfect tempo" for a number to really swing, he wrote: ". . . often, in spite of a good departure, the perfect tempo is not found, and it is only after the execution has gone on for a time that the tempo comes closer and closer to perfection. The 'Panassie Stomp' is a typical example. Here, after the opening piano chorus, the orchestra does not really 'find' itself until it reaches the splendid saxophone riffs which support the third chorus, played by Dicky Wells on the trombone, and only achieves its full height during the last two choruses of riffs, which are swung by the ensembles in a magnificent fashion."

Sweets and Prez and Bennie had the meat on "Shorty George," and old Base sprinkled a little spice in there to help keep things cooking and tasty. By the time we made that recording we had an arrangement, and that's what we played. But when we first put it in the book, it was just another head that I dictated. That's why it's listed as my tune, and I guess you could say it turned out to be one of our standards that people used to call for.

The main way we could tell when a number was a hit in those days was by the requests you kept getting for it. I mean, it was not a matter of how many copies of the record that were actually sold. I'm not going to get into that anyway. What I mean is, when you started getting requests for the same number in all those different towns, you knew something was happening. They either got it off the radio or the record itself, because otherwise they probably wouldn't know what number to ask for. They used to play a lot of instrumentals on the air in those days, not just pop vocals and novelties.

About a week after that record session we went into the Paramount Theatre over in Newark for seven days which took us up to the last day of November, and then we came back into town for a week in the Paramount down in Times Square for another week. The great dance team of Buck and Bubbles was on that show with us, and so was another dance act known as the Berry Brothers. Sister Rosetta Tharpe, the gospel singer, was also on that show with us, and, of course, we had Helen and Jimmy sing pops and the blues.

We went from the Paramount down to the Earle in Philadelphia, and on down to the Hippodrome in Baltimore. Then from there we swung back out into the Midwest for another string of those one-nighters that took us in and out of Cleveland several times and also to Dayton and Cincinnati. Then we came back to New York just before Christmas to be a part of John Hammond's "Spirituals to Swing" concert in Carnegie Hall.

Boy, did John have a fantastic lineup for that show. He opened that evening with three top boogie-woogie piano players. He had Albert Ammons playing an upright piano, and he had Meade Lux Lewis and Pete Johnson playing four-handed on a Steinway. Then he just had Pete Johnson and Big Joe Turner up there doing some of those same wonderful things I had first heard Big Joe singing as a bartender at a joint out on Independence Avenue and later at the Sunset and the Lone Star, back when I was learning my way around Kansas City.

Sister Rosetta Tharpe was on next, and John had her backed up by a trio that had Albert Ammons on piano, Jo on drums, and Big 'Un on bass. She sang some gospel songs that brought the house down. She sang down-home church numbers and had those old cool New Yorkers almost shouting in the aisles. There were a lot of people out there who had never heard that kind of singing, but she went over big.

Right after Sister Rosetta, John sent out a blues singer name Ruby Smith with the great James P. Johnson playing piano, and of course, that was just wonderful, too. Then there was a down-home church group from North Carolina called Mitchell's Christian Singers doing "What More Can Jesus Do" and "Ain't That Good News," and after them there was Sonny Terry with his harmonica.

The combo that John brought on to play a couple of New Orleans numbers featured the great Sidney Bechet on soprano sax and Tommy Ladnier on trumpet, backed up by three guys from my band, Dan Minor on trombone, Jo on drums, and Big 'Un on bass. They played the "Weary Blues" in up-tempo and followed it with "I Wish I Could Shimmy Like My Sister

Kate," and they were followed by another combo that John called the Kansas City Six, which also used Jo, Big 'Un, and Dan, and added Buck on trumpet, Lester on tenor, and Leonard Ware on electric guitar.

The first part of the program also had a down-home blues singer and guitar player named Big Bill Broonzy, backed up by Jo and Big 'Un, with Albert Ammons on the piano. Then in the second half my band came on, and I guess you could say that the special feature of that set was the number we called "Blues With Lips." John had arranged with Joe Glaser to have Lips come on as a guest performer, so that's how we had our first reunion since he pulled out from the Reno. Actually he had never played with the full band, but since what we played was a head that we just worked up, everybody was right at home and old Lips took care of business very nicely.

By the way, we had just added another man to our trumpet section before that "Spirituals to Swing" gig. That's when Shad Collins came into the band and joined Buck, Ed Lewis, and Sweets, and we have used at least four trumpets ever since, because using four gave up a richer harmonic structure.

Our set that night at Carnegie Hall also included spots for Helen Humes, who sang "Blues With Helen," and Jimmy Rushing.

—

During the first week in January, we recorded Helen Humes singing "My Heart Belongs to Daddy," and Jimmy singing "Sing for Your Supper." Then we swung back down to the Nixon Grand in Philly and the Howard in Washington and also hit a few other places like Norfolk, Richmond, and Baltimore, and came back; and just before we went into the Apollo for the first time that year, I cut five more of those honky-tonk standards using just the piano with Freddy, Jo, and Big 'Un. That's when we made "Oh, Red," "Fare Thee Well, Honey," "Dupree Blues," "When the Sun Goes Down," and "Red Wagon," also known as "Little Red Wagon" and "Your Red Wagon."

Right after we came out of the Apollo, we went back into the studio with the whole band, and in the next three days we made "You Can Depend On Me" and "Evil Blues" with Jimmie Rushing; "Blame It On My Last Affair" and "Thursday" with Helen; two instrumentals, "Cherokee, Parts I and II" (which took up both sides of the ten-inch 78-RPM record they used in those days), "Jive at Five," and "Oh Lady Be Good." By the way, the first tenor sax solo on "Oh Lady Be Good" is by Chu Berry. We borrowed Chu from Cab Calloway for that date because Herschel didn't feel well enough to make that session. Chu was one of the very top tenor men on the scene at that time. He had been the replacement for Coleman

Hawkins that Fletcher Henderson had finally settled on, and he was also the mainstay of Cab's band. Next to Cab himself, Chu was probably the best-known member of that band at that time.

We just brought him in for a couple of days or something like that, and then Herschel came back. We were getting ready to go out on the road and spend the rest of February out in the Midwest and down in Tennessee. Then we were going back to Kansas City for a day or so on the first of March, and also hit Topeka and then head back through St. Louis, Chicago, Detroit, and Cleveland, and spend the last two weeks of March in the Southland in Boston.

Herschel had been looking forward to that trip for months because this time we were finally going to make it back to Chicago. "Blue and Sentimental" had become a very big hit on the radio out there, and he had never had a chance to meet his fans and play it in person for them, because we hadn't even been through Chicago since we came out of the Grand Terrace on our way east. We were all looking forward to getting back out there again, and this time we were booked to play a dance in the Chicago Savoy Ballroom that very next week.

But as luck would have it, the only town in that string of one-nighters that Herschel made it to was Hartford, Connecticut. He turned out to be sicker than any of us ever realized. He collapsed on the bandstand in Hartford, and that's when we found out that what he really had was heart trouble. That was very serious, so he had to be rushed straight back to New York to the hospital, and naturally we were all pretty worried, but as we headed on out through Pittsburgh and Youngstown, we were still hoping he would be able to join us by the time we were scheduled to come back through Chicago for two days during the second week in March.

That was what we were hoping for on Monday, Tuesday and Wednesday. But then while we were in Toledo that Thursday, word came that we had lost him. He passed away at the Wadsworth Hospital on West 185th Street in Manhattan at twelve-thirty in the morning. Talk about shocking. We just couldn't believe it. Everything had happened so fast, and everybody in that band was so close and had such good eyes for each other. They had a lot of good eyes for each other in that band. I mean, I can thank God that the guys were always very wonderful.

So losing Herschel hit everybody pretty hard. But nobody missed him more than Lester. For a while, Lester really didn't want to go on. It was a problem every night just trying to get him to go on the bandstand, and then Jack Washington would have to spend most of the gig just trying to keep him up there. It was rough, and naturally the rest of us understood how he felt.

We used Skippy Williams on first tenor for the rest of that month. Then the replacement we finally settled on was Buddy Tate. I don't actually remember who brought his name up first, but it probably was Jo Jones. If I'm not mistaken, the first guy he thought about was Pimpy Washington, who had been in that band that I had taken down to Little Rock from the Cherry Blossom, and also with the last Bennie Moten band. But he was on tour with Walter Barnes's band out of Chicago. So then we got in touch with Buddy because he had also worked with us down in Little Rock after Lester left to join Fletcher Henderson, and he came with us in Kansas City. At first we had him alternating with Skip Williams, but then we decided that he was the one.

What settled it for us was the way he played "Blue and Sentimental" during a gig a couple of nights after he joined. I think we were probably playing on the college campus in Lawrence, Kansas, and I kept getting requests for that number because it was a hit all the way out there too, and I asked him if he knew it, and he said he'd try it, and he went out there and knocked everybody out, including Prez.

As a matter of fact I found out later on that Prez was really for him all along, and Buddy caught on beautifully. So we still had our special thing with two tenors, because Buddy was enough like Herschel, so he could take care of that business, and he also had his own thing, which meant we still had two different styles, tones, and everything. But truthfully, with Herschel gone, it couldn't really be the same thing for Prez anymore. He still did his thing, and he was just as great as ever, but he just didn't feel like battling Tate the same way, and we didn't really try to needle him into it.

We came back east by way of Chicago (where we had a couple of days off), Detroit, and Cleveland, and went on up to Boston, where we were booked in the Southland Club for the last two weeks of March. That was another wonderful gig, and it also showed how much difference our reception at the Famous Door had made in our status as a big-time band. To be able to settle down for a couple of weeks in the same place gave you a nice feeling, especially when you also knew that April was going to bring another week at the Apollo, our good old standby, followed by a whole week at the Royal in Baltimore, and still another whole week at the Howard, down in Washington. We had been in Baltimore and Washington quite a few times before, but not for a whole week.

But to get back to that gig at the Southland for a minute. Actually, at the end of the first week we popped in and out of New York for a record date. That was something arranged by John Hammond because we had finally come to the end of that awful contract with Decca, and John had set up our first session with Vocalion, for which he hired Liederkranz Hall at 111 East Fifty-eighth Street, because he said it had the best sound in town. So we came down for that Sunday and Monday morning and then left in time to be back in Boston that Monday night.

Three of the numbers that we cut during those two days became standards in our book. They were "Rock-a-Bye Basie," "Taxi War Dance," and "Baby Don't Tell On Me." I think "Rock-a-Bye Basie" is also worth mentioning for another reason. It has Buddy Tate's first recorded solo with us, and it shows just how quickly and smoothly he filled Herschel's chair, because he had been in the band for just a little over two weeks, which also tells you something else about the kind of spirit we had among those wonderful guys in that band.

That particular number was something that Lester, Shad Collins, and I got up, but Lester wanted Tate to have the tenor spot.

It really started out as a little something on a riff that Shad had brought into the band. Later on, after the recording made it one of our standards, we found out that Shad had probably picked it up from Dizzy Gillespie back when the two of them were in Teddy Hill's band together. According to my main man in the research department, Dizzy says that the fellows in Teddy's band used to call that riff the Dizzy Crawl.

What happened was that we made a head out of the riff that we heard Shad playing around with, and then later Jimmy Mundy made an arrangement from the head and put Shad's name on it and also added Lester's and mine for the parts we contributed. A hell of a lot of tunes come about like that, but what makes it a standard is the thing that somebody just happens to put on it.

Lester had the meat on "Taxi War Dance," and it was a very big hit with his fans when it came out, and some reporters have said that he told them that it was one of his favorite sides. Brother Dicky Wells had himself a nice little helping on that one, too, which has also been singled out by a few writers for special mention as belonging with some of the best work he ever did with us.

"Baby Don't Tell On Me" turned out to be another one of Jimmy Rushing's standards. In no time at all people were sending up requests for it everywhere we went, and they were asking for it from then on. People never got tired of hearing it, just as they never got tired of hearing him sing "Sent For You Yesterday" and "Good Morning, Blues," "I May Be Wrong," and "Going to Chicago." He also cut one pop side on that date. The title of that one was "What Goes Up Must Come Down," which didn't do as well, not because there was anything wrong with it but probably because Jimmy was becoming such a hit as a blues singer that people kind of overlooked the fact that ballads were just as much his thing as the blues.

We also cut two vocals with Helen Humes that weekend. The first was "If I Could Be With You One Hour Tonight," which, as I have mentioned, I first heard James P. Johnson play in the Rhythm Club one night right after he wrote it. The other one was "Don't Worry About Me," which she also took care of very nicely, and old Prez was right there giving her the same kind of support he used to give Billie.

The other instrumental we cut before going back to Boston that Monday was "Jump for Me." That was a little thing we had just recently knocked out, and Andy Gibson made an arrangement on it. At that time we were also calling it the "Southland Shuffle." Tate got a little solo spot on that one too, and there is also another little sample of how he sounded at that time on the record of the air check made when we went back into the Famous Door that summer.

The Southland Café was on Warrenton Street near the Braddock Hotel, just around a little curve off Tremont Avenue, and all of the top bands played there year after year. Duke, Cab Calloway, Jimmie Lunceford, and most of the other topflight outfits were in and out of there on a regular basis. We followed Andy Kirk in there, featuring Pha Terrell and Mary Lou Williams, and Chick Webb was due in behind us. It was a jumping place. They also had a very important radio wire in there, and those broadcasts were popular all through New England at that time.

There was also a regular floor show in the Southland in those days, and they brought a lot of headline entertainers in there from New York and the circuits. The band was really the top attraction, but the show was always pretty nice, too, and it was usually a real gas to be working with choruses and dance teams. As I've said a few times before, playing for acts had been one of my things ever since I first hit the road as a show-band musician.

I think just about everybody in the band would agree that the most memorable act in the Southland while we were there that first year was a dancer named Rubberlegs Williams. He used to break it up every night. We did a special thing with him out on the stage all by himself with the band playing the background in the shadows. Then when he came to those last choruses, there were spotlights that would also hit me at the keyboard and Sweets doing those little muted doodles with Jo riding the cymbals.

We recorded the music for that act for Vocalion as soon as we got back to New York. We called it "Miss Thing," and it took both sides of the ten-inch 78 RPM. I've forgotten who named that piece, but it was named for Rubberlegs himself, who was also a female impersonator as well as a dancer and a very raunchy blues singer.

The other instrumental that we cut during that session was "Twelfth Street Rag," featuring Lester and Sweets. The other sides were "And the Angels Sing" and "If I Didn't Care," two very popular ballads featuring Helen. But Benny Goodman had the commercial hit on "Angels," and a very popular vocal group named the Ink Spots did a novelty version of "If I Didn't Care" that was such a big hit that it became their trademark from a musical standpoint. Helen didn't do so bad with it, either, as far as I'm concerned, and she had old Prez right in there behind her again.

We spent most of May back out on the road doing one-nighters that took us down through Virginia, North and South Carolina, and Georgia, and then from Atlanta we swung back north through Chattanooga and headed directly for Chicago. We didn't play any one-nighters on that part of the trip because we had a record date that Friday, and we were opening in the Panther Room in the Sherman Hotel that Saturday night.

We cut two instrumentals that session. The instrumentals were "Lonesome Miss Pretty" and "Pound Cake." Mis Pretty was a takeoff on "Look Down That Lonesome Road." A lot of people associate "Pound Cake" with Lester, but he also had Jack Washington's baritone, Earl Warren's alto, and Sweet's trumpet in there with him on that one, and they all take care of business. We also cut "Bolero at the Savoy" with Helen on that date.

Our run in the Panther Room was just a sensational gig any way you look at it, and it stretched from the third week in May on through to the end of June. That was definitely one of the choice spots in the country at that time, and also for years to come. It was in the Loop district in downtown Chicago. Everybody knew about Hotel Sherman in those days because those regular radio broadcasts from there used to be picked up in so many faraway sections of the country. Three air checks of us broadcasting from there in June are in the album entitled *Count Basie at the Famous Door*. The tunes were "Jump for Me," "Darktown Strutters' Ball," and that's Tate doing Herschel's old chorus on "One O'Clock Jump" as we sign off.

It was while we were in Chicago that time that I got my first look at the alley of the Regal Theatre. That might not seem like a very big deal to some people, but it was for me. There was a very special little thing about going into the Regal that way, and I've never forgotten it, and of course, that also brought back that time when Bus Moten and I had sat up in the gallery looking at Dave Peyton's directing that fabulous pit band.

We had a really great time out there in Chicago that time. Everybody was just so nice to all of us everywhere we went. Those broadcasts and records had really done it for us. We had a lot of very special fans out there. I can't even begin to remember all of the parties and dinners and get-togethers and things like that that people invited us to and took us to. But I will mention one. Just about a week or so before we were due to close, a group of people gave a coronation banquet dance out in the suburbs at a place called Apex Road House, and during the ceremonies the mayor of Bronzeville put a crown on my head and called me the King of Swing Kings. The mayor of Bronzeville was to Chicago what the mayor of Harlem was to New York. His name was Robert Miller, and his assistant was J. L. Kelly, the head of the Waiters, Waitresses, and Cooks Union Local 444. Such local businessmen as Nelson Sykes, who ran the Brass Rail Café, and Warren La Rue, manager of the New Deal Café, were also present. And so was Alma Smith, the same Alma Smith who had been so wonderful to us when we were catching all that hell from Ed Fox at the Grand Terrace three years earlier. She was really very pleased because things were turning out so well for us.

Before we pulled out of Chicago, we also had another recording session for Vocalion. We did all vocals on that one, three with Helen and one with Jimmy. Pops were very big that year, and I guess somebody at Vocalion wanted us to cash in on a few, and Helen was so beautiful on them. This time we had her do "You Can Count On Me," "You and Your Love," and "Sub-Deb Blues." Jimmy's number was "How Long Blues," which we had already made another version of with the rhythm section.

The night after we came out of the Panther Room, we played a dance at the Lake Shore Club, and then we came back to New York by way of Gary, South Bend, Youngstown, and Columbus. Then, just before we went back into the Famous Door, we played out in Brooklyn and zipped down to Atlantic City.

We went back into the Famous Door during the second week in July, and they kept us in there right on through the rest of the summer. We had all of that network airtime out of there again, and everything turned out just as great for us as the year before. In fact business was even better. So much better that Al and Jerry had to expand the place to try to accommodate the steady stream of people trying to get in there.

That was the summer the World's Fair opened out in Flushing Meadows, so we got a lot of extra out-of-town people who had made us a sellout attraction the last time. And another thing about it was that there were a lot of regulars. A lot of people came back more than once. Some came back two or three times a week, and there were some that you got used to seeing in there almost every night. A lot of other musicians and show people did that, and quite a few others too.

Again I have to say that band was really swinging down there every night. The atmosphere was just so great, and another thing was all those wonderful Jimmy Mundy arrangements we had in there with us. That was when Jimmy was dropping all those firecrackers in there. At those rehearsals there was always something of Jimmy's to work on. A lot of times he would have two or three new things for us every week.

This was during the same time Jimmy was still doing all those killer-diller arrangements for Benny Goodman. Jimmy Mundy was something else. He had already become one of the top arrangers in the business back when he was in the reed section of Earl Hines's great band out in Chicago. I've been told that he did the arrangements on "Cavernism," "Fat Babies," "Lightly and Politely," "Up Jumped the Band," "Easy Rhythm," and I don't know how many other tunes for Earl's band. I don't know how many things he put in Benny Goodman's book either, but I'm pretty sure that "Sing,

Sing, Sing," "Swingtime in the Rockies," "Solo Flight," and "Fiesta in Blue" are his. I've lost track of a lot of the things he did for us, because for a while there were so many, including quite a few ballads, but the biggest were "Cherokee," "Miss Thing," "Easy Does It," "I Want a Little Girl," "Tune Town Shuffle," and "Super Chief."

Andy Gibson was also making quite a few additions to our book during that time: "Shorty George," "Jump for Me," "The Apple Jump," "Hollywood Jump," "Tickle Toe," "Let Me See," "Riff Interlude," "Louisiana," "It's Torture," "I Left My Baby," and "Beau Brummel," (which he had done back when he was in the trumpet section of Zack Whyte's Chocolate Beau Brummels out of Cincinnati) are all his. He had just about given up being a regular trumpet player for arranging when he was doing those things for us, because during this same time he was getting a lot of things together for the new band that Harry James had just organized since leaving Benny Goodman. By the way, Andy had been in the Lucky Millinder band along with Sweets Edison, and Sweets claims to be the one who got him to start doing things for us. Andy was a wonderful writer.

Buck Clayton was also beginning to write some things by the time we went into the Famous Door that second summer. He had done the arrangement of "If I Could Be With You" that Helen recorded back in February, and he had also written some things of his own that we never recorded. He wrote a little thing called "Baby Girl" back when we were still just a nine-piece group in the Reno, but for some reason we never did get around to it in those studio sessions.

Over the years he also did things for us like "Love Jumped Out," "Red Bank Boogie," "Avenue C," "Taps Miller," and "What's Your Number," which we recorded; and I don't know how many others that might be on air checks. Then there were also all those vocals that he might have had something on, because we just didn't pay all that much attention to things like that in those days. Somebody might work up something on some of the riffs and ensembles in the background of a tune, and sometimes nobody would think anymore about it. A lot of times things like that would happen during rehearsal, and we'd just put it in and keep going.

—

It was while we were playing at the Famous Door that I came across Catherine Morgan again. I don't think I had seen her since the time she almost got me fired in Club Harlem back when I was still with Bennie Moten. But that summer while we were at the Door, she was working across the street at Leon and Eddie's, and she used to come over almost every night and sit in the back in the corner and catch one of our sets.

She had been doing this for a while before I found out about it. One of the little fellows that worked there told me.

"Hey, who is this little cute one come down to see you all the time?" he asked me one night.

"Come to see me?" I just looked at him because I didn't know what he was talking about. But I was curious.

"Yes, sits back there every night. Changes her hairstyle all the time."

That's how I found out, and that's when I saw her again. She would just come in and sit back there by the wall and listen. I'm pretty sure she knew Al and Jerry, so she could just pop in in between her own sets over at Leon and Eddie's. Anyway, I saw her back there night after night, and if she was still there when I was on a break, I would smile at her or maybe point my finger at her on my way out front, but I didn't actually try to say anything to her at that time.

I didn't try to say anything to her until a little later on during the summer. The band had Sundays off, and sometimes some of us used to drive down to Atlantic City, and one of those Sunday afternoons I saw her down there. She was sitting at the bar with some friends, and I offered to buy a round of drinks for the whole party, and I never will forget what she said.

"Oh, the last of the big spenders, huh?"

I just smiled and aimed my finger at her and closed one eye like I was shooting at her. But she wouldn't let me buy her any whiskey. The others had shots and cocktails, but all she would order was a soft drink. So that's how I finally met her, but I still didn't get anywhere. She later said she had been warned against me. The people in the party she was down there with were from Philadelphia, and I found out that she told one of them that Mrs. Somebody, who ran a rooming house in Philly, had told her to stay away from me. Or maybe it was characters like me.

I just kept on trying to jive her a little bit that afternoon, and then when they got ready to leave I walked her out to the car with my little finger hooked into hers. Then when she got in, I aimed my forefinger at her again with my thumb cocked, and that's when I said something I remember to this day.

"That's all right. One of these days I'm going to get you. One of these days I'm going to make you my wife."

She just sat in the car and looked at me.

"Yeah?"

"Yeah," I said. "That's right. You'll see. One of these days you're going to be my wife."

She just looked at me and shook her head like she thought I was crazy as they drove on off. But when I went back to work that next week, I looked out from the bandstand for her, and after a couple of nights she started coming back again, but that was as far as things went that summer.

I also have to mention one other thing that happened while we were at the Famous Door that summer. Coleman Hawkins came back from Europe. He had been over there for about five years, and like quite a few other people, he just did make it back home before World War II broke out that September. According to an article in the *Defender*, he was met on the pier by more than five hundred musicians and fans, and there was also some talk about him forming his own band with MCA as his booking agent. I don't know anything about that. But I do know what he did as soon as he dropped his luggage off at where he was staying. He came right down there to the Famous Door looking for Herschel Evans.

He had heard that record of "Blue and Sentimental" in Europe, and it had knocked him out. But for some strange reason the news of Herschel's death, in February, hadn't reached him. So he came straight down there to check him out again, because of course he already knew Herschel from those times in Kansas City when he used to come in there with Fletcher Henderson's band, which means that he also knew that he was Herschel's main man.

Anyway, he came straight down there, and naturally everybody was happy to see him, but the main thing he was really interested in was Herschel on "Blue and Sentimental." Everybody was coming up asking him about various things about overseas and what he was planning to do, and all the time he was asking about Herschel.

"Where's Herschel? I want to hear what the cat's doing down here. That was some record. What's he doing now? Let me hear what this cat's blowing now."

That's how he found out that Herschel had passed away, and the news hit him pretty hard. That really put quite a damper on his big home-coming celebration. According to Jo Jones, Hawk sat around in his room for days playing "Blue and Sentimental" over and over. I don't really know about that from personal observation, and I don't actually know whether he actually had Herschel in mind when he cut "Body and Soul," as Jo Jones also says, but I do know that he had been very impressed with "Blue and Sentimental" just before he recorded "Body and Soul" that October.

—

The only studio recordings we made while we were at the Famous Door that year were two instrumentals and two vocals. What that actually meant in those days was that we made two ten-inch 78-RPM records, each with an instrumental on one side and a vocal on the other. One had Helen singing "Moonlight Serenade" with "Song of the Islands" on the other side, and the other had Jimmy singing "I Can't Believe That You're in Love With Me," with "Clap Hands, Here Comes Charlie" on the instrumental side. The big popular hit on "Moonlight Serenade" that year was the sweet band instrumental by Glenn Miller. But Lester's fans were pretty happy with what he did on "Clap Hands, Here Comes Charlie," which, by the way, had also been a number that Chick Webb used to get away on a few years before.

The week after we came out of the Famous Door, we did "Dicky's Dream" and "Lester Leaps In" with just Buck Clayton, Dicky Wells, Lester, and the rhythm section. We called that combo the Kansas City Seven, and when those two tracks came out, we started getting requests for them right away. Actually both of those tunes came from Lester, but we liked Dicky's solo on one of them so much that John Hammond decided to name that one for him, and Dicky has been getting requests for it ever since.

THE HOLY MAIN I

1939 = 1941

It was during the fall following that second summer at the Famous Door that we finally made our first trip all the way out to California. We left New York near the end of September and worked our way west from Buffalo, doing one-nighters in Cleveland, Indianapolis, St. Louis, Kansas City, Omaha, and Denver, which was as far out in that direction as I had ever been before. Then at the beginning of October we made it on out to the Coast.

We were scheduled to play a week at the Palomar Ballroom in Los Angeles. Then we were supposed to go to San Francisco for a two-week run at the World's Fair out on Treasure Island. But a promoter named John Bon-Ton booked us into Sweets Ballroom in Oakland a couple of days ahead of the date in Los Angeles, so that's how we happened to arrive in the Bay Area, where there was a very big surprise waiting for us.

When our train pulled into the station, there was an agent from the Oakland office of MCA looking for me. He came up and introduced himself.

"You are Count Basie, aren't you?"

"Yeah," I said.

"You're on your way to play the Palomar, right?"

"That's right," I said, and then I said, "Well, you don't have to tell me. The Palomar burned down."

I was just kidding, but he didn't laugh. He just looked at me, surprised, and nodded his head.

"That's right. How did you know?"

That was something. I wasn't ready for that. Nobody was. It was a very mysterious fire. The Palomar was the main café-ballroom for the Los Angeles and Hollywood area, and it was where the top ofay bands played. We were the first sepia band ever booked for a date there. We were supposed to follow Charlie Barnet in there and stay for a week or so, and when we got down to Los Angeles, we found out that all of Charlie's music and most of his instruments and equipment had been burned up. Only those musicians who happened to take their instruments home with them that night saved anything.

Actually our frustration didn't last very long. Willard Alexander had us booked into the Paramount Theatre by the time we got down to Los Angeles. The West Coast reporter for the Chicago *Defender* did a pretty good job on our arrival: "Despite the unfortunate fire that marred somewhat their auspicious appearance here, the famed group arrived in a highly jubilant mood. Like conquering warriors, they arrived in this city from Oakland, California, where they played a dance the night before, amid red hot tunes from a swing band provided by the local sepia section of the musicians' local and scores of friends and admirers who fairly overran the handsome new Union Station here.

"A parade was formed at the station and with Ed Bailey, president of the local, Elmer Fain, the business agent, and Leslie Hite, famed leader of the West's most outstanding band, in the vanguard, the orchestra and his troupe were escorted along Central Avenue, the main sepia thoroughfare, in grand and glorious style."

As soon as I found out about all of the music Charlie Barnet had lost in the fire, I let him make a copy of anything in our book that he thought he could use. Because I thought a lot of Charlie, and he has never forgotten that. From then on, he has always mentioned it, and he has always said, "Bill, anything you need, anything you want, just let me know."

Our little disappointment over not getting to play in that fabulous million-dollar ballroom was nothing compared with the situation Charlie and his band were in. And besides, we couldn't have been a bigger hit at the Palomar than we were at the Paramount. We did seven days in there. Then we played some ballroom in Los Angeles and a one-nighter down in San Diego before going back up into the Bay Area for two weeks at the World's Fair.

I think Billy Rose had something to do with that deal up there. I think that operation was losing money, and they brought Billy Rose in to put on some shows and turn things around. I don't remember who made the deal to get us out there, but I do remember playing that gig. We had to get up around five o'clock every morning to catch the six or maybe it was the seven o'clock boat out to Treasure Island, and it was cold in San Francisco that early in the morning, especially on the water. We had to wear overcoats to make that trip. It was colder than a mother all the way out there. And then around nine o'clock it turned hot out there on that island, hotter than the desert. But by the time we did our first show, at ten o'clock I think it was, I had my nip of scotch and I was ready.

We were out there for just about two weeks, which took us right on up to the end of October, and among the people that came to see us was my ex-wife, Vivian. She had moved out to California some time before that, and when she came up with a group of her girlfriends, she greeted me just as if we had never had anything but a ball when we were together. Nobody would have ever believed that she was the same woman.

I think I'll just leave the whole thing right there, because as far as I'm concerned I've mentioned too much about that particular person already.

After we closed at Treasure Island, we circled over to Sacramento for a night and came back to Los Angeles by way of a one-night stopover in Stockton, and then after one-nighters in Glendale and San Bernadino we spent a couple of days in Los Angeles recording for John Hammond in the Columbia Okeh Studio out on Vine Street. The instrumentals on that first day were "The Apple Jump," "Riff Interlude," and "Volcano." And that was also when Jimmy sang "I Left My Baby (Standing in the Back Door Crying)." Then that next day the instrumentals were "Ham 'n' Eggs" and "Hollywood Jump," and we made two vocals for Helen, "Between the Devil and the Deep Blue Sea," and "Someday, Sweetheart."

Then during the second week in November we headed back east by the southern route through Texas and Louisiana, hitting Fort Worth, San Antonio, Galveston, Houston, Henderson, and Port Arthur, and then Baton Rouge, New Orleans, and Monroe, Louisiana. Then we swung up to Little Rock and came back down to Birmingham, Alabama, and crossed over to Atlanta and dipped down to Jacksonville, Florida, for a couple of nights and headed north again by way of Macon, Georgia; Knoxville, Tennessee; Louisville and Bowling Green, Kentucky.

—

So by the first of December we were in Evansville, Indiana, and we went on from there to St. Louis and hit Chicago and Detroit, and finally came on back to New York by way of Columbus, Ohio; Huntington, West Virginia; Pittsburgh, and Baltimore. We spent the next couple of weeks around New York doing one-nighters in nearby places like Bridgeport, Trenton, Washington, and Newark. Then on Christmas Eve we did John's second "Spirituals to Swing" concert at Carnegie Hall.

John made a few changes in the lineup for that second year. He brought in the Golden Gate Quartet to do the spirituals, like "Gospel Train" and "I'm on My Way," and he got the great Miss Ida Cox, who was right up there in the class with Bessie, Mamie, Trixie, and Clara Smith, to sing some blues, and she was just great. He also added Benny Goodman's Sextet, which at that time had Charlie Christian on guitar, Lionel Hampton on vibraphone, Fletcher Henderson on piano, Arlie Bernstein on bass, Nick Fatool on drums, and, of course, Benny himself on clarinet. They played numbers like "I Got Rhythm," "Flying Home," "Memories of You," "Stomping at the Savoy," and "Honeysuckle Rose," and they also closed the program jamming "Lady Be Good" with us, Pete Johnson, Albert Ammons, and Meade Lux Lewis.

There was also something else that was different about the second Carnegie Hall "Spirituals to Swing" concert. John Hammond himself didn't serve as the master of ceremonies. He got Sterling Brown, a poet and professor from Howard University, to make the introduction and bring on the different numbers. Truthfully I didn't know very much about him and his books at that time, but he was an old friend of John's, and he knew a lot about music and history, and especially about blues singers. So it was a great honor to meet him.

John has said that he thinks the first year's concert had a slight edge over the second, but all I can say is that it was a real gas for us both times.

—

We opened the New Year in Philadelphia. Then we came back to New York and played a one-nighter out in Brooklyn, and about a week later we went into the Apollo for another one of those seven-day stands. Jackie Mabley was on the show that time, and so was Taps Miller, and of course, all of those fantastic Apollo dancers also known as the Harperettes had to be there. Jackie Mabley was not being billed as the fabulous Moms Mabley yet but had been a big headliner for a few years by that time.

That next week we went back down to the Howard in Washington for another seven days, and when we came back into New York the week after that, we went into the Golden Gate Ballroom up on Lenox Avenue at 142nd Street for fourteen days. The Golden Gate was in the same space in the same building where the Douglass Theatre once was, and at one time the Cotton Club had been upstairs in that building.

I don't really remember how our deal was set up, but maybe there is a clue in the promotional article that ran in the *Defender* under the heading "To Get Gold Piano": "Basie will be signally honored on his opening night by musicians of Local 802 paying tribute to his musical prowess by presentation of the world's smallest piano, constructed of old gold in its entirety, including the keys. It measures but 18 inches in length but will have the playing qualities of the regular 88-note grand piano. Nearly all the maestros now playing in and near New York will be on hand for the presentation ceremonies."

That may be some kind of clue, but the fact of the matter is that I don't remember anything about any gold piano. If they gave me one, I wonder what the hell happened to it. Maybe they did, but it also could have been a promo gimmick that didn't work out. I'm sorry, but I really don't remember anything about anybody giving me a gold piano.

Whether we were booked in there for two whole weeks because somebody was trying to compete with the Savoy I don't know, either. But according to the *Amsterdam News*, Moe Gale, Sigmund Gale, and Charles Buchanan, the owners and managers of the Savoy, moved in and took over the control of the Golden Gate by the first of April.

Whatever it started out to be, after that it was not the same kind of ballroom that the Savoy or the Roseland was. It was the kind of social ballroom that was usually rented by various organizations and concerns for special social affairs. Social clubs and civic organizations or whatever would just rent the hall for their affair, and who was putting on the occasion made their own arrangements for providing the music and the decorations, favors and refreshments, if any.

When we came out of there just before the middle of February, we did about a week of one-nighters that had us zigzagging down to Baltimore and back up to Orange, New Jersey, and up to Boston and back over to upstate New York and across to Connecticut, before swinging back to Boston to spend the last eleven days in February and the first three weeks of March in the Southland Café. It was at some point during that time before we went up there that Benny Morton left the trombone section and we replaced him with Vic Dickinson, another hell of a trombone player who came to us from Benny Carter's band, but who had also played with such fantastic bands as Speed Webb, Zack Whyte's Chocolate Beau Brummels, Blanche Calloway, and Claude Hopkins before that.

Shad Collins also left around that same time, and Al Killian came in as his replacement. Al had been with Don Redman's band before he came to us, and before that he had been with Teddy Hill, and he had also worked with Baron Lee. Al was something else in those high registers, and later he also took over some of the lead and lightened things up a bit for Ed Lewis.

It wasn't until the third week in March that we got around to recording again. Then in a couple of days we made "I Never Knew," "Tickle Toe," "Louisiana," "Easy Does It," "Let Me See," and "Let's Make Hay While the Moon Shines," and also two vocals with Jimmy, "Somebody Stole My Gal" and "Blues (I Still Think of Her)." Buck Clayton did the arrangements on these two. "Tickle Toe" was Lester's original, and Andy Gibson worked with him on the arrangement, and Jo and I also put a little something in there, but aside from a little four-bar middle by Sweets, Lester had all of the solo meat on that one. The rest of it is those ensembles and the trumpets accenting with Jo.

Andy Gibson also wrote up the arrangement on "Let Me See." It was Sweet's tune, but he didn't do it for himself. He just brought it in to the band, and the fellows picked up on it. Tate does a real nice get-off. Then after I follow him with thirty-two, Vic Dickinson takes over for a while, and then Lester picks it up and lays another one of his old good ones in there for us.

There was also a broadcast from the Southland that was recorded and released years later. We did five instrumentals and three vocals. I think that's the only record of us playing "Ebony Rhapsody" and "Take It, Pres." I don't think we ever made a studio recording on any of those. Another instrumental was "I Got Rhythm," which I understand is pretty hard to find these days. There were two vocals by Helen—"Darn That Dream," and "If I Could Be With You One Hour Tonight"— and Jimmy did "Baby, Don't You Tell On Me." The other instrumental number was "One O'Clock Jump," which we signed off with. Not long gao, somebody told me that the "I Got Rhythm" of that particular date is pretty hard to find, but with all the reissues coming out these days, I'm pretty sure it will turn up sooner or later.

During the rest of March we were back out on the road doing one-nighters in towns from Delaware to Maine. Then we spent the first week in Loew's State in Manhattan, the second week in the Flatbush Theatre in Brooklyn, the third in the Windsor in the Bronx, and a few days of the fourth in the Carlton Theatre out in Jamaica, Queens.

Then in May we were right back out there in that bus again, and we went through West Virginia and into Ohio and came back through Pennsylvania and Atlantic City, which put us in New York in time to go into the Apollo for the last week of the month.

Somebody thought up a very special promotion feature for our opening day and got the *Amsterdam News* and the Pittsburgh *Courier* to go along with it.

Then that next week the *Courier* followed up with a report which I will just quote as it came out, because it mentions a few little things that I probably never would have remembered after all this time.

In a riotous opening that saw 2,000 swing fans crowded into every available inch of the Apollo Theatre, and 1,000 in the lobby and street, Count Basie and his band, aided by Erskine Hawkins, Coleman Hawkins, Charlie Bar-

net and Benny Carter, put on one of the greatest shows this 125th Street house has ever seen, Friday.

It was a triumphant homecoming for the mighty Count. When the show hit at 11:30 A.M., the house was already crowded to capacity, with standees along the sidelines and back of the theatre. Among the audience were musicians from every large band not on the road, as well as prominent stage performers.

Fire department officials ordered ushers to close the doors, shortly afterwards, to prevent dangerous congestions. Those left standing in the lobby, and in the line at the box office waited patiently for the second show.

Jitterbugs completely stopped the show, by calling for repeated request numbers from Count and the boys. The Jump King completely ruled his subjects. When Coleman Hawkins, Charlie Barnet, Erskine Hawkins, Benny Carter and Lester Young stepped onstage for an impromptu, the audience went wild and rose to its feet. They were introduced by Symphony Sid, famed radio comic.

The roof was shaking when the curtain fell on the noisiest and the most enthusiastic opening of the season.

That was just about the way it was that day, and as I remember it, the rest of the week was also a sellout, even though that special jam session was for one day only. Of course, Jimmy Rushing and Helen Humes were a big hit every show, and the lineup for that also included such comedians and dancers as Willie Jackson, Alice Lovejoy, George Wiltshire, Hocha Drew, Tommy and Al, and naturally the sixteen Apollo chorus girls were in there doing their thing. The movie for that week was Jack Holt (remember him?) in *Within the Three Mile Limit*.

We spent the day after we came out of the Apollo recording for Columbia. That was when we did "Blow Top." Which reminds me that Tab Smith had come into the reed section by that time, because that was his tune, and he also did the arrangement on it. He had come in as a temporary substitute for Earl Warren on alto while Earl was out sick for a few days, but then we decided to keep him on. So that's when we started using two altos, which brought the reed section up to five pieces, giving us two tenors, two altos, and one baritone. Of course, Lester could also double on clarinet, and Jack Washington could also play alto and clarinet along with baritone whenever you needed him. And by the way, Earl could also double on baritone. I think maybe most people have forgotten that. Tate also doubled on clarinet.

I'm not really sure whether it was Sweets or Andy Gibson or somebody else that brought Tab in. I do know that Sweets and Tab and Andy had been in Lucky Millinder's band together. Of course, I had first heard Tab when he came down to Little Rock with Eddie Johnson's band from

St. Louis while I was down there with that band from the Cherry Blossom. He was a hell of a musician even then, and when he came over to us from Lucky, he was really together, and he was also doing some writing and arranging. Sometimes he used to sound like Johnny Hodges, but every time anybody said anything about having a tone like Johnny, he'd say, "What do you mean, I sound like Johnny? I'm Tab Smith, and that's who I sound like."

The other instrumentals we did on that same date with "Blow Top" were "Gone With 'What' Wind?" and "Super Chief." "Gone With 'What' Wind?" was really something from Benny Goodman's book. As a matter of fact I had sat in as a guest piano player in Benny's sextet when he recorded it for Columbia back in February while we were working at the Golden Gate. The full band arrangement was by Elton Hill, and I also dictated a few little changes here and there.

"Super Chief" was another one of those killer-dillers that Jimmy did for us. Tate and Sweets and Jo and I have the solo spots. The *Super Chief* was one of those super express coast-to-coast trains that used to go streaking across those Kansas plains like greased lightning, going west to California and east to Chicago and New York.

The day after that session, the band finally got a chance to take two solid weeks off for vacation, and I'm pretty sure that those two hard-earned weeks were just about the first real vacation the band ever had. It was just great for married guys like Tate and Earl; and Jack, Jimmy, Ed Lewis, and Jo had a chance to spend some time with their families for a change. Quite a few of those guys had brought their wives to New York by that time, and some of them had moved out of the Woodside to set up housekeeping in their own apartments. Some still had their families back out in Kansas City. I think Big 'Un's family was still out there at that time.

The only family I had at that time was my mother, and she was getting along very well. So I decided to take a little trip out to Chicago for a day or so. Actually I went out there to take care of a business matter, as well as have a little fun. But right away there was a newspaper story trying to make something of it. Dig this headline and article in the *Defender*:

COUNT BASIE HERE BUT IS NOT TO WED.

Count Basie was in Chicago Saturday and Sunday not merely on a pleasure trip and not to take on a mate as Harlem suggested in a flood of wires sent ahead of the famed band leader. Sunday afternoon, Chicago editors were flooded with wires advising them that Count had slipped out of New York and was to be married in Chicago Monday morning. This was all denied by Basie, who to prove the story false insisted that a couple of reporters stick with him while he was enjoying a few days off from

1. Backstage with Mister B. (Basie Collection)

2. With Freddy Green and the one and only Norman Granz. (Basie Collection)

3. The Combo at the Brass Rail in Chicago. Jimmy Lewis, bass; Buddy De Franco, clarinet; Gus Johnson, drums; Wardell Gray, tenor; Freddy Green, guitar, and Clark Terry, trumpet. (Driggs Collection)

4. Birdland Band number 1, also called the Lockjaw Davis–Paul Quinichette band because of two featured tenor soloists. Left to right front: Jimmy Lewis, Lockjaw, piano player, Ernie Wilkins, Marshall Royal, Paul Quinichette, Charlie Fowlkes. Rear: Freddy Green, Gus Johnson, Henry Coker, Reunald Jones, Johnny Mandell, probably Paul Campbell, Benny˙ Powell, Wendell Culley and Joe Newman. (Bill Mark Photo. Basie Collection)

4

5. First European tour. This line-up is also sometimes called the Two Franks Band, because Frank Wess, top right, and Frank Foster, third from top, have replaced Davis and Quinichette. Between the two Franks are Bill Hughes, trombone, and Joe Wilder, trumpet. Ed Jones, second from left, is new bass replacement. Mrs. Basie is front and center. (Driggs Collection)

5

6. Sixteen Men Swinging. Bill Graham has replaced Ernie Wilkins, Thad Jones has replaced Wilder, and the new drummer is Sonny Payne. (Basie Collection)

7. The Count from Red Bank, New Jersey, by way of Kansas City and Harlem is presented to HRH the Queen of England. (Basie Collection)

8. Joe Williams and sixteen men swinging the blues at Birdland. (Basie Collection)

7

8

9. In the studio with The Boss during the recording of *First Time! The Count Meets the Duke.* (Institute for Jazz Studies)

10. Honolulu stopover en route to Japan, 1963. Front row left to right: Buddy Catlett, Frank Foster, Freddy Green, Benny Powell, Don Rader, Sonny Cohn, unidentified, Marshall Royal, Old Base. Top downward: Charlie Fowlkes, Jimmy Witherspoon, guest vocalist, Frank Wess, Henry Coker, Al Aarons, Fip Ricard, Eric Dixon, Grover Mitchell and Sonny Payne.

9

10

11

12

13

14

15

11. Neal Hefti became a regular contributor to the band's repertory during the early combo and come back days and continued for about twelve years. Many of his items are widely known and still often requested.

12. Ernie Wilkins. In the old band the key sidemen—arrangers were Eddie Durham and Buck Clayton. In the present band the first main in-house man was Ernie Wilkins. Then there was Frank Foster, who never has all the credit due, Thad Jones and also Frank Wess.

13. Billie Holiday was the band's first female vocalist, and when she became a star single she still enjoyed doing things with the band. There were never any studio record dates. (Basie Collection)

14. Quincy Jones was an outstanding freelance contributor to the new band for many years. In 1963 four Jones/Basie albums were on the bestseller charts at the same time; two vocals, one with Sinatra, one with Ella, and two instrumentals, *This Time by Basie* and *Li'l Ole Groovemaker.*

15. Benny Carter is somebody who has always had class as a musician and also as a man.

16

17

16. Richard Wright, lyricist, Paul Robeson, vocalist in the studio to record a tribute to Joe Louis. John Hammond's idea. (Driggs Collection)

17. Benny Goodman and Sarah Vaughan always came by to check you out and wish you well on opening night whenever they had the time. Sarah has also shared headline bookings with the band many times right on up to the present.

18. With Ella Fitzgerald and Frank Sinatra— the First Lady of Swing and the Chairman of the Board. (Basie Collection)

19. Basie plus Tony Bennett equals a full house and a gas of a time not only over here but also in England. (Basie Collection)

18

20. Improvising with Fred Astaire on Astaire Time for NBC-TV September 1960.

21. Sammy Davis, Mister Entertainment. Just tell him what you want.

22. With Oscar Peterson. What he does on the piano is impossible, That's why he's such a monster. (Basie Collection)

23. Ole Base arrives on Amigo scooter. Left to right: Bill Hughes, trombone; Danny Turner, alto and flute; Willie Cook, trumpet, and Grover Mitchell, trombone. (Buddy Dunk Creative Photography. Basie Collection)

24. The Gipsy Trail one more once.
Don't ever say so many goodbyes in one
town that you're not up and saying
hello in the next.

24

*work in Chicago. "I just needed a rest and decided to take it in Chicago,
so I grabbed a plane and came here . . ." He was met at the airport by
Montel Stewart and Nelson Sykes. . . .*

I don't know who started that rumor, but they were way off on that one.

The first engagement on our schedule when we came back to work in
the middle of June was supposed to take place in the Armory in Newark.
It was planned as a big celebration in honor of me as a home-state boy
making good. But they had to cancel out. According to the city and army
people, a new War Department policy ruled out the use of the Armory
for social and civic events because of the war in Europe.

There were charges of discrimination, but I don't really know what the
score was, because we cut out that weekend for Rocky Mount, North
Carolina, and we spent the rest of the month doing one-nighters that took
us as far south as Johnson City, Tennessee. Then we came back up through
Ohio and Indiana, and we opened at the Regal in Chicago the day after the
Fourth of July.

That was our first stage date in Chicago, and it came at the same time
that the Negro Exposition, also known as the Negro World's Fair, was
going on in Chicago. So our show tied right in with the celebration of
our people's contribution to music, and we also had the audience jumping
with us all the way.

The headlines following our opening announced that we broke the
attendance record at the Regal, and the whole week was just fantastic.
Which just goes to show how things sometimes turn out. That time when
I came to Chicago on that record date with Bennie Moten and Bus Moten,
and I went to the Regal and saw Dave Peyton conducting that pit band
and I told Bus I was going to have my thing on that stage with my own
band some day, I didn't really have any idea about how fantastic it was
really going to be once I made it up there. I still don't know what made
me say that to Bus. All of a sudden I just heard myself saying it. But I
did say it, and I remembered it that week, and throughout the years I never
went back in there without thinking about it all over again.

Our next date after the Regal was a week in Cincinnati at a place called
Coney Island. Then after a one-nighter in Dayton, we went up to Detroit,
and I think this was the time when we played the Greystone Ballroom
and I ran into the dance team known as Billy and Milly, two of my old
friends, from the days back at the Reno Club. If this was that time, then
it was also the time when I ran into Catherine Morgan again.

That was when I finally really met her. She came into the Greystone
with Milly and Billy, who were old friends of hers too, and Milly was
going to introduce me to her, and I looked and saw her standing there
and I aimed my finger at her and said, "Bam!" I couldn't believe my luck,

because naturally Billy and Milly were all for me, and that just made it a very nice situation for getting better acquainted. At least that's the way I saw it, and of course, I tried to make the most of it.

So after the band finished the last set, the four of us went out somewhere. I don't remember where we went and what we said or anything like that, although I can guess what my line was. But one thing I do remember. When the goddamn waiter brought me the check, it was the biggest bill I'd ever seen in my life, and I like to have died. It was fifty dollars! Which was a hell of a lot of money back in those days. Geez!

I had to get Maceo Birch to come get me out of that, and when he came in there, I told him what had happened, and I said something like, "Damn, man. I don't need nobody handing me no check like this."

We were standing off to one side talking, and he looked at me and looked over at my guests and said, "You drank it, didn't you? You had the party, didn't you? So go ahead and pay for it."

But that time in Detroit was when I began to get tight with Catherine. After that, we really did some heavy going together. Telephoning and writing and visiting and sending and bringing presents and all of them kinds of things. We were really boy and girl from then on. It was almost ten years since I first spotted her and tried to talk to her back when I was with Bennie Moten, and she was, as she always says, only a fifteen-year-old girl from Cleveland dancing in the Whitman Sisters company.

I'm not saying that there wasn't a few others during all those years, because there are too many people who know better. But I'm not going to get into any more of that than I have to, because it really isn't an important part of this story. I think I've already said enough about how we work out the things we play to keep anybody from trying to make a lot of connections between our music and somebody's personal secrets that some people would like to gossip about. So I just don't see the point of going into things like that. If I was the kind of musician that wrote a lot of tunes about love affairs, maybe that would be a different matter. But when you come right down to it, as close as that band was, those guys didn't have to get all into each other's private business in order to play together.

—

We went back down south as far as Memphis and came back through St. Louis and Kansas City to Chicago, and that is where John Hammond held our next recording session. Jimmy Rushing did two great vocals on that date. The first one was "Evenin'," and the other one was "I Want a Little Girl." Both became standards that we still play. Helen's vocal was a little thing called "It's Torture," and Andy also wrote one of the instrumentals for that date. It was called "The World Is Mad" and it was another one of those numbers that took two sides of a ten-inch record. The second instrumental was "Moten Swing," which we finally got around to recording after all those years. By that time the arrangement that Eddie Durham and I had worked up for Bennie Moten had been through so many changes that what we were really playing was a head.

While we were in Chicago that time, we also played a week at the State Lake downtown in the Loop district. We opened on a Friday night, and the next night we also played a dance on the South Side at the Savoy Ballroom in honor of the crowning of a new mayor of Bronzeville and the winner of the annual Miss Bronzeville contest. Then on our way out to the Pacific Coast again by way of Kansas City and Topeka, we stopped over in Denver as we did the year before, and when we got to Los Angeles, we stayed in the Paramount Theatre eighteen days, which took us into the second week in September.

Meanwhile we also took part in the big Labor Day parade, and at one point the crowd wouldn't let us move on until we played something for them to have a jitterbug session right out there in the street. That's something I don't remember ever happening before, and everybody was having such a ball that we had a little trouble breaking away so we could get out to the Paramount in time for the curtain. While all that was going on, naturally I was too busy to keep up with anything else, but Jimmie Lunceford was also in that parade, and I understand that he and his gang also got stopped and had to play a little concert.

Then after running up to Oakland, we jumped all the way back to Oklahoma City and we spent the rest of that September in Texas, Louisiana, Mississippi, Alabama, and Georgia. A lot of that trip was the same as the year before, at least that's the way I tend to remember it. But your memory is such a tricky thing. Sometimes you try to remember something about a trip like that, and all you can recollect is playing in some hall somewhere and eating and talking and maybe partying a little, and then getting back on the bus and dropping off to sleep and then waking up somewhere out on the road, or pulling into the next town. But then, in another situation, it might all come back just like it happened yesterday. You might be somewhere or see somebody, and something reminds you, and you can say, "Oh, that was in Shreveport or Monroe or Greenville or Birmingham," and so forth and so on, and you can see the streets and buildings and people and everything. But then, in another situation, all you can say is "I think I must have been there if you say so, but I'm not sure. When was that?" I'm very good at that.

At the beginning of October we started back up the East Coast from Columbus, Georgia, and by the middle of the third week we had been as far north as Rochester and swung back to Detroit, and by the first we were back in the Apollo. Actually that gave us the rest of October in New York, because the only date we played the week after we came out of the Apollo that time was three one-nighters: one in Baltimore, one in Bridgeport, and one some other little place in Connecticut.

The recording session that John set up at the end of that month was for just four sides, two ten-inch 78 RPM's for the Okeh pop trade. Helen had a nice little tune called "All or Nothing at All," and another one called "The Moon Fell in the River." Jimmy's tune was about something that was on everybody's mind that fall. It was called "Draftin' Blues." The war in Europe was now going on into the second year when we made that record. The United States was not in it yet, but defense plants were already under construction and draft boards were already calling up men for military service. You didn't know when your number would come up, and you were going to have to report to the draft board. "Draftin' Blues" was not a new tune. My research assistant just recently reminded me that Maceo Pinkard, the same one who composed "Sweet Georgia Brown," wrote that tune back during the First World War.

The title of the instrumental that Buck Clayton arranged for that date fit right in with all of that too. It was called "What's Your Number?" The most important number at that time was not somebody's telephone number or the policy number for the day. I'm not saying that those were not still important, because they are still important right now, and not many people remember those draft board numbers, but they were very important when Buck wrote that jumping piece.

November was not a very big month for us. All we did during that whole month was about a week of one-nighters in New England. But there was another recording date for Okeh. We used Don Redman's arrangement on "The Five O'Clock Whistle" on that session. Buck Clayton had written "Love Jumped Out" for us, and the third instrumental was a great tune by Henri Woode and McRae called "Broadway," which turned out to be the last number that Lester recorded with us for a couple of years.

Somebody put out a very weird tale about how Lester had to leave the band because he was absent from the record date on Friday the thirteenth. As a matter of fact, the *Defender* actually ran a story on it with a headline that was two columns wide:

LESTER YOUNG LEAVES BASIE: . . . *According to sources close to the 'Jump King of Swing,' Lester was "fired" when he allegedly refused to show up for a recording date that took place on Friday the 13th. Lester is said to have asserted that Friday the 13th was definitely no time for music.*

Basie became enraged at this bit of insubordination and immediately handed Young, who was one of the mainstays of his powerful sax section, his notice after waiting for him several hours in the recording studios.

I don't know who put that out, but it was pretty ridiculous. In all of those years that I knew Lester, I never heard anything about him being superstitious until somebody made up that story. The truth of the matter was that he wanted to go out on his own and see what he could do with a little group for a while. And I really think another thing was Herschel's death. He had really wanted to leave right after that happened, and the longer he stayed right on in that same situation, the harder it was for him to get over it. Finally he just decided to make a little change.

And there was also one other thing that made him decide to leave when he did. By the beginning of December the band wasn't really doing too well financially. We were still working, but there were a lot of miles between gigs, so we were not really making any money. The problem, as I saw it there, was the way we were being handled by MCA. With Willard Alexander gone, things were different. Milt Ebbins, Willard's replacement, was okay. It wasn't his fault, but evidently there had been some policy changes in the front office. I don't really know what was going on up there, and I don't intend to get into all of that anyway, but things did get to the point where I really wanted to get out of my contract with MCA and go over to the William Morris Agency with Willard.

That's when those newspaper rumors about breaking up the band started, and there was also some talk about Benny Goodman offering me five hundred dollars a week to join his new band as a featured sideman. I'm not going to say how those rumors got out and became newspaper stories, but they didn't do our case any harm. The Chicago *Defender* ran a headline that stretched all the way across the entertainment page:

COUNT BASIE MAY BREAK WITH MCA MANAGEMENT: *In a final effort to straighten out his difficulties with his handlers, Music Corporation of America, Count Basie will take his case before James Petrillo, national chief of all musicians' locals Friday afternoon. The pow-wow will be held at New York's local 802 headquarters on Fiftieth Street, and Petrillo will make a special trip from his offices in Chicago to be present.*

We did reach an agreement with MCA for the time being, but in the meanwhile Lester had finally split, and that was why he didn't make that next recording session, which was on Friday, December the thirteenth. So we got Paul Bascomb to sit in with us on that date, so he is on "Stampede in G Minor," and "Rocking the Blues," and that means he is also on the two vocals we made that same day. We did "It's the Same Old South" with Jimmy, and "Who Am I?" with Helen. There is a special little story about "Stampede in G Minor." It was sent to me by a guy named Clinton P. Brewer, who was serving a life sentence in the New Jersey state prison at Trenton. At that time he had already been in prison for nineteen years, and he had learned to write music just to occupy his spare time.

Paul Bascomb also made two more sessions with us in January. On the first one, we did two vocals with Helen—"It's Square but It Rocks" and "I'll Forget." Then a couple of days later we came back and cut "You Lied to Me," another vocal with her, and there were two instrumentals, "Wiggle Woogie" and Andy Gibson's "Beau Brummel." Paul Bascomb had made a big name for himself as a member of Erskine Hawkins's Orchestra, which was once the Bama State Colleagues from Alabama State Teachers' College in Montgomery. The record everybody remembers him for is "Sweet Georgia Brown," one of the top tenor-sax solos of that time.

He was with us just for those few dates, and then by the end of January Don Byas came in. Naturally there was no way that anybody could ever really replace Lester in that band because there was nobody else in the world like him. He was an original, such a stylist. So I knew I might as well just forget about that. But Don was a real great cat on tenor too, and he fell right into things and made a place for himself without copying Prez. Don was from Muskogee, Oklahoma, and over the years he had played with Big 'Un and the Blue Devils (shortly after I left). He had been in Lionel Hampton's big band out in Los Angeles and also with the bands that Eddie Barefield and Buck Clayton had out there. Then he came east with Eddie Mallory and he also worked with Don Redman, Lucky Millinder, and Andy Kirk.

The first recording session that Don made with us took place in New York just a few days after he joined, and he got a little taste of "Jump the Blues Away" and also Skip Martin's "Tuesday at Ten." Tab Smith did the arrangement of "The Jitters" for us, and that's his alto sounding like Johnny Hodges and himself. That was also the session on which we did Jimmy Mundy's arrangement of "Music Makers." The one vocal we made that day was "Undecided Blues" with Jimmy.

That January was also the month when Vic Dickenson cut out, and we replaced him with Ed Cuffee. So Ed is also on all those same records we made on Don Byas's first date. I don't think he stayed with us for more than six or seven months, but that was time enough for him to do a whole string of dates with us. We went all the way down into Florida and spent the first week in February doing one-nighters in Jacksonville, Orlando, Tampa, Winter Haven, West Palm Beach, Miami, and Fort Lauderdale; and during the rest of the month, we came back up through Georgia, South Carolina, and West Virginia, and went all the way up to Boston.

We spent the last week in February hitting places like Orange, New Jersey; White Plains; Washington; Cleveland; and Buffalo. Then in March we headed out into the Midwest again, by way of Detroit, Milwaukee, Madison, Des Moines, Lincoln, and Omaha. Then we went down through Oklahoma to Texas and Louisiana and came back through Little Rock to

St. Louis and spent the first week of April there before moving on to Chicago for the next record date.

A very special added feature of that Okeh session in Chicago was Coleman Hawkins. That's when he played that great solo on "9:20 Special." Buster Harding did the arrangement on that one, and Hawk had a ball with us, and it turned out to be a good deal on both sides. A lot of people still get a big kick out of that record. The other tune he did with us that day was called "Feedin' the Bean." That was a head that we got up right there in the studio, and the name tells you just about what was happening. Bean was Hawk's other nickname, and I had the band feeding him like you feed the soloist riffs in a jam session.

That was also the same day that we made another one of Jimmy Rushing's all-time big popular hits, "Goin' to Chicago Blues." Everybody liked that one from the very first. Everywhere we went, as soon as we hit the intro you could hear that response out there, and then when Jimmy opened his mouth people were ready to start screaming and shouting. That's the way it was for the rest of Jimmy's life. And years later when we started doing it with Joe Williams, we got the same response. And to this day, every time we bring Joe Williams on as a guest star and we begin that number, there it is again.

Jimmy Mundy also had an instrumental called "I Do Mean You" on that session, and the other instrumental was arranged by Buck Clayton. It was called "H and J." That's Don Byas on the tenor solo and Tab on alto with Sweets's trumpet solo in between. The *H* and *J* initials in the title stand for Harry "Sweets" Edison and Jo Jones because they were the ones who came up with the tune and got Buck to do the arrangement on it.

That was the spring when Helen decided that all of those bus trips were getting to be too hard on her health, so she gave notice and cut out. I sure did hate to see her go, and so did everybody else, and for the record, that goes for Jimmy Rushing too, because in spite of gossip to the contrary, the two of them always got along just fine.

Meanwhile, back in January, we had also changed booking agencies. Willard Alexander helped us to work out a deal that could buy my contract from MCA. So we had shifted over to the William Morris Agency, where he was, and right away things had begun to pick up for us again. Our asking price improved, and so did our take-home pay. By the way, when we made the shift, Milt Ebbins came along to the Morris Agency with the same duties he had at MCA. He was the agency's road representative. Maceo Birch was still my personal road manager.

Shortly after Earl Warren came into the band back during our first year in the East, we had recorded him doing the vocal for a pop ballad called "Let Me Dream." So he was our third singer as well as our lead alto, who could double on baritone. He was a ballad singer. He was not a blues singer, and he didn't do jump tunes and novelties and things like that, but he was a first-rate pop-ballad singer, and we used him on a lot of live dates all along. But we didn't get around to recording him again until that Okeh session in the third week in May when we did "You Betcha My Life." Kenny Clarke sat in on drums for Jo Jones on that number and also on "Down, Down, Down," another one of those great instrumentals that Don Redman did for us. This is the same Kenny Clarke who became one of the top drummers during the so-called bebop period several years later.

We also recorded one of Jimmy Mundy's best-known arrangements on that date. It was called "Tune Town Shuffle," and it was named for the Tune Town ballroom outside St. Louis. That's Buddy Tate on the tenor solo and Tab Smith on alto, and Jo Jones back on drums.

Before our next recording session we had to bring two replacements into the trombone section. We got Robert Scott to replace Dicky Wells for a while, and when Dan Minor, who had been with us ever since Kansas City, decided to go out and try something else, we filled his chair with Eli Robinson. Since Dan and I had also been together in the Blue Devils and in the Bennie Moten band, I knew good and well that I was going to miss him very much. But Eli was a great replacement. He had played with such wonderful outfits as Speed Webb, Zack Whyte, McKinney's Cotton Pickers, Teddy Hill, and Lucky Millinder.

That session was held right at the beginning of July, and we just made four sides. One was a little novelty for Jimmy called "One-Two-Three O'Lairy," and the other side of that one was "Basie Boogie," which became a pretty big request number. Then we made another record with Earl Warren called "Fancy Meeting You." The other instrumental was called "Diggin' for Dex." It was arranged by my old buddy, Eddie Durham, and we named it for Dave Dexter, a reporter friend of ours from Kansas City. Buddy Tate and Don Byas got a taste of that one, and Jo Jones breaks it up.

That was the July that we went back into the Ritz Carlton up in Boston again, and part of the deal was that we were on the air coast to coast over NBC six nights a week. Hazel Scott was on up there with us that time, and she was just a sensational hit. They were really crazy about her up there and, I guess, you could say that the band didn't do too bad up there that time, either. According to the newspaper stories, we broke attendance records at the Ritz Carlton, and all during the time we were up there, I was being invited to make personal appearances all around town, and I don't know how many radio interviews I did.

There was also a "Count Basie Record Week" that was supposed to have been celebrated by our fans all over New England, and the jukebox operators and record wholesale people in Boston and a few other nearby places got together and gave me a big party at the Columbia record plant in Boston. The records that we made were going very well on the jukeboxes and also over the counters during that summer, and they were "I

Want a Little Girl," "9:20 Special," "Tune Town Shuffle," "Music Makers," and "Down, Down, Down."

That means that I also had to visit quite a few music stores during that particular week, and there was a big turnout just about everywhere I went. When I went to Sandler's Music Shop in Gloucester, Massachusetts, I was told that over 2,000 people were in the crowd, and the police had to be called out to control them, and when we finally pulled out, the manager or somebody told me that they had sold over 950 records that one afternoon.

Another choice gig we played right after the Ritz Carlton was the Surf Beach Club down at Virginia Beach. Then we swung out west again, and when we came back to New York near the end of September, we made two more instrumentals coupled with vocals. The first instrumental was Jimmy Mundy's "Fiesta in Blue," which he had written as a special trumpet show-case featuring Cootie Williams with Benny Goodman's band. Cootie had left Duke after quite a few years and joined Benny's new band back in November, and Benny had recorded Cootie's version in February. When Jimmy brought it to us, he and I decided that Buck Clayton was the one to do it, and I think we made the right choice; in fact, I'm pretty sure we did.

The vocal side of that record was an old standard called "My Old Flame." Jimmy Mundy did the arrangement on that one too, and the singer was not really our replacement for Helen Humes. Her name was Lynne Sherman, and she was the new bride of our co-manager, Milt Ebbins. And just in case that causes anybody to get any smart ideas about us doing that just as a novelty wedding present or something like that, I'd like to add that Lynne was a pro in her own right. She had sung with Benny Goodman's band before she even met Milt.

The other instrumental on that session was a little jump tune called "Tom Thumb," and the vocal side of that one was old Rush doing "Take Me Back, Baby," which turned out to be another one of his overnight hits, right up there along with "I Left My Baby," "Going to Chicago," and "I Want a Little Girl."

The big thing for us in New York at the beginning of the fall season that year was our gig at Café Society Uptown on East Fifty-eighth Street, over between Park Avenue and Lexington Avenue, not far from Bloomingdale's department store. It was our first club date in New York since the Famous Door.

There was also a Café Society Downtown, which was all the way down in Greenwich Village in Sheridan Square. That was the original Café Society which had opened right after John Hammond's first "Spirituals to Swing" concert at Carnegie Hall. As a matter of fact it was through John Hammond and that concert that Barney Josephson, the owner and manager of Café Society, hired Pete Johnson, Meade Lux Lewis, and Albert Ammons, three of the top boogie-woogie piano players in the country,

and right away that made Café Society the New York headquarters for
boogie-woogie. It was also the headquarters for Hazel Scott, and also for
Teddy Wilson and his combos; Billie Holiday was a hit in there, and so
was Lena Horne.

The club itself was so successful that after about a year or so Barney
opened up another one and called it Café Society Uptown, and when we
went in there that September, it was leaping! John Hammond still remembers that as one of the best club dates we ever played. The house musician
while we were there was Teddy Wilson, and for the dinner show we used
Buck Clayton, Buddy Tate, and Dicky Wells, plus the rhythm section, and
kept it soft and swinging.

Then for our main show set, we had the whole band stomping and
shouting, with Jimmy Rushing doing his thing on the blues and Earl
Warren getting to be a bigger and bigger feature as a pop singer. There
were also two CBS Radio broadcasts out of there every week. So the actual
sound of that band in live performance can be heard on a couple of records
that were made years later from air checks between September and November. There is a two-volume set put out by a collector's-item outfit called
Jazz Unlimited.

Both volumes have fourteen numbers. In volume one there is the band
doing "Tuesday at Ten," "Yes Indeed," "Tom Thumb," "9:20 Special,"
"Broadway," "Sweet Georgia Brown," "H and J," "Diggin' for Dex," and
"Swinging the Blues"; Jimmy singing "There'll Be Some Changes Made,"
"Take Me Back, Baby," "Going to Chicago," and "Baby, Don't Tell On
Me"; and Earl Warren singing "I Guess I'll Have to Dream the Rest."
"There'll Be Some Changes Made," "Tom Thumb," and "Diggin' for
Dex" are on volume two, but they were taken from different broadcasts.
The other vocals are Jimmy singing "My Melancholy Baby" and "I Want
a Little Girl." The other instrumentals are "Love Jumped Out," "Tune
Town Shuffle," "Every Tub," "Rocking the Blues," "Something New,"
"Topsy," "I Do Mean You," "Down, Down, Down," and one other tune.

It was also during that fall while we were playing at Café Society Uptown that John Hammond set up a studio date for Paul Robeson to record
with us. John and Paul were old friends, and John also knew Joe Louis
and Richard Wright, who had written a big, important book called *Native
Son* the year before that. I understand that all three of these cats used to
go into Café Society Downtown a lot. So John got the idea of doing a
record dedicated to Joe, with lyrics by Richard Wright for a twelve-bar
blues tune played by us and the vocal done by Paul Robeson. That's how
we came to make *King Joe, Part One and Part Two*. I think Jimmy Mundy
did the arrangement on it.

Just the idea of doing something with Paul Robeson was one of the
great thrills of my life. I was crazy about that guy. He was a great man.

He stood for something, and I mean if he was all for something, he would take a stand on it, even if it cost him jobs or even his whole career.

And he had a hell of a voice, one of the greatest you ever heard. But the strange thing was that he never had sung the blues. So John had Jimmy coaching him, and they got along fine, and when the time came for the takes, John had Jimmy standing right in front of Paul conducting and prompting him.

King Joe I & II was released on two sides of the regular ten-inch, 78-RPM record. The other record we made on that session had an instrumental by Jimmy Mundy called "Something New" on one side and "Moon Nocturne," a pop vocal by Earl Warren, on the other.

We did two more sessions in November. During the first week we recorded Earl singing "I Struck a Match in the Dark." That was one of our new production novelties featuring Earl. Originally it was supposed to begin with the stage all blacked out, and Earl was supposed to strike a match and that was the cue for the downbeat, but on the night we were supposed to premiere it, Jo Jones slipped a book of wet matches into Earl's pocket just as he went onstage, and when Earl got out there, nothing happened until I realized that somebody had pulled a prank on us. Of course, nobody took credit for it at the time. The instrumental on that release was "Platterbrains," another one of Tab Smith's arrangements. The other vocal was "All of Me," which was arranged by Jimmy Mundy for Lynne Sherman.

Our next session was in the middle of the month, and that was our last for that year. We did three instrumentals and two vocals. The first vocal was Lynn Sherman singing "More Than You Know." The other one is one more of old Rush's big hits of that time. It was called "Harvard Blues" and the lyrics were written by George Frazier, a Harvard graduate who wrote articles about jazz and was one of our biggest fans from Boston. The music was a straight twelve-bar blues arranged by Tab Smith. Don Byas gave us a very nice twenty-four-bar chorus on one, and "Harvard Blues" is the main record a whole lot of people remember as soon as you mention that Don Byas was in our band at one time. The rambunctious trombone in there behind Rush's vocal is Mr. Dicky Wells.

The three instrumentals were "Feather Merchant," "Coming Out Party," and "Down for Double." I did some dictating on the first two, and Jimmy Mundy did the charts. Sweets is the get-off trumpet on "Feather Merchant," and there is quite a bit of space for the piano. I don't remember who named that one. We were talking about it not long ago, and somebody mentioned the Feather Merchants in the "Snuffy Smith" comic strip.

"Down for Double" was Freddie Greene's tune, which Buck Clayton did the arrangement on. Dicky Wells had the trombone solo, and Buddy Tate took care of the tenor business, with Jo Jones getting in a nice little thing on the drum break, very snappy, really popping. "Down for double" means doubling the bet when you're gambling, which was something that went on quite often wherever we were. Somebody always had a little game going, cards or those little galloping dominoes.

George Frazier was one of our best-known fans from up in the Boston area, but another one of our biggest followers while we were at the Ritz Carlton that summer was a fine young lady named Sally Sears. She was very young, but she was pretty hip, and she really dug the band. She used to have her parents bring her to the roof garden on a regular basis all during the time we were up there that summer. So we got to be pretty good friends, and she talked me into promising to have the band come back up to Boston to play for her debut ball that was being planned for the fall. That is why we came up with the number called "Coming Out Party," which was the other instrumental on that mid-November session for Okeh. Jimmy Mundy did the arrangement, and we set it in a medium tempo in keeping with the occasion, but we also gave them a good solid beat to hop to.

—

When we came out of Café Society after six great weeks, we played the Strand down on Broadway before hitting the trail out into the Midwest again. I don't remember all of the places we hit on that string of one-nighters, but I do know that we went out west as far as Wichita because that was where I was on December 7. Somebody woke me up that Sunday morning because the news on the radio was about Pearl Harbor. So that's where I heard FDR making his speech declaring war on Japan.

Up to that time, the war was something you knew about from the headlines in the daily newspapers and the nightly radio broadcasts, and it was also the main feature of the newsreels in the movie houses. But it was still happening overseas in Europe and those places; and American soldiers were not really a part of it yet. The United States had been calling people into the service for training for a couple of years, and everybody figured it was just a matter of time before we would have to send troops in with the Allies. But all that changed with Pearl Harbor. From then on, everything was very close to home, and getting closer every day. Uncle Sam started building more and more bases and training camps and manufacturing more and more weapons and ammunition; and, of course, the main thing for us was that those draft numbers started coming up faster and faster.

That was a pretty big concern for most of the fellows because quite a few were classified as I-A. My main concern was training and going on those maneuvers. Somebody kept trying to tell me everything was going to be all right because I'd most likely be brought in as a musician and wouldn't have to do any fighting. But I told them I wasn't going anywhere. I said I ain't going to take all that training and stuff. I ain't going out on them maneuvers jumping in foxholes with them goddamn snakes and things out there in them swamps. I said I wouldn't, and I meant that. There was nothing they could do to me that was going to be worse than what them snakes were going to make me do to myself.

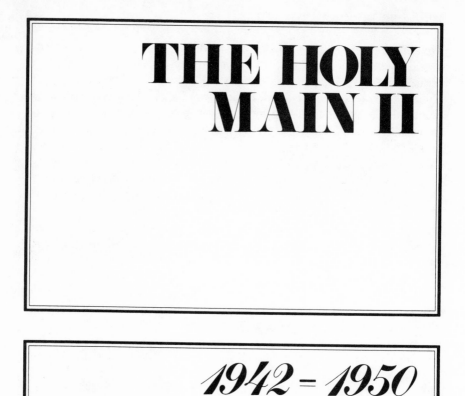

THE HOLY MAIN II

1942 = 1950

On the second Friday in January we went back into the Apollo, and during the week after that we recorded four more numbers for Okeh. That's when we did "One O'Clock Jump" with tenor spots for Buddy Tate and Don Byas, and a trombone solo by Dicky. Actually, that was a head arrangement, like the ones you make up on the spot when you have to answer a request. Somebody came up with that ride-out riff, like the one Bean used later on in one of his tunes called "Stuffy."

We also did a pop ballad for Earl Warren on that date. It was called "Blue Shadows and White Gardenias." Then we did a little novelty jump tune called " 'Ay Now."

At the end of January, the Pittsburgh *Courier* announced that we had won their poll as the best popular swing band in the land for the second year in a row. That kind of publicity was always good for business, and I must say our outlook for the year was not bad. There was even talk about us getting some spots in a few movies. I don't remember the details anymore. The newspapers had started printing rumors about a deal with Columbia Pictures, but there was nothing definite in that line for us yet. Meanwhile most of our dates during the first half of that year were in the East and the Midwest.

Our first big thing out in Chicago was around the beginning of March.

That's when we went into the Oriental Theatre in the downtown Loop district. With a big stage show doing four shows a day during the week and six on Sunday. There were some real headliners on that bill. Whitey's jitterbug group from the Savoy was out there, and so was Baby Lawrence, one of the great tap dancers. And then there were the dance teams of Apus and Estrelita, and also Rogers and Gordon vocals by Jimmie Rushing and Earl Warren. By the way, it was while we were in Chicago on that date that Maceo Birch rejoined us as co–road manager with Milt Ebbins.

Then we went into the Palace Theatre in Cleveland with Ethel Waters. Gordon and Rogers were also on that show, and on opening day the lines outside the box office started forming early in the morning, and in no time at all they had to put up the "Standing Room Only" sign. It was a great week. We had a lot of fans out there, and so did Ethel Waters, and of course, she was a showstopper. Everybody expected that, and that's what they got.

I was very happy about working with Ethel Waters. She was one of the great artists that I'd been crazy about for many years. It was a great pleasure for me just to be on the same bill with such a great star. I mean, that was something. That really gave me a great thrill.

After that week at the Palace in Cleveland, we went up to the Paradise Theatre in Detroit for another week, and then we came right back down to Chicago and went into the Regal for a week. It was around this time that Tab Smith left the band, and it was also while we were back in Chicago that April that we recorded "Basie Blues" and "I'm Gonna Move to the Outskirts of Town." Louis Jordan and the Tympany Five had the big hit on that one, but Jimmy Rushing gave us a good one on it, too. Somebody decided to call that instrumental "Basie Blues" because it was mostly just piano and some shouting brass choruses. I never did put my name on the title of any numbers. Somebody else named "Rock-a-Bye Basie" and "Basie Boogie," and I went along with the idea because it was good promotion for the band.

Our next stop after Chicago was Milwaukee. Apus and Estrelita and Baby Lawrence were on that show with us also, and according to the newspapers, we drew the biggest crowds in the town since Benny Goodman's big sellout up there two years before. That was supposed to be quite a trick, because we had played SRO in Chicago on two different one-week stands within the same month, and Milwaukee wasn't really that far away. I mean, it was no big deal for people from Milwaukee to catch shows in Chicago, but it turned out that they were waiting for us up there too, and a lot of our fans from Chicago came on up to Milwaukee to catch us again.

Our big event at the Savoy Ballroom that year was the battle of music we played with Lionel Hampton during the second week in May. Hamp had a hell of a band. He had started it a couple of years before that, after being a top-featured guest star in Benny Goodman's band for about four years, and it was one of the hottest outfits around, and as you would expect, knowing Hamp, it was also a great band for showmanship. This was another one of those Sunday-night contests, and according to the newspaper reports, there were nearly seven thousand people on hand for it.

Hamp had guys like Illinois Jacquet, Jack McVea, Dexter Gordon, Joe Newman, Ernie Royal, Milt Buckner, and Irving Ashby in that band, and they were out to get us. They never did let up. Of course, we were ready, too. Buck, Al Killian, Dicky, Don Byas, and Jo, and all those cats were just raring to go, too. They didn't even leave the bandstand between sets, except maybe for a few hot minutes to get a little taste and make a quick visit to the little boys' room. Otherwise they just stayed up there digging Hamp and his cats so we would know what to put on them during our next set.

The big number they dropped on us that night was "Flying Home." They got going on that thing just before our last set and kept on going on and on forever. Somebody said it was fifteen minutes, but it seemed like about an hour to me. When they recorded it a couple of weeks later, it was a hit as soon as it came out, and it was one of Hamp's biggest numbers, and it is still one of the great standards of jazz. It was also the record that made Illinois Jacquet famous. Everybody remembers his solo on that record, and a lot of people can still hum it note for note.

That was a pretty tough set to follow, so we decided to change the pace a little bit and swing in another groove for a while and then build up and go out popping. So we did, and I guess we must have done all right, because we didn't get run out of there. Of course, we had our fans and they stuck with us, and we were not about to let them down either. So when it was all over, the decision was that it was a draw, and we got the edge for musicianship, and Hamp had it for showmanship.

Toward the end of July that same year, we went back out to Los Angeles, and according to the newspaper reports, we "started out by erasing Glenn Miller's all-time attendance record at the Orpheum Theatre." We were also lined up for an appearance in a big movie musical starring Ann Miller, and we had two recording sessions in Columbia's Hollywood studio.

On the first one we cut "How Long Blues," "Farewell Blues," "Café Society Blues," and "Way Back Blues," using just the rhythm section. Then on "Royal Garden Blues," "Bugle Blues," "Sugar Blues," and "St. Louis Blues" we added Buck Clayton on trumpet and Don Byas on tenor. That was a kind of follow-up of something we did for Decca, when we made ten blues with the rhythm section not long after, we came out of the Famous Door several years earlier when we did "How Long Blues," "The Dirty Dozens," "Hey Lawdy Mama," "The Fives," 'Oh Red," and all of those things.

Our second session a few days later was a full band date, and we made three vocals with Jimmy Rushing and two with Earl Warren; and we also made two instrumentals. One of Jimmy's numbers was a remake of "For the Good of Your Country," which was released in place of the one that had been rejected back in January. Columbia also chose it over another wartime tune called "Lose the Blackout Blues," which we made that same day. But Jimmie's most successful number that day turned out to be "Rusty Dusty Blues," which was another one of those good ones that was already on the jukeboxes everywhere because Louis Jordan had made it a very big hit the year before. It was written by Mayo Williams, and it was just the kind of tune that people wanted to hear Jimmie do. Buster Harding did the arrangement on it for us.

Earl's first tune on that session was "Ride On," which was a little like a sermon, with the band doubling as a choir answering "ride on" in the background, and also with some nice little trumpet and tenor-sax comments in there by Buck and Don Byas. Earl's other number was a beautiful pop tune by Vincent Youmans called "Time on My Hands." The arrangement on that one was by Hugo Winterhalter.

The first instrumental was called "It's Sand, Man," which Ed Lewis brought in and Buck did the arrangement on. Don Byas has the tenor spot, and Mr. Dicky has the bones. The piano player is anybody's guess. The title is taken from a dance step that was in style at that time called the sanding and doing the sand. It was a light shuffle step that probably started with a dance act. It was a shuffle from side to side like spreading sand on the dance floor with your feet. In the jive language of that time, if you accused somebody of sanding you, it meant he was bowing and scraping around like a servant hyping the boss man. If you said somebody was a sandman, that meant that he was an Uncle Tom. But you could also do a little sanding to get next to a chick, especially if you were trying to get back in with her after having messed up.

The other instrumental was "Ain't It the Truth." I dictated that one, and Buster Harding did the arrangement on it. Sweets has the trumpet solo. I think it turned out pretty good, and it became a part of the book, and we kept it in there for quite a while. It was still one of our features when Lester came back to the band a year or so later. The title is another one of those old jive sayings like "tell me more," "honey hush," "well, all right," and so forth and so on.

Another thing about "Ain't It the Truth" is that it was the last instrumental we made for regular commercial distribution before the American Federation of Musicians recording ban that stayed in effect for a couple of years. The only recordings we made during that time were the V-disc transcriptions we made as a contribution to the war effort. The V stood for "victory," and those sides were made to be played over the Armed Forces radio and in service clubs as part of the troop-morale program. A lot of entertainers were asked to do those transcriptions.

One of the funniest things that I remember happening while I was in Los Angeles that time happened at a party at Hattie McDaniel's place. Hattie was a very big name in the movies at that time. A couple or three years before that, she had played in *Gone With the Wind*, and that had put her way up there. Anyway, she had just recently bought a mansion out on South Harvard Boulevard, and that's where the party was, and the Chicago *Defender* wrote it up with a big headline that ran all the way across the top of the entertainment page: "COUNT BASIE FETED ON COAST: Hattie McDaniel Is Hostess to Famed Band."

It was a hell of a party, and most of the show people in town must have been on hand, and also quite a few others. Ethel Waters, Clarence Muse, Lena Horne, Hall Johnson, Dorothy Dandridge, Cab Calloway, Les Hite, Timmy Rogers, Sunshine Sammy, and I don't know how many others, and also a whole bunch of local friends and some from out of town too. Naturally my good old buddy Stuff Crouch was there. So I really had myself a ball that night. But to tell the truth, I actually didn't realize that the party was supposed to be for me.

But that wasn't the funniest thing I remember about that party, because I just went on over there and had a great time because it was such a fabulous affair. The funny part was one cat that I just happened to notice. Right away you could tell that he was the kind of character that always manages to finagle himself in on something. I don't know what it was, but there was something about him that caught my eye, and old Sweets or somebody was with me, and I said, "Watch this cat!" So we kept an eye on him while he was circling around through the crowd, and then he finally made his way on over to the side of the room where the buffet spread was. We saw him pick up his plate and start working his way along the table. That was some real fancy spread, with all kinds of hors d'oeuvre and entrées and desserts and salads and fruits and cheese and all kinds of tidbits, and the table decorations alone were just fantastic.

We watched that cat moving along helping his plate, and then near the end of the table one of the decorations was a big crystal bowl with gardenias floating in it, and when he came to that part of the table, he reached over all cool and dignified and served himself a couple of those gardenias and put some salad dressing on them and moved on back into the crowd with his plate and a mouthful of gardenia. I couldn't believe it, but it's the truth.

Sweets and I almost died laughing. I can still see that cat putting that salad dressing on those gardenias. He found his way out of there, but he swallowed a mouthful of gardenia before he could get somewhere to get rid of it. Then later on, when he came back in, we walked up behind him, and old Sweets, or whoever it was, said, "Hey, how was that salad you ate there, buddy?"

＝

It was also during the late summer of that year that Catherine Morgan and I finally decided to get married—or, to let her tell it, I finally talked her into it. We had been seeing quite a lot of each other all during those three years since our first real date out in Detroit, the night that Billy and Milly "introduced" us at the Greystone Ballroom. Sometimes when the band had to be out of town for a long time and she was between jobs, she'd come out for a little visit, especially when we stopped somewhere like Chicago or Los Angeles, or someplace like that on a theater date.

Naturally she had her own career as a dancer and singer; and that is one reason it took her so long to make up her mind to tie the knot. I could appreciate that, but at the same time I also knew how rough it was out there trying to make it as an entertainer all by yourself, especially if you're a woman. But frankly I just wanted her to give it all up and be my wife. That was the way I felt when I first saw her way back when I was with Bennie Moten and she was just a little sixteen-year-old girl with the Whitman Sisters.

I just wanted her to settle down and make a home so we could have a family. That was what I always had in mind. It never was my idea just to hang out with her. Along with all of the jive I was always trying to talk to her, I was always trying to get her to marry me. So when she finally said okay, we got married that August. There was no big ceremony or anything like that. We just found a justice of the peace in Seattle and made it official on my birthday, and we spent our honeymoon on the road with the band doing another string of those one-nighters.

＝

When we went back out to the Coast that September, we had a little spot in a movie called *Reveille With Beverly*, a musical starring a tap dancer named Ann Miller. I remember that we used to have to get up very early to get out to the studio from the west side of Los Angeles back in those days, but I don't actually remember what we did. I don't even know whether I saw that picture when it came out. If I did, I don't remember it.

I don't remember very much about working out at the studio, only that Freddie Green went out there and got locked up. I think that was when we were working on *Reveille With Beverly*. Whenever it was, we went out on intermission or something, and he didn't have his draft card and couldn't get back in. Green likes to shop. When we are traveling, every time the bus stops somewhere for a while, he gets off and goes shopping. He likes to walk and shop. Any two minutes he gets, boom, he's gone.

But this time they caught him. When we came back on the set, nobody knew where the hell he was. He was out somewhere in the street looking in windows, walking. They checked him and he didn't have his card, so they picked him up and took him to jail, and when he didn't make it back in time to do the scene, Snodgrass had to sit in and fake it on the guitar. Freddie got out later on, but for a while we didn't know what happened to him.

It was also while we were out in Hollywood that time for our spot on *Reville With Beverly* that we did our first "Command Performance" radio broadcast for the armed services. According to *Metronome*, it went out to Allied troops in thirty-two countries. A lot of top-ranking stars went on those shortwave broadcasts. The ones on the program with us were Clark Gable, Bette Davis, Dinah Shore, Carmen Miranda, and Jerry Colonna.

That's when I met Clark Gable in person. I never will forget that, because he was my man. I was passing his dressing room and the door was partly open, and I saw him sitting in there reading something. I don't know whether it was a script or not, but he was just sitting in there by himself, and I just knocked and pushed the door all the way open. I guess I was really out of order busting in like that, but I couldn't help it. I just had to say something to him.

So I told him who I was and said, "This is really a pleasure for me. I hope you don't mind if I say hello."

"Of course not," he said. "I know who you are. I know all about you, Count."

A lot of movie stars like to try to keep their screen personalities when you meet them, so they are really not quite as open and natural as other people. But there are some that you might have thought would be a little stiff who are not, and Clark was one of them. He just looked up from whatever it was he was reading and turned around and crossed his legs and we talked for a few minutes, and later on out in the studio somebody got him to have his picture taken with me. That was a real gas for me.

Bette Davis was also very natural and very nice. She saw me sitting at the piano while we were getting ready to tune up, and she just came out of the booth and came right on over and introduced herself and sat on the bench beside me and started talking. That's how the photographers happened to get a picture of her with me. She was not asked to pose or anything like that; she just came on over and sat down beside me for a little while to tell me how much she liked the band.

And of course, Dinah Shore was very nice. She became a very good friend of the band. Whenever she was near somewhere we were playing, she'd come by, even if it was just a matter of popping in for a few minutes to catch a couple of numbers. I remember later on when we were playing at some little lounge next to the Chicago Theatre, where she was working for a week. She used to pop in and check us out and wave good-bye on her way home every night. Then, years after that, when she had her big TV program for Chevrolet, she wanted to do a show with us, and somebody else on the staff had another band in mind, and she wouldn't hear it.

"No, I want Basie."

I've never forgotten that either.

—

In November of that same year, we were headlined on a big variety show with Hattie Noels at the Orpheum Theatre in Los Angeles. The newspapers called that show another record-breaker, and it was a gas because Hattie Noles was something else. She was even better than she was when she was belting out those blues back when she was working at the Reno in Kansas City. And of course, there was our Jimmie, and we still had Earl on pretty ballads, and another headliner on that show was a great dancer and entertainer named Bill Bailey. Bill was very well known at that time, and his sister Pearl is still a headline singer and entertainer.

At the end of that December, we were back in New York again because we were booked into the Apollo for the Christmas show. The Apollo advertised us as its Christmas gift to New York theatergoers, and it was. We had some of the acts that had worked with us in the Midwest and out on the Coast. Bill Bailey, for instance, and also the great comic dance team of Apus and Estrelita. And of course, we had Jimmy Rushing, and I don't remember whether we used any of Earl Warren's vocals on that show or not. But we did use Thelma Carpenter as the featured female singer. I don't actually remember all of the little details about how we brought Thelma in, but I do know that she was recommended to me by Coleman Hawkins.

Pigmeat Markham was also on that big Christmas show, and so was Baskette. The Apollo was really like home base for those two cats. They always had them laying in the aisles in there. There was no other comedian that was a bigger favorite in Harlem than Pigmeat in those days. There were quite a few other big name comedians on the radio and in the movies, but when it came to live stage shows, Pigmeat was up there. When Pigmeat came on, the house belonged to him and his act.

Another feature on that program was an acrobatic team known as the Zoppys, and of course, there were the other regular Apollo production numbers with the chorus girls that were always just so great.

During the first month or so of that next year, we got a chance to spend some time back in New York playing local gigs and going out on nearby one-nighters and a few theater dates. Then, near the end of February, we played for the NAACP birthday dance at the Golden Gate Ballroom, and in March we went back out to Chicago for a week at the Regal and another week in Milwaukee. We also played Philadelphia and Boston in April, and in May we went back out to the Coast.

Our gig in Chicago that time was at the White City Ballroom at Forty-seventh Street and South Parkway, and from there we went down to St. Louis for another dance engagement. Then, after a stopover in Kansas City, we went on out to Los Angeles and Hollywood and stayed out there until October.

Catherine went along on that trip, and we lived over at my good friend Stuff Crouch's place. I don't mean we lived in his main house. Like a lot of people in Los Angeles, Stuff had a sort of small guest house in his backyard. It had a furnished sitting room, bedroom, bath, cooking facilities, and everything, and it was really a very convenient setup for light housekeeping. It was just what Catherine and I needed, because by that time we were expecting our first child.

The band worked on three movies for Universal Pictures while we were out there that time. There was a musical short called *Choo Choo Swing* that also had a great singing group known as the Delta Rhythm Boys in it. We did "Swinging the Blues," and Jimmy Rushing sang "Sent For You Yesterday." I don't actually remember what the Delta Rhythm Boys did on the short, because I haven't seen it for years. But they were also in another movie that we worked on while we were in Hollywood that time. That was one of those eighty-minute jobs called *Crazy House*. I don't remember very much about that one either, other than that it had Olsen and Johnson, those two crazy comedians, in it.

The other picture for Universal was *Top Man*. That was another full-length musical, and it starred Donald O'Connor. I've been told that we did "Basie Boogie" in a scene that takes place on a college campus, but if I ever saw that picture, it was so long ago that I've forgotten what the story was about. I will say that I remember that "Basie Boogie," as we called it then, was one of the numbers we were playing quite often those days.

I guess it must have been while we were out in Hollywood that time that we also did our little spot on *Hit Parade of 1943*. That was a Republic picture, and it also had a very beautiful singer and dancer in it named Dorothy Dandridge. Freddie Martin and his orchestra were also in that one, but that didn't have anything to do with what we did. My chief research assistant tells me that the cast included Susan Hayward, John Carroll, Eve Arden, or Gail Patrick, but I'm pretty sure we didn't spend much time around them because we were just on one scene or sequence. I think Dot Dandridge was playing the role of the singer with our band. There is a still shot of her singing and dancing on top of my piano, with the band mounted on a very fancy stand that can be raised or lowered.

Big 'Un was out there on the Coast with us for most of those movie spots, but by the end of the summer he had to cut out, and we didn't really know how long he was going to have to be away, so at first we had Vernon Alley in there for a while, and then the one we settled on was Rodney Richardson. Rodney was a very fine young fellow, and he did a wonderful job for us for what turned out to be almost four years, which was right on through the war. Naturally we were not very happy about losing Big 'Un, but he needed some rest after all that time knocking around with us, and there were also a few personal things he had to take care of. We didn't have any idea that he would be away as long as he was. But that's the way it went, and then he came back for three more years.

Sometime not long after we got our new bass player that September when we lost Big 'Un that first time, we picked up a new lead alto player named Preston Love to fill in for Earl Warren for a couple of months, and we spent the next six weeks doing about a month of theater dates and about another two weeks of one-nighters, and arrived back in New York near the middle of October.

That's when Earl came back off leave, and it was also when Don Byas cut out, and Lester came back and took over his old chair again. I don't remember why Don cut out at that time, and I've also forgotten how we happened to get back in touch with Lester, but according to Jo Jones, Lester was working with a combo somewhere on Fifty-second Street, and Jo went down there and found him and told him it was time to come back. I don't actually remember that, but it could have happened like that. Of course, the other tenor was Tate. Earl was back, and the other alto was Jimmy Powell. And Jack Washington was on baritone, and the only change in the rhythm was Rodney Richardson on bass.

—

Our big new thing in New York that year was the wonderful engagement we had at the Blue Room in the Lincoln Hotel, which turned out to be one of our three top midtown Manhattan showcases during the rest of the war years. The others were the Roxy Theatre and the Aquarium. Each time we went into those spots, it was for four weeks or more with an option to extend. I really don't know how we got into the Blue Room. The owner of the Lincoln Hotel was Miss Maria Cramer, and the band manager in there at that time was Jack Carney, but I understand that she was really the one that wanted us in there. I don't know where she had heard the band; I think she must have heard us at the Famous Door, but I hadn't met her before we went into the Blue Room.

The first time I actually met her was one night while I was trying to get myself a scotch and milk. It was either at a rehearsal just before we opened or during an intermission on the first night, and I was looking for a little nip of scotch and milk, and somebody introduced me to Miss Cramer, and she was just a wonderful lady.

We became very good friends, and she always spoke very well of the band; she also thought an awful lot of Thelma Carpenter. Whenever she would get a little flak about having us in that kind of room, she would say, "I'm sorry, but I want the Count in there. I'm very pleased with the Count."

She was just such a lovely lady. I will always remember how she used to come by backstage every night during one of our intermissions. I would look up, and there she was.

"Well, are you going to take a little walk and have a little nip?"

"I'm with you, boss lady."

"No. I'm with you, pal."

The little walk was really just in the little space right back there between two doors behind the bandstand. But she would come by there every night, and we would have our little nip together, and we'd talk for about five minutes or so. Every night. She just made everything so pleasant for us. No matter what anybody else tried to do, she made things pleasant. And she was the boss. I never will forget her.

—

When we came out of the Blue Room in January, our next big thing was in the Roxy Theatre at Fiftieth Street and Seventh Avenue beginning the following week. We were booked in there for four weeks, so that is where we were working when my daughter Diane was born in Cleveland on the sixth of February that year. Catherine had stopped off in Cleveland on our way back east from California in the fall, because she wanted to be at home with her parents when her time came. (Old Base stumbled out there for a hot minute somehow and made it back without missing too many shows, but I don't really remember anything about that trip because I was in a daze all the time.)

I guess we must have done all right in the Roxy because even before those first four weeks were over, arrangements had already been made to have us come back in there the next year and also the year after that. Of course, with the war going on and the draft boards grabbing musicians right and left along with everybody else, you never knew what to expect next, but in the meantime you had to feel pretty good about some of the good gigs that were coming our way.

Naturally you didn't have the freedom to stretch out when you were playing a stage show in a big midtown movie house like the Roxy and Loew's State and such places. All you had time for was about a half-dozen numbers, which was definitely not enough for our regular fans. But we played instrumentals like "Swing Shift" and "Basie Boogie," and Thelma sang Duke's "Do Nothing Till You Hear From Me," and Earl sang "I Couldn't Sleep a Wink Last Night," and Jimmy sang some blues.

Then Jo Jones did one of his features. And that band was as much together as it was in the Blue Room.

The draft had hit us again by that time, however. Our next loss to
Uncle Sam had been Jack Washington. Jack went into the Blue Room
with us, but I don't think he made it to the Roxy. The truth is, I don't
actually remember Jack leaving, but I do know damn well that his replacement on baritone and alto was Rudy Rutherford, who was also a hell
of a clarinet player. Rudy really had that sound on clarinet. That's him
on the V-disc take of "Kansas City Stride" and also most of the other
clarinet solos for the next year or so.

We were still playing in the Roxy when Catherine arrived back in New
York with Diane. I can still see Catherine coming off the plane wearing a
very fancy hat and carrying our child. I never will forget what a special
thrill it was for me to be bringing my family home from the airport that
day. Old Base and his wife and daughter.

That was when we moved into the Mayor La Guardia apartment building at 1274 Fifth Avenue, just south of 110th Street and right across from
Central Park. Earl Warren and his wife, Clara, were living in that same
building at that time, and they became Diane's godparents.

By the way, the minister who baptized Diane was Reverend Adam
Clayton Powell, Jr., the pastor of the Abyssinian Baptist Church up on
138th Street off Seventh Avenue. This was a few years before he began
doubling as congressman from Harlem, but he was already one of the
most outstanding leaders on the local scene and the national scene too. I
had known Reverend Powell quite a little while before that. I don't remember where I first met him, but he was the type of minister that really
got around in the entertainment circles, so he used to be in Café Society
Uptown all the time. He married my good friend Hazel Scott the year
after that. But I'm pretty sure I already knew him before I was ever in
Café Society.

When we came out of the Roxy, Miss Cramer brought us back into the
Blue Room in April. So anybody can find out just how that band was
popping at that time by listening to the air checks of the radio broadcasts
we made from there during the next eight weeks. There is one album
from the air check of a broadcast we did in April and another one made
up of selections from broadcasts we did in May.

The instrumentals on that April broadcast were "Jumping at the Woodside," "Avenue C," "Rock-a-Bye Basie," and "The Dance of the Gremlins." Jimmy sang "I'm Gonna Sit Right Down and Write Myself a Letter,"
and Thelma did "Tess's Torch Song" and "When They Asked About You."
There may be some other air checks from those April broadcasts, but I
don't know anything about them. At one time I used to have a lot of
those large transcriptions platters that the radio stations used to make, but

they were ruined when there was a flooding accident in the basement of
the house I had in St. Albans some years ago. But of course, quite a few
broadcast transcriptions of all kinds are now available from commercial
companies that specialize in all kinds of reissues.

Lester was featured on "Jumping at the Woodside" while we were in
the Blue Room, so there is another air check of him doing it on one of
those broadcasts in May. And, I mean, he was on it! There is also another
air check of "Dance of the Gremlins." The other instrumentals they picked
up on in May were "It's Sand, Man," "Swing Shift," "Circus in Rhythm,"
"Basie Boogie," "Greene," "I Found a New Baby," and "Ain't It the
Truth."

While we were in the Blue Room that spring, I also had a second little
gig going once a week. Because that was when I was working as a single
on "The Kate Smith Hour" on CBS every Friday night from eight to nine
Eastern wartime. Kate Smith was still one of the top singers on radio at
that time, just as she had been for years. People really looked forward to
her show every Friday night.

Her manager at that time was a fellow named Ted Collins, a real nice
guy. Buster Harding and I did a little number and named it "The TC
Blues" for him. He was a very big guy, and I'm not speaking of size. I
mean, he was a real heavy cat, and he was really in charge of things for
Kate Smith. He was the one who introduced her.

They had a great band on that show. I think it was called the Million
Dollar Orchestra, or something like that. What they wanted me to play
on there was blues, and I did all of Buster Harding's arrangements. To tell
the truth, though, I really felt peculiar up there playing the blues all the
time when they had such a bad boy playing piano in that band all that
time. His name was Teddy Wilson.

If I'm not mistaken, it was also while we were back in the Blue Room
that second time that Billy Eckstine got the arrangements from us that
I've been told he still mentions. He came by to see me. We got to talking,
and I guess he must have told me about the band he was trying to get
ready to take out on tour; and he says he mentioned not having enough
arrangements and that I told Snodgrass to let him copy anything in our
book he needed. Unless I'm mistaken, that was when that happened, but
I don't really remember very much about it. But if Billy says that's what
I did, all I can say is that it was not enough, whatever it was. Since I hate
him so much. I just hate him so much that I can't ever do enough for him.
He's just such a wonderful cat. He's one of my special people.

And by the way, that was a hell of a band he was putting together at
that time, too. At one time or another he had fantastic musicians like
Dizzy Gillespie on trumpet, Charlie Parker, Wardell Gray, Gene Ammons,
Budd Johnson, and Leo Parker in the reed section; John Malachi on piano,

and I don't know how many others in that band with him. I do know that he also had Sarah Vaughan on vocals. Nobody can ever forget that. Well, maybe I do know one dummy who could. But I'll come to that later.

A lot of those guys had been in Earl Hines's last great band with Billy. It was while he was Earl's vocalist that Billy became a big name singer with "Stormy Monday Blues," "Jelly, Jelly," and "I'm Falling For You." Sarah Vaughan was also the other vocalist in Earl's band at that time.

—

I think it was also that spring that Shadow Wilson first came into the band as a temporary replacement for Jo Jones. We already knew about Shadow and what he could do, because he had been with Lucky Millinder, Lionel Hampton, Earl Hines, and a few other top-rank bands by that time. Also I'm pretty sure that it was Jo Jones himself who brought him in, because Jo had to take a little time off to handle some personal matters.

Whatever it was that Jo had to take time off to take care of, he came back to work in a week or so. But then, when we went back out to Los Angeles later on that year, we lost him and Lester Young to the draft at the same time. I have to say we really were pretty lucky to be able to keep the band so intact with all the military buildup, especially after Pearl Harbor. We really hadn't been hit hard. But when they snatched Jo and Lester in the space of three days, that was a very big hit.

But we still managed to keep rolling. Lester's replacement was Lucky Thompson. Jo Jones had handpicked Shadow Wilson as his replacement, but Shadow was tied up in New York when Jo got his notice to report. So we had to get somebody to fill in for him for a while, and we got Jesse Price, one of my old friends from Kansas City, who was out in Los Angeles at the time, but then something happened and Jesse couldn't make a matinee we had, and we were trying to figure out who we could get to make that matinee for him, and that's when Milt Ebbins or somebody mentioned that Tommy Dorsey was playing somewhere in town, and we decided to ask Buddy Rich if he could come over. So I got him on the phone.

"You're damn right I'll do it!" he said.

So Buddy came right on over, and as soon as the cat who was the manager of that joint came in there and saw him setting up his drums, he came straight on over to me and started shaking his head.

"What in the hell . . . who's gonna play them drums?" he said. "What's going on here? What's happening?"

"Man, for Christ's sake, don't worry about it," I said. "You'll be all right when you hear this cat play these drums."

But he just kept right on grumbling.

"Aw, man, for Christ's sake. Now my whole day is all upset."

"Is it?" I asked. "Well, get ready to get unset then, because we're going to be rolling soon."

"I know, it's your band," he said, "but it's my joint."

"Yeah, and today it'll be my whole thing, won't it?" I asked. "Now, don't you worry about nothing. Everything going to be all right."

But he just kept shaking his head.

"Well, I ain't even gonna be here to listen to this crap that's gonna come up here now. You already got two or three new guys in there, and now you got a new drummer. Jesus Christ."

"Yeah," I said, "that's him."

Because the cat sounded so funny, he knocked me out, and I just laughed that one off, and he went on somewhere and I went on up to the stand and got ready for the matinee.

We opened with a tune called "It's Sand, Man," and when we jumped on top of that tune, everybody rushed out onto the floor, but instead of dancing, they came hopping down there and sat on the floor around the bandstand, and we had to do that number again. So we hopped right back on it, and they just loved it, and we went on running chorus after chorus for I don't know how many bars.

Then I guess we must have taken a short break or something, or maybe we were waiting for the crowd to settle down or something, and I saw the manager come running toward me and I turned my head in the other direction.

"Man, wait a minute," he said. "Hey, wait a minute, man."

"Aw, man, get away from me," I said.

=

Buddy Rich had to cut out and make it back across town to where Tommy Dorsey was working, so he said, "I got to go, but I'll try to make it back over here tonight. I think I can make arrangements to do it." He said, "If you want me to come back here tonight, I'll make arrangements to do it."

That's the reason why I love that cat and always will. He has done a whole lot of things. Buddy Rich really has. I'm talking about over many years, a whole lot of years. There's nothing he won't do for me. That's the way he has always made me feel about him. He has always been just a wonderful friend. You can always count on him. I don't even remember how all that got started, but that's the way it still is to this day.

Anyway, when I came back into the Plantation Club that night, I looked up there, and instead of everybody dancing, all kinds of people from out in Hollywood were sitting all on the floor, and I looked up on the stand and there was Buddy back on the drums, and then I looked over at the trombone section and there was Buddy's boss, Tommy Dorsey, himself sitting up there with his horn.

"What the hell is going on here?" I asked.

Everybody was there, and the joint was really jumping. That was a night we'll never forget, and there is also one more little detail I remember about it. While we were playing one number that we were having a lot of fun with, somebody tapped me on the shoulder.

"Hey, Base, what key you playing in?"

And I looked up and it was the world's wonder on the piano, Art Tatum.

"Don't give a damn what key we playing in, you ain't going to play. So you just might as well get on down off the stage. Yes. Get out of here."

I ran him off of there. I wasn't about to let that cat take over and disgrace me, and he knew it, and all he could do was laugh. We really had a ball that night, and Buddy Rich played that whole week with us. Then when Price finally came and the manager looked there and saw him, he came to me grinning.

"Where is Jesus Christ?"

"Back in Heaven," I said. Oh, boy.

—

When we came back east that fall, Jesse Price must have come with us, because he was mentioned in a review of our show at the Apollo. But I don't actually recall very much about Jesse being in that band, and I'm very certain he made it clear to us at the outset that he didn't have any intentions of spending any time out on the road with us. I remember that very well. So I guess we must have talked him into staying in there until Shadow Wilson could take over, and then he must have cut right back out for Hollywood. Because I remember him having something pretty good going for himself out there which he was not going to give up.

Anyway, Shadow came in that fall, and he stayed until Jo Jones came back out of the army, well over a year later. He was there when we started recording for Columbia again that December and made "Taps Miller," "Red Bank Boogie," and "Jimmy's Blues" featuring Jimmy Rushing, and Thelma Carpenter did Duke's "I Didn't Know About You." Then in January we did another one of those V-disc sessions, and we made "Taps Miller" and "Jimmy's Blues" again, and also with another "Take Me Back, Baby." The other instrumentals on that date were "Playhouse Number 2 Stomp," "On the Up Beat," and Don Redman's "Just an Old Manuscript," which we also recorded again a few years later for RCA Victor.

"Taps Miller" was named for a good old buddy of mine. Taps was a dancer and singer and variety-show performer, and we used to hang out together a lot, so when Buck Clayton and I were doing that tune, I said we would call it "Taps." I don't remember when we wrote it, but it must have been in the book for a while before we recorded it, because Buck had been in the service about a year by the time we had that session. Yet I do remember that we wrote that tune in Baltimore, whenever it was. Lucky Thompson plays on the second tenor solo. Everybody stretched out a little bit more on the V-disc track of that tune than on the original session.

The next session after that was about a month later, when we recorded Lynne Sherman singing "That Old Feeling" and a new tune called "This Heart of Mine," from a movie still in production at that time called *Ziegfeld Follies*. We used a thirteen-piece string section along with the full band on that one. As for the arrangements, my guess is that Milt and Lynne brought them in. They might have been done by somebody like Hugo Winterhalter, because he had already done a few background things for us before that. The arranger for the regular band instrumental we did on that date was Buck Clayton. It was called "Avenue C." Lucky Thompson had the main tenor spot on that date, and that's Sweets, not Buck, on trumpet.

It's pretty hard for me to keep track of all the changes of personnel in that band during that year. I think Thelma might have been one of the first to cut, because, according to our file of press clippings, by March she was working as a headlining single in a very classy East Side spot known as the Ruban Bleu. Then later on she went with Eddie Cantor, the great vaudeville comedian, and was featured on his radio show, one of the top variety shows on the air in those days.

—

Meanwhile the band went back into the Roxy Theatre for about four weeks that spring, and I'll never get over one particular thing that happened while we were in there that time. Sarah Vaughan and I still laugh and kid about it every time it comes up again.

Actually the joke is on me. Sassy, as we also called her, and I had become very good pals by that time. She was crazy about the band, and she was very friendly with the fellows, so whenever we were in the same town for a while, she used to drop by all the time, maybe every day, and just hang out backstage with them and also in my dressing room.

Now, during this particular stand at the Roxy, I was looking for a vocalist to fill Thelma's place. So I was holding these little auditions between sets. There was a piano in my dressing room, and that's where the guard at the stage entrance would send the prospects. I don't remember how long this went on, but sometimes Sassy would come by while this was going on, and sometimes I would ask her what she thought of this one and that one, and she'd point out certain little things, and I would agree with her.

Well, one day while she was there, somebody called up from the door to say that another one was on her way up. I think I had already heard two or three that day, and I was stretched out on the couch trying to relax for the next show. So I just mumbled something about being too tired to play for any more auditions that day, and that's when she stepped in.

"I'll play for you," she said. "Why don't you just lie over there and listen and let me play."

"Well, if you really don't mind," I said.

So she played and I let the girl sing, and afterwards I asked her what she thought, and we decided that we should listen to a few more. So this went on for a couple of weeks. She would come by there every day and play for me, so all I had to do between shows was lie on the couch and listen, and she even brought a little girl by there that she thought I ought to hear.

Now all I was thinking about during this time was what a great pal she was to be doing that for me. It wasn't until later on that I realized that all the while I was supposed to be looking for a vocalist I had had one of the greatest singers in the world coming by there every goddamn day, playing that piano so I could audition *other* singers.

I mean, she was already great then, and I already knew how great she was, but we were so close that I actually forgot all about what she could really do. She was just my buddy doing me a favor. That's all I thought about. It wasn't until George Treadwell mentioned it some time afterward that I finally realized what had happened. George became her manager, and they were also married for a while.

"Damn, Basie," he used to say. "You had the greatest singer in the world right there, and you had her playing piano for auditions."

Oh, boy. I'll never get over that. The next time I saw Sassy, I asked her why the hell she didn't say something since she was not working anywhere at that particular time. She just laughed.

"I thought you just didn't want me," she said. "I just thought I wasn't what you were looking for."

Oh, boy. By the way, she was a very good piano player. She was good enough to play piano as a member of *Earl Hines*'s band.

—

There were also a few more little changes in the trumpet section by the time we went to our next V-disc session in New York in the middle of May. Al Killian and Joe Newman left, and Karl George and Snookie Young came back. We had five trumpets on that date because Buck

Clayton was also there. I don't actually know how we swung that, because he was still in the service at that time. But he was stationed right over in New Jersey, and he was spending most of his time in the Theresa Hotel anyway, so I guess he must have been available, and then those V-discs were for the Armed Forces radio, so that might have had something to do with it, too. That's him following Mr. Bones on "High Tide." And that's my old buddy Taps Miller doing the scat vocal. That's Lucky Thompson on tenor and Rudy Rutherford on clarinet, and that's Sweets and Snooky in there doing the vocal with Taps.

That's also Lucky and Rudy on tenor and clarinet on "Tipping on the Q.T." and there is also a little eight-bar thing by J. J. Johnson on that one. I don't remember who brought J.J. into the band, but he was with us for a while. Then he went on and made a big name for himself as *the bop* trombone player.

We spent most of the spring in the East. Then we headed back out through the Midwest to California again. We had a very beautiful singer named Maxine Johnson as Thelma Carpenter's replacement for a while, but she didn't stay very long, and our next female vocalist was Anne Moore. She didn't stay very long, either. However, we did record one number with her on our next session for Columbia. It was called "Jiving Joe Jackson."

—

But the main change in the band that year happened in Los Angeles early that fall. That's when Illinois Jacquet came in. Lucky Thompson was planning to quit and stay out on the Coast and get his own little group together. At least that's what the rumor was, and Illinois must have heard it, because he just came over and said he was taking over the job. We were getting ready to go somewhere and I think Lucky was late, and when he finally made it to the bus, Illinois was already in his seat.

So Jacquet was in the reed section when we had that session for Columbia out there that October and recut "High Tide" for commercial release and also made "Queer Street." That's his tenor solo on "High Tide," and you can tell how much he liked Lester as soon as he starts in. He was crazy about Herschel and Lester, and he was sitting in Lester's chair and he knew what he was doing, and he was also having a good time. By the way, that was the date we also did "Jiving Joe Jackson," and the other vocal was Jimmy Rushing doing "Blue Skies."

We headed back east in late October. We began by making the big jump from Los Angeles all the way to Omaha for a week's stand at the Orpheum Theatre. Then we moved on from the Orpheum in Omaha to the Orpheum in Minneapolis for another week, and then in November we played one-nighters in Sioux Falls, South Dakota; the Skylon Ballroom in

Sioux City, Iowa; the Tromar Ballroom in Des Moines, Iowa; Municipal Auditorium in Kansas City; the Castle Ballroom in St. Louis; and Tomlinson Hall in Indianapolis.

Then we had a theater date at the Colonial in Dayton, the Trianon Ballroom in Toledo, and then from the Paramount Theatre in Detroit we worked our way back east to the Earle Theatre in Philadelphia and were back in New York. Then we went back to the Apollo three days after Christmas for the rest of the holiday season.

We recorded an instrumental called "The Mad Boogie" and a vocal with Jimmy Rushing called "Patience and Fortitude" right at the beginning of January. Dicky Wells had left us by that time, and in his place we had a very good man named George Mathews, but you couldn't help missing Mr. Bones in there, even though you still had a soloist in there as fantastic as young J. J. Johnson. There is only one Dicky Wells.

Then by the beginning of February, Jo Jones was back out of the army, and on our next session we cut "Lazy Lady Blues" with Jimmy Rushing, and three instrumentals, "Rambo Stay," "Cool" and "The King," which was one of Jacquet's big numbers with us. His other one was "Mutton Leg," which we made on our next session, along with "Hob Nail Boogie" and "Danny Boy."

Jack Washington and Walter Page also came back into the band that spring. So they were on that date, which was in July. Jack, like Jo, was back from the service, and he replaced Jimmy Powell on alto. Big 'Un just decided that he was ready to come back. Buck and Lester also got out of the service around that time, but they didn't come back. They both went on a touring group managed by Norman Granz called "Jazz at the Philharmonic."

Later on Illinois Jacquet also became a very big hit on "Jazz at the Philharmonic," but when he left us that summer, he started a little group of his own, and Joe Newman went with him. J. J. Johnson also left around that same time. So somebody brought Paul Gonsalves in on tenor to replace Jacquet; and Bill Johnson came into the trombone section for a while; and Snookie Young came back into the trumpet section. Paul was a hit right away. I think we were down in Baltimore when we opened up that first show with him playing "Mutton Leg." He was such a sensation we had to repeat the number. It was so terrific.

━━

That was the summer when we spent the last of July and most of August in the Aquarium Restaurant on Broadway. We got in quite a bit of coast-to-coast radio-network time while we were in there, and I also made a few guest appearances on other shows, which probably means that there are some air checks of all of that somewhere, too. I know for sure that there is an air check of me doing a guest show on a Benny Goodman show on the twelfth of August, because there is an LP of it.

We also made one commercial record session that August. We made a vocal called "Fla-Ga-La-Pa" with Anne Moore; a blues with Jimmy Rushing called "Good-bye, Baby," and a little thing called "Wild Bill Boogie." That was the last commercial session we had that year, but when we went back out to California that fall, we did a few broadcasts, and on those air checks of us in the Avedon Ballroom in downtown Los Angeles there are some pretty fair tracks of Paul doing "Sweet Lorraine" and "Mutton Leg," Jimmy singing "Don't Cry, Baby," and the band on a jump tune called "Step 'n' Fetchit," which I don't think we ever recorded in a studio.

The lineup of the band at that time was Ed Lewis, Sweets, Snookie, and Emmett Berry on trumpets; Eli Robinson, Ted Donnelly, George Mathews, and Bill Johnson, trombones; Jack Washington, Buddy Tate, Rudy Rutherford, and Paul, reeds; and our old rhythm section again, with Jimmie Rushing and Anne Moore doing vocals. And that's the way it still was when we came back east after spending Christmas in the Avedon and made our next records right at the beginning of that next January.

That was our first session under our new contract with RCA Victor, and four of the five things we did were vocals. We made two blues: Anne Moore on "Me and the Blues," Jimmy Rushing on "Brand-New Wagon." Then there was the band doubling as a vocal chorus on "Free Eats," a little novelty written by Freddie Green and Snookie Young; and we did Dusty Fletcher's old vaudeville hit called "Open the Door, Richard," with Sweets doing Dusty's part with Bill Johnson as his straight man. The only instrumental was "Bill's Mill," with Paul Gonsalves doing a nice little get-off chorus.

The only changes in the line-up for our next session, which was in March, were the vocalists. Ann Baker replaced Anne Moore and did "Meet Me at No Special Place," and Bob Bailey who had worked with us on stage shows many times, did "I'm Drowning in Your Deep Blue Eyes." We also did "One O'Clock Boogie" and "Futile Frustration" on that date. Then, between that time and the session we had in May, there was a change, because that was when Rudy Rutherford left after being with us for over three years. C. Q. Price was his replacement on alto. Nobody replaced him on clarinet at that time.

There were three sessions on three straight days in late May, and in all we cut over a dozen numbers. But on the first two sessions, we didn't use the whole band. We used Emmett Berry on trumpet, George Mathews on trombone, C. Q. Price on alto, Paul Gonsalves on tenor, and Jack Washington on baritone with the rhythm section, and we cut "Swinging

the Blues," "St. Louis Boogie," "Backstage at Stuff's," and "Basie's Basement" on the first day. I played organ on "Basie's Basement," and by
the way, "Backstage at Stuff's" was named for Stuff Crouch, my good old
buddy out in Los Angeles.

That next day we went back in there and made "My Buddy," "Shine
On, Harvest Moon," and "I never Knew"; and then Paul, Freddie, Jo,
and I knocked out a little version of "Sugar." The other number we cut
that day was a little something I worked up for Jack Washington. It was
called "Lopin'," and the Weasel took care of business, as he always did.
I don't know why it wasn't issued until some few years later.

On that third day we brought the whole band in and made three novelty
vocals and two instrumentals. Jimmy's tune was "You call Yourself a
Jungle King," which was about that same signifying monkey that Nat
King Cole's big hit number "Straighten Up and Fly Right" was about. The
vocalist on "Take a Little off the Top" was Sweets, and for "I Ain't Mad
at You" we brought in my old buddy Taps Miller. The first instrumental
on that date was "House Rent Boogie," and the other one was "South,"
an old Bennie Moten–Thamon Hayes tune from way back in the twenties.

—

Our big extended engagement for that summer was at Club Paradise in
Atlantic City. Actually business was not quite as good for us as it had
been over the past several years; bookings were beginning to fall off a
bit, and every now and then the band was having to take a few days off
without pay. But that gig at Club Paradise turned out pretty nice for us.

Everybody did have to take a little cut in pay because we had to reduce
our asking price to get in there, but we had a ball even with all those
long working hours and all those high Atlantic City living expenses. In
the first place the show itself was a gas. It was what the newspapers used
to call "an all-star sepia revue." It was produced by Ziggy Johnson, who
was right up there in the same class with Larry Steele when it came to
putting on great shows with beautiful chorus girls, singers, and comedians.
When it came to big production numbers with fabulous costumes and
sets, he was just great. For one feature number with the chorus, they
brought an organ in there for me. That's what that number "Paradise
Squat" is about.

As a matter of fact Larry Steele himself was our main competition
that summer. He was right there in Atlantic City at Club Harlem, with a
show called *Smart Affairs* that had Derby Wilson, Moms Mabley, Billy
Daniels, Top and Wilder, and a chorus line of twelve. That was our main
competition, but that was also one big reason why it turned out to be
such a wonderful run for us. Because our two groups had such a great

time hanging out together. And another thing was that so many of our old friends from all over the East Coast were always dropping down to Atlantic City.

Katy used to come down from St. Albans for the weekend and go back on Monday, which reminds me that I haven't mentioned anything about moving out of the La Guardia apartment building the year before, because we bought a new house out in St. Albans in Jamaica, Queens. As important as that move was, I can't really give much of an account of it because I don't remember very much about it. I remember something about Catherine getting me to go out there to look at places one of those times while I was in town, because a lot of new development was going on, and that's where a lot of uptown people were moving. But the way I found out that we had moved was during a telephone call while I was somewhere out on the road. We had been talking for a while, and then she told me.

"By the way, I have to give you our new address."

=

As long as our workday at Atlantic City was, the fellows still found a lot of time to have a lot of fun that summer. Jack Washington, Paul Gonsalves, and a few others organized a softball team and played a lot of games against teams that either had gigs in Atlantic City at that time, such as Harry James, Louis Prima, and also against a lot of local teams; sometimes they were firemen and sometimes policemen or maybe bartenders and workers and so on. We didn't get off until five o'clock in the morning, but sometimes there were two or three games a week, and I am talking about morning games.

I really think just about everybody enjoyed being in Atlantic City that summer. Because quite a few guys also had a chance to have their families with them during that time and take the children to the amusement places and the beaches along with all the other things that were going on. Certain families got together and made living arrangements to cut down on expenses.

But we didn't get to spend the whole summer there after all. We got a chance to go back into the Strand Theatre on Broadway for three weeks along with the movie *Deep Valley*, starring Ida Lupino and Dane Clark. So we had to cut out before the end of August instead of staying on until the end of the season after Labor Day. Pearl Bailey was the headliner on that show with us at the Strand that year. That was her first Broadway gig, and she was a hit. And so was the comedy team of Lewis and White, and the tap-dance team known as the Edwards Sisters.

We also used Bob Bailey and Jimmy Rushing, and we did very well in there. And when we came out the booking situation for the fall looked pretty good.

It always helps when you have a good run in a top Broadway showcase like the Strand, but we also decided to put a special package together for the fall season. So we had Ziggy Johnson turn the cabaret show that was such a hit in Club Paradise into a stage show for the theater circuit, and that was what we took into the Apollo when we came out of the Strand.

Somebody decided to call it *The One O'Clock Revue,* and there was a lot of talk about the big package stage deal being the new trend in show business at that time. In fact, Larry Steele also took the cabaret show he had over at Club Harlem and turned it into a stage show with June Richmond and about forty other performers, with music by Coleridge Davis. They took it out as *Larry Steele's Smart Affairs of '48,* and I think they opened at the Howard Theatre in Washington.

I wouldn't say that either one of those shows really set a trend. Neither one of those shows really got very far that year. And the main reason was those big all-star packages that the booking agencies started sending out. Sometimes there would be big-name singers, two or three name groups, and also a name band all in one package. Buck Clayton and Lester and Hawk and Roy and Illinois and Ben Webster and a whole lot of stars like that worked on those tours for a while, and that thing really caught on.

The bebop thing was also happening all during that time, and also there were not as many dance-hall bookings as before. But the other thing was those singing groups. That's when they really began to take the stage. I'm not trying to analyze the situation or anything like that. I'm just giving my impression of how things were changing at that time.

Anyway, we only had *One O'Clock Revue* out on the road for a while that fall, and then the band went back to one-nighters again.

What happened was that while we were in the Apollo, Howard Stanley, a young fellow from California, came up to catch the band, and he also liked the show so much that he decided to see if he could take the whole package to Los Angeles. So he went back out there and worked a few things out and found a spot out in Hollywood so we could redo the whole thing out there. If I remember correctly, he wanted to take the entertainers out there right away and start rehearsals and add a few features.

But I don't think the band made the trip with the others. I'm pretty sure we worked our way out there, because I think we went by way of the Dreamland in Omaha, and Denver, and the Rainbow Rendezvous in Salt Lake City, and then went on into Los Angeles and joined the rehearsals. I must say, Howard Stanley really liked us. He was a good friend, and he tried hard to make that thing go. But the show didn't work out. It seemed like the time just wasn't ripe for us on that one.

The band also played the Million Dollar Theatre. Then we went up the coast and up through Oregon, Washington State, and as far north as Vancouver. Then we came back to San Francisco and spent a week in the Golden Gate Theatre before coming back to Los Angeles for what was supposed to be three or four weeks at the Meadowbrook Club out in Culver City.

I don't think we did too bad at the Golden Gate so far as the box office goes, but the Meadowbrook, which by the way was once known as Frank Sebastian's Cotton Club back when Les Hite still had his great band out there, was a different story. The attendance was so far off that first week that the only way we could stay there for the other three weeks was to work only over the three-day weekends, and everybody had to take another cut in salary.

That was pretty rough on the fellows, and I could certainly understand how they felt, with Christmas coming on. But in the meantime we did have a few records to make before the end of the year because there was a new ban on recording that was all set to go into effect as of the first of January, and the people at RCA wanted to make sure that we had a big-enough backlog to tide us over.

Actually we had already started working on that backlog a month or so earlier. Altogether there were five sessions, one in the middle of October and three more in the middle of December. On that first one, we made Buck Clayton's "Seventh Avenue Express" and Buster Harding's arrangement on "Mister Roberts's Roost." The main solos on "Express" were by Tate, Sweets, and Mr. Bones, who was back in there by that time; and that thing was leaping all the way. According to the discographies, we also cut two vocals that day. One was supposed to be "Don't You Want a Man Like Me" with Jimmie, and the other was supposed to be "Blue and Sentimental" with lyrics for Bob Bailey.

The instrumentals on those December sessions were "Guest in a Nest," "Sophisticated Swing," "Just a Minute," and "Robbins Nest." Then we also made "Your Little Red Wagon" and "Money Is Honey" with Jimmy Rushing one day, and "Hey, Pretty Baby" and "Bye-Bye, Baby," the next. And we also did a couple of vocals with Jean Taylor on both of the same days. Jean was our new female singer, and she did "Baby, Don't Be Mad at Me," "I've Only Myself to Blame," "It's Monday Every Day," and "Ready Set Go."

—

Sometime right after the beginning of that following year there was some talk about a European tour for the band, but things didn't work out for that. In the meantime we pulled the *One O'Clock Revue* back together for a few more theater dates. I don't have any record of the places we took it, but according to the *Defender*, we did make it out to the Regal in Chicago, Ziggy's hometown, and I think we may also have taken it down to Baltimore and Washington. But I don't remember what happened down there, and I think we must have given up on it after that.

By early spring, after a couple of weeks at the Adams Theatre in Newark and one in the Apollo back in Harlem, we went to a few places down south. Then in May we went into the RKO Theatre in Boston. That was billed as another big all-star revue, and there were also a couple of very special added attractions: Billy Eckstine and the Nicholas Brothers.

After that, we headed out on a concert tour that took us back out into the Midwest to the English Theatre in Indianapolis, the Civic Opera House in Chicago, the Kiel Auditorium in St. Louis, and down to Louisville and back east and up to Buffalo for a week in the Town Casino, with a revue. I think we probably did pretty well until we got to Buffalo. I don't know what happened there. But we were not too hot there, and I think we had to send back to New York and get some help to make it through that week.

In June we went down to Rocky Mount, North Carolina, for the annual June German Dance at the Tobacco Planters' Warehouse, and according to the newspaper reports, we played two sessions that added up to over twenty-four thousand people. The first session was from ten to one, and the second was from two until five in the morning. That was the biggest crowd they had ever had up to that time. Naturally that many people couldn't get inside the warehouse. There were loudspeakers which carried the music to acres and acres of people outside.

We went back into the Paradise in Atlantic City again at the beginning of July, but we couldn't stay more than two weeks that time because we were due back in the Strand the third week in July. We had thought we were going to stay down there much longer than that; in fact, the club had actually been expanded to take care of the kind of overflow crowds we had drawn the last time.

But you couldn't turn down the Strand, and this time they had us booked in there with the world premiere of *Key Largo*, starring Humphrey Bogart and Lauren Bacall, two of the hottest stars in Hollywood that year. And on the stage they also had Billie Holiday, Stump and Stumpy, and the Two Zephyrs, and we also had feature spots for Jimmy Rushing and Bob Bailey. I think we went in there on a contract for three weeks with an option to extend for another two weeks, and I think they revised it and made it five weeks with options to make it six or seven weeks.

And that's how long we stayed. But by the end of that gig, there were quite a few personnel changes. Our first big loss was Jo Jones. One day somebody came up to my dressing room and asked me something that took me completely by surprise.

"What's happened to Jo Jones? Is he leaving or something?"

"Not that I know of," I said. "Why are you asking me a question like that?"

"He must be," whoever it was said. "I just saw him going out of here with his drums and sticks and everything."

And when I got down there to the stage level, Jo was gone. He cut out just like that, so I had to get busy and get somebody else for that very next show, and if I remember correctly, we got some young cat from a band up at the Apollo to come in there for a while, and then we got Shadow Wilson to come back.

—

When we came out of the Strand, we ran into a little trouble again because we had to make a few more salary adjustments. There were rumors that the band was breaking up, that Jimmy Rushing was cutting out to form his own group; but the way things turned out, the main fellows we lost were Buddy Tate and Ed Lewis. Buddy decided to see what he could do in another situation that would also let him spend more time in New York. Ed Lewis said he decided to give up music for a while.

Losing those two great musicians after they had been so much a part of the band for all those years made a very big difference. But we were able to bring Wardell Gray in as Buddy's replacement, and we got Jimmy Nottingham to fill Ed Lewis's chair as first trumpet. Wardell had been in Billy Eckstine's band, and before that, he had also played for Earl Hines and Benny Carter, and also with Benny Goodman's sextet. Jimmy had been featured as a high-note man in Lionel Hampton's great band, and also with Charlie Barnet and Lucky Millinder.

The band we took into the Royal Roost on Broadway at Longacre Square in the middle of September had Sweets, Emmett Berry, Clark Terry, and Jimmy Nottingham on trumpets; Dicky Wells, Ted Donnelly, George Mathews, and Bill Johnson on trombones; Paul Gonsalves, Earl Warren, Bernie Peacock, Jack Washington, and Wardell on reeds; Shadow Wilson on drums; Singleton "Cookie" Palmer on bass; and Freddie on guitar. And in spite of all those rumors and newspaper articles about Jimmie Rushing, he was right back in there taking care of vocals as usual.

There were a lot of newspaper and magazine people there to see how we were going to sound at our opening at the Royal Roost, and a lot of our friends also dropped by to wish us good luck. Naturally John Hammond was there, and Duke, Benny Goodman, Sarah Vaughan, and I don't know how many others also came in to dig us and lend their support.

The main thing a lot of people were wondering about was how much bop we were going to be playing. But as far as I was concerned, I didn't have any objection to new things so long as it all made sense, so there was little bop figures and also some bop solos, especially by Paul and Wardell and Clark Terry, but we also had those shout licks and choruses, and the rhythm had to be right. Because it really wasn't a matter of doing something different just to try to have a new sound; it all had to have feeling.

We did all right in the Royal Roost, and we stayed until early October. Then, when we headed out to Detroit by way of the Three Rivers Inn up in Syracuse, Shadow Wilson put in his notice, and we brought Butch Ballard from Philadelphia in on drums. We spent a week at the Paradise Theatre in Detroit, and then, after a big sellout gig in the IMA Auditorium in Flint, Michigan, we spent the rest of that fall barnstorming down south before coming back north and into Frank Palumbo's Click Club in Philadelphia in the middle of December.

I don't have any reliable documentation on how many one-nighters we actually made on that southern tour, but we did go all the way down as far as St. Petersburg, Florida. We played a big dance in the Manhattan Casino down there on Thanksgiving Day and came out of Florida for a night in the Memorial Auditorium in Atlanta at the beginning of December. I think we may also have hit Birmingham on that trip, but I don't remember anything special about being back there that time.

The Click was our last big out-of-town gig just before Christmas. Then on New Year's Eve we moved into the Apollo for the first week in January. Pearl Bailey was on that show with us, and so was Teddy Hale and the team of Patterson and Jackson. You could always count on a great stage show at the Apollo for the holiday season, and you could also bet on an even bigger turnout than usual. And of course, we also knew that there would be a lot of people there to check out how the new guys were working out. They might have missed those who had left, but I don't think they were disappointed over what they heard, because Paul Gonsalves and Clark Terry and Jimmy Nottingham were taking care of business. They were tearing it up.

Our first trip out of town in the New Year took us down to the Howard Theatre in Washington for a week, to be followed by another week at the Royal Theatre in Baltimore. But by the end of the month things were beginning to get tough out there. The Morris Agency was changing its policy on big bands. But we were able to line up enough dates to work our way back out to the Coast by spring, and while we were out there, we also went back into the recording studio for the first time in more than a year. That was when we cut "Brand-New Doll," "Cheek to Cheek," another "Old Manuscript," and "Katy."

Near the end of June we recorded Jimmie Rushing singing "She's a Wino," and "After You're Gone," and we made one instrumental entitled "Shouting Blues." Then in the middle of July we cut two more vocals, Jimmy doing "St. Louis Baby," and Taps Miller doing "Did You See Jackie Robinson Hit That Ball?"

The last tune that Jimmy Rushing cut with the band was on a session during the fourth week in July. It was called "Walking Slow Behind You." Of course, nobody thought about it as our last anything then, and I can't truthfully say that I can actually remember it like that now. But that is what it turned out to be. The two instrumentals we made on that same session were "Wonderful Thing" and "Mine, Too." The arrangements for both of them were made by our young third alto man. His name was C. Q. Price, and he was interested in writing in the new bebop style, which, as I say, was all right with me as long as it made sense and as long as it was swinging.

═

That turned out to be the last year for the band that I brought east from Kansas City. Actually the only ones left in there from the old Reno bunch, besides myself, were Jimmy Rushing and Jack Washington. The only others left over from those early days before the Famous Door were Freddie Greene, Earl Warren, Sweets, and Dicky Wells.

Anyway, things were drying up for big bands, and finally I just got tired of being out there on the road just catching those dates as we could catch them. So when we got to Memphis on the way back east from Mississippi and the West, I decided to lay off for a while. So that was it. I didn't tell anybody anything about what I was going to do until I did it. I didn't even talk to Jimmy Rushing about it beforehand.

I just made up my mind and then called everybody together and told them. I said I didn't know what was going to be happening next after I had a chance to take a rest and think about it. Because at that time I didn't know whether I was going to have a trio or six pieces or a big band or what.

"But I'll have somebody getting it together, and you will know," I told them, "and when you get your notice, that's where it will be."

I really didn't have any plans. I just wanted to get away for a while. I just wanted to have some time on my own to dig what was going on and see what would happen. And that's exactly what I did during those months until Willard Alexander got in touch with me about a job in a new club out in Chicago for about a month. To tell the truth, by that time, which was in the late fall, I needed to get back to work because I needed the money. So that's how I happened to come back to work during the first part of that next year, leading a six-piece combo.

I had spoken to Willard about booking me again, because I didn't go back to the Morris Agency, and the first thing he came up with was a deal with Milton Schwartz for me to take a small group into the Brass Rail. Actually Willard was the one who helped me to get that little outfit together. He was the one who suggested Buddy de Franco for clarinet, which I okayed. Then we got Clark Terry, and Clark suggested Bob Graf, a friend of his from St. Louis, for tenor. For drums we got Gus Johnson, and I don't remember who suggested Jimmy Lewis or where we got him from; but he came in on bass, and that was the combo we had out in Chicago during February and March of that next year.

By the way, it was while we were playing at the Brass Rail with that combo that I got my first taste of Joe Williams as a vocalist. He used to just come and stand out front there and do the last set with us every night, outdoors, out front, not even inside. We still laugh about that. One night he just turned up out there and started singing. I never will forget that, but at the time it never crossed my mind that one day he would be one of my biggest stars, my number-one son.

When we came back to New York, we became a septet. We didn't include Freddie Green in that group that we took out to Chicago, but when we got back he just came on in on his own. One night we were playing somewhere in midtown, and I came to work and there he was with his guitar and everything.

"What the hell are you doing here?" I asked.

And he just looked at me and looked at the wall or out in space or somewhere and shook his head.

"What the hell do you mean what am I doing here? You working tonight, aren't you?"

And that was it, and he's been right there ever since.

—

While we were back in New York that April, we had to add a few pieces to the combo to fill a booking at the Strand. I've been reminded that we had to expand in order to meet Musicians' Union Local 802 requirements for bands playing stage show dates. I don't actually remember any details about that contract. All I know is that the date came up and we did what we had to do to fill it. But there were a couple of things about that gig that I will never forget.

I will never forget the headline singer, because it was Billie Holiday, and unless I'm mistaken, that was her first performance back in New York for quite a while. I think her cabaret work permit had been revoked, and she could only play theaters. I'm not going to get into all of that, because it's not my story. The only point I'm trying to make is that it was a very special date, because she had so many fans waiting to hear her in person in Manhattan again.

She was definitely the big attraction on that date, and she looked great, and she was all ready to do her thing. But before the time came for her to do her first set, another great thing happened. One of the other acts on that show was the Will Mastin Trio with young Sammy Davis, Jr., and they went out there and when that kid started doing his imitations of famous movie stars and other singers, that audience went wild. I don't know how long they had him and that trio out there.

The applause went on and on, and they kept having to go back and take another bow until Sammy just had to stay out there and start his introduction for Lady Day. And that was pretty great, too, because he must have spent about two whole minutes just laying that introduction on her, and then he brought her on, and that was another standing ovation.

After that introduction she could have just taken a bow and walked off. It was wonderful—just marvelous. But when the audience finally settled back down, if there was anybody who had any question about whether Billie Holiday was still Miss Lady Day, she took care of that right away when she came on with "Fine and Mellow," "Billie's Blues," "Crazy, He Calls Me," and some of the other tunes that people knew nobody else could do like she could.

So that show was a big comeback for her, and it was also the real beginning of something big for Sammy Davis. As that group went on up higher and higher, everybody could see that Sammy was really the star of the act, but as far as Sammy himself was concerned, it was still the Will Mastin Trio with Sammy Davis, Jr. And that's the way it stayed until the trio retired from show business, and Sammy went on as a single.

=

I don't really remember very much about that expanded group we put together for that gig at the Strand. I do remember that we brought in Georgie Auld on tenor, J. J. Johnson as trombone, and Emmett Berry and Paul Webster came in with Clark Terry on trumpet; and I also remember that we got Tommy Potter to come in on bass for Jimmy Lewis because Jimmy hadn't yet gotten his 802 union card, so he couldn't work in New York City. Now, if I haven't mentioned anyone else who came in with us for that gig, I hope they will forgive me, because I didn't leave anybody out on purpose.

It's just that we made so many little temporary changes in that combo for one reason or another. When we made "The Golden Bullet," "Blue Heards Blues" and "Neals Deal" for Columbia in May, we brought in Charlie Rouse on tenor for Bob Graf, and added Serge Chaloff on baritone, and Buddy Rich sat in for Gus Johnson, just for that particular date.

Wardell Gray took over the tenor spot in San Francisco that September, so he was on our next sessions, which took place at the beginning of November when we recorded "These Foolish Things," "I'm Confessing,"

"One O'Clock Jump," "I Ain't Got Nobody," "Little White Lies," "I'll Remember April," and "Tootsie." The bass clarinet on those sessions is Serge Chaloff. By the way, it was not long after that date that Buddy de Franco cut out to get his own group together, and that is when I got Marshall Royal to come in on alto and clarinet.

I had known Marshall for a few years. He and his brother, Ernie the trumpet player, had been in Lionel Hampton's band, and he had also been a key member of that beautiful small band with Eddie Heywood at the Three Deuces for a long run. But where I really got to know him was out in Los Angeles, because he had also worked with my old running buddy, Les Hite. One thing I remember in particular is that Marshall used to give me some pretty good tips on the ponies when we used to go out to the racetrack. Which I did a lot. (That, by the way, was something Katy turned me on to. Katy loved to play the ponies; and so also got a big kick out of trying her luck on a few of those little games in the casinos. She got me interested but she didn't pass on any of her luck.)

Anyway, when Buddy split, I got in touch with Marshall, and he agreed to come in for a while. Actually he was not too keen on leaving California to come out on the old gypsy trail again, but not long after he joined us, I started getting another full band together again, and he changed his mind and ended up staying out there with us for almost twenty years as our lead alto and musical director.

You couldn't have wished for a better deputy to help you with a big band. He was not really an arranger or writer, but when it came to being the musical director, rehearsing the band, and also working with show routines and things like that, he was one of the best in the business. He was also a wonderful performer to begin with. He was a great section man, a strong soloist, and his feature spots were always a regular part of our repertory.

PART TWO

1951 = 1984

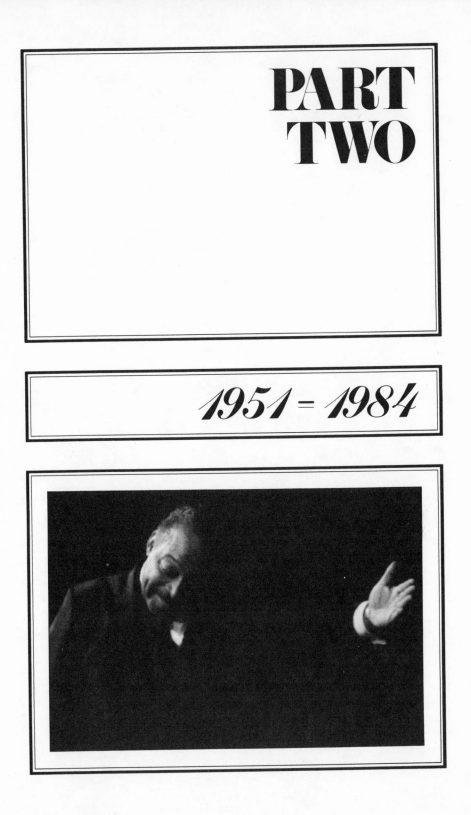

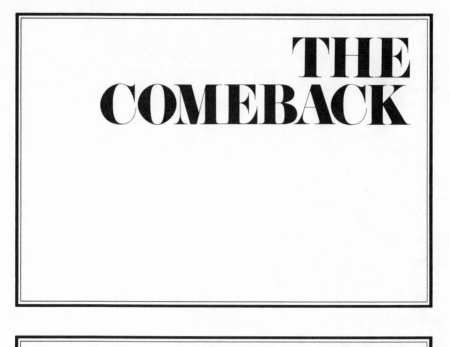

THE COMEBACK

1950 = 1954

The main one who was really responsible for me deciding to get a full band back together again when I did was Billy Eckstine. I have to give him a whole lot of credit for that. And no matter how much I give him, it will never really be enough. Because he was the one who just kept on after me and kept on after me and wouldn't let me alone until finally I just said, hell, I'd go along with it.

My co-writer has reminded me that a lot of people who were around during that time still like to think of the band that I began to work with that next year as the Birdland Band, and they have a point. Because Birdland, near the corner of the east side of Broadway at Fifty-second Street, was known as the jazz corner of the world in those days, and that was where things finally began happening for the new band, just as the Famous Door was where the first band really broke into the big time about fourteen years earlier.

So I'm not forgetting Birdland, and I'm not forgetting Norman Granz either. Because without all of those fantastic gigs in Birdland, it would not have been the same story for us, at least I don't think so; and I also have to say that all those records that Norman began bringing out on Mercury and then Clef and then Verve labels were also very, very important. That was the main way the new band got nationwide exposure.

Those first records were not big hits or anything like that, but there were disc jockeys playing them, and they were on the jukeboxes; and when we were out on those early tours, everywhere we went there were almost always some people waiting for us, mainly because they were already familiar with how the new band sounded on tunes like "Bleep Bleep Blues," "Sure Thing," "Why Not?," "Fancy Meeting You," "Cash Box," and "Tom Whaley" from those Mercury and Clef LP's that Norman was distributing all over the country, along with his *Jazz at the Philharmonic* releases that were so popular at that time. Because I really didn't give a damn about going back into the big-band thing at that time. I'm not saying that I didn't miss it.

Some people insist that all during that time with the combo I was always talking about how much I missed that bigger sound of the full band. Even my wife claims that I used to mope around the house grumbling and complaining about not being able to hear my music the way I was used to.

But the combo was doing all right. There was no problem about getting bookings for it, and those guys were burning it up every set, every night. It worked me a little bit hard, but I was getting used to it, and I was having a ball. I really was. But Billy came by to see us one night. I forget exactly when it was, but it was while we were working in the Capitol Lounge in Chicago. Whenever it was, he started in on me and that was just the beginning.

"Man," he said, "what you doing messing around out here with this stuff for?" Of course, all of Billy's close friends know damn well that he didn't really use nice little words like "crap," "stuff," "fooling around," "messing around," but we'll just pretend he did, because he really wasn't talking dirty to be nasty. That was just his way of showing how much he liked you. Instead of coming somewhere and telling how much he loved you, he would come in and cuss you out, just like some people show you how glad they are to see you by slapping you and pushing and carrying on like that.

"Man, goddamn, we don't need you out here with this old crap. We need you out here with a big band again."

And every time I saw him from then on, it was the same thing.

"Man, what you keep fooling around with little old one- and two-piece stuff for? Get your goddamn big band back together. Man, hell, you look funny up there messing around with that little old two- and three-piece crap. Stop kidding yourself. This is small garbage for you, Base. This ain't your goddamn thing. Hell, your goddamn thing is a goddamn big band, man." Now, he might have said, "your thing," but what he actually said was a word that begins with the letter *s*.

The thing about Billy was that he was really sitting on top of the world of show business at that time. He had a whole gang of hit records out, and he was getting top billing at some of the biggest theaters from coast to coast, beginning with the Paramount in Times Square. And that's the way it had been for a couple of years or so. Of course, he had already become one of the top band singers back when he was with Earl Hines's great band. And for a few years at the end and right after the war, he had also led his own wonderful band that had all of those great stars like Dizzy Gillespie, Charlie Parker, Fats Navarro, Sarah Vaughan, Budd Johnson, Gene Ammons, Art Blakey, and I don't know how many others in it. But at the time I'm talking about now, he was working as a single and he was the top male vocalist in the country, and everybody was talking about the great Mr. B. and everywhere you went you could hear that big, wonderful voice on the radio and the jukeboxes.

—

Things were really just great for him at this time, so he was not just jiving me. He really had some things in mind that he wanted me to do with him. He really meant what he was saying. He was doing a lot of concert series touring at that time. He had already been out with a big entertainment package show that had the George Shearing Quintet in it; and also another combo, which, according to my main man in the research department, had Benny Green on trombone, Joe Newman on trumpet, Eddie "Lockjaw" Davis on tenor, Tommy Potter on bass, and Kenny Clarke on drums. But he wanted a big band with him, and that's why he kept on after me.

"I need you out here with me, Base," he said, and he told me that he was getting ready to go back out on another tour to play a whole string of about 131 concerts, which, he said, was enough work for a new band to establish itself.

"There ain't no sense in you messing around like this," he kept saying. "You should be out here with me. So come on, Base."

"Why the hell don't you just come on out here, Base?" he said.

"Aw, man, I don't know."

And he said, "Come on." He said, "Don't worry about nothing. You don't have to worry about the money. We can take care of that. Just get your whole thing together again. And cut this crap out."

He kept on after me and kept on after me like that, and that's what convinced me to try it with a big band again, and that is what led to all of the wonderful things that have followed over the years. And that's why I hate his guts so much, and miss him so much when I don't see him for a while, and give him hell every time I'm lucky enough to run into him anywhere again. And whenever we are working together on the same bill somewhere, he is always subject to go out and introduce my set by telling the audience some joke about me, such as that I've been using that three-note tag phrase at the end of "One O'Clock Jump" ever since I first played it as an amen to the blessing for the Last Supper.

That's why as soon as I see him coming, I ask him, "When you going to stop telling all them lies on me?" And I know exactly what he's going to say.

"Watch your mouth, old man. Don't come messing with me. I'll kick your butt. Get out of my goddamn face. How you doing, Base? Goddamn, I love you."

=

Actually I had already been working with a big band every now and then. What we would do every time another theater date came up was add enough trumpets and trombones and reeds to bring the combo up to full band size, just as we did when we came back to New York from Chicago and went into the Strand with Billie Holiday after that first gig in the Brass Rail. And I also took another pickup band into the Apollo in April a year later; and I used most of that same lineup on a record date for Columbia when we made "Howz It," "Nails," "Beaver Junction," and "Little Pony."

Then we built the band back up to full size again, because we had this theater booking for the Strand again and for the Regal in Chicago, the Flamingo Hotel in Las Vegas, and the Paramount Theatre in Los Angeles.

I think it must have been while we were in the Strand that Clark Terry recommended Jimmy Wilkins for the trombone section and Jimmy's brother Ernie for alto. Clark says he also told me at that time that Ernie was also a pretty good arranger, so I'm sure he did, but it wasn't until Ernie had been in the band for a while that I realized just what a fantastic writer he was. He made a big difference. He had a lot to do with how the band began to sound from then on up to right now.

I remember being out west on one of those tours, and we barely made it to Denver, and we had to get in touch with my wife's mother, in Cleveland, and borrow enough money to get me out of that situation.

Maybe I have this trip confused with another time. I'm not sure. But we did make a trip out there with a show one time. It was a big show with Bill Bailey and also Norma Miller and her girls. I remember playing in Kansas City, because I took my good old dear friend Aunt Lucy to see the show. And we went on out to Las Vegas, and when we got there, nobody knew where Bill Bailey was. He and some of his people were traveling in his own car. So we figured he must have stopped somewhere for a break. Then it was almost time to go on for the first show and there was still no sign of him. Then the phone rang, and he had taken a wrong turn somewhere and ended up in Las Vegas, New Mexico!

Anyway, we did make it on out to California. But on the way back we couldn't make it any farther than Denver, so I borrowed some money from Catherine's mother and sent the other musicians back to New York and took the combo to the Capitol Lounge in Chicago. That's where Clark Terry decided to cut out. He put in his notice and went home to St. Louis, and the next thing we heard of him he was with Duke. As his replacement, we brought in another trumpet player from St. Louis named Paul Campbell. Ernie and Jimmy probably recommended him.

Chicago was also where Wardell left us, and that's where we got Paul Quinchette. I didn't know much about Paul at that time, but I do remember knowing that he liked Prez, which immediately fell right into the web of things, and we got along real well. He was absolutely excellent with the band, and pretty soon people were calling him the Vice Prez. I don't know what Lester thought of that, and I don't know what Lester called Paul.

From the Capitol Lounge we went on up into Canada, and I was in Toronto when I got the call from Willard Alexander about getting another full band together. As best as I can figure it out, that must have been right after Billy was talking to me in Chicago, because he was the real reason I told Willard it was okay. But if I remember correctly, the reason Willard called was that Birdland wanted to make a very special deal with us.

Then I called Charlie Fowlkes and told him to notify the people we needed to be ready to go into rehearsal when the combo came back to the Apple in a week or so. Charlie had been taking care of the baritone chair on just about all of those dates with the pickup band. So by that time I had gotten to know him pretty well, and I knew I could depend on him to fill the slots we needed. And in a day or so he called me back and said, "Nothing to worry about. I'll have everything assembled when you get here."

That was around the end of that summer, and we rehearsed in one of the studios in Nola's in the Brill Building on Broadway between Forty-ninth and Fiftieth streets, the same block where Jack Dempsey's restaurant used to be in those days, when Madison Square Garden was between Forty-ninth and Fiftieth streets over on Eighth Avenue. In our own lineup at that time, if I remember correctly, we had Paul Campbell, Tommy Turrentine, Johnny Letman, and Idris Sulieman on trumpets; Jimmy Wilkins, Benny Powell, and Matthew Gee on trombones; and in the reed section, Paul Quinchette and Floyd Johnson were our two tenors, Marshall Royal and Ernie Wilkins our two altos; and Charlie Fowlkes on baritone; and the rhythm section was the same.

Our first out-of-town job was in the Symphony Hall Ballroom in Boston in October, and after hitting a couple of other places up that way, we came back into town and went into the Savoy at the same time that Jimmie Rushing took a combo in there with Dicky Wells playing trombone for him.

In the middle of November we went down to the Academy of Music in Philadelphia on a package deal called "Carnival of Jazz" that also featured Dizzy Gillespie and his combo, Billie Holiday, and Buddy Rich. I think what somebody had in mind was the same kind of big package concert tour for us that Duke and Sarah Vaughan and Nat King Cole already had going at that time, but the only other trip I remember making with it was up to Buffalo right after Philadelphia. I think that was it for that, because by that time the Eckstine deal was already in the works for the early part of the new year.

Meanwhile in the middle of January we also started recording with Norman Granz, and on that first session we made "New Basie Blues," "Sure Thing," "Why Not?," "Fancy Meeting You," and about a week later we came back and did "Jive at Five," "No Name," "Red Head," and "Every Tub." By that time Joe Newman was in the trumpet section, and right away he was even more at home in the new band than he had been in the old one back during the war before he cut out to go with Illinois Jacquet. He took care of most of the trumpet solos on those sessions.

The tenor solos were why more and more people began calling Paul Quinchette the Vice Prez to Lester! But that's Candy Johnson's tenor on "Fancy Meeting You." Charlie Shavers was also with us on those two dates. He gets a nice little taste of "Jive at Five." Henry Coker was our new man in the trombone section, and that gave us another new soloist. That's his trombone in "No Name" and "Red Head." Everybody knew he was there from the very first.

Those sessions were the beginning of something very special. I'm talking about something that was a matter of business and also a matter of very special personal friendship. Norman Granz and I have been involved in a lot of recording dates and concert tours and various other kinds of bookings over the years, which have been just great for me, and our friendship has continued right on up to the present day, and as far as I'm concerned, that's the way it's always going to be.

Actually he and I had already been in touch with each other for a few years before I started recording for him that January. As I remember it, I first met him out in Los Angeles back during the war, or right after the war. Anyway, it was before he started *Jazz at the Philharmonic*. But he was already putting on those jam sessions somewhere every Sunday, and one Sunday I went over to one of them with somebody.

I don't remember exactly where that was, but I do remember that there were a lot of movie stars and other celebrities sitting all around in there, and also a lot of musicians. There was an all-star lineup on the stand, and the house piano player was Nat King Cole, and Norman came over and was talking to me, and he told me to listen to something Nat was getting ready to play.

That's what I recall. It is possible that I may have already met Norman somewhere even before that. But this is the time I actually remember. The number that Norman wanted me to be sure not to miss was "Body and Soul," and I had never heard a solo quite like the one Nat played on it. It was out of sight. Offhand I can't say whether Nat already had his first trio together at that time, but I'm pretty sure it was before he became very widely known.

I am also pretty certain that Norman came out to where we were working at that club out on Central Avenue. He came out there a number of times and we talked, and he was thinking way ahead even then. He was already beginning to put things together, and in a few years he was one of the top promoters, and he has done a lot for a lot of people. He has brought out a lot of people, and he has stuck by them.

Of course, there were some people who have had their differences with him. So naturally they have their ideas and their stories about him, which I won't get into, but you can't overlook all the opportunities and great favors he has done for people, a whole lot of people. That just goes to show that you can always find people to say things against somebody, but what the hell have the ones talking ever done for anybody? They all can say what they want to, but Norman Granz is still Norman Granz, and whatever he does, he just does it. He straightens things out the way he thinks they should be, because that's the way he is, and I think a lot of people have learned quite a lot from him. He's not afraid of anything. But I'm not going into any of that either. I'm just going to acknowledge all of the wonderful things he has put me into during all these years and say that nobody can ever take our friendship away—nobody. Ever. Norman is my man. Period.

It's like with John Hammond. There's only one John Hammond. Some people have their differences with him too. But as far as I'm concerned, John Hammond was the one who made the big difference in my life as a bandleader, no question about it. Without him I probably would still be in Kansas City, if I still happened to be alive. Or back in New York, and I don't know what for. There is certainly nothing I could be doing in New York now at my age at this time. Except maybe trying to be in somebody's band, and then worrying about somebody getting me fired.

There have been a few times when he didn't like something about what the band was doing as much as he did at other times, and he would tell me. He would say, "This is ridiculous, Bill," or something like that, and then sometimes he wouldn't come around for a while. Then if I'd see him somewhere or call him, I'd say, "I'm not expecting you. You ain't going to like this band nohow. But that's all right. I still love you, John." And he'd say, "Okay, Willum."

Even when he would write articles on things he didn't like about the band at different times, that didn't excite me at all. Because he was still my friend. He just wanted us to know what his opinion was, and that was that. As for anything else, he has always been right there, right *in* there and right tight when he thought that I really needed him. He's been a hell of a man. And he has never asked for a nickel from me or any of all those other people he's done so much for. And there have been quite a few of them. And he has even gone back and picked them up again after they had slipped out of sight, and he has uncovered them and brought them back and made a lot of people hear them that never heard them before. And all he wanted was to see the results of what was supposed to be happening.

—

Our first concert tour with Billy Eckstine got under way during the second week in February. We started down in Houston, and during the next month or so, we hit I don't know how many towns down south. One reason I guess I don't remember many details about all those one-nighters we played on that trip is that for me it was really mainly just a matter of knocking off one gig after another. Because all during that time I still was not really so sure that I wanted to be back in the big-band business yet. So I just left everything up to Billy, and I just went along, and of course, he was just wonderful, and he took care of everything.

Because that was the way we had agreed to handle it. When he finally talked me into it, I said, "Okay, I'll go out but I don't want nothing to do with it. You run it." And every time somebody came up to ask me about something, I'd just point right on over to him. He had his staff, and I think they sold most of that first tour to a fellow from Dallas named Howard Lewis.

The only thing you had to worry about with Billy was keeping him from getting into a fight because somebody was trying to pull some stuff. He wouldn't take any foolishness from anybody, no matter who it was— and still does not. So whenever something came up and it looked like it was going to be some stuff, I'd always say, "Don't tell him nothing about it, because that son of a gun will tear up something. Don't tell him nothing about it."

But he got results. One time somewhere on one of those trips, we were talking and he just happened to ask me how much the promoters or who-ever it was were paying me, and when I told him, he hit the ceiling. He said, "Man, that ain't no goddamn money." And he went to whoever it was and said, "Give this goddamn man some goddamn money. How the hell you expect this man to live off this kind of goddamn money?" And they damned near doubled my salary, and then about two weeks later he made them give me another raise.

We played on a lot of military bases during that tour, so sometimes we were flown from one place to another in one of those Air Force transport planes, which was still a pretty rough way to travel back in those days. Going by bus was bad enough. But this was during the Korean War times, and when you flew in a service plane, you had to get all hooked up in a parachute harness, and then the parachute pack was what you had to sit on as your cushion in those bucket seats along the wall.

So you sat facing the aisle like on the subway, and sometimes you also had to bundle yourself up in as many GI blankets as you could get to keep warm at those high altitudes, since those planes were not yet pressurized like the commercial airlines. Along with that, you could also hear all of that noise of the engines and propellers and the wind, and every time there was any kind of change in sound or motion, you could hear it and feel it. I never had been very excited about flying, and all that bumping around and carrying on didn't do anything to change my mind.

And of course, it would be just my luck to have the seat right by the exit. So if something happened and we had to bail out, I was supposed to be the first to jump. That didn't help my morale at all. Then, sure enough, on one of those hops somewhere down in Texas, we were sitting, already sweating it out, and just about the time we were supposed to be getting ready to land, one of the crew members came back there and started checking on something, and right away you could tell, or at least I suspected, that there was some kind of trouble. There was something wrong with the landing gear. So they were just circling around up there trying to straighten out whatever it was. It's a good thing that they got everything working again, because there was no way that I was going to be the first to bail out. I was not going to jump until the crew started hitting the silk.

—

When we came back into New York after that first southern trip with Billy, we went into the Savoy, and that is when Eddie "Lockjaw" Davis came into the reed section. I didn't know very much about Eddie at that time. My main man in the research department tells me that Eddie and Joe Newman had worked together, so Joe must have spoken to me about it, but if so, I don't remember what he said. I just remember that we were working at the Savoy for about three or four weeks, and we were rehearsing up there, and he used to come up and bring his little daughter. She was a very little child, and I was very fond of her because she was so cute.

That's what I remember, and every time I'd look up, Jaws would be sitting right there behind me on the steps near where the piano was. I don't remember whether Candy Johnson had already given his notice or not, but I do remember that Jaws kept saying, "You need me in this band." And I said, "No, I don't. I don't need nobody." But he'd say, "You need me in there." And I said, "I don't need you, man, and you ain't gonna stay with nobody no how."

But I did bring him in during that time, and right away he provided us with the same kind of tenor contrast to Paul Quinchette that Herschel and then Buddy was to Lester. But we did not use that contrast the same way as before. We didn't feature them on the same numbers as much. Mostly Paul had his tunes and Jaws had his. Of course, when we played some of the things from the old book, one would follow the other. But the contrast of those two styles was always there, and a lot of people still remember that band as the one that featured Paul Quinchette and Eddie "Lockjaw" Davis. I know what they mean, but they shouldn't forget that Joe Newman (also known as Pootman) was also one of the features of that band, and so was Henry Coker.

When we made our next records for Norman near the end of that July, Paul did his thing on that number that Ernie Wilkins worked up, from one of our signature themes called "Basie Talks," and sometimes also "Basie English," "Basie Kicks," and also "Basie." "Cash Box," "Bootsie," and "HFO" were also his. Jaws got to show his stuff on "Jack and Jill," "Bread," "Paradise Squat," "Tom Whaley," "Blee Blop Blues," and "Tipping on the Q.T.," which was a very cute arrangement, by the way.

The last day we were in the studio making those numbers, I also made my first two tracks with a fantastic young piano player named Oscar Peterson. We did "Blues for Count and Oscar," with Oscar on piano, me on organ, Paul and Jaws on tenor, Freddie Greene on guitar, Ray Brown on bass, and Gus on drums. Then we had the tenors lay out on "Extended Blues." Then Oscar sat with the band on "Be My Guest," and naturally he tore it up. He always tears it up. Hell, he can't help it.

At that time he was just making the scene as one of Norman Granz's stars. But that wasn't really the first time I had ever run into him. The first time I heard him was years before that when he was still a little youngster, so small that his feet could just barely reach the pedals, but he could play a lot of classics. He was unbelievable. I was playing at a theater in Toronto, and they brought him by so I could hear him play. Then the second time was years later, and I was up in Buffalo sitting in some place one night and Coleman Hawkins and I were sitting together talking with some friends, and Coleman said, "You got to hear this cat play piano. You never heard anything like him." So then they introduced him, and he came on and started playing, and this time he was *swinging*, and I mean, it was *there*. He was just terrific, and Hawk and I just sat there listening, and Hawk just sat there nodding his head and smiling.

"What did I tell you?"

═

The lineup on those records is just about the same one we were using on our first full band gig in Birdland that summer. We were in there for two weeks, and things went very, very well for us. We had been using Bixie Crawford as our vocalist on a few dates, but we didn't take her into Birdland with us because, if I remember rightly, it wasn't their policy to have band singers in there at that time. Of course, when it came to Mr. B. and Sarah Vaughan, that was something else. That was another story.

Those weeks we spent in Birdland that summer were just great for us in a lot of ways. It's always good for a new band to have a chance to settle down somewhere and play in one place night after night for a while. That's one of the best ways I know for really getting things together and also having time to rehearse and try out new things. You can always tell the difference when a band has a chance to settle down somewhere like that. You can hear it, and you can feel it.

And you couldn't wish for a better spot than Birdland. You were back in the Apple, and you were right on the main stem, right where everything was happening. You couldn't beat that kind of exposure, and the people running Birdland, from Morris Levy himself right on down to the washroom attendants, were all for us. It was just a wonderful atmosphere to be working in, and the people who came in there picked right up on what we were trying to do, and they began talking about us, and you'd see a lot of the same ones coming back as a regular thing, just like in the old days at the Famous Door.

The way Willard Alexander tells it, Morris Levy himself was the one who came up with the idea of having me come into Birdland with a full band. Before that I don't think they had used anything but combos, mostly stand-up groups. One time, according to Morris, they had tried an all-star aggregation in there called the Birdland Dream Band with Dizzy Gillespie, Charlie Parker, Miles Davis, and a lot of really outstanding musicians like that, but Morris says they never really got themselves together as a band, so it didn't work out.

I guess we must have had a little better luck, and Morris was very pleased with the way everything turned out. Business was good, and we got a few very favorable write-ups. Here is some of what *Downbeat* had to say: "*During two wonderful weeks in town recently, Bill Basie showed that far from having to piece together a clumsy rehash of his old band, he has managed to assemble an ensemble that can thrill both the listener who remembers 1938 and the youngster who has never before heard a big band like this.*"

The Birdland people loved that kind of review, and so did Willard Alexander, and so did I. But now I also have to say that as much as I liked that band—and I really did like it very much—I still didn't feel that we had really gotten it intact yet at that time, not to say that I could put my finger on anything in particular, because it really was nice, but somehow I just knew that it was going to be even better after we worked together for a longer while.

We went back out on another tour of one-nighters with Billy Eckstine that fall. It was still Billy's package, but this time Norman Granz also came in as the promoter. I don't know any more about what the arrangement was between Billy and Norman than I knew about the one with Howard Lewis.

We made one important change in the lineup while we were out on tour that fall, and that was on bass. Jimmy Lewis cut out in Denver, and that's when we got Gene Ramey to come in. I don't actually remember how his name happened to come up, but my guess is that Gus Johnson recommended him. They were old friends. They had been together when they were in that great rhythm section in Jay McShann's wonderful band, the same band that had Charlie Parker, Walter Brown, Al Hibbler, Orville Minor, and all those guys in it.

When that concert package tour with Eckstine was over, we came back to New York and, during the first part of that December, worked across the Hudson over in Englewood Cliffs, New Jersey, at the Rustic Cabin, which meant that we were really back in the Apple once more. So Norman Granz set up a few recording dates for us, but we just used the band on one, and on the others we used combos ranging from five to nine players.

The only change in the full band that we used to make "Sent for You Yesterday," "Let Me Dream," and "Going to Chicago," with Al Hibbler doing the vocals, was Gene Ramey. The rest of the lineup was the same as it was when we were in Birdland that summer. But in those combos, Buddy Rich sat in on drums. That was not hard to arrange, because Buddy and Norman were pretty tight, too.

The eight tunes we made on that session using Joe Newman and Paul Quinchette with the rhythm section were "Stan Shorthair," "Blue and Sentimental," "Count's Organ Blues," "As Long as I Live," "Basie Beat," "K.C. Organ Blues," "She's Funny That Way," and "Royal Garden Blues." I got a chance to use the organ on "Basie Beat," "K.C. Organ Blues," "She's Funny That Way," and 'Count's Organ Blues." I got a real kick out of that, and so did Norman, who was right there in the control booth during all the takes. I remember we really got with him because he left the door wide-open for me to do anything I wanted to do. We especially got along great because we both liked the same thing. We both liked the blues. Right up until today we still like the blues. Every time I go in the studio, he says, "What kind of blues you got?" And I say, "I don't know. What you want? Any kind you want."

My first job that next year was in Birdland. We opened in there on New Year's Day and stayed for two weeks. Lester and his combo were also back in there, alternating with us again, and we had a ball, as I was reminded once more not long ago when I was listening to some records made from air checks of a few of the radio broadcasts we used to make from there during that time. Lester and his little chickees, as he used to call them, Jesse Drakes, Roy Haynes.

Those air checks will give you a pretty good sample of what the band sounded like in a live performance at that time, and they are also very interesting because they picked up a few tunes that for one reason or another we never did record in a studio. I don't think we even had Paul Quinchette make a regular record of that number of his called "Prevue," and I don't think he ever cut "Basie Jones" on a studio date either. And the same goes for "Jingle Bells" featuring Lockjaw. I think that must have been a little something that somebody cooked up for the holiday season. I don't remember what happened to "Basie Loaded," featuring Joe Newman, Benny Powell, and Lockjaw.

A lot of Lester's fans will probably be very interested in those air checks of "Jumping at the Woodside" and those two of "Every Tub," because they feature him as guest soloist with the band. That was something that Birdland audiences really went for, and it was a lot of fun for the fellows in the band too. They loved Lester. He was the president.

During the third week in January, we went back out on the road doing concerts with Billy Eckstine again, and this time Billy took a wonderful singer named Ruth Brown along as a special feature. Ruth's big hit number was "Mama, He Treats Your Daughter Mean," and she scored big again with "Shake a Hand," and she didn't do too bad with "Cry, Cry, Cry" and "Jim Dandy" either. She could go out there and break it up with anything, and that's just about what she did every night. There she and Mr. B. had a duet that used to bring the house down every night, too, no matter where we went.

We swung back down through the South again with that package, hitting places like Richmond, Atlanta, New Orleans, Memphis, and a couple of dozen other places down there. Then, when we came back to New York in April, we went into a new club at 1680 Broadway called the Band Box. Mr. B. was the star on that show, too, and another feature was a combo led by a young piano player by the name of Dave Brubeck.

I don't actually remember whether Paul Quinchette left us just before we went into the Band Box after we opened there, but I do remember that Ben Webster came in with us for a while during the time we were there. But Ben was just filling in for a while. Paul's real replacement turned out to be a young fellow out of Oklahoma by way of Washington named Frank Wess, who was recommended by Billy Eckstine. Frank came in sometime in June. Then about a month later Lockjaw Davis cut out, and that's when we got another Frank for the tour, Frank Foster. Frank was just getting out of the army, and he was also recommended by Mr. B. and also by Ernie Wilkins.

We also had to make a few other changes in the lineup that summer. Gene Ramey cut out, so we got my old friend Milt Hinton to fill in on bass for a while before he left town to join Louis Armstrong's All-Stars. Then Al Hall filled in for a while, and when he split, Frank Wess recommended

Eddie Jones. Frank and Eddie had known each other as students at Howard University, and they had also worked together around Washington. It wasn't until he had been in the band for a week or so that I realized that he was from *my* home town and that I knew his family.

There was also a change in the trombone section. We had Johnny Mandel in there for a while after Jimmy Wilkins left. Johnny worked up a few nice little things for that book before he decided to move out to the West Coast. "Straight Life" was his tune. Henderson Chambers also filled that chair for a short time, and when he left, Frank Wess got Bill Hughes, another fine musician from the Howard University and D.C. scene to come in, and that was the beginning of Bill's long association with the band.

The only studio recordings we did that summer were the tracks of "Plymouth Rock," "Blues Go Away," and "One O'Clock Jump" that we did for Norman Granz on Clef. While we were out in Los Angeles in July, "One O'Clock Jump" was not issued, but Norman decided to issue "Plymouth Rock" and "Blues Go Away," along with some other new things in our current book that he was planning to have us record as soon as he could find the time.

We went back into the Band Box in July on the same bill with Duke. That was a great thrill. It was always a special treat for me just to be around the maestro, and frankly, like most other bandleaders, I hoped we would make a good impression on him. But it was the publicity people who promoted that gig as a battle of bands. Not me. They were thinking about how good a cutting contest would be for business. But I knew what Duke could lay on you if he wanted to. There was nobody who could lay the stuff on you that he could lay on you anytime he wanted to.

He had a hell of a lineup to call on, too. Johnny Hodges and Lawrence Brown were still out of the band at that time. But the great voice of Harry Carney was still in there on baritone, and he also had Jimmy Hamilton, Russell Procope, Rick Henderson, and Paul Gonsalves in that reed esction. He had Britt Woodman in Lawrence's chair in the trombone section with Quentin Jackson and John Sanders. He still had Ray Nance, Cat Anderson, Willie Cook, and Clark Terry on trumpets, and in the rhythm section with him he had Wendell Marshall on bass and Louis Bellson on drums. As for Clark Terry and Paul Gonsalves, both of them had left me to join Duke, so I knew what those two monsters could do.

Of course, our fans were always loyal to us, and I also knew that I could count on all of those wonderful youngsters in my crew to keep us from being run out of there in disgrace. After all, they wanted to make a good impression on Duke too. But don't ever let anybody put the idea in your head that you're going in somewhere and chop Duke. That's like being in the ring with Joe Louis and having your fans cheering you on from the ringside while you're getting your brains beat out. They're out there bragging on you, but you're the one up there facing all that stuff.

As far as I was concerned, everything was in good clean fun and on a very friendly basis all the way. We were just going in there and doing our little thing the best we could. Because Duke's whole thing was always so *beautiful*. It's so melodic and it took in everything—prettiness, swing— everything. It was just so wonderful. If you top that, where are you going? If he wanted something to swing, it was going to *swing*, and he was going to swing your behind right on *out* of there. Some people might not realize that. But I do. And I *know*. They can jump in there if they want to. Not me.

I can still remember walking down those stairs one night while Duke had this thing going on down there. I was just coming back from some- where and by the time I got halfway down there, all that music hit me. Wham! I had to turn around and go back up to that little bar upstairs and get another drink and then come back down a step at a time. It was too much. I had to go back and get myself together to face all of that.

When somebody asks me about him, I say you never know what's going to happen, for Christ's sake. I mean, he could take five pieces and make them sound like fifteen if he wanted to. They've copied his sound, or should I say *tried* to copy part of his sound, but they copy it with an orchestra with about a million people in it. They can't copy that sound with four or six men. Hell, it didn't matter to Duke if he went into a recording session and he had fifteen or sixteen men in his band and nine didn't show up. He'd just take those that are there and go on and do a side right there while they're waiting for the rest. If something like that happened, he could do it, and when you can do that, you're a champion and you're the boss!

He was just glorious. I loved him so much. I used to get a kick out of being near him. Just like I also used to get so much of a kick every time I'd get a chance to be next to and talk to another champion, one by the name of Joe Louis. Standing next to him, you felt so big. Just to sit down by Duke did me a world of good. There'll never be another one like him.

—

The show we went out on the road with that next fall had Sugar Ray Robinson, the super-great middleweight boxing champion, doing a danc- ing and comedy act as a special drawing card. Sugar Ray was taking a little vacation from the ring for a spell, and he decided to go into show business for a while. By this time he had already become one of the greatest fighters of all time as a result of all those great battles with Jake LaMotta, Rocky Graziano, Fritzie Zivic, and Kid Gavilan, to name a few, so the sportswriters had him going into retirement. But actually in a couple of years he came back and took care of some business in those terrific battles with Bobo Olson, Gene Fulmer, and Carmen Basilio.

Ray was another one of those all-time great champions who it was a big thrill for me to be hanging out with. One of the things I will always remember about that trip is how a group of us used to get together somewhere in a dressing room or a hotel and listen to the fights being broadcast over the radio, with him making his comments about how different what was probably happening in the ring was from what the sports announcer was telling you.

It was while we were out on that tour that I finally made up my mind that I was really back in the big-band business to stay.

When we came back into New York at the end of that tour, Norman set up a studio date, and we cut eight of the ten tunes he brought out in a twelve-inch album called *Count Basie Dance Sessions*. That's when we made "Straight Life," "Basie Goes West," "Softly, With Feeling," "Peace Pipe," "Cherry Point," "Bubbles," "Right On," and "The Blues Done Come Back." The other two tunes were 'Blues Go Away," and "Plymouth Rock," which I have already mentioned recording a few months earlier.

Then we went back into Birdland for the Christmas and New Year's holiday season. That made it two years in a row that we were in there for New Year's Day, and all you have to do to find out how great the band felt about that gig is just listen to the air checks of the broadcast on the NBC "All-Star Parade of Bands." At that time the band was still not yet as together as it became later on, but those guys were definitely taking care of business already.

Also, unless I'm mistaken, that was the time when the new thing we went down there with was Frank Wess playing the flute. Frank was an excellent flute player, but he had been with us for a little while before I found that out. Don Redman hipped me to him. We were uptown playing a gig somewhere, and Don came by and asked me how Frank was doing, and he said, "Has he played anything on the flute for you yet?" And I said, "Well, I didn't know about that." And Don said, "Why don't you try him?"

So one day at the Savoy we were doing a jam and I told Frank, "Why don't you take a couple of choruses on your flute? Did you bring your flute?"

And he looked surprised.

"Do you really want me to?"

"Yeah," I said. "Take a couple and let's see what happens."

So he went out there and played and broke it up, and as soon as I heard him, that was when I realized that we had a new thing to go back down into Birdland with. So that's how the flute thing started, because it seemed to me that it excited just about everybody that came down there.

"Hey, what is that?" they said.

"What's he doing, jazzing the flute?"

"Yeah," I said.

"Well. . . ."

And not long after, everywhere you looked, here come the flutes. Here come the flutes. Here come the flutes. Arrangers started leaving special spots for flutes. Later we also began to feature flute duets and little flute ensemble passages. We still do. They can put something different in somebody else's books, but Frank Wess is the man who really brought the flute into the jazz scene beginning right down there in Birdland.

SIXTEEN MEN SWINGING

1954 = 1959

That was the beginning of a very remarkable year for us. In March I finally got a chance to make my first trip to Europe. That had been in the works for a while, and when it seemed like it was actually about to come through, the kids in the band really began to look forward to it like a team getting ready for the World Series or something like that. As Joe Newman was telling my co-writer not long ago, "A few nights before we took off by SAS Airlines for Copenhagen, we were playing a date at an army base. The adrenaline was flowing like you would not believe. Everybody was just raring to go. Let me at it. Let me at it. The sections, the soloists. Everybody."

It was a very big thrill for me to be making my first trip overseas, but to tell the truth, I really think I spent so much of that flight trying my best to get a little rest and relaxation that I can just barely remember what that part of the trip was like. I can say one thing. I didn't like flying across the ocean any more than I had liked getting on those planes and going to all of those military bases back when we were touring with Billy Eckstine. I always used to expect a little help from Mr. Scotch or Mr. Bourbon in a situation like that, but I can't really say that either one of them ever really helped me. Maybe some. Not much. Not enough.

When we landed in Copenhagen, there were reception committees and reporters and photographers out at the airport to meet us, and when we got into town, there were more receptions and more interviews, which, I must say, was just wonderful, because everybody was so glad to see us and already knew so much about our music. They were really interested, and not only the reporters, but just plain fans were also coming up asking about members and happenings and personal things we hadn't thought about for years.

It was a great experience. But that also meant that you didn't get very much time to relax for just a few minutes on your own. Maybe some of the fellows got a little chance to break away for a little sight-seeing and gift shopping and maybe even a little other action, which I won't go into because it's none of my business. I didn't. Of course, I never have been very big on sight-seeing, so my main thing was just to enjoy what was happening and then get a little rest before the opening concert.

Which, according to the newspaper reports, was heard by eight thousand people, and which also got us some very nice write-ups. So we got off to a very good start, and that's the way things went for us from Copenhagen to Stockholm and Amsterdam, and from there to Brussels and Lille and then through Strasbourg and Metz and down to Lyons and Dijon, and then up to Paris for a couple of days. Then from Paris we went into Germany and played in Munich, Stuttgart, and Hamburg. Then the last three days we went into Switzerland and played in Basel, Zurich, and Geneva. Some of these were standard bookings, but as I remember it, quite a few were also on bases where American troops were stationed in Europe at that time. We didn't go to England on that tour.

I never will forget the narrow escape I had on the night we opened in Stockholm. One of the chief promoters took me out to dinner with Dean Dixon, the famous symphony orchestra conductor, and a heck of a fine guy, too, by the way. That was the night I met him for the first time, and that dinner was also the first time I ever ate raw hamburger, also known as steak tartare. It takes two hours to get through a dinner like that. You start out drinking vodka or something like that. Then they begin serving those raw hamburgers with all that spicy seasoning. They were mixing them all around the table, and we were having a little of that and a little of something else and then another drink and then some more and then another; and this went on and on, and they said we had plenty of time to finish dinner and get to the concert hall. But when we finally got to the main course, I couldn't even see it.

They had to get me out of there and take me to the hotel, and they put me in just about the coldest goddamn room I've ever been in anywhere in my life. There was no kind of heat at all in there. The only warmth I got was from a quilt they gave me. I really don't know what they all actually did to get me in there, but somehow they got me out of trouble in time for that concert.

That was my narrow escape. There was also a little surprise that I'll just mention. One of the American musicians that came by to see us turned out to be the little drummer that I had worked with back at the beginning of the time I spent with Gonzelle White and her Big Jazz Jamboree, the one who used to do all that fancy stuff when we were taking encores and curtain calls. He was doing very well over there, and he still looked almost the same as he did when I last saw him about twenty-five years before that.

I said hey, and called him by the stage name I remembered, and he grabbed me before I could say another word.

"Shhh . . . take it easy, man. That's not my name anymore. Don't nobody know nothing about that name over here."

I understood what he meant. I had spoken without thinking, and truthfully I realized that as soon as the word came out of my mouth and I saw that look in his eyes. I won't even repeat the name again, since I already used it in the Gonzelle White part of this story.

When we finally made it to Paris, that was really something. Everybody was looking forward to those concerts there. I guess I already knew how much the Frenchmen in Paris loved our kind of music long before Hugues Panassié and I met when he came to the States, way back during the time when we were in the Famous Door. I was jiving people about being on my way to Paris back during my first year out of Kansas City. I was playing organ in the Eblon Theatre, and when I got the telegram from Walter Page inviting me to join the Blue Devils, I went around telling people that I was on my way to Paris. And I showed them the address on the telegram, but I kept my finger over part of it so that they would think it was Paris, France, and not Paris, Texas.

But my head was already full of stories about Paris a long time before that. After all, I was a teenager when the AEF went overseas during the First World War, and all during the time, I was stumbling around to all those joints in Asbury Park and Harlem before I went out on the road with Gonzelle and ended up stranded in Kansas City. I probably heard as much talk from musicians and entertainers about Paris as any other city in the world. Somebody was always going over there and coming back with some more fantastic tales about how fabulous it was and how much they loved musicians.

So what can I say about coming to Paris that first time? Personally I had a ball. Everything was just great, and I think everybody else in the band can say the same thing. But I'm not going into any details about that, because there was so much happening in so many different places around town with so many different very nice people that I honestly didn't know where the hell I was most of the time. There was never any time to get away and be all by yourself and figure anything out on your own. But that's just a part of the dues you have to pay when you find yourself up somewhere as the main event. It's an entirely different thing from going somewhere on a visit. Instead of you going around getting a look at the city, it's more like the city getting a look at you. So when you finally get a chance, you try to catch up on a little of that shut-eye you always need before going to work, and you tell yourself that you have to come back to this wonderful place when you have time to get with it on your own.

We played four concerts in Paris that first time, and according to the reporters who were there for all four, we got off to a very good start and kept getting better right on through the last. That's also the way I felt things went, and I imagine that the fellows in the band felt the same way. By the time we came to the end of that program, they were really raring to blow. They were up for Paris. Yes, sir. No question about that.

I had a lot of stories hidden behind my brain about Germany. So it was a little strange when we first arrived there. But everything came out all right. At that time some areas had not repaired and rebuilt all of the wartime damage and destruction, but there were a lot of neat and fine-looking towns, too, and there were some little places that we went through that looked kind of weird. I remember some of those ruins of those castles in the mountains had looked haunted, like in stories from your childhood and old late-night movies.

But the people were very friendly. In some of the small places, they couldn't speak English very well. That was not usually the case, however. Most places you went, you found out that a lot of people could speak your language pretty well and understand you. But you couldn't speak theirs. That was a strange situation to be in, and sometimes just being able to understand just a few of their common sayings and expressions could have made things a little easier for me from time to time. I remember one time I didn't understand something, and it almost became embarrassing.

We were in a great big place in one of those German cities. I forget which one, but it was a beautiful hall, and we came on and all of a sudden the audience started doing a lot of stomping on the floor. I didn't know what the hell they were doing. I guess they must have been saying something, too, but that didn't help me, either, because I didn't know what the hell they were saying, chanting, or whatever they were doing. It was the goddamnest thing up there, because they could have been getting ready to run us off there, stomping on the floor like that. But of course, that was not what it was. They liked us.

We didn't get to play in England on that first tour, but the band went over so well everywhere we went that we were pretty certain that we were going to be making return trips in the near future; and we also knew that the English reporters who were covering most of our key concerts were so high on us that we couldn't have had a better bunch of advance agents.

—

When we came back to the States, we worked our way right on across the country and out to the Coast and back before going into Birdland that next time. Meanwhile we had to get somebody to replace Joe Wilder in the trumpet section, and Frank Wess recommended Thad Jones. It seems to me that I first heard him in Detroit. But he probably joined us in New York. Anyway, Thad just moved right on in and became one of us. When we went into the studio in June to make all eighteen of those tunes that Clef Records brought out in our next two albums, I don't think he had been in that section a whole month yet, but he was already with it, and that's his first recorded trumpet solo for us on "Ska-di-dle-dee-bee-doo."

Actually, most of those arrangements had already been in the book for a while by the time we made those recordings. We were already playing Ernie Wilkins's "Sixteen Men Swinging," Frank Foster's "Blues Backstage" and Neal Hefti's "Two Franks," just to name a few, before we left for Europe. But the book was growing all the time because arrangers were always bringing in new things.

We had all that wonderful stuff that was being worked up by writers that we already had right there playing in the band, and Neal Hefti and a few others were also bringing in their things from the outside. By this time we had picked up around a dozen originals from Neal, and I think Norman recorded just about all of them. There is something of his on each one of those first albums of that new band.

I had already known some of our other outside writers like Andy Gibson and Buster Harding for years; in fact, we were still playing some of the things they had done for the other band. But I didn't know very much about Neal Hefti before he did those first things for us. I'm not sure who introduced us. It might have been Norman, or it could have been Willard Alexander. But anyway Neal came by, and we had a talk, and he said he'd just like to put something in the book. Then he came back with "Little Pony" and then "Sure Thing," "Why Not?" and "Fancy Meeting You," and we ran them down, and that's how we got married.

I think Neal did a lot of marvelous things for us, because even though what he did was a different thing and not quite the style but sort of a different sound, I think it was quite musical. We still have some of Neal's things in the book. One thing that he did for us a little later on called "Li'l Darlin' " has become one of our standards.

With all the new writers we had bringing things in there and all the changes in the lineup of those sections, it was like we were starting to build a whole new book. But that was not really so, because I was still using a whole lot of material from that other library, and I still do. Our audiences have never stopped asking for tunes like "Jumping at the Woodside," "Swinging the Blues," "9:20 Special," "Every Tub," and all those things, and the new guys seem to get as big a kick out of them as anything else.

So what we were really doing and what we are still doing to this day is adding to the book. Naturally there are some changes, because so many of the people writing and playing were different, and hell, I was different, too. But when you talk about the difference in the sound and style of those two bands, the one in the Famous Door and the one in Birdland, the Old Testament band and the New Testament band, as my co-writer likes to say, you have to remember how that other band was sounding on some of the things we were playing just before we broke up.

Some people call the new band an ensemble band, but we already had some of the same ensembles in the band that recorded "Wonderful Thing," "Mine, Too," and "Normania," which became one of the numbers the new band used to hit with. We just changed the title to "Blee Blop Blues."

But like I've said so many times before, I really haven't been very interested in making all those distinctions. The band in the Famous Door had its thing, and the one in Birdland had its, but they were both swinging. The new band didn't have the stars in it that the other band had, but the band was jumping, and every one of those soloists was taking care of business.

But the thing about it is, to me, the band is *always* changing. Every time we come back from vacation, I'm listening for different little things, even when it's the same lineup. And naturally when I put somebody new in there, he's going to bring something different, and I'm always excited to find out what he's going to have to put in there. Truthfully, every time one of those cats walks out to the solo microphone, it's a big thrill for me to hear how he's going to come on this time. You never know.

  —

We spent the last part of July and the first part of August back in Birdland, which by that time was really beginning to feel more and more like home base for us. We were beginning to be able to count on being booked in there for three- or four-week stands about four times a year. That was really a beautiful deal for us because everybody could look forward to being at home for about a month in the summer, about a month around Christmas, and maybe another few weeks in the spring, and there was still some time off for vacation. By the way, there are also air checks of the band in there that time, and I think they gave you a nice little taste of the way things were popping in Birdland that summer.

In the middle of August we went out to Chicago and spent the next two weeks at the Blue Note, which at that time was the number-one jazz spot out there. So things were popping out there too. But the main reason I remember that particular gig was something that happened during intermission of a dance we were playing on the South Side at the Trianon. Rennald Jones, my lead trumpet man, came to me all excited about a singer he had just heard.

"Hey, Base, hey, man," he said. "I've just been down the street there, man, and there's a cat down there you ought to hear. Yeah, man, you ought to hear this cat singing the blues. He's really something, man. You got to hear this kid, Base."

"Well, hell," I said. "If he's that good, why don't you go back down there and get him and bring him up here on the next break and I'll see him."

And that's what happened. By that time the other place was on a break, too, and as soon as Jonesy brought him in, I saw that it was the same young singer that used to come stand outside in the Brass Rail and sing along with the combo I had in there three or four years before.

Well, he just came on in there and got up and sang some blues, and he broke it up; and I made my decision right then and there. I didn't have to figure anything out or anything like that. As soon as he got into his thing, I knew the band could use him right away.

"That's great," I said. "That's wonderful. Now I tell you what. I leave here in the morning, so go get your suitcase packed and be down at the Blue Note ready to get on the bus before nine o'clock."

So that's how that marriage got started although he wasn't able to come with us until a few months later. He actually joined us in New York a few days before Christmas. He got there just in time to get himself together a bit and get right on the bus for a swing down through Washington, Maryland and Virginia, and he's still on the trip that began on that bus that many years ago. I don't recall whether I actually remembered his name from that time at the Brass Rail. But he wasn't with us very long before a whole lot of people everywhere knew who Joe Wililams was.

There was a little static at first, but not for long. When the time came for us to go back into Birdland, they didn't want to take him. They didn't want to have to pay that extra tax or something you had to pay to bring a vocalist in there. And nobody knew anything about Joe Williams yet, so somebody said, "No, we just don't want a singer. The band doesn't need a vocalist."

So I said, "Okay. That's all right. I'll take him in with me. I'll just take it as my responsibility." And Joe went in there and knocked them out. So then here they come, and I said, "So, you don't want him, huh?" And they said, "Hey, wait a minute. This is a different thing now." And I said, "Oh, yeah? It sure is. We're going to sit down and do a little talking now. We going to do a little business."

Then when we went down to Philadelphia a little later on, the owners of that place didn't want him at first, either, but when we closed in there, we had an open week before we were due on our next gig. So what happened? *They wanted to extend him as a single.* They didn't say anything about extending the band. They wanted to make a side deal with him for that week.

—

But to back up a bit, one night in early October, we went into Carnegie Hall in the opening spot on a big concert package. I don't know whether anybody made any tapes or transcriptions of that or not, but it was a hell of a show. It was an all-star gig. The two featured singers were Billie Holiday and Sarah Vaughan. The Wild Bill Davis Trio was there with Wild Bill on that organ, and so was the Modern Jazz Quartet, with John Lewis on piano, Milt Jackson on vibes, Percy Heath on bass, and Kenny Clarke on drums.

Then there were also two instrumental solo features. They brought Charlie Parker on with the Modern Jazz Quartet in Milt Jackson's spot, and we backed Lester on a head arrangement of "Stomping at the Savoy" that was a real gas. Some of our musicians also backed Billie on her set.

For our own spot we came on with Frank Foster getting off with "You for Me." Then the other Frank, Frank Wess, did his thing on "Perdido," with his flute on one solo and his tenor on the follow-up. So then we sent both Franks out there together on Neal Hefti's "Two Franks," and of course, they tore it up. I don't remember how many other numbers we had time for, but I'm pretty sure that Joe Newman and Thad Jones and Coker and Marshall got a little taste before we took it out.

At the end of the month, there was a big Sunday-night banquet at the Waldorf-Astoria given for me by a committee headed by John Hammond, Willard Alexander, and Allan Morrison, who was then the New York editor for *Ebony* magazine. According to the invitation, what they were celebrating was my twentieth year as a bandleader. Now that I think about it, I don't know just how they figured that out to be twenty years at that time, unless they began back with the time I was elected to lead that band at the Cherry Blossom when Bennie Moten went over to Club Harlem with George E. Lee. Which is very interesting because, after all, just about everybody, including me, went back to Bennie Moten after we went down to Little Rock and got stranded. Most people think I first became a leader at the Reno Club, which was not until after Bennie passed away, which didn't add up to twenty.

But I'm pretty sure I didn't question anything like that at that time. Truthfully, the whole thing was such a big surprise that I had a big enough hustle just to make it. Then when I did get there, I was in for an even bigger surprise. There were about four hundred and fifty people up there on the Starlight Roof that night. That's a lot of friends in one room at the same time. You have to be moved by something like that, no matter how much applause you're used to hearing when you come onto the bandstand every night.

My father and a bunch of people from my hometown were there; and a whole string of speakers including Congressman Adam Clayton Powell and his wife, Hazel Scott; Nat King Cole; Lena Horne; Benny Goodman; Joyce Bryant; and Marshall Stearns got up and said a lot of nice things about me. Dr. James Parker from Red Bank also said some nice things about my childhood days that must have surprised the hell out of all those house folks who really know what little old Willie Basie was really like back in those days.

Old Lips Page was the emcee, but the big surprise of the evening came when they opened the curtain down at the other end of the room and I saw all the musicians from the old band that John Hammond had rounded up to turn the occasion into a reunion. He had gotten Jack Washington to fly in from Oklahoma City. Lester took time off from a gig in Chicago. Walter Page, Jimmy Rushing, Jo Jones, Earl Warren, Buck Clayton, Ed Lewis, Dan Minor, Emmett Berry, and, naturally, Freddie Greene, who was and is still working with me, were all sitting up there ready to roll, with Erroll Garner on piano.

I sat there and listened to those characters for a while, and then I had to excuse myself from my table and go up there and join them. I don't think that surprised anybody. As far as John Hammond was concerned, it was only a matter of how many bars I could take before I made my move. And the guys on the stand started in on me the minute I got there.

"Here he comes. Hey, man, what you doing up here? You supposed to be the guest of honor. It's your party."

And I said, "You damn right it's my party. And that's just why I'm not going to let you dirty dogs have all the fun!"

So Erroll let me take over, and we hopped on a few old things like "Every Tub," "Sent For You Yesterday," and, of course, the "Jump." Then we ended the evening with my current band, and they got a special kick out of playing in the presence of all those guys from the old days.

By this time, that current band was really getting there. But before the year was out, we found ourselves with a hell of an emergency on our hands. Shortly after we opened in Birdland for the Christmas holidays, Gus Johnson had an attack of appendicitis and had to go into the hospital for an operation. That was just two days before Christmas. But that just shows how fate works sometimes.

Because the guy we brought in to pinch-hit for Gus was Sonny Payne, and he came in and hit a home run with the bases loaded. That was not any reflection on Gus at all. Absolutely not, because Gus, even up to this very minute, is still one of the great drummers. He's got a great sense of timing,

and he can hold things together. Everybody speaks of him as being a great
man for backing a band. He can set things behind a big band or any kind
of band or any kind of group. It doesn't make any difference. He's a great
drummer even if he's just playing by himself. He can do it from one and
two on up. He's just an all-around great guy to have in your organization.

But fate is a funny thing. Sonny Payne came in there, and right away
he touched off a new spark in that band, and we had to keep him as much
as we all loved Gus. Naturally people noticed that Sonny was more of a
showman than Gus was, but I wouldn't say that showmanship was what
made the difference. It was not that easy. You can't see any stick twirling
and trickerlating on those next records, but you can hear and feel a difference in the band.

—

When Ernie Wilkins decided to give up his chair in the reed section that
following January, his move didn't really have any big overall effect on
the sound and drive of the band, because he continued to write for us. In
fact the real reason he got out of the band was to be able to stay in New
York and concentrate all of his time on arranging and composing. So that
is what happened. He was no longer performing in the reed section when
we recorded the arrangement of "Everyday I Have the Blues." Bill
Graham was playing Ernie's book at that time; but Ernie was responsible
for the Joe Williams's vocal that turned out to be the first really big hit
release of the new band.

But that's getting a little ahead of the story, because in the meantime
something else was added to our deal with Morris Levy. As of the middle
of December, Birdland had been in business for five years and was still
jumping, while most other clubs in the Fifty-second Street area had gone
under. So as a feature of the fifth-anniversary celebration, Morris decided
to take a Birdland package show on tour. It was called "Birdland Stars of
1955," and in that first lineup they had Sarah Vaughan, Erroll Garner,
Lester Young, George Shearing, Stan Getz, and my band.

The program always opened with the band. Then Stan Getz and his
group would come on, and then George Shearing would close the first
half. That would take about an hour. Then after intermission the second
set would open with the band back onstage again, and we would also back
Lester for his set. Then Erroll and his rhythm section would take over
until it was time for Sarah, and she would take it up to the finale, which
brought everybody back out.

That was the show Morris took out in February. We went up to Boston
and came back to Newark for an early show at the Mosque Theatre, and
then cut straight back to the Apple and played a late show at Carnegie

Hall that same night. Then we hit the road and swung down to Richmond, Norfolk, and Raleigh, and came back to Philadelphia, and after that we headed west out of Rochester and didn't get back east until March.

It was a lot of traveling and a lot of work, but we also had a lot of fun on that tour. I won't go into all of that. I'll let somebody else get all of those tales together, because that's another book in itself. But there is one little incident that I will mention. I don't know how it all got started, because the family feeling and team spirit that was building up in that band was just wonderful. There was team spirit in each one of the sections, and it all added up to what was good for the band as a whole. Everybody wanted to make the band a success. So however this thing got started, it was all in fun, and that's the way it stayed. But by the time of the Birdland tours, the band was also divided into two groups that were always challenging each other in the games we used to play on the road and in various places, games mainly like softball, which may have been how it got started.

Anyway, on one side there were the little guys like Joe Newman, Sonny Payne, Frank Wess, Frank Foster, Benny Powell, and so on; and they called themselves the Midgets. And the others, the big guys like Poopsie, Coker, Eddie Jones, and Bill Hughes, were known as the Bombers. Naturally since I was the chief, I didn't take sides, but when we were touring on a package show, I would line up on one side or the other. Usually the big guys would have to go with the Bombers, but naturally Lester insisted on being one of the Midgets. He was really too big to be a Midget, but he had to be with the underdogs, which was a joke, because the Midgets were the ones who were always coming out on top, beginning with softball and going right on through most of the other horsing around.

Well, Morris Levy was classified as a Bomber, and he was having a ball with all of the games and pranks, and when the tour went out to Kansas City, Morris went around to the novelty stores and bought up a supply of water pistols for the Bombers to attack the Midgets with. So they had the Midgets on the run, and then, according to Joe Newman, Sonny Payne found out where Morris had his supplies stashed, and the two of them stole them for the Midgets.

That's what led to what happened to Morris in Kansas City. We were at the Municipal Auditorium, and several of us were standing near the bus talking with some local people—reporters, officials, and businessmen— if I remember correctly. And they were asking about who was in charge of the tour, and somebody said Morris Levy.

"You mean, Morris Levy, the manager of Birdland, is traveling with the show?"

"That's right."

"And he's in Kansas City right now?"

"Right now."

And right at that exact split second, we saw three or four of the Midgets heading in one direction, chasing a Bomber, shooting at him with water pistols. He was splitting, but they were gaining on him, and just as he got to about a few feet from where we were, he tried to make a fast cut to go around the bus and he slipped and ended up under it.

The people standing there talking to us just sort of glanced at what happened, and then turned right back and continued the conversation.

"I'd like to meet him."

"Well, that's no problem. Here he is."

"Where?"

"Right there under the bus."

"Under the bus? What's he doing under there?"

"The Midgets," I said. "The Midgets ran him under there. They were after him."

"The Midgets? Who are they? Is this some kind of gag?"

So I told them about the Midgets and the Bombers. But then when Morris came out from under the bus, it turned out that he had just had a serious accident. That fall had actually broken his arm. The minute the Birdland people back in New York were told about that, they started burning up the telephone wires to Kansas City, and Morris had to explain that it was all part of a game. Because as soon as he said that the Midgets were chasing him, they thought he was talking about a mob trying to cut in on the business.

"The Midgets? Who the hell are the Midgets?"

Morris had to explain fast. His business associates in Chicago were ready to put somebody on the next plane to Kansas City to help him take care of the situation. But Morris said it was all in fun and the joke was on him.

Another show that we got hooked up with during that late spring and early summer that didn't work out so good for us was the Alan Freed "CBS Radio Rock 'n' Roll Dance Party," which had a coast-to-coast network broadcast every Saturday night. Rock-and-roll music was the big commercial thing at that time, and there were a lot of kids out there who didn't want to hear anything but that, but rock 'n' roll was not our thing.

As I told a reporter from *Down Beat* magazine at the time, I knew after the first week that this wouldn't work out. I just don't think we fit into that kind of program. I think it's a real cute show if he has a band that knows how to play that rock 'n' roll. But we don't fit in any kind of way.

I remember he had a heck of a thing going at a theater down on Fourteenth Street somewhere, and we used to get down there around eleven o'clock and you couldn't get near the place for the crowd. Sometimes the theater was already full before the ticket windows opened. The kids would just break in, and it was a job to get them out of there so they could be admitted properly.

I remember that, and I also remember how things went. The first acts would go on, and the kids would all be jammed in there having a ball and applauding and shouting and whistling. Then when it came time for us to go on, just about all of them would get up and go outside to get their popcorn and ice cream and everything, and we just played our act to an almost empty house. Then when we finished our set, they would all come back in. No kidding.

So we would just go downstairs and play poker until it was time to go on again. That's the way it actually went. Those kids didn't care anything about jazz. Some of them would stay and come down front and stand and listen and try to hear it as long as they could, and we would try fast and slow, and it made no difference. That was not what they came to hear. To them we were just an intermission act. That's what that was. It didn't mean anything else but just that. You had to face it.

—

During the two-day session on which we made "Everyday I Have the Blues," we also did that band's first best-selling instrumental. In fact, I don't think we have ever had an instrumental that became so popular so quick and has remained such a big crowd pleaser as Wild Bill Davis's arrangement of "April in Paris." I'm talking about thirty years right on up to this day. As soon as that record hit the jukeboxes, everywhere we went, audiences started imitating that jive line I used for the tag. "One more time. One more once."

Actually Wild Bill, who had his group in Birdland while we were in there that summer, was supposed to be in on that date, but something happened to the little truck he used to haul his organ around in, and lucky for us he didn't make it. He was supposed to play it with us as we had been doing it together in Birdland.

Now, I'm not saying that I actually fixed his old wagon so that he couldn't get there, but it sure turned out to be a big break for us, so, as I told him, I'm glad it happened. Because we went right on and made "April in Paris" anyway, with the band using exactly the same arrangement he played on the organ with us as a special feature down in Birdland. It was a big break for us, because the band got a big hit. But if he had been there, it would have been mainly him. Because Wild Bill played it with a sound on that organ that was just unbelievable. The sound he got on that one instrument was as wide as a whole room, any room. Oh, it was big. Big as a whole band.

—

We didn't make any more studio recordings until that next January, and that's when we made the other numbers for the *April in Paris* album. We had done "Big Red" the week before, but we didn't make "Low Life," "Slats," and "Lollipop" until that June.

Meanwhile we went back out on another Birdland tour, and so did Sarah and Lester, but this time Al Hibbler was added as a vocal feature, and the others in the package were Bud Powell on piano, Al Cohn on tenor, Conte Candoli on trumpet, and Johnny Smith the organ player, whose big hit had been "Moonlight in Vermont." I don't remember anything about that tour that made it any different from a lot of others I had gone out on, but I do recall a little something about a couple of other things the band did that spring.

We went out to Las Vegas for a concert in the Congo Room of the Sahara Hotel, and things were quite different from that first time when we were booked into the Flamingo Hotel in that package show with Bill Bailey and Norma Miller and her girls. This time we took the band there for a two-night stand following the midnight show, and it was a real blast. Everybody was hot on that opening night. On the first set Joe Newman and Thad Jones took care of "Shiny Stockings" and "What Am I Here For?," and we were off and cracking. We just kept things going with Frank Foster on "You for Me," and with Frank Wess and Joe Newman chasing each other on "Midgets." Then Joe Williams came on and took charge with "Everyday," "The Comeback," and "Roll 'Em, Pete." That wrapped up the first set, and for the second we had "Corner Pocket" and "April in Paris" and turned Sonny loose on "With Friends" and brought Joe Williams back, and when we took it out, everybody wanted more.

At the end of that August, we went back to Europe for another tour, and on the way to Stockholm we touched down on British turf for the first time. But it was just a five- or six-hour stop at the U.S. Air Force base at Burtonwood, and we put on a little show for the GI's and that was about it for England. We were looking forward to a trip to London and all those other places, because we knew we had a lot of friends over there, just as we had in France, but at that time the arrangements just hadn't been worked out yet.

So we went on to Sweden where we opened with an outdoor concert for a crowd of over six thousand in Folk Park, in a town called Gavle. It was a beautiful place, and the people were just so wonderful that you had to put out for them. And as soon as I brought them in on "Jumping at the Woodside," I knew the band was already hot, and when I followed that with "Shiny Stockings," I knew I had a bunch of monsters up there that night, and they would never let up. I wasn't counting the tunes, but the reporters came up to me afterwards and wanted to know if there was any reason why I had chosen *thirteen* instrumentals. I said no, we just reached a certain point and I let Sonny Payne loose on "With Friends." Then it was time for Joe Williams, and he broke it up all over again.

That was the eight o'clock concert. Then at ten we went into a big

circular hall to play a dance, which really turned out to be another concert, because the place was supposed to have a normal capacity of two
thousand, but the police estimated that there were actually about six
thousand people packed in there. I mean, they were pushed right on up
against the music stands.

—

We finally got to make our first tour of Great Britain in April of that next
year, and it was just wonderful. We got right off to a real cracking start
at Royal Festival Hall in London on the same day that we arrived, and
that was the way it was everywhere we went for the next three weeks.

I don't think anybody in that band will ever forget that particular opening night. We hadn't had any sleep because we had come right off the
bandstand after our last set at the Blue Note in Chicago and headed
straight out to the airport for the flight directly to England. When we arrived, there were all of those receptions and interviews. Then when we
went to the theater to get set up, we found out that in all of the rush and
excitement, somebody had left all of the music back in Chicago.

That was impossible. But there it was, and after all that advance buildup
we were going to have to face that premiere audience full of very experi-
enced and very serious listeners, with nothing but a bunch of empty music
stands up there in front of us. That was enough to shake anybody but
those guys in that band. They were something else. They had been looking forward to that gig, and they were not about to let a little thing like
that get in the way. They said, "Hell, don't worry about nothing, chief.
We can play all that stuff from memory anyway."

And they did. They just went on out there and took everything in their
stride, and the audience responded just the way you dreamed it would.
While you were playing, it was so quiet you could hear a pin drop, because
everybody was digging every note, no room noise, no buzzing, no ruffling
and shuffling, just listening. Then their applause let you know that they felt
that you were worth all the time they had spent waiting to hear you in
person.

We played two shows that evening, one at six and the other at nine,
and they both were memorable for us, not just because the band was such
a big hit in such a fantastic place with such a classy and appreciative audience, but also for another reason. Somebody had told us about the royal
box. When it was lit up, that meant that a member of the royal family
was attending the programs, which was a very high honor. We were so
busy deciding what we were going to play that I didn't have any time to
think anything about it.

But right after we got started, I noticed that the lights had come on, and somebody passed the word that Princess Margaret and her party were there. That made everything about that evening even more extra special than it already was. There was a special kind of excitement. I'm not going to try to explain it, but it got to you, and the band was right there with it. Naturally I was just *dying* to look up *there*.

You could always count on those characters in that band to lay it on 'em in a situation like that, and I guess they must have gotten that extra little message across, because when we were getting ready to go back onstage for the ten o'clock show, we got word that the royal box was all lit up again. The princess had decided to come back, and she stayed there right on up to the end of that one too.

Nobody could remember that anything like that had ever happened before. So it was headline news: "ROYALTY SALUTES BASIE BAND.   Princess at two shows." That's the way the *Melody Maker* ran it.

The greatest compliment to jazz. On Tuesday night Princess Margaret paid an unexpected and unannounced visit to see Count Basie at the Royal Festival Hall—and she stayed for four hours.

She was with a party of six which arrived at about 6:20 P.M. (just after the first concert had commenced) and left just as quietly by the artists' entrance as the concert ended. . . . But shortly after 9 P.M. the swirling Princess and her party were back in the Royal Box for the second concert. And on more than one occasion, she led the applause—particularly for Sonny Payne's favorite show-stopping drum solo.

We also played some very fine dates in Scotland and Wales on that first tour of Great Britain, and when we came back, we had our regular thing at Birdland, and there was also another trip out on the road with the Birdland stars. Billy Eckstine, Sarah Vaughan, and Jeri Southern were the top featured vocalists in the Birdland lineup for that year. The featured combos were Bud Powell's Trio, Phineas Newborn's Quartet, Terry Gibbs's Quartet, and there were also star sidemen like Lester, Zoot Sims, and Chet Baker.

In June we were booked into the Starlight Roof Room of the Waldorf-Astoria for a few weeks. That, so I was told, was another of those big first-time things for a sepia band, but what actually happened was that we just went on in there and played the gig, and it was a big sellout and everybody had a ball, and we were extended, and when we finally cut out, we already knew that they wanted us to come back. By the way, speaking of sepia performers, the other big headliner in there at the same time that summer was Ella Fitzgerald.

We also went up to the Newport Festival that July, and that performance was released on the last album we did for Verve before Norman Granz gave up the record business and moved to Europe. So in September we began recording for Morris Levy, our old friend and boss at Birdland, who was starting a new company called Roulette Records, and our next records came out as a part of what was called the Birdland Series.

All of the tunes were written and arranged by Neal Hefti. Teddy Reig was the recording supervisor on that date, which was the beginning of a long business and personal relationship for the two of us. Teddy was to be our main man for recordings on all of our Roulette dates for the next ten years or so, and also for a few years after the Birdland and Roulette things ended.

I'm pretty sure it was Teddy's idea to put out a whole album with the band featuring one arranger, and during the following years right on up through the time when we went back to Verve (owned by MGM), we also made albums featuring originals or arrangements by Quincy Jones, Benny Carter, Billy Byers, Chico O'Farrell, and Sammy Nestico.

That first one of Neal's turned out very well. We still have "The Kid From Red Bank," and "Li'l Darlin'" in our current book because we still play them, and when we don't, we get requests for them. I don't know whatever happened to my copy of that first Roulette album, but I remember it as the one with the atomic bomb on the cover.

Between that summer and the first Roulette record date we had to replace three chairs in the lineup. We brought Al Grey into the trombone section when Bill Hughes gave us his notice. Lockjaw came back in on tenor, and Frank Wess began playing the alto book when Billy Graham had to cut out; and Snookie Young came back as our main first trumpet man when Reunauld Jones split. That's how we happened to have three tenor soloists on that album, the two Franks and also Lockjaw, who got the meat on "Flight of the Foo Birds," "After Supper," "Whirly Bird," and "Double-O."

The lineup on those tracks is the same one that we had when we went back over to England a week or so later for our second tour, which turned out even better than the first. Right after our opening concert in Royal Festival Hall the write-up in the *Melody Maker* came out under a big headline: "Basie Does It Again." It said, "On the strength of Count Basie's first London concerts, I'd judge his 'new' orchestra potential greater than its predecessor. . . . The band performs with even more life and fire than it did in April."

And that was just the beginning. Because it was on that second trip to England that I got one of the biggest thrills of my life. We had a spot on the Royal Variety Show at the London Palladium, also known as the Command Performance, the great entertainment event of the year which the royal family attends, and I was introduced to the queen. You can't beat that, not in Great Britain.

It was a three-hour variety show, and I don't know how many other acts there were, and I'm not even going to try to guess. But I do remember that Judy Garland and Mario Lanza were also there. I don't know whether they were the first American singers to participate, but everybody said that we were the first American band ever invited.

Our spot gave us just enough time for about three numbers, and you couldn't take any encores. So we opened with a little chart, spotlighting the piano, called "The Kid From Red Bank," and that sparked them up and started things popping. So we laid our "April in Paris" on them, and when we went into that one more time and one more once routine, they were ready to give us a standing ovation. But there was still enough time for one more number, so I decided to go out with Sonny Payne, breaking it up on "Old Man River," which he definitely did. Most definitely.

The headlines we got for that one short set were really something. "BASIE BAND IS ROYAL SENSATION." That was the way it came out in the *Melody Maker*, and the article under it said, "The number one hit of the 1957 Royal Variety Performance was the Count Basie Band. Basie was acclaimed a smash hit by even the least jazz-conscious of the press."

On the souvenir program the Royal Variety Show is called the Royal Performance in the Presence of Her Majesty The Queen. It is really an annual benefit show to raise money in aid of the Artists' Benevolent Fund and Institution, a charity of entertainers, and the queen and the queen mother were sponsors of it.

So the queen and members of the royal family came to the Palladium and sat in the royal box during the program, and then afterwards she received the performers. That was not a matter of having a private audience with her or anything like that. She came down out of the royal box; and there was a formal reception right there in the theater, and she greeted each of the performers as you moved along the line.

My position was between Vera Lynn, the singer, and one of the ballet dancers. The chairman of the fund was the last, so he was the one who "presented" you.

"Count Basie, Your Majesty," he said, and I did my little bow.

"Your Majesty," I said, and she nodded and smiled.

"Count Basie," she said, and congratulated me and also thanked me, and that was about it. But when I moved on to Prince Phillip, he and I had more of an exchange.

"Well, Count," he said, sounding very hip, "I see you really had a lot of them out to hear you tonight."

"That's right," I said. "Almost too many."

"Oh, you had them swinging, and for a good cause."

The queen mother was also there that night, and she gave me a big smile, and that was enough for me. Princess Margaret was not there, but somehow I have the notion that she was probably the one who put the royal family hip to what our current band was about. She knew quite a lot about us. From time to time she used to catch the band in places outside of London, and she also came to a recording session and a broadcast.

That just about wraps up that part of the story. However, there is also another part, or really another side of it. *The next morning the band got put out of the place where they were staying.* It was a place somewhere over in the West End section of London, and it was not a regular hotel but more like a very special kind of place that rented transient apartments. I don't know what happened, because I had been put up elsewhere, but I do know that everybody was feeling very excited after the performance, and I guess some of the fellows and some of their happy fans must have gotten a little too carried away with all the celebration and afterpartying, and they forgot where they were. Anyway, when they woke up that next day, the band was asked to resign or withdraw its residence or something like that. In other words they were being kicked out. Nobody could believe it.

But that is exactly what happened. I don't think it had anything to do with color. Those people just didn't want the attention the band was attracting. It was like they were asking you to resign from a club or something like that, not because of something you shouldn't have done, but you were attracting the wrong people or maybe just too many people.

I'm not going to try to speak for the fellows on that matter, because it was their story, not really mine. But I will say that I don't think anybody was too upset by what happened. I think they just took it as one of those things. Actually I think they mostly took it as a big joke. Anyway, however, they felt it didn't have any bad effects on the way they played the rest of that tour. They broke it up everywhere we went.

—

That was Lockjaw's first trip to England. But he was already well known over there from the records he had made with us a few years before and also with various other bands and combos. So there were a lot of people over there waiting to hear and see him in person, and he did not disappoint them. He was a hit everywhere he went, and he was always one of the musicians the reporters singled out for special mention.

It was a great trip for him, and I think that gave him a few ideas about some things, so on the flight back he started talking to me. Jaws is a great talker, especially when he starts sipping on that scotch and milk. That's what he had done all the way from New York to London on the flight going over. But as soon as he started in on me on that flight coming back, I knew he was about to work up to something, so I beat him to it.

"You don't need to tell me nothing," I said.

"What are you talking about?" he said. "What do you mean?"

"You asked me for this job," I said. "I did not ask you. You got the job and now you're thinking about something else. Before you tell me what you have to tell, I know what you got on your mind." Because I knew that he had had his little group and they broke up, maybe because he had gotten a little fed up with them. But I think he was kind of getting a little heartache for that again.

"What are you talking about?" he said.

"Well," I said, "I know. Tell you what you do. You need your own thing. Now, look, when we get back, my joint will be ready to open in about a month, or something like that. Why don't you go and work in there? That's what you need."

And he said, "What are you talking about?"

"You want a job with your own thing?" I said. "You got a job in there."

He just looked at me. I said, "See how you like it. Because you need your group. I don't know why you broke it up nohow."

He didn't say anything for a minute or so, and then he said, "Well, you know, maybe. . . ."

So that's what he did. He went in there to work, and he was supposed to be in there for a few weeks or a month or so or something like that, and it turned out to be more like about a year. That was a great thing for him, and a great thing for me because everybody liked him and business was good the whole time. I think his little band broke up after that. I don't really know why.

But speaking of that second time that Lockjaw was in the band, it brings me up to the point where I had my own little club uptown on the corner of Seventh Avenue and 132nd Street. That was a deal I got into during those Birdland days, and before very long it had become one of the recognized spots in Harlem. I never did take my band in there because the place really wasn't big enough, but over those years we had a hell of a lot of topflight groups and singers in there. Also from opening night right on up to the end, a whole lot of friends we made in Birdland became regular customers up there.

We called it COUNT BASIE'S, and the corner where it was located was next to the garage where people from downtown used to park back during those days when Connie's Inn was so great. Right on the corner that used to be known as Harris's Corner, across the street was where Big John's used to be, and a few doors down 132nd Street was the place where they used to sell those hot dogs that I used to take to my room and eat in bed way back before I left town with Gonzelle White and ended up stranded in Kansas City. I'll never forget that.

Life is strange. It really takes some surprising turns. I never would have thought that that place on that corner would ever be mine. Back during those early days I used to walk along that sidewalk and see people going in there, but I never could. You *could* go in if you wanted to and could afford the prices. But Big John's was the place that was a little closer to my reach, and I couldn't make it in there but so often, either.

It was a real gas to be the owner of your own club, especially when it was so popular. And by the way, right next door going uptown on Seventh Avenue was one of the most solid night spots in Harlem at that time, Well's famous "Home of Chicken and Waffles!" They had entertainment in there, too, but evidently their business was good for us and ours was good for them, because my place was popping.

As the years went on, however, I began to realize that all the business we were always doing wasn't adding up to very much profit. That's when my wife, Kate, entered the picture. When I went into that deal, I didn't bring her in at all. I wouldn't let her touch anything because I thought I knew everything. So things went on and went on for a few years, and then one day we were talking about it, and that's when she got to me.

"The club is doing all right," I said.

"Okay," she said, "so where's the money?"

"Business is fine. Look at the crowds we always have in there."

But she said, "Where is the report?"

"Everything's all right," I told her again.

But that's when she came in. She got a chair and sat back up in there by the railing where she could see the whole scene, and she started checking out everything. Then she showed me how the club really had been making a lot of money and asked me where it was going.

"Who is getting the money?" she asked. "You're right. The business is here, and somebody's got to be making money, but where's yours?"

So what could I say? She was a pretty smart cookie. She went back in there and jumped right in on that operation and started taking over, and she saved me. But after a while business did begin to fall off, and we finally had to let it go. But it was a jumping place for years.

—

Lockjaw's replacement in the reed section was Billy Mitchell. He went into Birdland with us in December, so we still had three tenor solo men, because Frank Wess was still taking solos on tenor and also on the flute, although he had moved over to the second alto chair. Billy came to us from Dizzy Gillespie, and before that he played with Nat Towles, Lucky Millinder, and also with Lunceford, and with Thad Jones and his brother in a band out in Detroit. In fact Thad may have been the one who recommended him. Billy stayed with us for just about three years that first time, and he also came back a few times after that.

We made that second Neal Hefti album while we were in New York that next April. That is the one that came out under the title of *Basie Plays Hefti*. All the tunes were very musical. That's the way Neal's things were, and those guys in that band always had something to put with whatever you laid in front of them.

In June we finally got all the way back out to the West Coast again for the first time in three years, and everybody was glad to be touching base with all the wonderful friends out there once more. But another special thing about this particular trip was that it was the first time we played in the Crescendo, Gene Norman's fabulous club out on Sunset Strip. Which added one more great spot to our list of favorite places to settle down in for a while before hitting the road again.

Number one, of course, had to be Birdland. Then there was also the Blue Note in Chicago. There were a lot of other great places, too, and I wouldn't want to slight any of them. There were all those places in towns like Boston and Philly and San Francisco, just to name a few. But there was something about the Crescendo that put it way up there. It was a big, beautiful room, right where one of the busiest parts of the Strip was in those days, and the regular Hollywood, Beverly Hills, and Los Angeles customers were so hip, and so were the out-of-towners who made that scene. They were real fans of our kind of jazz.

But about Birdland. We played in there so many times over such a long period that they didn't even bill us like other headliners anymore. They would just put a sign up like those lights that run around that building down at the south point of Times Square, and the lights just said "Basie's Back." That's all, and people knew, and they came and a whole lot of them got into the habit of coming back. Some were there night after night, and others used to make it several times a week while we were there, just like back when I had that other band in the Famous Door. And of course, some of these were the same people from the Famous Door. There were quite a few of these, but naturally most were the younger set. Take Morris Levy himself, for example. He was one of our biggest fans, but back when we were playing at the Famous Door, he was still too young to get in there.

The band was always ready to go whenever we went back into Birdland. But the thing about that gig was how those cats hit that last set. No matter how hot they were all night, there was always something special about that last one. It was like they were warming up for that two o'clock show. Sometimes I used to save special tunes just for that set, because I knew we were going to be burning, and I mean blazing.

There was a little bar upstairs on the street level. It was called "The Magpie," and that's where I used to go to have a little taste and get ready for that last set every night—every morning, really. It always used to be crowded in there at that time because that was also where the musicians and entertainers from the other shows in the Broadway area would be getting off from work, and they'd stop in there on their way downstairs to catch our last set every night. And of course, a lot of other people would be in there because they were the kind of fans who just like to make the scene and hang out with people in show business, and also because it was a great little place. The main reason, though, I would say, was that everybody knew that our last set was going to be dynamite.

Then there were also those closing nights. They were also something extra special. Everybody was sure to be there that night to say good-bye, especially people in show business. On some of those closing nights, it was nothing to have a whole string of busy people like Sammy Davis, Frank Sinatra, Pearl Bailey, Dinah Washington, and you name them, coming by to do a number or two with us just for the fun of it. Morris Levy still gets excited when he remembers those nights.

I have never bragged on anything, but the band I had by the summer of that same year when we played that first gig in the Crescendo was one I could have bragged on. When you had Joe Newman, Thad Jones, Snookie Young, and Wendell Cully up there in the trumpet section, you had everything you needed. We had Henry Coker, Benny Powell, and Al Grey on trombone, and the reed section had Marshall Royal on alto and clarinet, Frank Wess on alto tenor and flute, Frank Foster on tenor, Billy Mitchell on tenor, and Charlie Fowlkes on baritone.

In the rhythm section with me and Freddie Greene we had Big Eddie Jones walking that bass, and Sonny Payne was really in charge of those drums by that time. Hell, I'd find myself just sitting back listening. Everything was crackling so good. Frankly I felt pretty lucky to be along in that band, because I'd just as soon sit and listen because everything was cracking so evenly.

Those guys in that band, they really were something else. They just wanted to get up there and play, and when the time came, they were ready, and they did it, and it was scorching. Then, even during the intermission, especially when we were playing dances on those one-nighters, you could find most of them standing around not more than fifteen or twenty feet away from the bandstand. What can I say? That band was really a shaker.

In May we hooked up with a sensational new vocal trio known as Lambert, Hendricks, and Ross (for Dave Lambert, Jon Hendricks, and Annie Ross), who were beginning to create quite a stir in some circles, especially for the way they came up with their own swinging lyrics for some of our instrumentals.

Their thing was to put words in for what the instruments were playing on certain passages or on arrangements. In a way it was like scat singing, but scat singers just riff with vocal sounds and made-up words and nonsense syllables of jive lyrics, whereas what this trio was doing was putting words in there note for note for ensembles choruses, just as they did for the solo instruments, and the words always told a little story. They had to do a lot of tongue twisting to make those words get some of the licks and runs in those solos by Lester and Dicky and Sweets and Herschel and Tate and so on, but that was all part of the excitement that was already their trademark.

That was also the year we did the theme for *M-Squad*, a weekly crime-fighting series like *Gangbusters*. There were several very popular shows like that at that time, and they all used to come on with a very strong hip-sounding theme that set the mood for things happening in a big city. When the people producing the series came to see us, they already had a rough notion for a theme. But the one we finally came up with was really a head that Frank Foster and I hit up on and dictated to the band, like almost at the last minute.

We recorded "M-Squad Theme" on a session in New York in October. In November we made an album with a very popular young singer named Tony Bennett. It was called *Strike Up the Band*. Ralph Sharon, Tony's regular accompanist, worked up the score for that session, and he also played the piano on most of those numbers. I'll let the reader figure out which ones I sat in on.

We also did about a dozen other tunes with Tony in Philadelphia and New York before the end of December; and down through the years since that time, we've done a lot of things together that have turned out very well for both of us. We've done club dates on both coasts, theater specials abroad, and a few festivals too.

On another date during that same December we also recorded five numbers for an album of ten originals by Quincy Jones. Then January, after we did our Christmas holiday thing in Birdland, we made five more, and that album was called *Basie, One More Time*.

Then we took off for Europe again, and during the first week in February we played in Switzerland at Theatre Beaulieu in Lausanne and also in Kongresshaus in Zurich. My main man in the research department has come up with recordings made from a couple of those performances in Switzerland, and also in England, and I'd say they are a pretty fair sample of the program we were presenting on that tour. In the one from Lausanne and Beaulieu we played "Shiny Stockings," "Her Royal Highness," "Bag o' Bones," "Whirly Bird," "The Deacon," "In a Mellow Tone," "The Midgets," "Old Man River," "Basie Boogie," and "Cute." For the one called *The Count in England*, the selections were "The Moon's Not Green," "Brushes and Brass," "Bag o' Bones," "Who Me?," "The Deacon," "Plymouth Rock," "April in Paris," "Fancy Meeting You," and Joe Williams singing "Five O'Clock in the Morning," "Roll 'Em Pete," and "Every Day." Of course, the program also included other things, some by request and some just to change things up a bit. Those two releases also remind me that we had already added new things like Thad Jones's "HRH (Her Royal Highness)" and "The Deacon" and Frank Foster's "Who Me?" featuring Snookie Young, before we recorded them for Roulette.

We hopped directly from Zurich to England and opened at the Royal Festival Hall in London the very next day, which was a Saturday. Then for the next two weeks we were booked solid. Here is the itinerary: the Gaumont State Theatre in London that Sunday, then the Odeon in Newcastle, the Odeon in Glasgow, Scotland, the Odeon in Leeds, the Gaumont in Hanley, Colston Hall in Bristol. Then we came back into London for the weekend and played the Gaumont Hammersmith on Saturday and the Davis Croydon on Sunday, and on Monday we were at the De Montfort in Lancaster, and between there and that last Sunday at the Empire in Liverpool we played the Odeon in Birmingham; the Gaumont in Cardiff, Wales; the Gaumont in Southampton; the Granada Walthamstrow back in London; and the Free Trade Hall in Manchester.

===

In the two-day recording session we went into back in New York near the end of April, all the tunes were things we had already been playing for a while, because they were written by current members of the band and one former member, Ernie Wilkins, who was still a part of the family because he was a charter member of the new band. "HRH (Her Royal Highness)," "Speaking of Sounds," "Mutt and Jeff," and "The Deacon" all came from Thad Jones.

I still can't get over that Thad. There he was, sitting up there listening to everybody and never opening his mouth about what he could do. Then he threw a couple of things down there. I think Marshall Royal knew something. I think Marshall had seen the sheets, and he was the one who told me one day at rehearsal.

"Hey, Base," he said, "why don't you look at these things?"

So I did, and we went over them, and wow!

Thad's things were always very exciting. And you never knew what he was going to write next. He wrote some things that were just fantastic. And he can play that horn the same way. I'll always remember one little thing he used to play on the horn, "Mama Talking Soft." That really knocked me out. Anytime Thad brought something in there, you'd better watch it, because he always had something happening.

Frank Foster had three numbers ready for that session, including "Who Me?," which featured Snookie Young, and which Snookie had been breaking things up with all during the tour we just got back from.

STOMPING GROUNDS AND STOPPING PLACES

1959 = 1964

It was not quite a month after we made *Chairman of the Board* that we went back in the studio to make a long-overdue album with Billy Eckstine. That really wasn't work. We just went on into those two sessions and had a ball, just like we used to have beginning back when he took us out on those tours and also on the road with the Birdland Stars.

Billy, and Bobby Tucker, his piano man, knew what he wanted behind him, and those guys in that band tried to give him everything he asked for. So we can still include any of those tunes on the programs every time we are lucky enough to work together somewhere. After twenty-some-odd years, they still go over not just with the part of the audience that remembers the old days but also with young people who never heard them before.

==

At the end of that May, there was a big conference of radio and television disc jockeys and officials of the big recording companies down in Miami, and on the last day Morris Levy had us fly down from Birdland to play for a big party that Roulette was giving for the disc jockeys. It

331

was held in the grand ballroom of the Americana and was called a Breakfast Dance and Barbecue, like back in Kansas City, because there was a big spread of barbecued spareribs right in the ballroom that night, and then we played on into that next morning. They started serving ham and eggs and hot coffee.

According to Morris Levy and the Roulette people, there were three thousand guests there for that party. And from what I could see from where I was, I could tell that it was one of those fabulous balls that people were going to be talking about for years to come. But of course now, I wasn't down there for the whole thing, and even though Kate went along, I was pretty busy working from the time we got there until the time we left, which was that next morning. Because we had to get back to New York in time for our first set at the Birdland that night.

All I can really say about that night is that it was jumping while we were down there, and we have the record to prove it, because Roulette recorded us live. I don't actually remember how many numbers we played from the time we hit until five that morning, but Roulette issued eight of them in an album called *Breakfast Dance and Barbecue*.

—

We also went back to the Starlight Roof in the Waldorf again that June, and that was the time Ella Fitzgerald was the other headliner. So what can I say? The only thing Ella knows how to do is just go out there and be wonderful. But as I remember it, she was there for just a few weeks. Then she had to cut out for another gig that Norman Granz had waiting for her somewhere. The band, with Joe Williams billed as an extra added attraction, had been booked into the Starlight Roof for the whole season, which was right through the month of June.

Up at Newport that year, our set was scheduled as the closer for opening day, which was a Thursday. But by the time we began our first number, it was actually about a quarter past midnight. We kind of set things up with a few tunes from our current book. Then we brought Joe Williams out, and he did "Shake, Rattle, and Roll" and "Well, All Right, Okay, You Win," and left the crowd all sparked up even higher, and that's when the Lambert, Hendricks, and Ross Trio joined us and made its festival debut with "It's Sand, Man," and there was no letdown in the audience at all. They were a hit by the time they finished the first couple of numbers, and when they got through their thing on a cool tune by Horace Silver called "Doodling," that crowd wanted to keep them out there. But it was time for the wrap-up then, so we brought Joe Williams, and the four of them took off on "Every Day," and from that we made a fast segue right on into the outchorus of "One O'Clock Jump."

By the end of that summer, we made it back out to the West Coast and back into the Crescendo, and while we were out there, we recorded enough tunes for another album featuring Joe Williams.

Which brings me to our first record date with Sarah Vaughan. After all the years we had known each other and all the times we had worked together, we finally made it into a studio while we were back in New York that December for three short sessions. We taped enough for a nice little album, but of course, everybody knew that we hadn't even begun to scratch the surface of the wonderful music that Sassy can lay on you.

As usual, we were in New York during that time of the year because we were spending the holidays at the Birdland. Then before we hit the road, we went uptown to the Apollo, which gave us another week to make a few personal pop calls on my own little club just seven blocks up Seventh Avenue. As a matter of fact you could say my club was also represented at the Apollo that week because the other featured group on that bill was Eddie "Lockjaw" Davis with Shirley Scott on organ and Arthur Edgehill, who was just about the house band at that time. The headline comedian that week was my old friend Pigmeat Markham, who could never be anything but great with that audience in the Apollo.

It was while we were out in Chicago that February that we finally found a permanent replacement for Wendell Cully in the trumpet section. His name is Sonny Cohn. He came to us after a number of years with Red Saunders, and he has been with us ever since, which is twenty-plus years, and for the last ten years he has also doubled as our road manager.

I remember being back in England for another tour that next spring, because that is where I was when I got word that my father had passed away. I flew back to New York, and about all I had to do was to get to Red Bank for the funeral, because Katie had made all the necessary arrangements for everything else.

I have to say that Katy always came through beautifully in circumstances like that. She really knew how to get things done. She was also always just wonderful with my family, from the time she and I finally became boy and girl, right on up to Dad's funeral, and even afterwards. Because later on she was the one who decided that we should have a family plot in the Pine Lawn Mausoleum in Farmingdale, Long Island, and the first thing she did was to relocate the remains of my mother and father there from Red Bank.

She also had a lot to do with me and Dad being as close as we had become during those last years, because from the time that he and my mother separated, I was always closer to my mother than to him. Mama spent the rest of her life with me in New York. But when Katy and I got married, she made a special thing of seeing to it that we acted more like father and son than we had been for all those years.

Katie was just wonderful about things like that, and that's why I have to give her so much credit for the consolation I had when Dad passed on. All along she had been the one who was right there to see that he and I didn't get out of touch because I was always out on the road somewhere. She made sure that he didn't have to go wanting for anything that we were able to provide, and when we decided to replace the old house where I grew up on Mechanic Street with a nice little one-story pad, she was the one who stuck close to the scene, checking on things, not me. As usual, I was mostly out on the road.

Right after we came back from England in April, we went to work on the tunes for another album with Sarah Vaughan. It took us two sessions, and when we finished the second one in the middle of May, we had eleven tracks. As far as I'm concerned, every one of them was right there, right where it was supposed to be.

During that same month, I also did a couple of sessions for a Roulette album with strings. That was strictly a studio group. The only musicians from the band I had at that time were Freddie Greene and Frank Wess. In the rhythm section with me and Freddie, we had George Duvivier on bass and Jimmy Crawford, the drummer from that great band that Jimmie Lunceford once had. I don't know who was in the string section and who was on harp, but Herbie Mann was on flute, along with Frank Wess and Andy Fitzgerald, with Illinois Jacquet taking care of tenor.

When we went back into the Waldorf for the Starlight Roof season that year, the other headliner on the bill was a very popular singing group known as the Hi-Lo's. Joe Williams also went back up there with us again as an extra added attraction.

During the month that we were settled into the Waldorf doing those two shows a night, there was plenty of time during the day for us to get things done in the recording studio. It was also when the fellows in the band had more time to work up their own compositions and arrangements. So this time somebody, I think it might have been Teddy Reig, came up with the idea of the current band doing a whole album of things from the old book as a twenty-fifth-anniversary tribute, and we ended up with a two-record album called *The Count Basie Story* that had twenty-three of our old standards in it.

The main arranger for that project was Frank Foster. Somebody else may have been in on one or two of those, but Frank did the rest of those charts, which he transcribed from the old recordings and reworked for the current band without getting too far away from the originals.

When we came out of the Waldorf, we had a one-nighter in Philadelphia on our way down to Atlantic City for a couple of nights, and then before coming back to New York for our summer thing at Birdland the second and third week in July, we hit the Newport Festival on the fourth. We didn't get any days off until the end of July, and that was only for about a week. In the meantime we made another studio album during our stand at Birdland. It was released under the title of *Not Now, I'll Tell You When*, which was also the name of one of the tunes.

By the third week of that August, we were working our way back to the West Coast by way of Buffalo, Detroit, Kansas City, and Denver, and by the second week of September we were in Los Angeles for our thing in the Crescendo once more. But just before we opened in there, we spent a couple of days in the Universal Sound Studios making the first of those Benny Carter albums that I mentioned earlier. All of the numbers that Benny wrote for that session were related to life in Kansas City, and he named it *Kansas City Suite*. And I think Benny liked what we did with it, and that meant a lot to me. Naturally we put some of those numbers in the book that we used when we opened at the Crescendo that same week.

The following week was when we taped a TV program with Fred Astaire. It was one of a series of specials called *Astaire Time* that Fred was doing for NBC, and he had used Jonah Jones and his combo on the others. But this time he had asked for us, and the terms and all of that had been worked out through Willard Alexander's office in New York earlier that summer, and it was during that time that Fred and I had finally met for the first time. He was stopping at the St. Regis, and he invited me to come over so we could talk about what he wanted to do, and as soon as Willard and I got there, I knew the whole thing was going to be a ball.

He was waiting for us, and you never met a nicer guy. I had been a big fan of his for a long time, and right away it turned out that he had been following what my bands had been doing down through the years.

"Well, Count Basie," he said, taking my hand as I stepped into his suite. "So nice to meet you finally."

"My pleasure," I said.

"I'm so happy we could get together. I've been looking forward to this for a long time."

"Same here," I said, because he really had been a big favorite of mine for many years.

We sat and chatted for a few minutes, and he said some very nice things about liking the music over the years and then he asked me about various tunes, and then he mentioned "Sweet Georgia Brown" and said he thought maybe he'd like to build something around that.

"Beautiful," I said. "How do you want to do it?"

"I tell you what you do," he said. "You make a tape of 'Sweet Georgia Brown' and get it to me."

"You got it," I said.

"Well, good," he said. "That's just fine. We'll go from there."

And that was it for that first little get-together. So what I did was have a whole arrangement made to go with the piano solo, and when I took it to him out in California, he had his chauffeur pick me up at the airport, and as soon as we got to where he was and I handed it to him, he had somebody put it on the machine, and he jumped right on it and every moment in that arrangement got something from him.

On the program he did a solo dance to "Sweet Georgia Brown." We did "Not Now, I'll Tell You When" from our new album. Joe Williams sang "It's a Wonderful World," and we also did a blues thing behind Fred and Barrie Chase, and he was very pleased about how well everything turned out, and so were we. Actually the show turned out to be such a hit that NBC decided to rerun it that next February, which was only five months away.

I also have to mention another nice thing about doing that wonderful TV special with Fred. Somehow or other he found out that I liked to play the ponies. So he said if I desired to go out to the track at any time while I was in town, just let him know and he would have his man pick me up and take me out to his box at the track, which I did. And of course, that was a ball. To tell the truth, I don't remember whether I won anything out there or not. I probably didn't, but I sure did have a great time.

We also played in the Hollywood Bowl one night while we were still working at the Crescendo that time. Then we headed back east by way of Dallas; Stillwater, Oklahoma; and Fayetteville, Arkansas; and by the end of the month we were beginning a week at the Regal in Chicago. By the way, when we got back to Chicago that time, the Blue Note had been closed down for several months. Naturally I had heard that bad news, but it's when you actually come back into town that something like that really hits you like a death in the family. Chicago was still a jumping town, however, and by that fall there was a new club trying to get under way, and we were invited to be one of the first bands it featured. It was called Robert's Show Lounge.

—

We went back into Birdland on the second Thursday in December that year, and we stayed in there through the first week in January. That was Joe Williams's last engagement in there with the band before going out on his own as a single. So the annual Birdland Chitterling Supper for the closing night of our holidays turned out to be a farewell party for him, which went on until the next morning. (For the record, Joe didn't actually leave the band until we closed at the Apollo that next week.)

I don't have to tell anybody that before very long Joe had made it big as a single attraction. And everybody also knows that over the twenty-some years right on up to this day he has maintained his family ties with the band. No telling how many guest appearances he has made with us. Sometimes he makes two or three a year with us, mostly on special concerts, but sometimes also for a few nights or even a week or more in a row. And no matter where we are, whenever he walks out there and takes over that mike, it's still like he's back home, even to this day when the only ones left from the time he was with us are Freddie Greene, Sonny Cohn, and old Base himself.

The last night up at the Apollo was when Joe Newman also decided that it was time to make a change. That was some pretty bad news, because Pootman had been our main spark plug in the trumpet section for all those years, and he was still the chief soloist in that department. He was also a wonderful section man, and nobody showed more cooperation when it came to the making of a good show for the whole band. Back during the time when we were dropping most of the trumpet solo choruses on him, I don't remember him ever complaining about being overworked. He just went on out there and took care of business, just out of team spirit. And whenever you mentioned anything about how his chops were holding up, all he ever said was something like "Hell, don't worry about nothing, chief. I can make it."

You don't run across wonderful guys like that every day, so naturally you'd like to keep him as long as you can. But when I asked him if there was anything I could do, he said he didn't have any complaints, and that it wasn't about money. He just wanted to try something else, and I could understand that, so I wished him well and told him he could always come back whenever he wanted to. And that offer still stands.

—

After the Apollo we did another week of one-nighters in the New York and nearby New England areas before going down to Washington to play for one of the big dances celebrating the inauguration of President John F. Kennedy. There were five Inaugural Balls that night. We played the one held in the District Armory, which must have been the biggest. The others were at the Mayflower, the Shoreham, the Statler, and the Sheraton Park.

That was most definitely another one of those big highlights in my career. But truthfully, there's not a hell of a lot that I have to say about it, because I was so busy just making the gig that I didn't get to see the Inauguration Parade or even the ceremony, because it was all we could do to get down to Washington from Fort Dix, New Jersey, through all of that rough winter weather. There was a big snowstorm by that afternoon, which snarled up traffic everywhere in the area.

But the weather didn't stop those people down in Washington from stepping out that night. I can't speak for those other balls, but I can vouch for what was happening at the Armory, and it was leaping, very definitely.

As I understand it, the new president planned to drop in on all of the five parties. He and the First Lady started the evening at the Mayflower, and the Armory was his second stop. Of course, everybody knew when he was making his entrance, and then you could see his party in the executive box up in the balcony. But to tell the truth, I have a clearer picture of his father in my mind than of the President. His father really seemed to be having a lot of fun. I looked up there one time and saw him with his coat off. I don't know what that was about.

I don't remember knowing when the President cut out. I've been told that the First Lady went back home after they left the Armory and that the President went on to the other three balls without her. But speaking of First Ladies, my own number one was also present at that occasion. Kate had been very active in the Kennedy campaign, so she probably would have been a part of the big victory celebration even if the band had not been invited to play.

Joe Williams and Joe Newman were not the only ones we had to replace during the first few months of that year. Al Grey and Billy Mitchell also cut out, and the two of them got a little group together. We got Quentin Jackson to take over Al's chair, and that meant that we still had a big plunger voice in the trombone section, because Quentin, also known as Butter, had handled those parts in Duke's band, and that's where it all got started, with Tricky Sam Nanton, my old friend from the old days when I was in and out of Leroy's and also Smalls' place on Fifth Avenue.

We didn't try to replace Joe Williams with another Joe Williams. Our next male vocalist was Ocie Smith, and he was not like Joe at all. But he came on in there and took care of business in his own way, which was not easy when you have to follow somebody who had built up the number of fans that Joe had all across the country. But Ocie was very good with the band, and I was very pleased with him, and when he checked out, he did so with my good wishes.

He came to me and said he wanted to go out and see if he could make it as a single, and I said go ahead and let's see what happens. That's the only way to find out. So he went on out and took his chances, and the move paid off for him. He had a couple of hits before long, and he was on his own.

Our replacement for Billy Mitchell was Budd Johnson. Budd had been a key man in Earl Hines's great band from the late thirties right on up to the time Earl let the band go. Budd was the straw boss of that band at one time. He also wrote some great things and took some great tenor solo choruses on numbers like "Second Balcony Jump" and "Grand

Terrace Shuffle," for instance. He could also double on alto or clarinet Budd had also worked with Dizzy and as musical director for Billy Eckstine's big band. And he had written arrangements for Georgie Auld, Woody Herman, Boyd Raeburn, and Buddy Rich. When he joined us that spring, he had just come back from a short tour of Europe with Quincy Jones's new band. He came with us and started taking care of business right away. I don't think it should be too hard to spot him in there on albums of our records and broadcasts between that spring and that fall.

Not long after Ocie came into the band, we also found a new female vocalist by the name of Irene Reid. Somebody brought me a demonstration tape of her singing "Alexander's Ragtime Band," and by the time she got about sixteen bars into that thing, I knew we could use her.

"Where is she?" I asked.

"Uptown," somebody answered, and I told him to go get her. So that's how she came in, and she was with us for a year or so, and she was a very strong asset for us. She could shout some blues, and she also had her own way doing tunes like "Yes, Sir, That's My Baby," "Almost Like Being in Love," "Them That's Got," "Easy Living," and "Alexander's Ragtime Band," of course.

There are tapes of Irene and also of Ocie singing with the band in Sweden during the summer of the next year after they came with us, but so far as I know, they never have been issued. I don't think the studio tracks of Ocie singing "Don't Push, Don't Pull" and "Don't Worry About Me" and Irene doing "Alexander's Ragtime Band' and "Easy Living" were ever issued, either. Those were done during the same time that we were making the Benny Carter album called *The Legend*.

By the way, Irene also did all right on her own after she decided to cut out. And I can say the same thing for another vocalist who was with us for a while a little later on. His name is Leon Thomas. He didn't do a lot of studio recording with us. He's on two albums, *Pop Goes the Basie*, and *Basie Picks Nice Winners*, and that's about it. Maybe there are some air checks from some of those live broadcasts from somewhere. If so, they are worth listening to, because Leon did an excellent job with us.

My next extra-special thing that year came in July when we made an album with the Boss himself. Somebody came up with the idea that Duke and I record a battle of the bands, but I knocked that notion out as soon as it was brought up. So what we did was put our two bands together, and we cut four tracks from his book and four from mine. His four were "Battle Royal" and "Wild Man," two new things he had written, featuring Louis Armstrong in a couple of spots in a movie called *Paris Blues*;

Billy Strayhorn's "Take the A Train;" and "BDB," a little blues thing that he and Billy cooked up just for that session to feature the three of us on piano.

Our four tracks were Freddie Greene's "Until I Met You (Corner Pocket)"; Thad Jones's "To You"; Frank Wess's "Segue in C"; and Frank Foster's arrangement of our old standby, "Jumping at the Woodside." I think all of the fellows in both organizations had a ball that day, and that is exactly the way it was supposed to be. We shared the section work and the solos on every number, using Duke's rhythm section on his and mine on mine, but with the two pianos there on all numbers (except "A Train"), with him comping for his soloists and me for mine.

I was not about to touch "A Train," not with Billy *and* Duke there. I said, "Let Billy do it himself," so he and Duke took it. Of course, all three of us got our little taste of *BDB* (which stands for Billy, Duke, and Basie). Sonny Payne paid Sam Woodyard a little friendly drum visit on "Battle Royal," and they trade a few bars just before we take it out, but, like I said, there was no battle. It always was rough enough just to have Duke there when you're playing, let alone trying to chop him. Of course, you always tried to do your best whenever he was around, but that wasn't about battling him. It was about pleasing yourself by measuring up.

==

We also went back to Europe in the middle of that July, and this time we made the trip just to play at the jazz festival down at Antibes. We were over there for about a week, and we stopped in Paris on the way back, and our next gig in New York was up at Freedomland, and that took us into the first week of August.

Between then and the middle of September when we went back into Birdland for two more weeks, we were busy making it from one town to another throughout the Northeast and as far out into the Midwest as Detroit, counting the first week in January. That was the third time we were in Birdland so far that year, and there is a Roulette release made from a broadcast recorded either that time or the time before. It is called *Basie at Birdland*, with no date given, but it was probably taped during June and September, because Budd Johnson is one of the tenors; and the "Whirly Bird" track with the vocal by Jon Hendricks, who was in on the June gig, is on it.

==

Later on that fall we cut a second album of originals that Benny Carter laid on us. *The Legend* was the title of the album. By the way, Benny

Carter himself also sat in on alto on those sessions, but he wouldn't take any solos. He just didn't think it was fair to take even one little solo away from a regular member of the band. Hell, the only reason he sat in at all was to fill in because Marshall Royal had to be absent to take care of a family emergency. So he just sat in as a favor to me, so we wouldn't have to go out and hire a replacement for Marshall; and what actually happened was that Frank Wess shifted from second to first alto, and Benny played second for Frank.

That's all we could get him to do on an album featuring his own compositions, and when the fellows kept on after him and kept on after him to take at least one solo, he begged off by saying that his chops were not up to it. But all you have to do is check on what condition Benny Carter's chops were in at that time is listen to an album he made for Impulse called *Further Definitions*. Incidentally, another substitution in our lineup for that album was on guitar. Freddie had to be away, so Sam Herman sat in for him.

Later on that month Budd Johnson cut out. His last gig with us was at the Howard Theatre down in Washington, and that's the spot Eric Dixon filled when he joined the band the first time. He didn't replace Budd directly. We had a couple of others in there for a short time, and Eric came in after we got back to New York. Eric was another one of Frank Wess's recommendations, and like Frank, he can also play flute, and also clarinet if he has to, as he did on the small group sides in a cut that following March.

On the first Thursday in December, we began our annual holiday run in Birdland for what turned out to be the last time. I was aware that Birdland, like a lot of other clubs of that kind, was going through some changes, but I can't say that I remember coming out of there that first week in January feeling that it was all over any more than I did the last time we played in the Blue Note. I don't think anybody said this is it or anything like that.

We just had our usual closing night send-off and came on out and spent the second week in January up at the Apollo again, and then we worked our way south along the Atlantic seaboard on down to Miami, and then over to Nassau and down to Kingston, Jamaica, splitting a week between the two. Then we came back into Florida for a few more dates, and that was the extent of our bookings during the midwinter resort season down there that year.

Then we headed back north into winter weather, and we spent the last three weeks of February out in the Midwest and the first part of March getting back into the Apple for two weeks at the Jazz Gallery. It was right near the end of that stand in the Jazz Gallery that arrangements were made for us to take a seven-piece combo to the Van Gelder Studio in Englewood Cliffs, New Jersey, and cut nine tunes for Bob Thiele to be released on Impulse Records. We used Thad Jones on trumpet, Frank Foster on tenor, Eric Dixon on tenor and flute, and Freddie, Sonny "Big Ed" Jones, and the Chief.

Those were Eric Dixon's first studio sessions with us, and we gave his flute a little workout, and we also used him on clarinet. Except for a short break or two, Eric has really been a member of the band right on down through the years, and as this is being written, he has been serving as our musical director for about a year.

—

We flew out of New York for England and Europe during the last week in March and toured over there until the first week in May, and when we came back, we went straight on out to Seattle for a one-week engagement at the World's Fair before working our way down to San Francisco for another week and then spending June on the road back to the East and July in the New York and New England area. During this time we started recording some things for another album of originals by Frank Foster.

That was the summer Sonny Payne ran into a few personal problems, including a four-way automobile car crash on the New Jersey Turnpike, and had to be hospitalized. That's why he didn't make the trip to Europe with us that time. We got Louis Bellson, husband of our old friend Pearl Bailey, to fill in for him on that tour. So Louis was the drummer on all of those tapes we made in Sweden in August. Then Sonny was ready to come back to work after a few weeks.

Meanwhile Ed Jones didn't make it back to Europe with us on that trip, either. He wanted to try something else, so he cut out. He left music as a full-time thing and began a new career with IBM. He had been studying for that all during the last few years he was in the band. He carried books everywhere and studied them every chance he got. He even read them backstage between sets, and as soon as we got back on the bus, he'd tuck that bass away, and wham, he would be right at it again. I remember that very well, because his seat was near mine. So when he finished everything, he made the shift and started right in, and he has done very, very well, as we all knew he would. After only a few years he had worked up to be a division manager in the IBM organization.

He hasn't really given up music completely, however. He has come back and played on reunion programs with us and guest shots with other groups from time to time, and I've been told that sometimes he might even take a leave to go out and play a few gigs just to keep in touch with what's happening.

Before we got Buddy Catlett as the replacement for Ed Jones, we had Art Davis on bass for a while. But Buddy made the trip, and so did Fip

Ricard, who came in on trumpet when Snookie Young decided that he had had enough of the road for a while and settled down with the NBC studio band.

Buddy Catlett came to us from Jaws Davis's current group. He had also been with Quincy Jones, and he turned out to be one hell of a bass player, a beautiful bass player. He could find some notes you would not believe. He was such an excellent bass player, just marvelous. When you heard those strings popping, they would still be so melodic—*djoom djoom djoom djoom / djoom djoom djoom dejity djoom djoom djoom*—oh, boy! Buddy Catlett was one of the most wonderful bass players I've ever played with.

When we got back from Europe, Quentin Jackson also decided to settle down in one place for a while, so he cut out in New York. That was the chair that Grover Mitchell came in to fill when he came into the band the first time. Actually he took over from Rufus Wagner about six weeks after Butter cut out, but he became the permanent replacement, and he has been in and out of that chair for the last twenty or so years. As this is being written, he has been back for three years.

At the very beginning of that October, we finally got around to making our first records with Frank Sinatra. That was something that both Frank and I had been looking forward to for a hell of a long time. I won't try to go into any explanations of all the reasons why we hadn't been able to get together before, but by that fall everything had fallen into place. We were just about at the end of our longtime deal with Roulette Records, and Chairman Frank had started his own record company, Reprise Records, and he said, "Let's do it."

So we went on out to Los Angeles and did ten tunes in two four-hour sessions. All of those tunes were standards, which I'm pretty sure he had recorded before (and had hits on). But this time they had been arranged by Neal Hefti with our instrumentation and voicing in mind.

I don't remember any snarl-ups or anything like that at all on those sessions. Frank is a perfectionist, and he believes in thorough preparation and hard work, but he also likes for things to hang loose. I remember the rehearsals and the takes going down very smoothly, and I also remember friends and well-wishers like Sammy Davis, Benny Carter, Dinah Shore, and a whole bunch of others dropping by those sessions and sticking around as long as they had time to spare. That's the kind of gig that was, and when we finished, Frank said something like "We must do this again sometime."

Which we did. Two more times on record, and I don't know how many times in theaters, a few of them with Ella, the First Lady of Swing. We made the next album a little less than two years later, with Quincy Jones as arranger, and then in January, about a year and a half after that, we did *Sinatra at the Sands* with him during a run of about a month in Vegas.

Quincy did the arrangements on all of the tunes for that album too, and speaking of the kind of preparation Frank likes, he found out that the band had a couple of days open just before we were scheduled to go into the Sands with him, and he arranged to have the band fly out to Vegas from Chicago at his own personal expense two days in advance just to have us on hand for extra rehearsals. That's Frank. Whenever he steps out on that stage, he knows what's happening, and he's ready.

You'll never catch him coasting. I'm pretty sure he could have coasted in the Sands, and it still would have been great. But that's not Frank. He might look like he's taking it easy up there, but that's just your impression, and that's because he's such a pro. And to me he has always been such a sweetheart of a guy.

Our Yuletide gig in the Apple that year was not in Birdland, but at a new spot called Basin Street East over on Forty-eighth Street off Lexington Avenue, just diagonally across the street from the back of the Waldorf. Birdland had gone through some changes, and it really wasn't the same kind of club anymore. A lot of jazz clubs were folding, and before long Birdland went out of business, too. But Basin Street East was popping. Nipsey Russell, the stand-up comedian, and Joe Williams, our old vocalist, were also on that bill, and we stayed in there right on through the first three weeks in January.

—

That was the beginning of another very remarkable year. I think I can say that the whole year turned out to be one of the great high points of my career as a bandleader. When we came out of Basin Street, we spent a couple of days recording an album of pop standards for Reprise. The arrangements were by Quincy Jones, and they were really heavy, and we just went on in there and did them and ended up with a Grammy.

We spent February and March doing mostly one-nighters in the East, the South as far as Fort Lauderdale, and as far out into the Midwest as Iowa. But in April we made it back into New York for a few days during the second week, and also during the fourth week, and in six studio sessions for Verve we taped enough material for the albums released as *More Hits of the '50s and '60s* (arrangements by Billy Byers), *Li'l Ole Groovemaker in Basie* (with all compositions and arrangements by Quincy Jones), and *Basie Land* (with compositions and arrangements by Billy Byers).

—

When we hit the trail again at the end of that April, we went back to one-nighters in the New York and New England area, with a few little jumps out into the Midwest, and then when we headed for California by way of Ohio and Michigan in the third week in May, we knew that we were starting out on the longest distance the band had ever traveled. Because actually we were finally on our way to Japan for the first time.

That was our destination when we took off from Los Angeles, but on the way we also had a two-day stopover in Hawaii for our first gig in Honolulu. That broke the jump a little bit, which was just fine with me, because as excited as I was about going to Japan, I don't really like to fly anywhere. So as usual, I tried to get well acquainted with Mr. Scotch and Mr. Brandy, but they didn't help at all. They never have, but I had to try something, and I was still drinking a little bit in those days, so that was it.

I don't remember getting around Honolulu very much that first time. I just remember spending a little while by the beach with some people and also in the beach bar. Our gig was in the Kaiser Dome on Waikiki on that Thursday and Friday, and both nights we played a concert from seven-thirty to nine, and then at nine-thirty the room opened as a cabaret with no beverage service and a show, and we played dance sets. I don't remember making it out to any other spots on that stopover. But I liked it there.

We flew from Honolulu to Tokyo on Japan Air Lines, and when we landed, there was a big reception committee waiting for us at the airport, including a group of as many girls as there were members in our party, and they presented each of us with a bouquet of flowers. Then we were taken into a nearby room for television interviews. Then we were driven to our hotel, and the band was free for the rest of that day. Of course, everybody had guides, and somebody translated for them, but I decided to take it easy that first night and get myself together for the next day, so I didn't even leave the hotel that first night.

There were some more interviews during a big press conference at the Golden Akasaka Club early that next afternoon, and then later on there was a big party with music, a local orchestra known as the Blue Coats. That was when each one of the fellows was called out on the stage and formally introduced, and they were Al Aarons, Sonny Cohn, Don Rader and Fip Ricard, trumpets; Benny Powell, Henry Coker, and Grover Mitchell, trombones; Marshall Royal, Frank Wess, Eric Dixon, Frank Foster, Charlie Fowlkes, reeds; Freddie Greene, guitar; Buddy Catlett, bass; Sonny Payne on drums; and old Base sitting at the piano like the sparrow, so everybody would have something to keep their eyes on. Jimmy Witherspoon took care of the vocals on that trip, and he was quite a hit.

After the reception everybody was taken back to the hotel for an early dinner because our opening concert in Kosei Nenkin Hall was scheduled for six that evening. Everybody was ready, and it was a good kickoff, and the audience response was just so great you had to feel right at home. There were a lot of people who already dug the music from way back, and a whole lot of other people having a good time getting with it.

The Japanese are really something. They are right on the ball. They are busy, and I mean it seemed to me like they were busy twenty-four hours a day, continuously working. They intend to get something done, and they get it done. They're constantly learning new things. It really was an exciting experience over there, and everywhere we went we met such wonderful people.

One of the beautiful people I met on that first trip was Nabuo Hara, and he turned out to be one of my great friends in Tokyo. Somebody took me to see the show at the Nippon Theatre, and I thought the band on the program was marvelous, and I mentioned that I wanted to go and meet him. So they took me backstage with a translator, and I told him how much I enjoyed hearing his wonderful band. It was known as the Sharps and Flats, and I found out that it was the most popular band in Japan. When Nabuo Hara came to hear us, he brought me a little present, and that's something he has continued to do every time I've gone back to Tokyo, right on down through the years to this day. He also brings two big bottles of sake for the members of the band.

On the last couple of days of that first trip our bands played on the same bill in the Golden Hakisaki, one of the top spots in Tokyo. It was really some place, with a stage that could accommodate three bands, and there were no lulls. You'd be backstage, which was down on another level, and when the band onstage played its last number, your band would be in place and play its theme. They'd go down to the backstage level, and your bandstand would come up to the auditorium level, and by the time you finished your theme, you were in the place where they had been. No lulls. I actually saw three big bands rotating in there like that one night. I never saw anything like that before anywhere.

By the way, I think they must have more big bands in Tokyo than we have in the whole United States. Just in Tokyo. That's the way it seemed to me. I think they must have had at least two great big bands in each one of those big clubs over there, and they were good bands, full of good musicians. They can play anything they hear. I mean, they're such exact musicians that sometimes when they work from recordings or live performances, they write in the mistakes without realizing it. That's just how precise they are.

Which reminds me of something that happened to me over there on one of those trips. We were playing somewhere, and we were programmed to come on after the house band, and I happened to arrive a little late, not late for my set, but a few minutes before the first band was supposed to hit. So I was pretty sure that I had enough time to come in through the main entrance and catch part of their set from the audience.

But when I stepped inside the lobby and heard the music, I said, "Damn, the band is on. Am I that late?" Because it was those Japanese cats playing one of our tunes as a tribute to us, and for a couple of bars they had me fooled. I said, "Jesus Christ!"

—

When we came back from Japan, we spent the rest of June and the first week of that July working in California, and then just before heading back east on a string of one-nighters that took us back into Freedomland for about a week. We rehearsed and taped a TV guest appearance with Judy Garland and Mel Torme in Hollywood to be aired in November. It was Judy's show, and she sang "I Hear Music," "The Sweetest Sounds," and "Strike Up the Band." The band's instrumentals were "One O'Clock Jump," "I Can't Stop Loving You," and I did "Memories of You" on the organ. Mel Torme's numbers were "I Got My Love to Keep Me Warm" and "Don't Dream of Anybody Else But Me."

Then our next special thing was our first album with the First Lady of Swing. It was released as *Ella and Basie*, and the tunes were Quincy's arrangements. And as usual, when you're working with Ella, it was more like a ball than a job.

That two-day *Ella and Basie* session was Benny Powell's last record date as a regular member of the band. He had been with us for just about twelve consecutive years by that time, ever since he was really still just a kid. So when he decided to split and check out a few other things for himself, it was like a member of the family coming in and telling you that he's ready to make his next move. You know you are always going to miss him no matter who comes in there to replace him, because during those years you've seen him continue to develop as a wonderful musician and as a wonderful person. He had become the fine, clean-cut gentleman that he still is to this day.

So naturally you hated to lose Benny, but luck was with us on his replacement, because that was when Bill Hughes came back to the trombone section of the family after an absence of about six years. Bill is another one of those excellent musicians who is also a clean-cut and very reliable gentleman, and he has been a mainstay in that section ever since, which as of now is twenty-plus years.

—

We spent all of that August and September and the first few days of that October in Europe again. The very next day after we closed at Freedomland, we took off for Scandinavia and started playing all those folk parks and concert halls and theaters. Some of the gigs in the parks were for dancing, but I don't remember playing any club dates up there, and I don't think we did. I think it was three whole weeks of those parks and halls in Sweden, Norway, Denmark, and Finland with no time off between dates except for travel.

Then during the last week in August we swung down into Germany and toured on the main part of the Continent until the second week in September, and that was when we began our sixth tour of Great Britain. After a while all the rest of those tours run together in your memory unless somebody happens to remind you of something that happened somewhere at some particular time.

But there are several special things that I do remember about being back in England that September. That was the time when Jimmy Rushing hooked up with us for a string of dates over there. It was also the time that we shared billing with Sarah. And it was also the time when I looked out of the train window and saw those clotheslines and started remembering my childhood in Red Bank and decided to write a book about my career as a musician.

Those programs on the concert circuit in Great Britain always opened with the band playing a set of instrumentals, and then Jimmy would join us for two or three vocals, mostly from the old book, and that would take care of the first half. Then, after intermission, the program would begin with Sarah and her trio. Then to wrap things up, the band would come back on to back her on three or four other things, with "Bill Bailey" as a closer.

We were back in Paris for a few days at the very beginning of October. Then as soon as we came back to the States, we zipped right on out to Los Angeles for a spot on the Jerry Lewis TV show, and we headed back east. We also did a TV show with Edie Adams. We finally got a chance to take a week off for vacation at the very end of the month. Then November was mostly a month of one-nighters, and December was the same, right on up to the week before Christmas, when we opened in Basin Street East for the holiday season and stayed in there until the second week in January.

ONE MORE TIME AND ONE MORE ONCE

1964 = 1976

There were no plans for us to go back to Europe that next year, and we didn't get around to our second trip to the Far East until about eight years after the first, but in the meanwhile the band began to pick up some very choice bookings in places like Miami Beach, Las Vegas, Lake Tahoe, and Disneyland, Hollywood, and San Francisco that became a regular part of the annual itinerary that we have followed for the past twenty years.

That was also the same summer that we made the second album with Frank Sinatra, which I've already mentioned. We did that in Hollywood, right after we came down from Lake Tahoe in June. We still had our own two Franks in the reed section when we made those tracks, but that was their last record date with us. Frank Foster cut out when we closed at Basin Street East at the end of July, and Frank Wess split a few weeks later. We had Sal Nestico in Frank Foster's chair for a while, and then Jaws Davis came back for his third round with us. The replacement for Frank Wess on alto and also on flute was Bobby Plater, who was also an excellent arranger and co-composer of "The Jersey Bounce," who did a very fine job as a musical director later on. He was another one of Charlie Fowlkes's wonderful recommendations. Everybody liked him, and he spent the last eighteen years of his life with us.

We also went back out to Tahoe for the first eleven days in August and worked our way back into the Midwest and did a thing in Detroit with a fine young singer named Nancy Wilson, who had become a very big attraction during the last four or five years. Then around the first of September we finally got a chance to cut our first album with Sammy Davis, Jr. It was a Verve album, and Quincy Jones was the chief arranger for those sessions. By the way, this was during the time that Sammy was trying out the *Golden Boy* musical on the road before bringing it to Broadway.

In the meantime four of our record albums had made it to the best-seller list in *Billboard* magazine. The first was *Sinatra-Basie*, from that first session with Frank. Then we got lucky with Quincy's charts for *This Time by Basie: Hits of the '50s and 60s*. That was a big surprise, but *Ella and Basie* wasn't, because something good is bound to happen when you work with her. Quincy made the charts for that one too, and also for *Li'l Ol' Groovemaker, Basie*, which was another surprise best-seller, because it was just an album of straight instrumentals with the band popping and grooving.

Speaking of charts, some people think of this band as being more of an arranger's band than the old band. Sometimes they make the other band out to be mainly a head band, as if we were always jamming. But that wasn't really the case. We did have a lot of heads on things, and as I've been saying for years, those heads sounded as great as the charts. But I wouldn't want anybody to forget that some of the most popular things in that old book, tunes that we are still playing to this day, were put in there by some of the greatest arrangers in the business. What about all those things by Eddie Durham, Jimmy Mundy, Skip Martin, Andy Gibson, and Buck Clayton? And what about those charts that we got from Fletcher Henderson back when we were just starting out in Kansas City?

And what about the fact that this band also plays a hell of a lot of those old heads? We play "One O'Clock Jump" every night and "Jumping at the Woodside" almost every night, just to name a couple. The guys in the current band love the stuff from the other band as much as anybody else, and the thing about it is that we don't have to get into a sentimental bag to play those things. They just jump on any of them as part of the band's thing, just like they did with that *Count Basie Story* album. Of course, we don't have the same stars as in the first band. But we still have guys in there who are stars in their own right, and they have to do their thing just like Herschel and Prez and Buck and Sweets and Dicky and those cats did theirs.

There is also another thing you have to take into account when you're talking about those two bands, and that is the record business. In the old days the record companies used to issue those ten-inch singles with one three-minute tune on each side. But when long-play microgroove records came in, those companies began to issue ten- and then twelve-inch discs with from twenty to thirty minutes of music on each side. So that meant when you went into a recording session you were really working on an album that usually called for anywhere from several extended numbers to as many as sixteen regular three-minute tracks.

Naturally that spurred arrangers to bring in more and more arrangements at the same time, and that is really how we got into whole albums of tunes from just one arranger. It really wasn't a matter of having to get all those new charts for the book. Actually it was the other way around. We had to have new material for those recording dates, and then we would keep some of it in the book for a while, either because it was something we happened to like, or because it would help boost the album, or because it was something we began to get requests for after the record came out.

Now, as for the charts themselves, when we were recording things that we had been playing and swinging with for a while, we had no problems. But with new things it's a different ball game. I mean, sometimes we might have a rehearsal of a new thing right in the studio, and the band might play the arrangement perfectly, but I don't think you ever get the actual feeling that it should have when you do it that way. It might cook; but if you've been playing things for a while, then they will have settled down. Because there'd be a lot of changes in the feelings by the time you get into a studio. Because there are probably a lot of different shadings of things in different choruses, and you need time to work out the different ways that things have to be done in there, and sometimes there is a big change from the way you first played it, simply because you know more about it.

But of course, now there are some arrangers that can write things that are flowing and just fall right in place as you work through them. Benny Carter, for instance. Benny can do things that are wonderful that we just run right through. But there are different types of things. But when we have had a chance to run them down beforehand, they are done pretty easy when we go into the studio.

When it comes to the things we do by the guys in the band, sometimes we have pretty good luck when we do them right on the spot. Because these guys are a part of it, and they know what they know from playing together, and that's the way they write. So they put things in that they've been hearing while we're out there doing those one-nighters. Which is when we can really jump on a lot of little things that you don't have time to put in when you're doing concerts. You can really get the feelings out when you're doing dances and one-nighters and, of course, also when you have a chance to settle down someplace in a club. Then you can really jump on them. But you don't have a lot of places where you can do that, not like Birdland and the Blue Note and a few other places.

When you're not lucky enough to get arrangements that are easy-flowing, and you have to have that extra push, then you got to have musicians that have been used to that sort of thing. And it's not likely that you're always going to have a band full of those kinds of people. When you have that kind of person, you know you can settle them down in there again, and they can cut it. Or they can walk into the back room and take a cork or two out of something and throw back their heads, and then come on back in there and bam (and of course, I had been in that room throwing back my head too).

"Bam! Let's get 'em!"

And there it was.

We've done things like that and really got to them. Of course, you've got to have confidence in your writers too. Most of the guys who write for us know what I like to hear. They have made studies of the band and know just about where things should lie and who should have them. They don't say this is for the first trumpet and so on. They say this is for so-and-so. They know by name who should take the solos or what have you. That makes a big difference, and that's the whole story of how things have gone down with us all through the years.

We've had success with them, and sometimes you stumble. Anybody can fall up against a rock and make a few stumbles every now and then. Not that we haven't tried, and not that the arrangements weren't right, but sometimes we just haven't put the color in where it's supposed to have been and didn't get the feel of the thing. There was nothing wrong with the arrangement. Further down the line, after a while, it settled in. We hit it and we have it.

Sometimes when the band doesn't get it right, I can tell by the expression on each one of the guys' faces whether it's exactly what they want. And I talk to them.

"Is that what you want to hear?" I ask them. And if they are a little slow, that tells me something.

Take Benny Carter, for instance, whom I've known for about a thousand years and respect so much because he is so beautiful in so many ways. We'll be doing one of his things, and when we make a take on it, I always check with him.

"Well, what do you think, old man?" I always ask him, and right away I can always tell if we've missed something. If he hesitates, I just cut right in.

"How was it, Benny?"

Then he'll have to say something.

"Well, it's all . . . right. . . ."

"Do you want to try it over?"

"Well, yes," he'll say, and you can tell he's relieved. "Why not try it once more?"

So we'll try it a couple more times. Then he feels that you have shown a lot of interest in what he's trying to do, that you're really willing to try to understand what's going on. But speaking of Benny Carter, I remember one time, to skip ahead a bit, when I was asked to do an album with Jackie Wilson, who was a top rock-and-roll singer in those days. One of his big hits was a tune called "Lonely Teardrops." Well, when they asked Jackie who he wanted to write and direct the thing, I suggested Benny Carter, and he looked at me.

"Benny Carter? He can't write rock and roll."

So I told him. "What the hell or you talking about?" I said. "He can write *anything*. You're talking about Benny Carter. Hell! Just tell him what you want."

And that's who we got, and Benny put down some music on that album, believe me. Benny jumped on top of that thing. And Jackie sang it, and it's musical and it's well played. So I looked at the band.

"Now what you guys going to say? Ain't a goddamn thing you can say. That's *it*, and I ain't changing *nothing*. Ain't nobody going to tell me *nothing* about Benny Carter's writing. *Sheet*, get out of here. That's the way it goes or nothing goes."

Benny Carter is a special kind of man, and he has been that kind of man for years. He's one of the all-time great arrangers, and both as a musician and a person he has always had class. He is a hell of a bandleader when he wants to be. He is one of the all-time great alto men and also an excellent trumpet player.

When you're talking about Benny Carter, you're talking about a master arranger. And Quincy Jones is another one. In the first album he did for us, there's a beautiful thing called "For Lenny and Lena" that I like so much and was happy to do because Lenny Hayton and Lena Horne were such wonderful friends of mine. By the way, it was Lenny who turned me on to the yachting caps that I've been wearing for a few years now. I liked the way he looked in his and had to have one for old Base, and now it's kind of like one of my trademarks. Quincy also did that *This Tune by Basie* album, with "I Can't Stop Loving You" in it, that won us a Grammy Award, and those others that I have already mentioned. Quincy is a pro, and you can't get away from guys that are pros. You cannot get away from them to save your life.

Like Neal Hefti. Neal has done a few albums for us down through the years, and we rehearsed them and played them. Neal is definitely one of the outside arrangers who has studied the band and can write assigned spots to particular musicians by name.

Sam Nestico's thing also flows easily, and you can just use them right down without a whole lot of trouble. Sammy was recommended by Grover Mitchell, our first-chair trombone man. Grover and he became friends when they were on the same base in the service. Sammy was the bandmaster. They've remained good friends, and Grover got him to do a few charts for us that turned out very well. That's how it started. He is an excellent arranger, and in recent years he has written quite a few things for us. What he writes is very melodic, and he does pretty things that tell definite little stories down in there.

You have to have confidence in your writers. I'll take a chance with each one of the guys I've named and any arrangements that they bring in, because I respect what they're trying to do. All down the line those guys have been awfully nice to us. They've done everything that they could do just to help us do something and make the band sound right on their arrangements.

—

We settled in at the Sands Hotel in Las Vegas for most of December 1964. Then we went back to Hollywood and spent that Christmas season in the Coconut Grove. Unless I'm mistaken, that was the first time we had ever had to be out of New York during the whole holiday season. And as great as Coconut Grove was, you could tell that the fellows really missed being in the Apple.

After we came out of Coconut Grove the second week in January, the next big thing was President Lyndon Johnson's Inaugural Ball. That was another one of those good years, and so were the ones that followed. We made another European tour during that September and October and then skipped the year after that. But we were right back over there the next May and June, and then during the year after that, which was 1968, we were over there three different times.

The first time was in April. I remember that April trip very well, because it was the week Dr. Martin Luther King was assassinated, and we canceled a couple of dates in the Washington and Baltimore area. I'm pretty sure that everybody can remember exactly where he was when the news of that great tragedy came. I was in Montreal on a one-nighter in a theater before heading back down to New York and Washington.

We went to Germany and Holland for just a couple of weeks and came back on the first of May. Then in July we went over again to play at the festival at Antibes, and we also went down to North Africa for one date in Tunis before hopping up to our old stomping ground in Scandinavia one more time. We did all that in nine days. But when we made that third trip over there during the last week of that October, we began in England and traveled to Copenhagen, Stockholm, Brussels, Madrid, Milan, Munich, Düsseldorf, Lyons, Paris, Berlin, in that order and came back by way of Barcelona around the middle of November.

It was Christmas in the Apple for us once more that year. We went into the Riverboat, a big downstairs club in the Empire State Building, at Fifth Avenue and Thirty-fourth Street, and stayed in there through the

New Year's party. Then, after ten days off and ten days at the Tropicana in Las Vegas, we hit the southern trail to the resort scene down in Florida, and when we came back to New York, we spent the last of February and the first half of March in the Copacabana.

The trip to England, Switzerland, and Germany in 1969 began during the third week in April and lasted until the first week in May. Then, after a very busy summer that took us to Harold's in Reno, Basin Street West in San Francisco, and the Steel Pier in Atlantic City, we made our first trip down to South America during September.

That was a nine-day trip, which we spent in Argentina and Chile, and it was very interesting to be in that part of the world. But of course, as usual, we spent all of our time either working or getting to the next job. We performed eight out of those nine days down there. There wasn't any time for sight-seeing, except for what you could get a glimpse of on your way from one place to another, and that was also the way it was for shopping.

But it is a very beautiful part of the world, and there are some wonderful cities down there. We touched down at São Paulo going down, and in Ecuador coming back. But we didn't spend any time there. We spent most of the tour at the Opera Theatre in Buenos Aires, and originally we were scheduled to go across the river to Montevideo, Uruguay. But that was canceled, and the only other city we played was Santiago, Chile.

The newspapers gave us some good write-ups, but as I remember, things were also a little strange down there. Of course, there were friends and fans waiting for us down there, just like in those countries in Europe, and we made some wonderful new friends. But I also have to say that there are a lot of people who were not really ready for us at that time. They were very nice, but you could tell that most people were not really with it yet, and to tell the truth, I was kind of glad when it was all over and we cut out from down there.

Actually we ran into bad luck as soon as we landed. We had a problem just getting through Customs, because there had been some kind of mix-up over our immunization papers, so everything was held up until everybody was examined again, although we had already been cleared before we left New York. That was just great. Then just as we were winding things up in Santiago, the hotel where the band was staying caught on fire, and they had to evacuate those premises in a hurry, as sleepy and tired as they were.

—

The four Caribbean cruises on the *Queen Elizabeth II* and the one we made on the *Canberra* were another ball game altogether. That whole thing turned out very nicely all around. Our first QEII began on the first

Monday night of that next January. We sailed from Pier 52 at the end of
Fifty-second Street on a ten-day cruise that took us down to Kingston,
Jamaica; and Bridgetown, Barbados; and back by way of Charlotte Amalie,
St. Thomas, in the Virgin Islands; and it was almost as much a vacation
for us as for the regular passengers.

Each member of the band was provided first-rate accommodations for
two. We worked only one set, which means we had twenty-some hours free,
so there was time for some sight-seeing and shopping when we hit those
ports of call with our wives. Naturally, most wives were very pleased to
be able to go along on all of those cruises, and they had a wonderful time
relaxing and getting all that first-class *QEII* service, including the deck
games, the movies, and the swimming pools, not to mention the food and
drinks. It became an annual thing with them for five years.

Incidentally, among the passengers on that first cruise were Sarah
Vaughan and also Eubie Blake and his wife. Sarah was just taking a break
from her busy schedule. But naturally, she did a couple of things with us,
and she also took part in a few jam sessions on the Q4 bar. Eubie was his
usual fun-loving self. He claimed that he was warming up for his eighty-
seventh-birthday celebration, which was coming up soon. He picked a
great way to get ready.

But I don't think anybody enjoyed that cruise any more than Kate. She
really fell in love with the climate and the pace of things down there in
those places. She went on every cruise we made during the next four
years, and by the time we made the last one, we had sold our house in St.
Albans and moved down to Freeport on Grand Bahamas Island.

I'm not saying that we found the house on one of those cruises. That's
not the way that whole big change came about. We found it while we were
in the Bahamas on an excursion with the Rinky Dinks, one of Katy's social
clubs. Actually I found it.

One day while we were out on a sight-seeing trip, we began to look at
places that were new real-estate developments, and we just happened to
pass one particular house that you could walk all the way around to the
back of, and while I was just meddling around back there, I tried one of the
sliding doors and found that you could get inside. So I called Katie and we
walked through, and I just liked the way it looked inside, and so did she.
But I remember that Dr. Rene Sabbagh, a good friend of mine from Brazil
who comes up and travels around with me and the band from time to
time, was along on that excursion. He said what he thought the price range
was going to be. I said, "Well, hell, I might as well stop thinking about
this one then," and I put the whole thing out of my mind.

Because I knew that I didn't have any business getting upset about it
if it was going to cost the kind of money he was talking about, even though
I really did like it. And I also saw two or three others definitely worth

considering. But hell, I wasn't even ready to buy a doghouse at that time, which is what I should have been thinking about, since I stayed in the doghouse so much. Actually I stayed in the doghouse so much over the years that there were a lot of houses out on the road that I was paying enough rent on to be buying. Actually the main reason I was down there on that excursion was to help get myself out of the doghouse one more time. You can't be Peck's bad boy as often as I have always been without getting caught every now and then. But that's another story.

Anyway, I just forgot about a new house for the time being. But it's funny how things turn out, because a little later on Kate and I were talking about something or other, and suddenly she brought the subject up again.

"By the way," she said, "you know that little house you liked so much down on the island?"

"What about it?" I asked, not really thinking anything.

"Well, you'd better try to get two or three more gigs together, because I've put four or five dollars down on it."

And I said, "Aw, no!"

And she said, "Oh, yes!"

And that was the beginning of our love palace. It really was the start of something big for me, for just me and Katy and our daughter, Diane, and Graf the puppy. That's when we really started living as a real family. It was our house of happiness. The house in St. Albans was just a house so far as I was concerned, and I wasn't there very much anyway. I'm just speaking for myself, not for Katy, because she really became a part of that community in a way that I never had time even to think about.

She did so many things in that community. And she had a special thing about children. She was always saying, "This is my little girl. This is my little boy." And of course if they were all her little children, they were mine too; because I thought what she was doing was just so wonderful, and the way the kids responded was so beautiful. Anywhere you saw them, it was always beautiful smiles and greetings.

"Hello, Mom."

"Hello, Dad."

But that is really her story, and I'm not going to get it any further, except just to say that when we bought the lot next door in St. Albans, we put an Olympic-size swimming pool on it, and it really became like a neighborhood thing for quite a few kids. And when we sold the house because we were moving down to Freeport, we held on to the pool so it would still be available to the kids.

Anyway Katy closed the deal on the new house in the Bahamas later on that fall, and as I always have to say, I know it seems strange to people who lead a more settled life than I ever have, all I can truthfully remember about how and when we actually made the move is that Katy took care of it, and that by the time the band went into the St. Regis in the middle of that next January we were in our new place, and I was flying down to the island on my off days.

—

But to get back to the first *QEII* cruise. That was really an easy gig for us. Our set began at eleven and went until midnight. We didn't use any standard program as we do on a regular show. There were some passengers who wanted to dance and some who wanted to listen, and also some who were fans of ours. So we just relaxed and changed things around a bit every night. That way there was something for people who wanted to hear some of the older things as well as for those who expected things like "April in Paris" and "Shiny Stockings," and other selections from the current book and the pops on some of our recent releases.

It was not long after the first *QEII* cruise that Marshall Royal, who had been our rehearsal director all those years, became ill and had to take some time off. We brought in a temporary replacement, but then when Marshall recovered, he didn't come back. I think he just decided to give up the road at least for a while. He didn't really have to come back out there, because his services were very much in demand right there at home in Los Angeles. There were all kinds of work laid out for him in studios and groups around town whenever he wanted it. We still had Bobby Plater on alto. We brought Bill Adkins in for a while, and for a couple of years we had Curtis Peagler. As for Marshall's job as musical director, for a while everybody just sort of pitched in, and then it fell to Bobby Plater for the rest of the time he was with us.

I'm going to let Jaws Davis account for all the details of how many times he was in and out of the band when he tells his own story. All of those records he made with us speak for themselves and people who caught the band live when he was in it remember him very well. But I would like to give him special credit for the job he did while he was my road manager.

He was one of the best. I don't care what anybody else says. Eddie did a good job. He was tough, but he was fair. And he was honest, which is more than I can say for some others we've had in that job over the years. He was very honest about everything dealing with business matters.

But he could get pretty rough when it came to personal relations. He wouldn't stand for any stuff from anybody. Sometimes I've had to cool him down because he could rub some people the wrong way. That's why I'm pretty sure that some other people will have their side of the story to tell. Because they couldn't bend him in any kind of way at all. If something went wrong, he was for straightening it out right on the spot. If somebody in the band screwed up, he was right on him. He'd come right to me.

"What are you keeping this man for? You know he's always going to mess up."

That's when I'd have to pull him back, because sometimes he would forget that we were dealing with musicians, although he was a musician himself, and a good one. He did his job, both as a musician and as a manager, and that's what he expected everybody else to do. He didn't make any allowances for personal weaknesses. So I still say he did a good job, although he did stir up some resentment. That's my side of the story; I'm not saying that's the only side.

By the way, as far as the other band managers I've had over the years are concerned, if I say what I really think about some of them, it would change this book into another kind of story. That's why I haven't tried to give any more of a running account of them than I have. I'll just say that all of them could talk a lot and also talk very loud and count that money and separate it. They could really separate that money. But the thing about it was when you checked up, every time you found a mistake it was always in their favor. I'm not going to name any names, but one cat made something like a twelve hundred dollar mistake on one goddamn payroll. I mean, within a few months after I had rehired him for old times sake. When members of the old band heard about it, they didn't want to believe it.

"What, again? Not again."

Jaws was also a big talker, but he always was straight when it came to money matters. Since Jaws cut out, my trumpet man, Sonny Cohn, and I have been sort of co-road managers. So now when things go right, I take all the credit and when the schedule gets fouled up, I can always blame him. That's the way things have been in that department for the last twelve years.

As much as we had liked our first trip to Japan, and as eager as everybody was over there for us to come back the following year or sooner if possible, it was actually about nine years before we got around to making our second trip over there, and that was a part of a four-week tour that began the second week in January 1971 and took us down into Southeast Asia and also down under to Australia for the first time.

I remember that we liked Japan just as much the second time as the first, probably more, because we already had so many friends over there, like Nabuo Hara, leader of the Sharps and Flats Orchestra, who came to greet us with a present for me and a couple of big bottles of sake for the members of the band. Japan was just great. But I really don't have very much to say about those places we hit on the way to Australia, because I was mostly just scared all of the time. They were shooting at planes over there during that time.

One little trip to somewhere over there, I was in one of those little three-seaters, and you could sit back there and look right down on where all that trouble was. George Wein, who was booking that tour, was the other passenger in that little plane that day, and when he looked at me, he could tell that I had just about had it.

"Well, Bill," he said, "what you gonna do?"

"Hell, man," I told him, "I don't know what you gonna do, but as soon as they get this damn thing back on the ground, I'm getting out of this whole mess."

I told him I was not going anywhere else over there in those war zones, and when we came down, we went on talking about it, and I told him to count me out. But old George could dig it.

"Well," he said, "I guess I'll have to take your place. Don't worry about it. I'll go."

George himself is a good piano player, and he was actually getting ready to fill in for me on the next gig. But that's when I said to myself, I ain't gonna be *that* chicken. If the rest of the guys in the band were going, I had to go, too. And besides, George had his father along with him on that trip, and he needed to stay with him. But that definitely was no sight-seeing trip for me. All I was concerned about was when we were going to get the hell out of there.

So if I've forgotten about what I saw in those places over there, that's exactly what I intended to do. Hell, I was trying to forget it as fast as it was happening. But we did make our scheduled appearances in Okinawa, Manila, Hong Kong, Rangoon, and Bangkok; and we found fans and made new friends at every stopover. As a matter of fact, sometimes you run into quite a few hip people in places like that. They come up to the bandstand to tell you about when they came to hear you somewhere in Europe or the States. That's not really unusual. There are people in all those places from Europe and the States; and there are also local people who have traveled in the States and in Europe, or maybe have gone to school in one or the other.

And then, too, there are also people in all of those places who had been listening to us on the radio for years. They could get those Armed Forces broadcasts and also the Voice of America, and you could also find our recordings in some of those shops over there, especially after the Japanese started reissuing them, but actually, as I've been reminded, that was also a part of the territory that the British record companies had already been shipping stuff to for years.

Anyway, the local advance publicity and newspaper coverage must have been up to par, because the turnout was okay, and the promoters seemed to be doing pretty good! When we got down to Singapore, according to the local paper, *New Nation*, we played a one-nighter in the Orchid Lantern room of the Tropicana Nightclub. The capacity was three hundred fifty persons, and we drew almost three hundred at eighty-five dollars a seat.

—

When we finally made it all the way down under to Australia, it was not so strange as some of those other places, because it was almost like being somewhere in England. Of course, you ran across quite a few people in those other places who spoke English, but everybody in Australia speaks English, and that in itself made things seem a little more familiar. We arrived right at the beginning of February and spent a little more than a week there and in New Zealand.

We landed in Perth, and there was a reception committee with a little band waiting to greet us, and they played one of our numbers, and it was very nice. I know that we spent the next week playing in Adelaide, Melbourne, and Sydney. But as usual, most of it is just a blur to me now, because you really didn't settle down long enough to let anything soak in. You were always moving on to the next gig. But I do remember how wonderful those audiences were, and the people in general were just so fine, and so many of them knew so much about what we were playing.

And another special thing I also remember is the sound of some of those halls we played in down there. They had a natural sound that was just beautiful, just fantastic! I don't trust my memory on certain kinds of details about all those trips to different places down there, but I never will forget that sound. It was really a great pleasure.

I liked Australia very much. I'm not saying that I actually saw a hell of a lot of it on that first trip, but I definitely knew that I would like to come back again and see some more. Then when the chance came, about eight years later, that's why Katy went along. I knew she would really have a good time down there, and she did, and the people down there liked her very much.

According to our files, we played four concerts in three days on that first visit to Australia. Then we headed back to the States after two or three days in New Zealand and a stopover gig at the Hawaiian Village in Honolulu. Then we worked our way back east from California, and in the middle of March we made our second *QEII* cruise. Then in the middle of April we took off on another tour of Europe and England that lasted right on through to just about the end of May, and in that little space of time hit thirty-nine cities in nine countries. It's hard to believe, but that's what it was, and Ella Fitzgerald will vouch for it, because she was with us some of those places.

The run in the St. Regis in 1972 took us right up to the end of the first week in February. Then after a swing up to Windsor, Canada, and a one-nighter at Mr. Kelly's in Chicago and two weeks at the Tropicana in Las Vegas, we went back out to California near the end of the month, and that's when we spent a three-day session making an album with Bing Crosby.

I don't remember who got that one through, but I was very thrilled at the idea that we were going to be doing something with the Bingle. I thought it was just wonderful. He had been such an important part of the scene for so long. He had put his own personal touch on so many fine tunes that had become standards down through the years. Whenever old Bing took to a tune, there was never any question about who that was. His personal touch was a standard in itself.

We did eleven tracks during those three sessions. There was no problem running them down; but they didn't turn out as great as I had hoped. I don't really know what happened that everything didn't come off better than it did. I really don't know, but I don't think that was really Bing's shtick. I don't know. So I'll just say that we didn't hit his groove on that one. But I was still very happy about the whole thing, because it gave me a chance to do work with him.

I really think Bing was right at home when he could have his pipe and Pops. I think that was really his life, anything he and Louis could do. They fit so good. That's what I was thinking about all during the while we were in the studio those three days. If old Louis just would have walked in there on any of those numbers, everything would have fallen in place. That's all it would have taken. Bing and Pops were sometheing together.

Which reminds me of one of my big regrets and also of another one of my greatest thrills. I will always regret that I never did get the chance to have the pleasure and great honor of doing a recording with Pops. Because it was always such a great thrill to play with him. He was just so wonderful. Anytime we were playing somewhere on the same bill with him and his group, it was always something special.

The memory of one time in particular just popped into my mind. Our groups were on the same card at a theatre in Philadelphia. I never will forget that. My band had the opening set, and just a little while before we were supposed to go on, word came that Thad Jones was not going to be able to make it until a little later on. It was just one of those unexpected things. Because Thad never gave us any trouble about anything like that.

Anyway, that left that first chair open, but I just figured that we could go on without too many people missing him right away. So we just went on and hit, and I heard those trumpets and heard that goddamn audience going wild and looked up there, and old Pops had snuck up there and was sitting in Thad's chair; and when we got to the trumpet solo spot, he took it and you never heard so much clapping. Old Pops was having a ball.

As it turned out, Thad did arrive before the set was over, but he made

Louis stay right on out there in that first chair. That was something no-body could ever forget. It was just such a special experience. And after that, old Pops would check by every day, just in case Thad got held up again.

"Man, what you doing here this early?" I asked him that next day or the day after. "That man ain't never going to be late no more. He ain't never late. That's the only time I've known him not to make it on time."

Old Pops just grinned.

"Hell, man, you never can tell. So if you need me, I'm here, daddy. And I like to listen to these cats, too, you know."

But you can bet that Thad was not about to let anything get in his way again that week. Oh, but that was such a wonderful week with old Pops in Philadelphia. Old Pops. He was *everybody's* main man. One of a kind.

When we came back east after those sessions with Bing, we spent the middle fourteen days in March on another *Queen Elizabeth II* cruise. That's the time when we went to St. Thomas in the Virgin Islands, St. Lucia, Caracas in Venezuela, and Port-au-Prince in Haiti, a five-thousand-mile round-trip for sixteen hundred passengers. The main stop I remember was Port-au-Prince, because as soon as we went ashore I wanted to get back out of there. The poverty of the place was just unbelievable, and I never will forget the horrible, narrow escape we had on a sight-seeing trip.

A party of us hired a guide and went on one of the little tours to look around and also eat at one of the local restaurants. But right away the poverty was so unbelievable that I knew I wasn't going to enjoy the trip. And I didn't. We saw some interesting historical landmarks downtown, but it was also a pretty sad scene, and it didn't get any better in those other sections. Then we stopped somewhere, and we saw a bunch of school-children. Hildegarde Bostic, who was along with us, wanted to give them some change, and she started to get out of the car, which was a hell of a mistake.

Those kids stampeded, and all of a sudden we were all in trouble. Hildegarde almost had her arm torn off, and then we thought those poor hungry kids were going to rip that car apart trying to get to us for more handouts. It was an awful experience. The guide had warned us that it was dangerous to get out of the car with those kids clamoring around like that, but none of us realized that it was that dangerous.

I also saw some projects that the Haitians had under way to try to rebuild and improve things down there, and if they get them finished, it would be very straight down there, but there were a lot of pitiful condi-tions. It was very discouraging. I just wanted to get back on board the ship and get the hell away from there as soon as possible.

As far as I was concerned, that was the worst part of that whole cruise scene. I wouldn't say that you didn't see some strange sections in some of those other ports of call down there, but in the main everything was fun and relaxation. That's what those trips were about and the passengers were wonderful. And of course Kate and I were right at home with all of those little clicking wheels and felt tables and galloping bones and slot machines. Oh boy. Then, on that last trip, Miss Sarah came along again but this time she was a star attraction, which means she probably had even more fun than when she was just a passenger. Cannonball Adderley was *also* a feature attraction that time around. And by the way, we hit Bermuda on that one, and that was another gas.

=

We spent most of the fall of 1973 overseas. We went to Europe and also to Japan and Hawaii between that time and the first week in December.

We took off for England and Europe the day we came back to work. We opened in Birmingham, England, and worked our way to Berlin by the end of the month. Then we began the first day of October in Hamburg and came back to Bristol, England, and did a TV show in London before playing one-nighters. Then before coming back to London for a couple of days, we crossed over to Rotterdam for one night.

That brought us up to the middle of October, and our itinerary for the rest of the tour took us to eight countries, including Spain, and back to the States with a little break of about nine days before heading out to the coast and Japan from St. Louis.

The towns on our itinerary for Japan that November were Mito, Tokyo, Niigata, Tokyo, Sapporo, Iwata, Aomori, Tokyo, Kanazawa, Matsuyama, Nagasaki, Kumamoto, Nagoya, Osaka, Kyoto, and Sendai. On the second of December, we stopped over in Honolulu for a one-nighter at the Coral Ballroom en route back to San Carlos, California, for a week in the Circle Star Theatre. After that, it took us about nine days to work our way back east for our well-earned Christmas vacation.

=

The band as a whole didn't do a lot of studio work in 1973. We used it on four of the tunes we did with Teresa Brewer in February for an album produced by Bob Thiele to be released on his Flying Dutchman label. But the other five, which we made in April, were backed by a combo made up of Sonny Cohn, Henry Coker, Eric Dixon, and the rhythm section. On the other two albums I recorded that year, I played with a combo made up of Sweets Edison, J. J. Johnson, Lockjaw Davis, Zoot Sims, Irving Ashby on guitar, Ray Brown, and Louie Bellson. Both of those sessions were for Norman Granz's Pablo Records. The first was called

Basie Jam and the second, which we made the very next day, was called *The Bosses*, and it featured Big Joe Turner, the all-time boss Kansas City blues singer.

Special bookings that broke up our regular schedule of Stateside one-nighters in 1974 were the gigs we played at Caesar's Palace in Las Vegas and at Disneyland in July and the trip to Europe, which began at the end of September and lasted right on through October. The itinerary covered a lot of the same territory as the year before, but we had more time off in more places.

There may be some tapes of some of those dates somewhere, but the only studio recordings from that year that I can account for are two combo albums for Pablo Records that Norman Granz set up for me and a few of my old friends. The first was with Ray Brown on bass and Louie Bellson on drums, and it was released under the title of *For the First Time*. And it was all fun, because we just went on in there and did them.

That session took place in the summer. We did the other one while we were out in Los Angeles in December, and it was the first whole album with that incredible monster by the name of Oscar Peterson on piano, and with Ray and Louie plus Freddie Green. All you have to do is listen to that monster firing all those fastballs by me on every one of those tunes to understand why we called that album *Satch and Josh*.

Satchel Paige was already just about the greatest pitcher in the world when he was playing with the Kansas City Monarchs back when I was out there; and Josh Gibson of the old Pittsburgh Greys was the most fabulous catcher and also as great a slugger as Babe Ruth. Sometimes they used to work together in all-star games, so over the years they also became pretty good friends.

There is an old story about how one time before a big special game somewhere, Josh went up to old Satch and asked him for a favor.

"Hey, look, man," he said, "my mother is going to be at the game today. So what about giving me one good one so I can hit it out and make her feel proud?"

And old Satch just nodded and winked at him.

"Ol' buddy, just leave it up to ol' Satch."

But when the game started and Josh came to bat, old Satch smoked the first strike by him before he could get the bat off his shoulders. He stepped out of the batter's box surprised, and then he told himself that old Satch just did that as a setup to make things look real. But when the second pitch came, it was another smoking strike, so old Josh figured he'd better remind him.

"Hey, Satch," he said, "hey, man, remember my mother's up there in the stands. Come on, man, lighten up."

But old Satch was already shaking his head as he went into his third and last windup.

"No way, man. No way. No way."

That's that monster, and I'm poor Josh. Norman Granz has had Oscar's group and my band do quite a few things together over the years, and as a special little novelty after Oscar's segment of the program, Norman has brought the two of us out, and we used to do three things together. We'd play a few bars each, and he'd play a chorus, and I would stumble through one, and he'd catch me stumbling along and pick me up and help me. He was wonderful.

But some nights he'd forget, and I'd have to hit the piano real hard to let him know I was still there, so cut it out, and don't get carried away. He was wonderful. But he was also terrible. Sometimes I'd just think about how I was going to have to be with that monster that evening, and my whole day was ruined.

Yet I am always very happy every time Norman has us on the bill together. I'm right out there in the wings, listening to him, because he's impossible. He's got a special piano he plays. It cost sixty thousand dollars or something like that a few years ago—no telling what it costs today—and they send that piano everywhere he plays.

I just sit there in the wings just looking and listening, because what he does is really incredible. I mean, it's impossible for anybody to sit down at the piano and play and think that fast. Impossible. You can't think that far ahead. So he just puts his hands on the keyboard, and his fingers will just play. He doesn't even look at the piano. He just puts his hands out. And I am sitting there, looking at him out there smiling because his fingers have just played something he wanted to hear.

I'm waiting out there in the wings with a *baseball bat*. Then, when it's over, he comes over toward me, asking how I liked that tune.

"Rotten," I say. And he just comes on into the wings and puts his hand on my shoulder, and I knock it away.

"Get your goddamn hand off me. Don't touch me."

And when the concert or the tour, or whichever it happens to be, is over, I'm so relieved because I don't have to wake up every morning with my day already ruined as soon as I remember that I have to go out there and face him in the evening.

"Thank goodness. Good-bye."

But he's so sweet, you have to love him. He's just great, just so great. And that Swedish bass player named Niels Pedersen he carries around with him ain't no amateur, either. He plays bass like Oscar plays piano. Then when Oscar really gets *heavy*, he calls for the boss, Ray Brown, to jump down in there, pounding and walking through there. Old heavy you. Ray is also a longtime friend of Norman's.

I also made a small combo album with Zoot Sims on tenor, John Heard on bass, and Louie Bellson on drums that next April in New York. It was called *Basie and Zoot*. Then, while we were at the Montreux Jazz Festival in July, Norman Granz made another combo album from a live jam session that I was in with Roy Eldridge on trumpet, Johnny Griffin on tenor, Milt Jackson on vibes, Louie Bellson on drums, and that fantastic Swedish bass player. There were just three tunes on the whole album: "Billie's Blues," "Festival Blues," and "Lester Leaps In." I think everybody had a little fun that day.

The band had come down to Montreux from Ostend, Belgium, after the beginning of our summer tour of Europe in Malino, Sweden, and going to Copenhagen, Denmark. After Montreux we went down to Antibes and Marseilles and came back across France by way of Orange to Vienne, near Lyons, and Evian, near Geneva. Then we played in Perugia, and from there we flew down to North Africa, to Tunis and Carthage, before coming back to the Apple.

The only full band studio recording session we had that year was in Los Angeles while we were filling an engagement in Disneyland during the last week in August. That was a two-day session, and all of the material was written and arranged by Sammy Nestico. That was Sammy's third album for us. His first was *Basie Straight Ahead*. The second was *Have a Nice Day*.

By this time, there had been a few important changes in the lineup. Actually these changes had started back in January when we had to get a new drummer, and somebody recommended a very young fellow by the name of Butch Miles. Butch came to us from Mel Torme's outfit. He was a real crowd pleaser, like Buddy Rich and Sonny Payne, and he picked up on things very nicely, and he was also interested in sticking around for a while, which he did, for about four years.

Charlie Fowlkes had also come back and taken over his old baritone chair from Johnny Williams. And Eric Dixon had also come back and taken over his old tenor spot after a couple of other replacements, including Harold Onsley, cut out. The other tenor was Jimmy Forrest, who was actually filling the chair Eric had left a year and a half before. So they were our two tenors for the next few years, with Eric also doubling on flute along with Bobby Plater, the first alto man. The other alto man by this time was Danny Turner, who came in from Machito as the permanent replacement for Curtis Peagler. Danny shared the alto solo feature with Bobby Plater, and he could also double on flute and clarinet.

I'm not even going to try to account for all the changes in the brass sections over the last several years leading up to that summer. I'll just say that the mainstay in the trumpet section was Sonny Cohn, and some of those who stayed a little longer than the others were Waymon Reed and Pete Minger, with Paul Cohen coming in from time to time. There are quite a few others who didn't stay very long or were just there on a record date.

Our mainstay in the trombone section was, and still is, Bill Hughes. Al

Grey had also been back in his old chair, and he stayed for several years before cutting out again. Curtis Fuller was also in the trombone section for a couple of years before Dennis Wilson, who is still with us. The other trombone player by that time and from time to time for a few years afterwards was Melvin Wanzo. And I'm sure that everybody remembers Richard Boone, for his vocals on "Boone's Blues" and "I Got Rhythm."

The bass player on that August session was John Duke. There had been several other people in there after Norman Keenan cut out, but John Duke was the one who stayed with us for the better part of two years, which means he was also on two more albums, *I Told You So* and *Prime Time*.

On our way back east, we stopped off in Kansas City and played an outdoor concert in Swope Park Mall on the first of September. Then we came on back into New York for our two-week special at the new Uris Theatre (now renamed the George Gershwin Theatre), across the street from the Winter Garden on Broadway between Fiftieth and Fifty-first streets, with my man Frank and everybody's First Lady of Song.

Frank Sinatra and Ella Fitzgerald on the same bill of fare. So Frank just went on and followed his usual warm-up routine of rehearsals at his own expense. He rented NBC Studio G for Wednesday, seven to ten P.M.; Thursday, three to six P.M.; and also for Friday, one to four P.M., before moving over to the Uris for a last run-through from five to eight. We had that Saturday off and played at the Chateau Pelham in the Bronx that Sunday and opened at the Uris that following Monday.

What can you say? It was fourteen days of standing ovations. That was a foregone conclusion. They both have about a billion fans in New York, and neither one of those two champions has ever let up on any audience anywhere. If you go somewhere to hear either one of them, they're going to knock you dead. So what else can you expect with both of them up there on the same program? Slaughter.

We began our fall tour of Europe in London on the third of October and spent the rest of the month hopping to The Hague, Paris, Brussels, Burghausen, Munich, Frankfurt, Helsinki, Stockholm, Milano, Köln, Hamburg, Berlin, Nancy, Antwerp, Zurich, Geneva, arriving back in Great Britain in time for Edinburgh, Scotland, and a few days off in London before a fournight gig in Ronnie Scott's wonderful place.

I'm pretty sure that was the first time we were ever booked into Ronnie's club, which was definitely one of the top jazz spots in Britain. I think the only other time I had ever taken my band in Ronnie's before that was the time when somebody arranged for us to hold a rehearsal with George Frame in there, in preparation for the show we did together. Anyway, doing a regular gig in there was a great pleasure because, as I told my friend Max Jones, the reporter, I liked the sound in there, and the atmosphere was, as his article quoted me as saying at the time, "just delicious."

As I also said at that time, I really think we could have stayed in there for at least two weeks without any letup in attendance. But as a matter of fact, we already had something even bigger than that on the schedule. Because Thursday of that next week was when we opened at the London Palladium with Frank, and this time it was Frank and Sarah. That's Frank for you again. This was his first season at the Palladium, and he could have sold the place out by himself. According to the newspapers, the whole town had Sinatra fever. So here he comes with Sarah Vaughan and Basie. But that's Frank.

His first warm-up session was the day after we closed at Ronnie Scott's, which was that Sunday. The command performance was on Monday. Then we worked out with Frank and Sarah again that Tuesday and Wednesday and opened that Thursday. The first night audience was everything that you would ask for, and the show got better and better every night.

We came straight back to the Apple on the next day after we closed at the Palladium and had one day off. That brought us up to the last week in November, and we didn't get but three more days off between then and the last week in December when we broke for a nice long Christmas vacation after a short week's stand at the Royal York in Toronto, followed by a night in the Civic Auditorium in Allen Park, Michigan.

I remember zipping back to New York and heading straight to Freeport to spend some time just taking it easy in my little love cottage on Confederate Walk with Katy and Diane and our dog Graf, and of course, I also planned to pay a few visits to the money that I had been leaving at the casino during the three years since we moved down there.

—

The first thing we did when we came back to New York at the end of the second week of January 1976 was an album of eight original instrumentals and two standards arranged by Bill Holman, a West Coast reedman who has also played and written things for Charlie Barnet and Stan Kenton. We called that one *I Told You So.*

This was another release that Norman Granz was producing for his Pablo label, but the sessions actually took place in RCA Studio A on Forty-fourth Street and Sixth Avenue, and we were in there for three afternoons, and I think that they turned out okay, considering the fact that the charts were all new to us. As I've said before, when you have something in the book for a while, you just go on into the studio and do it, and that's it. If I remember correctly, the band hadn't seen any of those charts for the session beforehand, but I also have to say that I don't remember anybody having any problems with anything, either.

That's the way it goes. Which reminds me of something else I'd like to mention. Sometimes somebody will come up and say, "You have a swinging band. What about all those things you do with those headline singers and all of those pop things? How do you really feel about working on that kind of gig?" When somebody asks me about something like that, I say I feel just great about it. Because in the first place, I like the tunes, and also the people are wonderful to work with. And I also think it's just great to have musicians who can play different kinds of things. It's how the band plays that matters, how it does its own thing on those tunes. Well, it could be a whole arrangement or just a little tune. If somebody gets something started, that could be it.

A whole album can get started like that, I think. Maybe there will be one little tune that will catch on and change the whole deal, right from the beginning. If you get a good feeling and good guys are playing, good guys who want to play and they think everybody around them is all right, believe me, you got something going. You got one going, even if you have to take a walk, even if you have to go into another room and throw your head back a few times.

It is a big mistake to think that the band is going to take any session lightly just because the material might happen to be something you call a pop tune. All you have to remember about the kind of musicians I'm talking about is that they don't have to have the greatest tunes in order to have a great jam session. Somebody is subject to get something going on anything.

It's the way you play it that makes it. What I say is, for Christ's sake, you don't have to *kill* yourself to swing. Play like you play. Play like you *think*, and then you got it, if you're going to get it. And whatever you get, that's you, so that's your story.

You don't have to play anything loud until you *need* it, and you don't *need* it until you really *feel* it. Then it's *you*. Like I always say, I think a band can really *swing* when it swings *easy*, when it can just play along like you are cutting butter. I haven't ever heard but a few guys who could really do that, and I never did tell them what they were doing, because I didn't want them to know what I was stealing from them. But that's all you need.

I think you can make five thousand people out in a park or a stadium somewhere listen as quietly as a hundred people in a room. They'll listen, and they'll make those who are not listening shut up. You can hear them going *shhhh*—until those others settle down. That's the kind of thing that decided me about what I like to listen to.

And that's another reason why Duke was the boss as long as he lived. He *remained* the boss. He *stayed* there. And he didn't have to go any further up on the ruler than three or five, and when he went on up to seven or eight, he was getting ready to get your *ass*. Get out of here. There'll never be another one like Duke.

Sometimes I've heard people saying, "Duke ain't playing nothing tonight. What's the matter? Something must be wrong with him."

And I always tell them he just don't want to get anybody yet.

"Don't make him want to get you."

People forget about that sometimes, and they really should know better. I know a couple of bandleaders who thought they had caught him on an off night, but that was a big mistake. Because when you try to take advantage of a situation like that, you're asking for it.

Because when he comes back up there on the stand, *the red-hot number you worked up to so you could bring the house down*, will be the one that he'll use as his *warm-up* number! And he will *play it for you* as if to say, *"Oh, is this the tune you mean?"* Or he can play your *theme song* with so much stuff in it that you don't want to touch it anymore that night.

Sometimes people forget about that until they get smart. Sometimes he's just holding his musicians back. And they're raring to go. Sometimes you can hear them up there grumbling.

"When are we gonna play something? Goddamn, man, ain't we going to get to play something tonight? Come on, Duke, let's play something."

I've known people who've decided that nothing was happening and got up to leave but before they could get to the door they heard something that changed their minds. And I've heard the waiters kidding them.

"Oh, we thought you were leaving. Would you like the same table?"

One of my greatest satisfactions is that he always liked me and always encouraged me. He never did drop it on me. He never did. I know what he could drop on you, and if he put any of his really heavy stuff on you, damn if you could play your own things as well as you usually could, because instead of hearing yourself, you'd be up there hearing *him*.

He was always nice to me whenever we were on the same bill somewhere. If some of those guys in his band started to get carried away because they didn't want to let him down and you asked him to lighten up, he would. One little battle just didn't mean that much to him when it was the two of us. I don't care what anybody else says. Old Duke. I sure do miss him. Nobody was sadder than I was when he left us. I was out on the Coast, but nothing was about to keep me from getting back to New York to be at St. John the Divine to pay my last respects. Everybody should have been there, and quite a few were. He achieved so much and set such high standards for everybody.

Johnny, Harry, Ben, Blanton, Ray Nance, such great voices and now Cousin Sonny. They're all together again now. But thank God the music is still here for us.

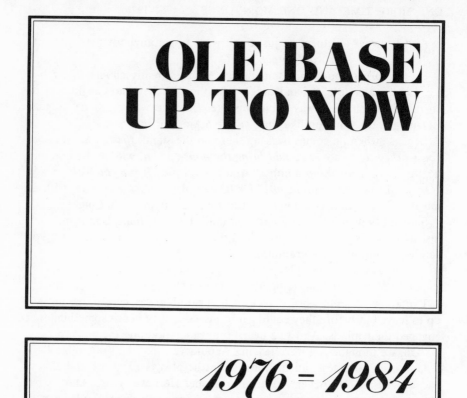

OLE BASE
UP TO NOW

1976 = 1984

After that recording session for Pablo at the RCA Studio, we started in on a string of one-nighters through the New York, New Jersey, Connecticut, Pennsylvania, Maryland, and Virginia area, and then came into the Apple at the beginning of February for three dates and a CBS television show before I flew out to Los Angeles for a guest shot on John Denver's TV show. The outlook for the band was just as bright as it had been at the same time the year before. And that is exactly the way things turned out so far as choice bookings and our rates were concerned.

There were more one-nighters in every section of the country than we could handle. There were stands of a week or more in theaters like the Schubert in Los Angeles and great hotels like the Deauville in Miami Beach, the Sahara and the Aladdin in Las Vegas, and amusement centers like Disneyland. And there were also all of those places in Europe and the Far East that were still as much a part of our gypsy caravan route as a lot of our Stateside stopping places.

=

But as it also turned out, while all of those wonderful and profitable things were continuing to happen for the band, I myself was heading for some very serious trouble. It was one of those things. You're so busy doing what you're doing that you're not paying any attention to whatever warning signals might be right in front of you, and then, like all of a sudden, there it is, and you don't really know what's happening to you, and when somebody tells you what it is, you still can't really believe it.

We spent just about all of April in Japan, beginning in Tokyo and then moving out on a string of one-nighters in seven cities. Then we came back to Tokyo for a couple of days and took off again for seven more and ended up back in Tokyo for the flight to San Francisco.

Our tour of Europe that year began with four days in Nice during the second weekend in July, right after the Jazz Festival Dance in Roseland Ballroom. We were over there for eighteen days, and we worked fifteen of them. We were in Nice for another jazz festival, and then, after a couple of days in Paris, we went up to Copenhagen and circled back to Amsterdam and then crossed over to Arhus and hit Göteborg on the way to Stockholm, and then we were in Oslo and Halmstad and Hälsingborg, and the last town we played over there before coming back to New York for a couple of days off before going to the Steel Pier in Atlantic City was Malmö.

I spent the first half of August at home down in Freeport, and all of our dates for the rest of the month were in the Northeast. Then, beginning on the first of September, we had a very nice little four-day deal in a brand-new Las Vegas spot called the Aladdin Hotel. I remember that things were really popping in Las Vegas while we were there from Wednesday through Saturday. The response to the band was very good, and when we were not working, you could visit your money at the tables and the slot machines, and there were also the ponies in the afternoon.

When we closed at the Aladdin that Saturday night, we had to zip directly to Los Angeles, because we were opening a one-week run at Disneyland on Labor Day, that Monday. Which we did, and then the day after that was when a very strange thing happened to me.

We were staying at the Players Motel in Hollywood, and when I woke up, I felt a pain in my chest, and I just thought it was indigestion or something like that. I just felt like I needed to belch but couldn't, and I couldn't relieve the congestion or whatever it was, and when I began to sweat, I called Paul Probst, one of our staff men who travels with us and helps with the equipment, wardrobe, and stage setup and valet service, and when he came in, I was perspiring an awful lot. Then the next thing I knew, I was lying over in his arms, and he was wiping the sweat off me, and I had a *terrible* pain in my chest.

Then I was lying in bed, and I must have passed out again, because the next thing I realized was that the medical emergency crew was there giving me a regular going-over and getting ready to take me to the hospital.

"Looks like you had a slight heart attack," one of them said. "It's a good thing this gentleman called us in time."

"We have to carry you," another one told me.

But I said I didn't want to go, and then I insisted that I was not going to be carried out on a stretcher. I didn't realize just how dangerous it was for me to walk down those steps, but I insisted, and when we got outside to the ambulance, they stopped.

"Now, you know you're going to have to get in this thing."

And that's all I can remember, because I passed out again.

That was a strange feeling. I didn't even know what hospital I was in. I vaguely remember seeing Norman Granz and John Williams standing outside the door in the hallway at some time or other, and I also remember being in another ambulance going into another hospital. That was when I went into the Cedars of Lebanon Hospital. The first hospital was Hollywood Presbyterian, and I don't really have any conception of how long they kept me there before they transferred me. I just remember being all hooked up to the EKG machine and the doctor talking to me.

"You've had a heart attack," he said.

"Oh, yeah?" I said. "Is that what this is?"

Because I really couldn't believe it.

It just didn't seem all that serious, and I never felt that I was going to die. But they kept me in Cedars for about two weeks, and I really did get some rest in there. I had a nice room and television, and I could play it all night if I wanted to, because they didn't give me any time to go to sleep. I didn't have anything to do other than get up for breakfast. You had to get up in time for them to do what they had to do in the morning, but all night and most of the day all you had to do was take it easy.

When they finally let me go home, they said I still needed to rest for a while longer before going back to work. So I stayed in Freeport, but I really didn't feel like I needed all that much rest, because before long I was doing a lot of walking all the way around Confederate Walk, which is really a half-mile circle, and I would do that a few times every day.

Then, after a while, I just didn't know what to do with myself, and I missed being around and seeing what was going on. And it also looked like the band was doing too well without me. They took off on a twelve-day vacation beginning the first Monday in October, as was already planned. Otherwise they were working just about every day as usual, and bookings were still coming in as usual. As straw boss and music director, Bobby Plater was really filling in as the leader for rehearsals and calling the tunes during performances. Sonny Cohn just went on doing his job as road manager, and to fill in on piano for me they had Nat Pierce some of the time, and at other times they had Junior Mance and Sir Charles Thompson.

When they came back from vacation in the middle of October, they worked their way to New York from the Midwest, and they then spent most of November in the East before heading south at the end of the month. The first time I actually saw them again was when they came down to Florida right at the beginning of that December.

They were booked for the Dade County Auditorium in Miami on the first, and Williamson's Restaurant in Fort Lauderdale the next night. So Kate and I decided to go over there and catch them and we did, and they really sounded good, and they were doing very well. I sat in on a few numbers, and I almost stayed with them then. But we decided that I should wait until the schedule was a little easier. It was nice to be back working, but you can also work too hard.

So I went on taking it as easy as I could in Freeport for a while longer, and then I went back to work when they came back from Christmas vacation the first Thursday in January. That was at the University of Redlands out in Redlands, California, and from there we went to San Francisco for a couple of days and then on to Sun City and Scottsdale over in Arizona, and I felt pretty good, but the next couple of days had been left open for free time in Phoenix for my benefit anyway. Naturally everybody wanted me to take it easy, and you couldn't argue with that, but to tell the truth, after all that time off I was tired of doing nothing.

By the way, I have been asked how much time I spent practicing and playing the piano and organ at home while I was there all that time. The answer is none. With me it is a matter of working out with other musicians. I never just sit at the piano practicing by myself for hours. Actually I don't even have a piano in my house down in Freeport. I have a little Hammond organ, and I might hit that a lick or two every now and then in passing, but that's about as far as that goes.

The first recording session after I came back to work took place in the SunWest Studios in Hollywood when we came back into Los Angeles from Vancouver during the third week in January. We took it easy and did eight tunes in three days.

In the lineup at that time we had Pete Minger, Lyn Biviano, Bobby Mitchell, and Sonny Cohn on trumpets; Al Grey, Curtis Fuller, Bill Hughes, and Mel Wanzo on trombones; Danny Turner, Bobby Plater, Jimmy Forrest, Eric Dixon, and Charlie Fowlkes on reeds; and the rhythm section was John Duke on bass, Freddie Greene right where he was supposed to be, and Butch Miles on drums. These are the guys who pitched in and cooperated so beautifully to help keep things going while I was away.

And then when I came back, everybody was just so considerate. Naturally they were all trying to act like nothing had happened, but you could feel the concern. You knew they all were keeping an eye on every move you made, ready to say something anytime they thought you might be about to do something a little strenuous.

"Hey, watch it now. Take it easy, Chief."

They didn't ever really bug me with it or anything like that. You just knew that they intended to do what they could to help you take care of yourself.

＝

When we left California near the end of that January, we were booked into the Sahara Hotel in Las Vegas for a week, and from there we went down to Disney World in Orlando, Florida, and stayed down there filling other dates in that area until we came north during the fourth week in February for a week at the Westbury Music Fair, followed by seven days at the Valley Forge Fair in Philadelphia, which took us through the first week in March.

By this time I was getting pretty much used to being back on the road again, but we took ten days off beginning the second week in March just to break things up a bit. Then when we came back, we spaced the dates so that we worked only eleven out of the next sixteen days before taking a nice long vacation of about two and a half weeks in April, before taking off for Europe. We went over on a five-day-week schedule that time, so with the time off it took us from the last full week in April up to halfway through the third week in May to make it from London to Paris by way of fourteen one-nighters.

I made that trip without any trouble with my health, and the band was very well received everywhere. I really felt very good. I was following my diet and keeping at my exercise routine, which at that time was mainly getting out and taking a good walk every day. But we didn't push my luck. So after a couple of weeks' vacation that lasted up to the first Saturday in June, we went on a very light schedule that called for only twelve dates spaced out over the next twenty-seven days.

Then after our Newport Jazz Festival concert at Carnegie Hall on the first of July and the annual jazz-festival dance gig at Roseland Ballroom that next Monday night, we took off to Europe again, and after a stop-off in Paris to play for a private party, we spent the next five days at the jazz festival at Nice. Then we moved on into Switzerland, and the Pablo record which was taped during our performance at Montreux is a pretty good sample of what was happening in the band that summer.

This time around we went up to The Hague from Montreux and then cut back down to Spain, but we spent the last week up in Scandinavia. Then after a couple of weeks off, we came back to work in the middle of August. We opened with a one-nighter at the Meadowbrook in Cedar Grove, New Jersey, and then after another one-nighter at the Coliseum

Theatre at Latham, New York, and another at Robin Hood Dell, we headed west by way of Chatauqua, New York, and Hotel Pontchartrain in Detroit, and arrived in Disneyland just in time for the big party to celebrate my seventy-third birthday on opening night at the Plaza Gardens.

Actually that whole week of Disneyland was like a birthday party, with everybody making a special point of wishing me well. And so were the next two weeks, which we spent in the Sahara Hotel in Las Vegas. It was really beautiful. You couldn't ask for a better way to wrap up the story of my comeback from my heart attack.

—

Since that time, things have settled into a routine that I have been able to handle very well without too much trouble. We have cut down on the number of working days per week whenever possible, and we have definitely increased the number of vacation breaks we take each year. The schedule is now set up so that we get from ten to fifteen days off just about every five or six weeks.

But the market for the band is even bigger than ever. We seem to be picking up more and more followers of all ages every year, and we get more calls for dates than we would have been able to fill even when we were out there grabbing everything we could get. We just have to re-schedule them when possible. We still do a lot of one-nighters all across the country, some in theaters and auditoriums and some in ballrooms, and that also includes dates on college campuses, just as it always did. Club dates are usually for more than one night and so are quite a few theater concert dates, especially those big concert specials that we are lucky enough to do from time to time and place to place with Ella or Sarah or Frank or Tony, and also with the Mills Brothers once in a while.

Engagements running for a week or ten days, and sometimes more in Disneyland or at Knotts Berry Farm or at the Fairmont Hotel in San Francisco, Harrah's in Lake Tahoe, and at top spots in Las Vegas like the Desert Inn or Caesar's Palace and the Sahara and also at the Royal York in Toronto are still regular events on our annual schedule. It is always a special treat for road musicians to have stopping places like that to look forward to during the year, and the guarantees that they bring you in on are not bad, either.

It's been a while since we've had the chance to settle down in New York like we used to do back during the days of Birdland, the Starlight Roof season at the Waldorf, and Basin Street East. If I'm not mistaken, the last time was a week at the Riverboat over five years ago. But of course, we still think of the Apple as our home base, and we are in and out of there all the time. But actually we have had longer dates in places like Detroit and Cleveland and St. Louis than in New York. Most of our gigs during the past few years have been performances at Carnegie Hall and Avery Fisher Hall in Lincoln Center, or public dances at the Roseland Ballroom during the Jazz Festival, or private parties at the Waldorf and also one at the Hotel Carlyle. However, when we have been booked for a couple of nights in clubs like Art d'Lugoff's Village Gate or the Savoy (in midtown), those places have been sold out even before the notices came out in the *Times*, the *News*, and the *Post*.

During the last five or so years, we've also been back to Australia once and back to Japan four times, and Europe four times. That was our second trip down under and out back, and Kate made that one with us. She had a wonderful time down there, as I knew she would, and she also made a big impression on people down there.

===

I'll just pass on over most of the little physical ups and downs that I went through during those months following my comeback, because once you hit your seventies, you can't really expect to feel in tip-top condition every day anyway. So you just hang on in there, and you go on out and make the gig, and you feel much better doing that than you do just lying around worrying about yourself.

But I do have to mention two things that have happened since that time. The first hit me in October of the same year that we made that second trip to Australia. By the way, at the time we didn't realize how heavy that year had turned out to be. We spent part of February and part of March in Australia, most of July and part of August in Europe. Anyway, we had just finished ten days in Las Vegas at the Desert Inn with Tony Bennett and had moved on up to San Francisco on our way to an autumn tour of Japan and *wham*!

I came down with a hell of a case of shingles, and we had to cancel the whole four-week tour of Japan because I had to go home to Freeport and take it easy until the beginning of the year. Which I did, and the tour was rescheduled for that next March, with us doing only a little over two weeks right after coming back off a two-week vacation beginning near the end of that February.

We also took another vacation of about twelve days beginning the first Monday in May. But we hadn't been back out on the road for more than two weeks when this other thing which I call this arthritis thing hit me one night.

When I had that heart attack, I really didn't feel like anything that serious was happening. I did have some discomfort and pain, but it didn't really scare me. It just felt like indigestion or something that would go away if I could belch. But this other thing really hit me. I felt it coming on, and then all of a sudden there it was. It hit me like a brick. It really shook me. Everything was spinning, and I couldn't stand up and walk, and I couldn't control *anything*.

That really scared the hell out of me because I didn't really know whether I was going to make it from one minute to the next. And nobody knew what the trouble really was. When the doctor came, he knew it was not another heart attack, but he didn't know what was really happening either. So they sent for Kate, and meanwhile they checked me into the hospital in Chicago and ran a lot of tests on me. They kept me in there for only three days, and what they said when they released me was that I was suffering from fatigue and a viral infection.

Whatever kind of infection it was, it also brought on this arthritis thing that I haven't recovered from yet. When Kate checked me out of the hospital, I was in a wheelchair because I still hadn't regained my balance. It was all I could do just to get on my feet by myself, let alone walk anywhere, even with two walking sticks. But I did feel back together enough to go on a few more jobs, and with Katy out there with me to make sure that I didn't do anything drastic, I hung in there for about a week and a half and got through a couple of days at Resorts International in Atlantic City and Belmont Park the last weekend in June before cutting out for some time off in Freeport.

I spent the whole month of July at home following a daily program of rest and special exercise, and when I came back to work at the end of the first week in August, I did so with my doctor's approval, because by that time I had made a lot of progress, and I was really back up to handling it. But there was one big difference, because I was still having some trouble standing up alone, so my main way of getting around, and also for getting to and from the bandstand, was my new Amigo motor scooter.

And just to make sure that I kept on taking care of myself like I was supposed to, Katy came out on the road with me in spite of the fact that her own physical condition was not really very strong at that time. Actually we had been concerned about her high blood pressure for the last few years. That was one reason her trip to Australia with us the year before had been so important. I was very concerned about how well she could hold up on a long trip like that, and when she made it without any trouble, I thought we were very lucky, and I was very relieved when she settled back down at home.

But with my condition as it was, she insisted on coming back out. So she made arrangements to keep things running smoothly for Diane at home, and over the next couple of years she spent almost as much time on the road with me as she spent down in Freeport.

Of course, the fellows in the band just picked right on up from where we left off and went right on taking care of business, just like they always do when we get back from vacation. The main difference was the way I had to get on to the bandstand. I would drive the scooter out to the piano stool, and then somebody, usually Grover Mitchell, who had rejoined the band in Tokyo that March, would give me a hand in making the switch. Other than that, everything was back to normal, with us filling the same choice bookings as before and drawing the same sellout audiences that gave us the same great receptions as before. By the middle of October we were on our way to Europe again, and we stayed over there until the middle of the third week in November.

Our first studio recording after the arthritis thing put me on the motor scooter was for the Pablo album entitled *Warm Breeze*. Following that Norman also led us to *Farmers' Market Barbecue* and *Me and You*.

That turned out to be the last album I made while Katie was alive, and she didn't get to hear it because we lost her last April while I was up in Toronto. She was at home in Freeport, where she had been since late fall because her doctor had advised her to stay home and take it easy and watch her weight.

So I knew she was not in the best of health, but all during the time while I was at home during the Christmas break, she didn't seem to be having serious problems either. She was just her usual self, and that's the way she was when I came back to work in January, and that's how she sounded on the telephone every day.

Then all of a sudden she was *gone*. My Katy, my baby.

And that's about all I'm going to say about that at this time. I'm just going to let her rest. I think just about everybody can understand that, and I know that anybody who has been through something like this can also understand why I decided that the best thing for me to do was come right on back out on the road a couple of days after the funeral. And I have no doubt at all in my mind that this is what she wanted me to do.

As a matter of fact, she really hadn't expected me to get back down to Freeport until after I finished a two-week tour of Japan at the end of May.

In the meantime we made another album for Pablo Records just before we took off for Tokyo. That one has not been released yet, but I can say that the way the band sounds on it and on those other three albums before it is a pretty fair sample of what old Base and the bunch are laying down on any night these days.

Of course, now when something happens to turn maybe just one guy on, and he takes off, that might spark the whole band into something special, and we sound even better. Something like that is subject to happen anytime. And naturally I also like to think we're always getting better and better all the time. The present lineup is still a little young in places, but that's like with a racehorse. You have a thoroughbred, but you have to train him to make him into a racehorse.

Take our young drummer. He's just reaching twenty. I call him the third Dennis and Number Three, because we also have young Dennis

Wilson on trombone and young Dennis Rowland the singer. Number Three is already a good drummer, and one day he's really actually going to be a monster. The main training he needs is how to close up his ears and not think about anything but himself and listen to the orchestra and not just himself too much, and keep his eyes on the sparrow. Then we can get so we can just look at each other and tell exactly what's going to happen. That's the way all of our rhythm sections have done. We have always stayed within each other, and we knew where to put it all the way down the line.

Actually the whole band works like that, especially since these ailments began to slow the old sparrow down a bit. They know what I want, so when I start somewhere on the keys and old "Arthur" grabs me, they know where I'm going and that's where they take it for me.

As for the old sparrow himself, like I've said time and again before, it's always a big thrill for me to hear what's going to happen every time we hit and every time one of those guys walks out there to that microphone. It's never really the same. Something different and exciting is always subject to happen, and I'm waiting to hear it.

—

So that just about brings things right on up to old Base as of now, which is my eightieth year, and I'm still kicking around out here on the old gypsy trail with my own thing. And that is exactly where I intend to be for as long as I keep on having as much satisfaction and enjoyment as I'm still getting out of it. I certainly don't have any plans for retirement in the foreseeable future, since I still am playing music, or at least *trying* to play it, as much as I ever did.

I shouldn't have to say that it is not a matter of money, but I will, just for the benefit of people who wonder and worry about things like that. It is not because I'm still hard up for bread after all these years as a headliner. Naturally I don't think that you can ever really have it made when it comes to your financial situation. But so far as being able to retire without being forced to give up a lot of the conveniences and pleasures that I've become used to, Kate saw to it that I took care of that some few years ago. She left things in very good shape for me and also for Diane.

But truthfully, playing music has never really been work. Not to me. Of course, if you are a professional musician and that's the way you make your living, that does make it a job because that means you have to get hired, and you get paid, and you can also get fired. But I still say that money has never really been a very big consideration with me personally. I really would rather not get into any discussion about it.

I'm not saying that I don't think money is important. It is very important, because as a bandleader I always have to try to get the top rates for my musicians. You have to do what you can to keep your band together and also make it stand for something. Then you can get the right people in there. So in that sense it is a business. Because you have a whole organization to keep together and that means all those bookings and all that traveling.

But all of that is just a part of the dues you have to pay to have the kind of band to make the kind of music you like. However, I still say the main thing for me is the music. That's what excites me. That's what keeps me going. The music and people having a good time listening to it. People dancing or just patting their feet.

And by the way, the main thing about being the Chief is that you get to call the tunes. (And set the tempo. And the mood.) Otherwise I just think of myself as the sparrow, and I just say keep your eyes on the sparrow. You can't have but one leader. You can't have four leaders. When you get away from having one leader, you're going to have a mixed-up band. That's why I tell them in my band, "Keep your eyes on the fellow at the piano. The sparrow. He don't know nothing, but just keep your eyes on him and we'll all be together on what's going down."

As far as all the traveling and bumping around is concerned, that just means that I'm still lucky enough to be doing what I was always dreaming of doing way back when I was still in my boyhood days playing hooky from school and hanging around listening to the show people and helping to take water to the elephants when the carnival used to come to Red Bank. I know that some people think of all of this as the same old grind. I don't, and I never have. I didn't look at it that way back during all those years when you didn't know whether those old buses were going to make it to the next town in time for your next gig, and your eating and sleeping accommodations were Jim Crow even when you were the hottest attraction in the biggest theaters and auditoriums or the top night spot in town.

Some people seem to be mainly concerned about that aspect of your life as a musician. So maybe they will think I haven't mentioned enough about it. If I haven't spent a lot of time complaining about all of these things, it's not because I want anybody to get the impression that all of that was not also a part of it. It was. So what? Life is a bitch, and if it's not one damn thing, it's going to be something else. I already knew about all of that beforehand just as you would just have to know about what you have to go through to become a prizefighter or a football player or something like that. You don't let that stop you if that's what you really want to be. The fact is that I really didn't run into very much along that line that I didn't already know about. In other words it was not news to me, so I just went on trying to do what I was doing.

It is also a matter of not giving myself a lot of credit for being more high-minded about a lot of things than I ever actually was. I'll just say that I was out there trying to do what I was trying to do, which was to play music and have a ball. I'll just say that I was not surprised when things got strange in one way or another. I'll just say that I didn't intend to let anything stop me if I could help it, and that should tell you something.

Actually, when I look back at everything, it seems to me that the biggest problem of my whole career was how I was going to get into Bennie Moten's band. That was the number-one band in the West, and I told myself that it was the one I had to be with. But how the hell was I going to get in there when Bennie Moten himself was the piano player? I was still really trying to find out what was happening in Kansas City, and Bennie had been playing piano all those years, so what did he need me for? But I had to get in there because that was where it was. And somehow I made it.

As far as I personally am concerned, nothing that I've had to deal with out here has been any rougher for me to take on than that. When I remember all of that now, it seems to me that I must have been the only musician in the world who thought it was possible to break into that band as a piano player. But that didn't stop me. I was not discouraged at all. I guess I was too busy trying to plot my next move to be discouraged.

When it came to all those other tough or strange situations that my co-writer calls "occupational hazards" of those days, we just took care of them somehow or other and kept on going, and if I've forgotten to mention some of them, I guess that means they were not really worth mentioning. And of course, there is also the matter of not bringing up some run-in you had with somebody this many years after all of the circumstances have changed and you have become friends. Somebody else might want to deal with something like that in another book. I don't want any more in this one than I put in here.

That also goes for personal relationships of a very intimate nature. I've said that I was Peck's bad boy from time to time and place to place, and I've also said that I spent a lot of time in the doghouse, and that's the way I'd rather leave it. Because when it comes to naming names and going into details, I just don't see the point of doing that just to give somebody something to gossip about.

And besides, that is another thing about still being active. I might bring up something that happened over fifty years ago, but it is not as far in the past as you might think, because every so often I still get back to all of the towns in every part of the country that I ever performed in, and that means that I have never really been out of touch with people in all those places down through the years. And whenever and wherever the people you're talking about are not still around, there are still their children and grandchildren and even great-grandchildren to be considered. I don't want to have to face them. Hell, I don't even want to have to imagine what they'd be saying behind my back.

I also don't want somebody out there waiting to waylay me around some corner somewhere because I have finally exposed some secret and confirmed some suspicion that has been nagging somebody all this time. That's dangerous. And if you come up spilling the beans about something nobody *was* suspicious about, that could be *even more* dangerous. I know you can get away with putting almost anything in a book these days. But I don't want any more outhouses in mine than I have already put in here. People have been doing very well by my music up to now without all of that! Because that's not what it's about. All you have to do to start getting with it is pat your feet.

So to wrap things up for the time being, I'll just say whatever happens from here on in I can't complain. I've had my breaks, and I really can't squawk. Whatever else happens, I'm still going to have to say I've been blessed. I've been very lucky. Fate has been very good to me. It really has, and I'm thankful. That's why I never sit down to a meal without first pausing to give thanks. Every time I think about how many years I've been able to do what I enjoy doing and make a pretty good living and also make a name for myself and a reputation that stands for something, I realize how much I have to be thankful for.

And of course, I was also *game*. I was always game. I have to put that in here, too. *If something came up, I was willing to try it.* That doesn't mean that I was always changing what I was doing because I was out there trying to latch onto the latest thing to come along. Some people are like that. Not me. Naturally there are things that come up over the course of the years, and you have to adjust to them because that is the way life is. But I've seen people get away from who they are and what they can do—something they are just wonderful at—just because they think they have to try to be something else. You don't have to do that. You don't have to leave from where you are. I've never forgotten that. You can still be yourself and grow and keep up with the times. If you are going to grow.

When I say I was always game, I mean being willing to take a big chance on yourself because you want to do what you want to do, because when I say that I'm thinking about how I jumped at the offer to go out on the Columbia Wheel with Katie Krippen, and the things I did out on the TOBA with Gonzelle White's Jamboree, and how I got my job playing organ at the Eblon Theatre in Kansas City, and how I left the Eblon the first time to join the Blue Devils and the second time just to see if there was any way to get with Bennie Moten. And so on to how I did what I did to take over that job at the Reno and start that Three, Three, and Three outfit that got me the attention that brought me back to New York and into the big time.

I was always willing to say, "Let's see what happens," when something came up that looked like it might help me get a little closer to where I wanted to be, and since that's the way I still am, that really is old Count Basie right on up to date, motor scooter and all. As my co-writer says, autobiographies don't have endings. It's like when I segue into the out-chorus of "One O'Clock Jump" to wrap up a dance set or a concert or a stage or nightclub show. I'm not saying this is the end. I'm just saying that's all for now. I'm saying: *to be continued, until we meet again.* Meanwhile, keep on listening and tapping your feet.

AFTERWORD AND ACKNOWLEDGMENTS

The person other than Count Basie himself most directly responsible for engaging me as co-writer of the Basie Memoirs was the late Willard Alexander of Willard Alexander Inc., Exclusive Artists Management Agency, a longtime Basie business associate, then serving as project director.

Willard's first choice had been Alec Wilder, the very highly regarded song writer ("When We Were Young," "It's So Peaceful in the Country"), composer and co-author with James Maher of *American Popular Song*, who was a life-time Count Basie fan. But according to Willard, Alec immediately recommended me as his own first and only choice, and advised him to get in touch with me right away.

At the time, I had no intention of interrupting my work on the second part of a proposed three-part work of fiction, because I had already done so to write *Stomping the Blues*. So to stall him I told him that Alec was an old friend and booster of mine, and suggested that he check out a couple of my books for himself and call me back if he was still interested, which he did—and this time he insisted that I let him set up a luncheon date for me and Basie. I said okay, and that's how it started.

Because as soon as we got through our jive greetings and gave the waiter our selections, Basie said he had dipped into the two books Willard had sent him and had liked them. Then he asked me if I had any ideas about what kind of story his life would add up to, and I started a very brief outline beginning not with his birth but at a crucial turning point in his musical life, explaining that although the main thing would be the story-line, the sequence of the chapters could be a matter of orchestration like the choruses in a Kansas City arrangement, which would also work like a movie senario. He lit a cigar, took a couple of puffs, put it in the ashtray, and sat listening as if from the piano with a soloist at the microphone, and before the waiter could get back with appetizers, he had made up his mind.

"Say Al," he said, picking up his cigar, "is it all right to call you Al? Man, why don't we just relax and hang out a little and enjoy our snack. Because as far as I'm concerned, this interview is over. As you know, I've had quite a bit of experience holding auditions over all these years, and it really don't take but just a few bars for me to tell when somebody can voice my stuff and fit into my situation. This thing is all yours if you can see your way to take it on, and I sure hope you do because I been dragging my butt on it for about umpteen goddam years and ain't got nowhere."

So the next day Willard called again and made a working proposal that

I turned over to my agent. There was no publisher's contract yet, so there was no long-term advance, but in the meanwhile Basie had authorized him to take care of all expenses incidental to my traveling with the band and to Basie's home in Freeport in the Bahamas from time to time, the transcribing of taped interviews, and the preparation of the manuscript.

That's how it all started, and from then on, Willard's cooperation was not only prompt and efficient but also enthusiastically supportive. Members of his staff were also as pleasant as they were professional. They always kept me up to date on the band's constantly changing current itinerary and quickly facilitated the establishment of necessary chronological sequence of the band's development by making office archives of Master Routing Sheets and pertinent contract data readily accessible.

As for actually working with Basie himself, it was as much a pleasure as it was an honor. When he asked me to take on the project as co-writer, he really meant take it over. At our very first working session, I found out that along with functioning as his literary accompanist and orchestrator, I was also expected to assume all of the responsibility for the progress of things, and from then on, he acted as if he had to do whatever he could to meet *my* schedule. At the beginning of every session, he always asked what I wanted him to talk about, and at the end he always expected me to suggest the place and time of our next get-together. Sometimes when he was on a heavy performance schedule he would say, "Okay now, let's get to bar 19 so I can get some rest," and at other times he'd say, "I'm not nodding on you I'm just breathing heavy." But at no time did he ever become irritable or disagreeable, even when he made himself work while he was not really feeling very well.

Interviewees who graciously permitted me to make tapes that provide extremely useful background and corroborative data were Eddie Durham, Dad Minor, Buck Clayton, Benny Powell, Joe Newman, Billy Eckstine, Sonny Cohn, Eric Dixon, Frank Foster, Buddy Tate, Budd Johnson, Johnny Williams, Grover Mitchell, Willard Alexander, Norman Granz, Morris Levy, Teddy Reig, and that raconteur *par excellence*, Jo Jones, whose colorful reminiscences could be edited into a statement of some literary as well as documentary value. There were also casual but very helpful backstage chats with Freddy Green, Joe Williams, Bill Hughes, Frank Wess, Sweets Edison, Jimmy Lewis, Dicky Wells, Sarah Vaughan, Henry Snodgrass, Bob Porter, and Phil Schap among others.

Expert assistance always so generously forthcoming from Alice Adamczyk, Betty Gubert and Charles Finney at the Schomberg Center in Harlem and from Dan Morganstern and Ed Berger of the Institute for Jazz Studies at Rutgers and from the staff of the Performing Arts Library at Lincoln Center which helped to make long hours of indispensable microfilm and vertical file research a pleasure rather than a chore.

Basies' own collection of photographs was greatly enriched by contributions from Frank Driggs, whose authority in the field of jazz documentation is second to none, and from Bruce Ricker, producer of *The Last of the Blue Devils*. Debby Thomas Ryan, photo specialist at the Schomberg Center was also very cooperative. David Chertok was especially generous. He gave me private showings of all the Basie footage in his extensive collection of jazz films.

Chris Sheridan, who is currently completing a comprehensive Basie Discography in England, was a rich and ready source of information about the changing line-up of sidemen over the years, and also about the band's overseas itineraries. Interviews with various Basie musicians by Stanley Dance and collected in *The World of Count Basie* produced excellent references to spur Basie's own reminiscences.

As will be news to no one familiar with Count Basie's phenomenal career, you could always rely on John Hammond for moral support and other assistance as needed, and he was also an eager and occasionally dissenting first copyreader of the finished manuscript as each chapter came back from the typist. Unfortunately, neither Alec Wilder, Willard Alexander nor Count Basie himself lived to read the book as published. Alec passed away before the work on it reached midpoint. Basie survived only two and a half months after we finished the first draft (incidentally, the last chapter had been taken care of about a year earlier). But Willard did have a chance to inspect and concur with the draft that was submitted to the publisher.

ABOUT THE AUTHOR

ALBERT MURRAY is the author of *Stomping the Blues*, an indispensable book about the meaning of jazz, which won the ASCAP Deems Taylor Award for music commentary in 1976. He has also conducted seminars on criticism for Music Writer's Institute Fellows at the Smithsonian (1975–1979), and has given USIA-sponsored lectures on the literary implications of the blues at Bonn University and the University of Berlin.

He was once an instructor in the English Department at Tuskegee and has also been O'Connor Professor of Literature and Professor of Humanities at Colgate, Writer in Residence at Emory University, Adjunct Professor for Creative Writing at Barnard, and Woodrow Wilson Fellow at Drew University.

His Paul Anthony Pruck lectures at the University of Missouri on ethical implications of literary esthetics were published as *The Hero and the Blues*, and his essay "The Visual Equivalent of the Blues" was the theme essay in the Mint Museum Catalogue *Romare Bearden 1970–1980*.

His other books are *The Omni-Americans, South to a Very Old Place* and *Trainwhistle Guitar*, the sequel to which will be *The Spy Glass Tree*, his current work-in-progress.